THE
MORAL
VISION
OF
POPE
FRANCIS

Recent Titles in the Moral Traditions Series

David Cloutier, Andrea Vicini, SJ, and Darlene Weaver, Editors

Art and Moral Change: A Reconsideration
Ki Joo Choi

The Structures of Virtue and Vice
Daniel J. Daly

The Aesthetics of Solidarity: Our Lady of Guadalupe and American Democracy
Nichole M. Flores

Radical Sufficiency: Work, Livelihood, and a US Catholic Economic Ethic
Christine Firer Hinze

Tragic Dilemmas in Christian Ethics
Kate Jackson-Meyer

The Fullness of Free Time: Leisure and Recreation in the Moral Life
Conor Kelly

Beyond Biology: Rethinking Parenthood in the Catholic Tradition
Jacob M. Kohlhaas

Growing in Virtue: Aquinas on Habit
William C. Mattison III

Beyond Virtue Ethics: A Contemporary Ethic of Godward Spiritual Struggle
Stephen M. Meawad

Reenvisioning Sexual Ethics: A Feminist Christian Account
Karen Peterson-Iyer

Tomorrow's Troubles: Risk, Anxiety, and Prudence in an Age of Algorithmic Governance
Paul Scherz

Wealth, Virtue, and Moral Luck: Christian Ethics in an Age of Inequality
Kate Ward

THE MORAL VISION OF POPE FRANCIS

EXPANDING THE US RECEPTION OF THE FIRST JESUIT POPE

Conor M. Kelly and
Kristin E. Heyer, Editors

GEORGETOWN UNIVERSITY PRESS / WASHINGTON, DC

© 2024 Georgetown University Press. All rights reserved. No part of this book may be reproduced or utilized in any form or by any means, electronic or mechanical, including photocopying and recording, or by any information storage and retrieval system, without permission in writing from the publisher.

The publisher is not responsible for third-party websites or their content. URL links were active at time of publication.

Library of Congress Cataloging-in-Publication Data

Names: Kelly, Conor M., editor. | Heyer, Kristin E., 1974– editor.
Title: The moral vision of Pope Francis: expanding the US reception of the first Jesuit pope / editors, Conor M. Kelly, Kristin E. Heyer.
Description: Washington, DC : Georgetown University Press, 2024. | Includes bibliographical references and index.
Identifiers: LCCN 2023037931 (print) | LCCN 2023037932 (ebook) | ISBN 9781647124557 (hardcover) | ISBN 9781647124564 (paperback) | ISBN 9781647124571 (ebook)
Subjects: LCSH: Francis, Pope, 1936—Ethics. | Social ethics. | Christian ethics.
Classification: LCC BX1378.7 .M664 2024 (print) | LCC BX1378.7 (ebook) | DDC 241/.042—dc23/eng/20231204
LC record available at https://lccn.loc.gov/2023037931
LC ebook record available at https://lccn.loc.gov/2023037932

∞ This paper meets the requirements of ANSI/NISO Z39.48-1992 (Permanence of Paper).

25 24   9 8 7 6 5 4 3 2   First printing

Printed in the United States of America

Cover design by TG Design
Interior design by Integrated Books International

For all our colleagues, in both the academy and the Church, already working so diligently to expand the reception of this first Jesuit pope.

CONTENTS

Acknowledgments   ix

Introduction *Conor M. Kelly and Kristin E. Heyer*   1

PART I: FOUNDATIONS

1   The Moral Theology of Pope Francis: Contextual, Collaborative, Charitable, and Not Always Clear   15
    Lisa Sowle Cahill

2   Responsive Listening: Giving Recognition and Empowering the Voices of Those Long Ignored   33
    James F. Keenan, SJ

3   Pope Francis: Virtue Ethicist?   49
    Conor M. Kelly

4   Pope Francis's Ecclesial Ethics: Mercy, Subsidiarity, Justice   65
    Elyse J. Raby

5   Pope Francis's Social Ethics: Advocacy for Economic Justice and Equity   81
    Thomas Massaro, SJ

6   The Preferential Option for the Poor: Incarnational Theology in the US Context   98
    M. T. Dávila

PART II: APPLICATIONS

7 An Ever Wider We: Pope Francis's Migration Ethics 117
   Kristin E. Heyer

8 Pope Francis, Antiracist? Revealing the Heart in a Time of Racial Reckoning 133
   Maureen H. O'Connell

9 The Twilight of Dissent: Pope Francis and LGBTQ Persons and Morality 149
   Bryan N. Massingale

10 The Work of the Spirit, or Machismo with a Skirt? Feminism, Gender, and Pope Francis 166
   Megan K. McCabe

11 A Discerning Bioethics: Pope Francis's Threefold Approach 183
   Andrea Vicini, SJ

12 Pope Francis's Peace Ethics: Beginning from the "Wounded Flesh of the Victims" 200
   Laurie Johnston

13 Pope Francis's Ecological Ethics: A Constructive Application for a Climate "Revolution" in the US Catholic Church 216
   Daniel R. DiLeo

Conclusion *Conor M. Kelly and Kristin E. Heyer* 234

List of Contributors 255

Index 259

ACKNOWLEDGMENTS

While authors readily admit that no book is ever the result of one person's work alone, this book more than most underscores the collaborative efforts required to transform the kernel of an idea into a written text. As a coedited project, the book has put us in touch with so many wonderful colleagues whose direct contributions and support have led to the finished volume.

We want, first, to thank the eleven theologians and ethicists who responded so graciously to our unsolicited inquiries asking them if they would like to participate in a still very fluid project on "the moral theology of Pope Francis." They each said yes, effectively agreeing to add to their workload so that our hopes for the book could be realized, and we thank each of them here.

A crucial part of our plans for the book was a conference that would bring all our contributors together to workshop chapter drafts and agree on common themes to guide final revisions. This workshop occurred in October 2022, thanks to the generous support of the Jesuit Institute at Boston College and the Institute for the Liberal Arts at Boston College. We are grateful to both institutes for the financial support and expertise they offered as we hosted the conference on campus. We would like especially to thank James Keenan, SJ, the director of the Jesuit Institute, for his enthusiastic support of the project from the beginning and Toni Ross, the associate director of the Jesuit Institute, for her tireless logistical work on behalf of the conference. Three of our contributors—James Keenan, Lisa Sowle Cahill, and Bryan Massingale—participated in a public panel during that conference and we thank them for their willingness to tackle the complicated questions of Pope Francis's moral vision in that open forum.

When we first brainstormed this project, we spoke about potential publishers and immediately agreed that Georgetown University Press would be the ideal home for this volume, given the excellent, admirable work the press is doing in the area of Catholic theological ethics, particularly in the Moral

Traditions Series. We are therefore grateful to be working with Georgetown University Press and would like to thank the director, Al Bertrand, for his encouragement of the project and his willingness to travel to Boston to join us for the conference. We are additionally grateful that this volume will appear as part of the Moral Traditions series and thank the editors for their support. We also wish to express our gratitude to the two anonymous reviewers, whose constructive comments improved this volume; to Alfred Imhoff, whose careful copy edits have made every part of this book clearer; and to Rachel McCarthy, whose production management has made the final version a reality.

Finally, as two lay theologians working to raise families while also contributing professionally to the life of the Church, we are especially cognizant of the support and sacrifice from our spouses and children that are the sine qua non of all our written work. This book is no exception, and so we happily close with a special thank you to Kate, Clare, and Ryan; and Mark, Owen, and Luke.

INTRODUCTION

Conor M. Kelly and Kristin E. Heyer

From the moment Jorge Bergoglio was first introduced to the world as Pope Francis, on March 13, 2013, it was clear to all observers that his pontificate would not be constrained by the normal conventions. Eschewing both the regal clothing and the pomp and circumstance traditionally associated with the leader of the Roman Catholic Church, Francis appeared on the balcony of Saint Peter's Basilica in an all-white cassock, its color the sole clue to his expanded responsibilities. In case anyone failed to appreciate the significance of this preference for sartorial simplicity, he then offered a modest wave of his hand to greet the crowd, as if to stress that his newly added title did not replace his humanity. His first words as pope were similarly jarring, describing the "duty of the Conclave" not as the task of electing the pope but as the responsibility "to give Rome a bishop." He went on to underscore his unpretentious approach to the job of guiding the world's largest Christian denomination by prefacing the requisite apostolic blessing with a personal request. "Before the Bishop blesses his people," he paused, "I ask you to pray to the Lord that he will bless me: the prayer of the people asking the blessing for their Bishop."[1] From his choice of name to his choice of clothes, from what he said to how he said it, Francis sent the message from the start that his ministry as the vicar of Christ would be anything but business as usual.

THE CHALLENGES OF DISCERNING FRANCIS'S VISION FOR MORAL THEOLOGY

After more than a decade, it is evident that the early signs of a distinctive approach to the papacy were not mere illusions, but a genuine foreshadowing of what was awaiting the Church under this servant of the servants of God. With a new emphasis on collegiality in ecclesial governance and a transformed set of public priorities for the global Church that rejects culture war issues in favor of a deeper concern for the plight of the poor and marginalized, Francis has modeled a unique form of papal leadership with far-reaching implications for virtually every aspect of the Catholic faith. Catholic theology is not immune, and yet Catholic moral theology—particularly in the United States—has still not grappled fully with the emphases of his pontificate.[2]

There are, of course, a variety of reasons for this gap. As John Allen noted during the leadup to Francis's apostolic visit to the United States in 2015, "American Catholicism poses two unique challenges for a pope who's an economic populist, and who's vowed to dial down the rhetoric on the wars of culture. Nowhere else is there such a strong Catholic infrastructure dedicated to defending capitalism, and nowhere else is clarity on the 'life issues,' such as abortion and gay marriage, such a defining feature of Catholic identity."[3] Ten years into Francis's papacy, these peculiar US obstacles persist, slowing the reception of Francis's leadership among US Catholics. Commentators frequently point out that the episcopate in the United States remains especially attentive to "life issues," as the culture war would define them. Though this is not the style of every US bishop, the national bishops' conference in the United States has continued to prioritize culture war concerns more strongly than Francis's vision would seem to commend.[4] And, related to Allen's first point, there are institutional structures in US Catholicism that have no qualms using the support of their significant financial backers to openly criticize this pope and counterprogram his agenda.[5] Still, both these trends would have only a minimal impact if ordinary US Catholics refused to journey down the same path. At the level of the faithful in the pews, however, there is broadly—but notably not universally—a willingness to double-down on culture war issues and a reluctance to engage critiques of economic excesses.[6]

Part of the problem is the power of partisan politics, which is particularly strong in the United States. As a result, US Catholics mimic a broader trend, in which "many Americans let their political ideology or partisan identity shape their faith and political behavior."[7] The political alignment has led to a far less robust reception of Francis in the US Catholic Church, as the faithful read each new priority through the lens of their preferred political party and increasingly opt to resolve any cognitive dissonance between their partisan identity and Catholic commitments by defaulting to the former. The other part of the problem is that US Catholics are fully enmeshed in US culture, which valorizes a form of individualism and a vision of economic liberty that is at odds with Catholicism's understanding of the human person as an inherently social creature with concomitant social responsibilities.[8] As M. T. Dávila explores in chapter 6 of this volume, these cultural entanglements create a sizable gap between Francis's priorities and the concerns that emerge most naturally for US Catholics.

Both these dynamics provide an important nuance to the narrative that the lackluster reception of Francis's pontificate in the United States is chiefly an episcopal problem. Though it may be true that the US bishops have been less vociferous in their promotion of, for example, the Catholic responsibility to confront climate change outlined in Francis's 2015 encyclical *Laudato si'*, the power of partisan identities and the contours of the broader US culture mean that even the most vigorous campaign would have encountered headwinds that may well have led to the exact same outcome, wherein individual Catholics' concerns about the environment mirror partisan divisions.[9] Consequently, Catholics (and Catholic theologians) who are apprehensive about the limited impact of Francis's papacy in the United States cannot simply adopt an outwardly critical stance that blames external forces such as episcopal structures for the unenthusiastic response. Instead, we, as US Catholics, must be willing to point the finger back at ourselves to ask how we are exacerbating the problems we have identified, and we must take the initiative to champion change in a way that starts closest to home.

When applied to the realm of moral theology, this internal gaze reveals that the greatest challenge hindering the extension of Francis's leadership into the field comes not from external pressures, real and consequential though they may be, but from features that are peculiar to the way Francis wields his teaching authority on moral matters. Put simply, Francis does not operate as a moral theologian, nor does he intend to. More concerned with the "pastorality of doctrine," which Elyse Raby emphasizes in chapter 4 of this volume, Francis has had neither the patience nor the inclination to develop an explicit moral methodology, lest this slow down his efforts to deal directly with the pastoral concerns that demand immediate attention. Moreover, as Bryan Massingale highlights in chapter 9 of this volume, Francis has been much more willing than any of his predecessors not only to accept but also to countenance disagreement and public debate, further muddying the waters on what "the moral theology of Pope Francis" might mean. As Lisa Sowle Cahill and Conor Kelly respectively outline in chapters 1 and 3 of this book, Francis does not work with the established categories of one moral system alone but pulls pieces from multiple approaches in an effort to provide the most expedient response to the ethical issues in front of him.

This characteristic response, arguably more than anything else, makes it exceptionally difficult to translate Francis's vision for the Church into the field of moral theology. Unlike in other areas, such as ecclesiology, where the implications of the pope's teaching are explicitly connected to the questions that drive the field, Francis's interventions in ethics do not map neatly onto the categories and concepts that define moral theology. This is not to suggest that Francis has little to offer the work of moral theologians. On the contrary, the defining features of his pontificate are just as consequential for moral theology as they are for every other area of the Catholic faith. The challenge is that anyone who wants to explore these connections has more work to do, because Francis's approach to moral questions has to be reverse engineered, so to speak, from his various pastoral interventions on a wide array of ethical issues.

CRUCIAL EMPHASES IN FRANCIS'S PAPACY FOR MORAL THEOLOGY

Due to the intellectual extraction required to make sense of Francis's vision for ethics, his influence has seeped into Catholic ethics more slowly than it has in other areas of theology, and consequently Catholic moral theology has not yet fully grappled with the emphases of his pontificate. The delayed, and thus incomplete, reception of Francis's insights has harmed the field, because the changes at the heart of the "Francis revolution" are especially pertinent for moral theology's efforts to show how faith can be put into practice in the concrete particulars of ordinary life.[10] Consider the message Francis communicated with his first solo-authored text, *Evangelii gaudium*. "Christians have a duty to proclaim the Gospel," he insisted, but "instead of seeming to impose new obligations, they should appear as people who wish to share joy. . . . It is not by proselytizing that the Church grows, but 'by attraction.'"[11] By emphasizing the *joy* of the Christian life, Francis has reminded all Catholics that the heart of their faith is a dynamic relationship with Jesus Christ, who "came that they may have life, and have it abundantly" (Jn. 10:10). While Catholic moral theology has always shared this goal, its means of encouraging the faithful to pursue a more abundant life have not always aligned with this end, and in fact have frequently undermined it. How often has Catholic moral theology looked like a list of "obligations" imposed rather than an invitation to a new way of life that is meant to be enjoyed?[12] While the negative moral norms (e.g., "thou shalt not . . .") are always ordered to the positive goal of the human person's full flourishing as a creature made in the image and likeness of God, there is a definite tendency in Catholic moral theology to stress those negative norms in a way that eclipses the positive vision. Francis's summons to return to the joy at the heart of the Gospel thus has far-reaching potential for the field of moral theology, provided that moral theologians and theological ethicists are willing to do the work to translate Francis's insights into their discipline.

Clearly, Francis wants his ecclesial influence to extend to the work of moral theology. In *Amoris laetitia*, for instance, Francis concluded the exhortation's influential eighth chapter with the note, "The teaching of moral theology should not fail to incorporate these considerations."[13] Notably, this request covered not only the reclamation of "the highest and most central values of the Gospel" that he had similarly encouraged in *Evangelii gaudium*, but also an application of Francis's appeal to mercy, which was a central feature of the synod on the family that generated *Amoris laetitia*.[14] This concern for mercy represents a second central theme with significant implications for the field of moral theology, where a merciful application of the law can make all the difference between a defensive rejection of Catholic teaching and a welcome engagement with the deeper vision of hope that this teaching promotes. As Francis explained in his reflections on the Jubilee of Mercy he instituted in 2015–16, "etymologically, 'mercy' derives from *misericordis*, which means opening one's heart to wretchedness," a disposition that would encourage moral theology to be more understanding of the human failings and constraints of circumstance that frequently contribute to a person's descent into sin.[15] Indeed, Francis intimated as much, albeit not with direct reference to the work of moral theology, when he appealed to the teachings of Saint Francis de Sales and asked, "if you have a little donkey and along the road it falls onto the cobblestones, what should you do? You certainly don't go there with a stick to beat it, poor little thing, it's already unfortunate enough. You must take it by the halter and say: 'Up, let's take to the road again, . . . and we will pay more attention next time.'"[16] If moral theologians more fully embraced this orientation toward mercy and sought consistently to recognize the wretchedness facing "the faithful, who very often respond as best they can to the Gospel amid their limitations," then the field would necessarily look different, in the best way possible.[17]

By insufficiently attending to Francis's priorities, such as the primacy of the Gospel for the life of faith and a renewed emphasis on mercy as the Church's guiding disposition, Catholic moral theology is certainly failing Francis, who has a plain desire to lead the Church into new territory. In fairness, one could *theoretically* argue that some distance from the pope is not inherently a bad thing, given the role that dissent plays in Catholic theology, where canon law notes that responsible dissent may actually be a duty for faithful Catholics who find an inconsistency or outright mistake (as judged by their primacy of conscience) in Catholic teaching.[18] In practice, however, two factors indicate that this is not a plausible defense for the gap between papal leadership and theological practice occurring in the rejection of Francis.

First, although there have been a few high-profile cases in which theologians have explicitly questioned the legitimacy or authority of Pope Francis's teaching, such as the *dubia* submitted by four cardinals in response to *Amoris laetitia*, the current lacunae in moral theology have arisen not from a direct engagement with and dissent from Francis's leadership on moral matters but primarily from a failure to engage his moral vision at all. Properly understood, dissent can only emerge after a careful consideration of magisterial teaching, because every Catholic is supposed to approach magisterial authority with a charitable disposition that presumes assent on matters of faith and morals.[19] There is no room for a "pocket veto," whereby a Catholic might register dissent merely by ignoring a specific teaching and refusing to take its ramifications seriously. The limited application of Francis's leadership currently plaguing moral theology thus does not rise to the level of official dissent, because it falls far short of the preconditions required for such a weighty judgment. The gap between pope and people in this area is thus much more difficult to justify as a sign of robust dialogue in the Church; if anything, it is an illustration of how much of that dialogue is missing.

Second, moral theology's forestalled engagement with Francis's vision for the Church is not simply an unjustified rejection of papal leadership. It is also, more fundamentally, a liability for the field, which is limiting its own potential as a result of its unwillingness to engage with and respond to Francis's invitation to return to the most fundamental priorities at the heart of the Catholic faith. The summons to reclaim the joy of the Gospel and to embody a missionary form of mercy could be transforming the field in ways that would allow Catholic moral theology to reach the kinds of people who most need to hear the call of God's love. Instead of turning outward through an application of Francis's central themes, Catholic moral theology has turned inward, rehashing old debates in some of the same academic terms that leave the conversation inaccessible to outsiders. Arguably, much of this failure to flourish is unintentional, emerging from an inattentiveness to Francis that, in the most charitable interpretation, can be traced to the difficulties of interpreting this pope's unsystematic approach to ethics. While this explanation may mitigate the field's culpability, it can do nothing to lessen the opportunity costs moral theology incurs by not engaging Francis's invitation to radical renewal more fully.

THE AIMS OF THIS BOOK

Cognizant of this toll, we have gathered a leading group of Catholic theologians and theological ethicists from across the United States to reflect on the impact Francis's leadership and vision can and should have on our field, because we do not want the missed opportunity of his papacy to continue until it is too late. Through their chapters, the authors do the heavy lifting necessary to tease out the implicit resonances with moral theology that lurk below the surface of Francis's episodic treatment of concrete ethical questions. The result is not a full-fledged "moral theology of Pope Francis," because this would be an artificial imposition on a pope who frequently appears to be making a concerted effort to avoid the pigeonholing that such a categorization would inevitably entail. Instead, what emerges is better characterized as the moral vision of Pope Francis, for this is much more consistent with his style of leadership, which exhorts by inspiring a wider imaginary more than it pronounces in carefully curated dicta.

While the authors examine a host of practical ethical issues in the quest to establish the moral vision of Pope Francis, two features are intentionally designed to generate consistency across the volume so that a coherent account of this vision can emerge from the detailed analyses that each expert provides. First, all the chapters in this book have an explicit US focus. While we do not want to ignore Francis's global influence, we recognize that the United States is something of an outlier in its underattentiveness to Francis's leadership, due to the cultural influences noted above. We therefore want to develop concrete applications of Francis's moral vision for the US context. The US emphasis does not reflect a lack of awareness of the global impact of Francis's papacy, however. On the contrary, the consideration of US implications is rooted in an examination of the work Francis is doing throughout the Church and around the globe, with the authors in this volume routinely mining not just the major encyclicals and most publicized messages that would be most familiar to audiences in the United States, but also his speeches and comments originally directed at particular local communities far from the boundaries of the United States. The point of this careful study is to draw out the key themes that define Francis's moral vision so that they can then be applied to the current US context, where more work must still be done to expand the reception of this pope. Other projects can, and we hope will, explore similar applications for other local contexts across the global Church, but we have prioritized US reflections here because we are especially attuned to the unique obstacles and interruptions the Francis revolution has experienced in this country.

Second, this book places a unique emphasis on the Ignatian influences shaping Francis's pontificate and thus his approach to moral theology. As the first Jesuit pope, Francis brings a distinctive set of experiences to the Chair of Peter, all of which have been colored by the charisms of the Society of Jesus and the emphases of the Ignatian spirituality that serves as the animating principle for the Jesuits' apostolic mission. Throughout their chapters, the authors in this volume draw on their own experiences in Jesuit contexts to interrogate how parallels between Francis's approach to ethics and the richness of the Jesuit tradition can help Catholics appreciate the novelty and dynamism of Francis's moral vision. Thus, some authors point to the role of discernment in Ignatius's *Spiritual Exercises* to illuminate Francis's characteristic emphasis on conscience and discernment in moral matters. Meanwhile, others explore how the pastoral demands of life in a missionary order give insight into the pope's prioritization of mercy and openness to some degree of flexibility in the application of rules. Still others examine how Ignatius's promotion of an imaginative form of prayer and attention to the movement of the Spirit in the affections shapes Francis's penchant for conveying his key messages through evocative stories and imaginative gestures that aim to stir the heart in order to shift the mind and not the other way around. These Ignatian connections are not coincidental overlaps but serve as substantive links that promote a deeper understanding of what Francis is trying to achieve. By interrogating these links, the authors generate both a cohesive theme uniting the chapters and the details of a fuller account of Francis's moral vision so that the application to the US context can proceed more effectively.

STRUCTURE OF THE BOOK

The collection begins with a set of chapters addressing Francis's foundational and methodological emphases, which are followed by a series of chapters elaborating his vision across a range of applied ethics areas. At the outset, in chapter 1, Lisa Sowle Cahill frames Francis's approach to questions of moral theology as following through on conciliar reforms and postconciliar revisionist proposals. His mode is marked by decentralization (and relatedly, inclusive discernment), the priority of the poor, attention to mercy guiding right reason, and empowerment of social movements. Cahill traces how his pastoral prioritization of compassion over "analytic stringency" make an impact on Francis's moral teachings and posture. In chapter 2, James Keenan, SJ, analyzes how the pope's preference for encounter and inclusive listening orient his focus toward recognition and accompaniment of those on various peripheries. By tracing Francis's work with the World Meetings of Popular Movements alongside the pope's encyclicals and commitment to synodality, Keenan reveals Francis's consistent commitment to empowering and heeding long-marginalized voices. The chapter draws on the practice of the *anamchara* (soul-friend) to illuminate how these emphases make an impact on the pope's approach to conscience, as well.

From these overarching emphases that shape the pope's moral vision, the next several chapters specify his approaches to fundamental moral theology, social ethics, and ecclesial ethics. In chapter 3, Conor Kelly poses the question of whether the pope's moral theology can be characterized as virtue ethics. Given Francis's emphases on contextual discernment, character formation, and moral growth, Kelly elaborates on the ways the pope acts like a virtue ethicist, even as he is ultimately more oriented to an encounter with God rather than any idea or individual virtue. The chapter indicates ways Pope Francis's approach and traditional virtue ethics might mutually strengthen one another. In chapter 4, Elyse Raby suggests Francis's ecclesial ethics is in fact marked by three virtues in particular: mercy, subsidiarity, and justice. She shows how these virtues shape his ministerial vision, ecclesial reforms, and response to the ongoing clergy abuse crisis—and how the three virtues are both interrelated and reflective of his Ignatian formation.

Rounding out the book's first, foundational part are chapters treating the pope's social ethics, in general, and understanding of the option for the poor, in particular. In chapter 5, Thomas Massaro, SJ, takes up the ways Francis's "new grammar of deep social concern" plays out in his economic ethic, identifying continuities, innovations, and implications for the US context. He notes how exclusion emerges as a key motif across the pope's structural critiques of various forms of social injustice, as evidenced in his pointed critiques of exploitative economies. Francis grounds his teachings on economic justice in a Church that sides with the poor, which subsequently connects to Dávila's chapter 6, taking up the pope's understanding of the option for the poor itself, through his gestures and teachings alike. She traces the origins of the principle in Latin American liberation theology, tensions between magisterial and liberationist understandings, and the ways in which Francis understands and centers on an option for the poor. Francis's use of conflict in *Laudato si'*, understanding of poverty as solidarity, and practice of encounters place him in the liberationist tradition and pose a challenge to US ecclesial priorities. In the volume's part I, then, distinct priorities shaping Francis's moral methodology and center of gravity begin to come into view.

Part II of the volume springs from the foundational emphases elaborated in part I, addressing Francis's engagement of particular social issues in order to further illuminate his moral vision. Picking up on Massaro's acknowledgment of Francis's "structural eye," in chapter 7, Kristin Heyer elaborates on the pope's social framing of an issue close to his heart: migration. She indicates how his attention to both structures of injustice that propel and harm migrants and to affective dimensions of in/hospitality reflect his Ignatian influences and move beyond the dominant "crisis management" migration paradigm. In chapter 8, Maureen O'Connell likewise engages Francis's attention to affect in her treatment of his engagement with the virus of racism. For example, she highlights the role wonder plays in his moral method and how it can interrupt white supremacy. O'Connell also praises the pope's praxis of naming dimensions of racism and framing it as injustice, even as she probes areas in which antiracist teaching and praxis can further push his approach and wider Church praxis.

In chapter 9, Bryan Massingale retrieves the principle of probabilism to characterize the Church's approach to LGBTQ persons under Francis's leadership. Massingale traces how the pope's words and actions on LGBTQ moral questions, together with his approach to the synods—especially, his encouragement of *parrhesia*—have allowed for the toleration of a plurality of positions, laying groundwork for doctrinal progress. Following upon this emphasis, in chapter 10 Megan McCabe highlights the subtle shifts in the pope's approach to gender and feminism, conceding some continuities with his immediate predecessors, while identifying other new directions driven by his pastoral sensitivity to lived experience. She stresses how Francis's softening of rigid gender roles and fostering of women's ecclesial participation evidence significant progress. And in chapter 11, Andrea Vicini, SJ, draws on the foundational chapters' emphases on discernment, attention to concrete experience, and the option for the poor to characterize Francis's approach to bioethics. He emphasizes the centrality of human dignity and of a spiritual relationship with Jesus to inform discipleship in facing bioethical challenges; even given this Christological focus, the pope's bioethics initiatives encompass an inclusive, shared common good and avoid a single-issue agenda.

In the final, applied chapters, the volume takes up Francis's peace ethic and environmental ethic, and their implications for the US Catholic context. In chapter 12, Laurie Johnston emphasizes that what distinguishes Francis more than his conclusions on the use of force or peacemaking is the place he begins: the most vulnerable victimized by violence, rather than, primarily, geopolitical leaders. Tensions between a sense that just war theory has outlived its usefulness and its defense persist in papal addresses. The pope's employment of dramatic gestures as a mode of nonviolent peacemaking and a "polyhedric" vision of peace as the fruit of "reconciled diversity" also set his approach apart. And in chapter 13, Daniel DiLeo takes his inspiration from just such dramatic gestures, arguing for the need to shake up apathetic responses to Francis's environmental ethic. He traces the pope's elevation of the urgency of the cry of the Earth and its connection to the cry of the poor in *Laudato si'*, and how, reflective of our discussion of partisan politics above, US Catholics generally received its summons along party lines. In response, DiLeo draws on Francis's ecclesiological and popular movement writings to propose that US Catholics pursue diocesan net zero carbon commitments through community organizing, advocacy, and nonviolent direct action, if necessary.

In the conclusion, the editors assess the volume as a whole and draw out three themes from the preceding contributions that define the moral vision of Pope Francis and that should guide the field of moral theology in the United States. The conclusion presents the primacy of the poor, a respect for ambiguity, and the importance of structural analysis as Francis's key contributions to moral theology and explains how moral theologians can incorporate these insights into their work in the United States. Ultimately, the conclusion ends with a forceful reminder that the value of these changes is not an improved alignment with the pope but a more faithful following of Jesus Christ, yielding a Christocentric moral vision that befits the first Jesuit pope.

NOTES

1. Francis, "First Greeting of the Holy Father Pope Francis: Apostolic Blessing 'Urbi et Orbi,'" March 13, 2013, www.vatican.va/content/francesco/en/speeches/2013/march/documents/papa-francesco_20130313_benedizione-urbi-et-orbi.html.
2. There are notable exceptions beyond the United States, but even internationally, interventions in moral theology have been limited in scope (e.g., focusing on the implications of one specific document or the impact of Francis's leadership for one particular ethical issue) or have had only a limited impact. As subsequent sections of the introduction detail, this volume is designed with an intentional emphasis on the US lacunae. For two international examples, see Aristide Fumagalli, *Journey in Love: Pope Francis' Moral Theology*, trans. Salesians of Don Bosco (Melbourne: Coventry Press, 2019); and Stephan Goertz and Caroline Witting, ed., *Amoris Laetitia: Wendepunkt in der Moraltheologie?* (Frieburg: Herder, 2016).
3. John L. Allen Jr., "Are US Bishops Really Resisting Pope Francis?" *Crux*, December 6, 2014, https://cruxnow.com/church/2014/12/are-us-bishops-really-resisting-pope-francis.
4. For illustrations of how this limited reception has played out in the US bishops' conference over the years, see Michael Sean Winters, "US Bishops, as a Group, Still Resist Pope Francis' Pastoral Impulse," *National Catholic Reporter*, November 15, 2017, www.ncronline.org/opinion/distinctly-catholic/us-bishops-group-still-resist-pope-francis-pastoral-impulse; and Michael Sean Winters, "In 2021, It Became Obvious the US Bishops and the Pope Are Singing from Different Hymnals," *National Catholic Reporter*, December 29, 2021, www.ncronline.org/news/opinion/2021-it-became-obvious-us-bishops-and-pope-are-singing-different-hymnals. Cf. Francis in Antonio Spadaro, "A Big Heart Open to God: The Exclusive Interview with Pope Francis," *America*, September 30, 2013, 26.
5. See, e.g., Christopher White, "Boston's Cardinal O'Malley Defends Francis Against Attacks from EWTN Critics," *National Catholic Reporter*, December 17, 2021, www.ncronline.org/news/people/bostons-cardinal-omalley-defends-francis-against-attacks-ewtn-critics;

and Tom Roberts, "The Rise of the Catholic Right: How Right-Wing Billionaires Are Attempting a Hostile Takeover of the US Catholic Church," *Sojourners* 48, no. 3 (March 2019): 16–23.
6. On the nonhomogeneity of US Catholics, especially across racial and ethnic lines, see Gregory A. Smith, "8 Facts about Catholics and Politics in the US," Pew Research Center, September 15, 2020, www.pewresearch.org/fact-tank/2020/09/15/8-facts-about-catholics-and-politics-in-the-u-s/.
7. Robert G. Christian III, "The Roots of American Catholic Polarization," *Church Life Journal*, April 1, 2019, https://churchlifejournal.nd.edu/articles/the-roots-of-american-catholic-polarization/.
8. For the particular form of individualism regnant in the United States, and its contrasts with Catholic theological anthropology, see Conor M. Kelly, "Everyday Solidarity: A Framework for Integrating Theological Ethics and Ordinary Life," *Theological Studies* 81, no. 2 (June 2020): 414–37, esp. 420–22.
9. For details on the US bishops' presentation of climate change as a pressing Catholic concern, see Sabrina Danielsen, Daniel R. DiLeo, and Emily E. Burke, "US Catholic Bishops' Silence and Denialism on Climate Change," *Environmental Research Letters* 16, no. 11 (October 2021): 114006. For the current partisan division on climate change among US Catholics, see Jeff Diamant, "The Pope Is Concerned about Climate Change: How Do US Catholics Feel about It?" Pew Research Center, February 9, 2023, www.pewresearch.org/fact-tank/2023/02/09/the-pope-is-concerned-about-climate-change-how-do-u-s-catholics-feel-about-it/.
10. Austin Ivereigh, "The Francis Revolution: This Pope Has Reasserted the Church's True Power," *America* 228, no. 3 (March 1, 2023): 66.
11. Francis, *Evangelii gaudium*, November 24, 2013, no. 14, www.vatican.va/content/francesco/en/apost_exhortations/documents/papa-francesco_esortazione-ap_20131124_evangelii-gaudium.html.
12. Lisa Fullam provides a fine illustration of these emphases in the realm of sexual ethics: Lisa Fullam, "Thou Shalt: Sex Beyond the List of Don'ts," *Commonweal* 136, no. 8 (April 24, 2009): 14–17.
13. Francis, *Amoris laetitia*, March 19, 2016, no. 311, www.vatican.va/content/dam/francesco/pdf/apost_exhortations/documents/papa-francesco_esortazione-ap_20160319_amoris-laetitia_en.pdf.
14. Francis, no. 311. On the importance of reclaiming the centrality of the Gospel in *Evangelii gaudium*, see Francis, *Evangelii gaudium*, no. 39.
15. Francis, *The Name of God Is Mercy: A Conversation with Andrea Tornielli*, trans. Oonagh Stransky (New York: Random House, 2016), 8.
16. Francis, 13–14.
17. Francis, *Amoris laetitia*, no. 37.
18. On the legitimacy of dissent and its potential value, see Charles E. Curran and Richard A. McCormick, eds., *Dissent in the Church*, Readings in Moral Theology no. 6 (New York: Paulist Press, 1988).
19. For more details on the nuances of this disposition according to the different levels of teaching authority, see Richard R. Gaillardetz, *By What Authority? Foundations for Understanding Authority in the Church*, rev. ex. ed. (Collegeville, MN: Liturgical Press, 2018), 205–11.

PART I
FOUNDATIONS

I

THE MORAL THEOLOGY OF POPE FRANCIS

Contextual, Collaborative, Charitable, and Not Always Clear

Lisa Sowle Cahill

Pope Francis is a Vatican II–forward pope. He makes good on reforms in moral theology that some "revisionist" theologians proposed in the years after the council, but which were resisted or at least very cautiously incorporated by Paul VI, John Paul II, and Benedict XVI. As a pope and not a theologian, however, Francis (like his predecessors) is reluctant to make radical changes in traditional moral teaching. As surfaced by episcopal debates at the two-part Synod on the Family,[1] not all regional churches are prepared to accept the same reforms, even if promulgated from the Vatican, especially in the areas of gender equality, sex, marriage, and family. The Synod on the Amazon, by comparison, exposed the resistance of some regional churches to Vatican reform initiatives on justice issues like climate change, the extractive industries, and the political participation of indigenous peoples. As the leader of a globally represented and culturally diverse Church, Pope Francis has the daunting responsibility to maintain ecclesial communion while moving Catholic practice and theology ever closer to the "Church of the poor" as he can best envision it.

To fulfill this responsibility, Pope Francis emphasizes three keynotes of the council—the contextual nature of moral truth, the Gospel's inspiration of moral theology, and the priority of the poor.[2] First, Pope Francis approaches morality and social justice from the local, the contextual, the contingent, and the popular.[3] *Gaudium et spes* set "the nature of the human person and his acts" as the standard of objective morality,[4] later interpreted to mean the human person as relational and historically situated (more on this history below). As most directly explained in *Amoris laetitia*, following Aquinas, *objective* knowledge requires contextual discernment, which for Pope Francis should be collaborative. For Pope Francis, a premise of the "responsive listening" that James Keenan (in chapter 2 of this volume) likewise illustrates with Pope Francis's turn to the popular movements, is that the listener is also a learner. Authentic listening changes power dynamics. Pope Francis is clear that listening to "the poor" involves an active alliance with the poor, such that the disempowered gain voice and agency.

Second, for Pope Francis, love, "mercy" ("the true face of love"[5]), and "connectedness" with other persons and creation (*Laudato si'*) are the driving forces of Christian morality. This accent expresses the call of *Optatam totius* for a more integral biblical formation of moral theology.[6] At the social-ethical level, Francis calls for mutual "care" across religions and moral traditions (*Fratelli tutti*). And *third*, "the poor" have a prior claim on initiatives of justice and of ecclesial inclusion. *Gaudium et spes* announces the keynote, "The joys and the hopes, the griefs and the anxieties of the men of this age, especially those who are poor or in any way afflicted."[7] Pope Francis calls for a "Church of the poor" (as reflected across *Laudato si'*, *Amoris laetitia*, *Querida Amazonia*, and many other speeches and writings). These three values or commitments are interdependent.

CONCILIAR-ERA ANTECEDENTS: THE CHARACTER OF MORAL REASONING

Pope Francis's stress on the contextuality of moral-political reasoning and on the animating role of love in just moral discernment has roots not only in conciliar theology and ethics but also in paraconciliar and postconciliar developments in Catholic moral theology. These can shed light on how Francis both takes his lead from the council itself and from some Catholic forebears, and formulates a distinctive approach that, while going back to Aquinas and the Gospel, is more successful than midcentury moral theology in transcending the frameworks of manualist morality and of elitist Eurocentric social teaching.

The Second Vatican Council (1962–65) was convened by the charismatic Pope John XXIII, who sought collaboration with the modern world and its humanistic and scientific modes of inquiry. *Gaudium et spes* specified that the "objective standards" of morality are not based fundamentally on Church authority but on "the objective nature of the person and the person's acts" (no. 51).[8] This was quickly taken not only in a personalist but also in a contextual and social direction in moral theology, in which the grounds for "objectivity" were reinterpreted. In an influential move, Richard McCormick reworded "the nature of the person and the person's acts," by repurposing a line of an official commentary on *Gaudium et spes*.[9] That commentary offered "the human person integrally and adequately considered" as a key to the meaning of "the objective nature of the person."[10] McCormick repeated the commentary's phrase in numerous writings, rarely reminding readers that it is not actually to be found in the conciliar document itself. Often, he conveyed it simply as the perspective of the council or of *Gaudium et spes*. For example, "Vatican II proposed as the criterion not 'the intention of nature inscribed in the organs and their functions' but 'the person integrally and adequately considered.'"[11]

To set markers or parameters for what that might mean, McCormick invoked Louis Janssens's definition of personhood. The person is a responsible subject; a corporeal subject; part of the material world; essentially directed toward other persons; a social subject requiring social and political life; a historical being, original and equal; and called to know and worship God.[12] The personalist-leaning criterion of Vatican II was a repair effort that led the way not only to healing and renewal but also to the reinvention of moral theology.

Post–Vatican II moral theologians, no matter how revisionist, never saw their proposals as breaks with the tradition, but rather as a radicalization of its history and heritage. They returned to vivifying roots (in Aquinas and in casuistry that took seriously context, and context-specific analogies among cases, rather than legalist deductions from principles) that had been all but cut off by manualist legalism and neo-Scholastic methods. Though principles like double effect had been wielded like mathematical formulas, the revisionist moral theologians argued the objective relevance of contexts, options, and how agents personally discern situations and intend to resolve conflicts of value. A frequent target, or at least paradigm case, was the 1968 "birth control encyclical" of Paul VI, *Humanae vitae*. The ensuing debates generated too much controversy and literature to cover here.[13]

Suffice it to say that the centerpiece of the debate was the so-called principle of double effect, a standard tool of the manuals evolved to handle acts having both a good and a bad outcome, while still avoiding "utilitarianism," interpreted as tolerating "intrinsically evil acts" for the sake of a greater good (the greatest good for the greatest number). According to the moral-theological use of the principle, an evil effect could be permitted under certain conditions, the most important being that the act in question was not already categorized as intrinsically evil. Critics of the standard use of this principle (Richard McCormick was salient among the Americans, using his annual

"Notes on Moral Theology," in *Theological Studies*, as a forum to air his views) complained that the grounds of this categorization were unclear and inconsistent, that certain acts were ruled out without adequate regard for circumstances or intention, and that the category "intrinsically evil" amounted to a device to exempt from scrutiny things that the magisterium had already defined as mortal sins. These involved mostly sexual and, to a lesser extent, biomedical ethics. Critics asserted further that the only really necessary criterion of acts with "double effects" was the proportion of good to evil. Hence, they were dubbed "proportionalists" (as well as relativists and, inconsistently, utilitarians) by defenders of the tradition, who felt vindicated by John Paul II's *Veritatis splendor*. This encyclical, without naming names or analyzing anyone's published arguments, brushed aside proportionalists as "not faithful to the Church's teaching, when they believe that they can justify, as morally good, deliberate choices of behavior contrary to the commandments of the divine and natural law."[14]

It is fair to say that neither side of this debate produced a fully coherent defense of their position, for the proportionalists did not succeed in explaining clearly and consistently what differentiated their method from utilitarianism. The traditionalists, in turn, never explained, in logical terms, just why something could be deemed intrinsically evil on the basis of its physical structure alone; nor why the stipulated conditions of double effect were the necessary and sufficient determinants of an act's morality. What the revisionist and "proportionalist" theologians were essentially doing was making sociality and contextuality integral and essential to "objective" moral truth, even in so-called personal ethics. There is no moral truth that can be isolated, understood, and realized apart from its personal, relational, and social dimensions. Yet their first line of recourse was a critique of neo-Scholastic terminology, which they tried to redefine rather than replace. Putting new ideas into an "old wineskin" turned out to be a dead end. Proportionalism was gradually abandoned as a moral methodology. As Aline Kalbian has insightfully argued, its former theorists went into new forms of virtue ethics and casuistry, as well as emerging fields of social ethics, such as feminist ethics.[15] McCormick summarizes the years after the council as instilling in moral theology a sense of "historical consciousness," from which "a sense of tentativeness is inseparable."[16]

Pope Francis also works within the Thomistic intellectual-theological framework. In chapter 8 of *Amoris laetitia*, he elaborates a context-sensitive moral epistemology and ethics grounded in the thought of Thomas Aquinas.[17] Aquinas's ethics is framed around the concept of the natural law, a way of articulating that people in every culture grasp that deprivations of necessary goods violate human dignity, while access enables flourishing. According to Aquinas, "the light of natural reason, whereby we discern what is good and what is evil, which is the function of the natural law, is nothing else than the imprint on us of the Divine light," and "the rational creature's participation of the eternal law."[18] Indeed, to "do good and avoid evil" is the very essence of morality.[19] Human beings know the basic goods because we have a natural inclination to seek them, as essential to a secure personal existence and to the welfare of human societies. Aquinas gives three examples: to preserve life; to procreate and educate the young; and to live cooperatively in political society.[20]

But these goods and inclinations are experienced and known differently in different cultures. Pope Francis sees that "culture is a dynamic reality which a people constantly recreates; each generation passes on a whole series of ways of approaching different existential situations to the next generation, which must in turn reformulate it as it confronts its own challenges."[21] *Amoris laetitia* appreciates that, while many basic principles of the moral and social life apply across cultures, cultural experiences are various, and "real life" involves a good amount of unpredictability. Moreover, each culture will present its own enabling and obstructionist factors, regarding realization of goods and just institutions. It follows that adaptation, creativity, and negotiation among conflicting or obstructed goods are included in the meaning of moral responsibility.

Aquinas seems to agree: In terms of the "general principles," moral truth ("practical rectitude") is "the same for all and known by all." However, the more moral reason gets into practical details and contingencies, the more what constitutes "rectitude" will vary, and the harder it may be to know what rectitude means practically speaking.[22] Moral reason deals with truth in action. No single solution can fit every case, eliminating the need for discernment, doubt, difficulty, or compromise. This follows from a basic premise of Aquinas on which Pope Francis relies: all moral reason is practical reason. *Amoris laetitia* validates this principle on the basis of family life.[23]

As Pope Francis explains, a deciding subject, couple, family, or community may "be in a concrete situation which does not allow him or her [or them] to act differently [than to depart from the pertinent norm] and decide otherwise without further sin."[24] Variable concrete objectivity should not call into question valid universal rules.[25] Yet rules are not as important as attunement to the particular. An unusually strong statement comes from Aquinas's commentary on Aristotle's *Ethics*. Of "general knowledge of the rule and the particular knowledge of the practical discernment [Aquinas] states that 'if only one of the two is present, it is preferable that it be the knowledge of the particular reality, which is closer to the act.'"[26] The bottom line is that knowing the rules is less important than knowing the realities of the relevant situation—where objective moral truth is ultimately found.

Justifiable rule departures can be due to shortcomings of the agent— or to limits and barriers within the situation itself. Pope Francis draws on a caveat of Aquinas: "Saint Thomas Aquinas himself recognized that someone may possess grace and charity, yet not be able to exercise any one of the virtues well . . . because the outward practice of that virtue is rendered difficult: 'Certain saints are said not to possess certain virtues, in so far as they experience difficulty in the acts of those virtues, even though they have the habits of all the virtues.'"[27]

This brings us to Pope Francis's recommendation that discernment be an inclusive, dialogic, and self-correcting process. Discernment as a model for reaching spiritual and moral judgment has an anchor in Pope Francis's Jesuit formation, in the *Spiritual Exercises* of Ignatius Loyola. Ignatius certainly recognizes that discerning Christians are members of faith communities, the Society of Jesus being an obvious example. Yet his advice for discernment primarily turns the attention of the person inward, in a stance of personal, prayerful reflection.[28] Ignatius outlines personal attitudes or dispositions that are conducive to discernment, an "examen" in which the person invokes the presence of God. Ignatius observes that discernment may be approached with inner clarity, conflict, or blankness and confusion.[29] To reach discernment, the person should consider prayerfully, while asking for and trusting in God's guidance. Authentic discernment is confirmed by an inner state of peacefulness and an experience of God's blessing. A spiritual director is essential; and a faith community is assumed; yet the discernment process occurs primarily in the interiority of personal prayer.

Francis's approach to discernment (regarding both the family and, even more obviously, the environment), is different in focus. *Amoris laetitia* holds out a model of communal discernment regarding eucharistic participation by civilly remarried Catholics, in which couples are accompanied by a priest through a reflection on whether and how well they have met their marital and family responsibilities. Sometimes accompaniment is as important as decision-making, because particular barriers to righteousness and justice cannot be surmounted. This is another way in which Francis expands upon Ignatius. Clarity, interior peace, and assurance of God's blessing may not be gifts that are given. Human life is complex; prayerful discernment cannot always overcome quandary, incompleteness, and conflict. Then what may be called for is ongoing negotiation of the possible, illumined but not regulated strictly by moral ideals or norms.

THE COHERENCE OF CHRISTIAN MORAL REASONING, LOVE, AND DISCERNMENT

Pope Francis likewise is interested in context and the social conditions that impinge upon moral options, both individually and for communities, including families. Yet he is not a proportionalist. He does not argue his case in terms of double effect, nor for that matter, against double effect. Nor has he rejected any traditional teachings. Unlike the majority of the debaters from the 1960s through the 1980s, Pope Francis seems willing to live with a certain amount of intellectual ambiguity for the sake of practical moral truth and pastoral authenticity vis-à-vis the reality of people's complicated lives.[30] A gap in moral-analytic coherence may be inevitable in some existential conflicts of responsibility; yet gaps may be bridged and practical truth may be attained when discernment is guided by compassion.

Love, Compassion, and Discernment

A conciliar-era development (yet with roots in *Quadragesimo anno*[31]), that is highly influential for Francis, is that moral discernment requires not only the intellectual virtue of prudence but also the deepening virtue of love—understood as compassion, solidarity, and active commitment to others' welfare.[32] According to Francis, "discursive reasoning" is inadequate; also essential is "the affective connaturality born of love."[33] Love and solidarity are not equated with what Aquinas calls the Christian theological virtue of charity (which flows from saving grace), but they can be expressions of it.[34]

Pope Francis is mindful that families can be "crushed" by social conditions.[35] Families struggle to find solutions to burdens, threats, and internal injustices, more or less successfully. As Pope Francis cautions, when responsibilities pull in different directions, conformity to a general moral rule "is not enough to discern and ensure full fidelity to God in the concrete life of a human being."[36] As the 2015 Synod *Relatio* warns, "'pastors are to avoid judgments that do not take into account the complexity of various situations.'"[37] Pope Francis agrees, denouncing the application of moral laws "as if they were stones to throw at people's lives."[38] This is a good example of the way Francis's "responsive listening" brings practical results, when informed by charity and solidarity. If pastors genuinely listen to the experiences and insights of families, they will in some instances adjust their conceptual frameworks, their moral judgments, and their ecclesial approaches.

Francis is not confined to the moral-theological framework of the Vatican II era, which even for the revisionists, concerned the derivation and application of natural law principles conceived primarily as guides for right reason, along with the intellectual virtue of prudence. Reason still has a place in the moral theology of Pope Francis, but "an approach to casuistry inspired by Pope Francis would emphasize that the moral law has to be interpreted according to the intention of the lawgiver—Jesus Christ."[39] Jesus Christ understands that people in the midst of brokenness may be doing the best they can. For Pope Francis, solidarity, compassion, and what he terms "mercy" are the essential guides to right moral reason, which is not limited to logical and systematic analysis. This is a pastorally informed insight that goes back to Vatican II but is integrated more explicitly into Francis's normative thinking.

The Vatican II era "breakthrough" on the morally transformative coherence of love and discernment owes much to the iconoclastic and groundbreaking work of Berhard Häring, captured in a personal tribute by Charles Curran. Curran read Häring's *The Law of Christ* in Italian as a doctoral student at the Gregorian University in 1959.[40] Until that point, Curran's education in moral theology had followed the purpose of the moral "manuals": preparation of confessors-to-be to identify sinful acts by degree within legally specified categories. "Law was the objective norm of morality."[41] Häring's book opened Curran's eyes to the fact that the center of Catholic morality should be responsibility, not law, and that responsibility concerns the entire moral life. Christian moral responsibility is nothing other than one's response to Christ, the Word of God; it consists in love of God and neighbor, nourished by Scripture: "In God's presence, we also find our neighbor and the way to fellowship and community in the Church and the broader human society."[42] Curran maintains that *The Law of Christ* was a transitional work, yet the era's most important moral-theological intervention, because it set the tone and standard for so much to follow. In James Keenan's view, *The Law of Christ* was a "decisive break with the more than two hundred year moral manual tradition . . . of 'moral pathology,'"[43] when truth and its discernment were almost entirely reduced to the defense and application of moral prohibitions, at least in the "personal" sphere.[44] Häring's work crystallized a broader movement to recontextualize morals within the entirety of the Christian life, and to recalibrate moral truth to the concrete responsibilities of agents, as they respond to God and others in a complex and dynamic world. For example, the Decree on Priestly Formation calls for moral theology to be more nourished by the Bible, bringing to light the "calling of the faithful in Christ and the obligation that is theirs of bearing fruit in charity for the life of the world."[45]

Love or charity is especially important to the honest appreciation of moral truth, when moral reality is fragmented and painful. Love is also the sustaining power that lifts and guides the seeker. As Pope Francis expresses it, "In every situation, when dealing with those who have difficulties in living God's law to the full, the invitation to pursue the *via caritatis* must be clearly heard. Fraternal charity is the first law of Christians (cf. *Jn* 15:12; *Gal* 5:14)."[46] For Francis, in the new approach initiated by Häring, discernment should be outwardly as well as inwardly directed. Discernment has to do with relationships, with people, and most especially, with empathy, compassion, and love. Teachers and pastors are urged "to enter into the reality of other people's lives and to know the power of tenderness,"[47] encouraging awareness of where God's grace is operative in people's lives.[48]

In one of his notoriously spontaneous in-flight exchanges with journalists, the pope responded to transgender people with a more generally pertinent remark: "Life is life, things have to be accepted as they come. . . . Not to say that it's all the same, but in each case. Welcome, accompany, study, discern and integrate. This is what Jesus would do today."[49] With this comment and other gestures (e.g., meetings with LGBTQ Catholics[50]), Pope Francis places himself on the side of the learning Church and the pilgrim Church, not only of the teaching Church. In *Amoris laetitia*, he speaks personally and with humility, respecting consensus views of the synod, sometimes confirming (or omitting to confirm) that he agrees with others' views.[51] He does not "magisterially" cancel these out; nor does he operate on the premise that ecclesial authenticity requires a united episcopal front.

Collaborative discernment as an ecclesial practice is embodied in Pope Francis's preference for "synodality" and "a synodal Church."[52] Collaborative discernment as an ecclesial-political practice is manifest particularly in the two-part Family Synod leading up to *Amoris laetitia* and in the Amazon Synod, which shifted the balance of authority from Rome to the Amazonian peoples. At the Amazon Synod and in the follow-up document, *Querida Amazonia*, Pope Francis invited Catholic leaders and leaders of indigenous peoples from the region, as central to the ecological, cultural, and ecclesial vision of the Amazon's future.

Here we see another dimension of Francis's version of discernment: structural sin and unjust practices can undermine the discernment that agents and communities undertake because they are formed in communities or institutions in which vision and dispositions are distorted. Turning inward to individual reflection based on erroneous premises—or finding assurance in interior peace that amounts to complacency in a preexisting mind-set confirmed by personal, ecclesial, or political allies and authorities—does not amount to genuine discernment.

In a generally appreciative commentary on the *Exercises*, Anne Arabome notes that "discernment does not happen in a vacuum." A woman studying the *Exercises* "may be living her life in response to the warped expectations of her religion, culture, or society," and not rarely "might have been raised in a faith tradition that does not give her the room to think or imagine for herself."[53] Arabome points out that Ignatius himself compares the evil spirit to a weak woman; and characterizes women as susceptible to the wiles of the evil one acting as "a false lover."[54] Discernment about the family, for instance, may be "warped" by a gender bias and a culture of ecclesial control over sexual relationships; discernment about ecological justice is warped by a cultural bias, economic interests, and too great a distance between powerful decision-makers and indigenous stakeholders. Going beyond Vatican II, Pope Francis not only calls for collaborative discernment and for widening the circle of collaboration but also for privileging the wisdom and agency of those marginalized by current normative systems.

THE PRIORITY, VOICE, AND AUTHORITY OF THE POOR

The third Vatican II value of Francis is the Church of the poor. Numerous assessments of Francis's intellectual and pastoral history have noted that he has a distinctive "spin" on liberation theology's "preferential option for the poor" (which was eventually incorporated into the writings of predecessors, especially John Paul II[55]), going back to his ministry among the urban poor of Buenos Aires. Jorge Bergoglio came under the early and lasting influence of the "theology of the people" of the Argentinian priest-activists Lucio Gera (a theologian and university professor) and Rafael Tello (a lawyer and professor of philosophy).[56] The perspectives of both, and subsequently of Bergoglio, were shaped by the Argentinian bishops' Episcopal Commission for Pastoral Practice (Comisión Episcopal de Pastoral Prioridades, created in 1966) for the implementation of Vatican II.[57] For the theology of the people, "the simple and poor" in Latin America "are the ones who . . . alone have human dignity and common culture without the privileges of power, possession and knowledge." Indeed, the cultural values and symbols of the poor can be "the seed in the nonpoor of a conversion to the poor, bringing about one's liberation and the liberation of all."[58]

To a reader fifty or more years later, this perspective on "simple and poor" *campesinos* and indigenous peoples, not atypical for its time, seems problematically romanticized and condescending, almost instrumentalizing poverty in the cause of "the liberation of all." As is obvious when we consider feminist or Black liberation movements, for example, oppressed classes are not free of their own internal stereotypes, blind spots, and structures of injustice (e.g., race and gender hierarchies). This was captured with concise eloquence in the title of a book about African American women's studies: *All the Women Are White, All the Blacks Are Men*.[59] Yet positively, the theology of the people identified that systematic conceptualization, logical analysis, and facility with textual analysis—marks of intellectual prowess in Western thought—do not capture the genius of indigenous knowledges or those of people with little formal education. As Pope Francis affirms in *Querida Amazonia*, "Each of the peoples that has survived in the Amazon region possesses its own cultural identity and unique richness, . . . which is hard to conceive using mental categories imported from without."[60] Although the theology of the people seems to place elite theologians, academics, and clergy as the liberators, guardians, and mediators of "popular" theological creativity and authenticity, it is also tacitly empowering these voices by demanding that they be heeded across the Church as a whole. In the second decade of the twenty-first century, Pope Francis will much more directly affirm popular political self-determination and action.

For Pope Francis, moral realities and the obligations they entail can be best understood by those with direct experience and a personal stake in the resolution of dilemmas and conflicts. This is clearly illustrated both in *Amoris laetitia*, with its appreciation of the grace present in divergent family situations; and in *Querida Amazonia*, where wisdom about ecological challenges is to be found with the peoples of the Amazon, not with ecclesial elites in Rome. In a groundbreaking move of *Laudato si'*,[61] Francis directly calls into question John XXIII's premise (in *Pacem in Terris*) that government, political, and civil society leaders are generally of "good will" and can be persuaded to enact reforms justly. He turns instead to popular political agency, already recognized by Paul VI, especially in *Quadragesimo anno*.[62] In *Laudato si'* and in addresses to the World Conference of Popular Movements, Francis sees popular momentum as a positive force for the common good. He does recognize that "populism" too can be morally co-opted and become a perpetrator of injustice.[63]

Laudato si' calls out the lack of political will in the wealthier nations as the fundamental reason why efforts to regulate and modify climate change fail. United Nations summits produce one "ineffectual outcome document" after another, because implementation is voluntary and the greatest emissions-producing nations have the least incentive to comply. Pope Francis understands that climate control is at an impasse because such countries "place their national interests above the global common good."[64] This is why the empowerment of the poor is an essential move in favor of the common good. Pope Francis is hopeful that "local individuals and groups can make a real difference" because

> they are able to instill a greater sense of responsibility, a strong sense of community, a readiness to protect others, a spirit of creativity and a deep love for the land. They are also concerned about what they will eventually leave to their children and grandchildren. These values are deeply rooted in indigenous peoples; . . . public pressure has to be exerted in order to bring about decisive political action. . . . *Unless citizens control political power—national, regional and municipal—it will not be possible to control damage to the environment* [emphasis added].[65]

At about the same time that *Laudato si'* was under construction, Pope Francis began (in 2014) to sponsor the series of World Meetings of Popular Movements. His address at the second one, in Bolivia in 2015, is virtually a magna carta for a popular mobilization to replace the "globalization of indifference" with a "globalization of hope." Popular movements are key to the fight for social and structural justice: "You, the lowly, the exploited, the poor and underprivileged, can do, and are doing, a lot. I would even say that the future of humanity is in great measure in your own hands, through your ability to organize and carry out creative alternatives . . . and through your proactive participation in the great processes of change on the national, regional and global levels."[66] Francis calls upon the peoples of the Amazon to discern causes and potential solutions of ecological challenges to their region that affect the whole planet;[67] and intentionally uses his own role to empower their agency, while also to the extent possible getting out of their way. Their cultures and cosmologies are sites of authentic religious experience and "the good life."[68] That being said, Catholic networking is imperfectly inclusive and just—it, too, can be co-opted by powerful interests and systems, like patriarchy. For example, a "gender lens" identifying the impact of injustices on women or promoting women's agency has not been a strong suit of Catholic organizations, or of Pope Francis. Neither *Laudato si'* nor *Querida Amazonia* nor *Fratelli tutti* spotlights women's potentially huge contribution to the popular mobilization for which *Laudato si'* calls, and that women are already realizing.[69]

CONCLUSION

Looking back over Pope Francis's contribution to moral theology as a whole, its most radical mark is a *decentralization* that follows on contextual discernment, the empowerment of the laity (at least in theory, and in some contexts), the Church of the poor, and the prioritization of love and compassion over analytic stringency and established magisterial positions. Pope Francis has taken the highly significant step of calling upon Catholics at the local level to creatively apply Catholic moral teaching, not only to resist wealthy landowners, economic neocolonialism, or the extractive industries but also to rethink the Church's own constraints on gender, sex, and family. Francis acknowledges, and even urges explicitly, that the Church's magisterium must listen to and learn from the moral realities and insights of "the faithful." Local episcopacies and individual bishops, pastors, or centers of Catholic theology may or may not follow this lead. But the reality is that "the Church" extends around and beyond such authorities and includes sites of Catholicism that creatively generate more diverse Catholic identities and practices.

Even when authorities insist on uniformity, Catholic laity (and, for that matter, clergy and bishops) may openly resist episcopal demands, whether they concern adherence to sexual teachings or to the urgency of action against climate change. In the United States, for example, the majority of Catholics support same-sex civil unions (if not marriage), yet over 40 percent are inhospitable to immigrants who they think "are invading our country."[70] These are both "Catholic nonconformist" positions, emerging at the intersection of subsets of Catholic and cultural values. This leaves Catholicism with a new set of challenges, both *magisterial* and moral-political: how to avoid confirmation bias, widen consultative circles, settle moral differences, and prevent schism.

Bryan Massingale's study of probabilism (chapter 9 of this volume), as a more flexible approach to "dissent" from Catholic teaching, is enlightening in this regard. By retrieving the venerable tradition that a "solidly probable" moral analysis may be adopted as a guide to discernment and action, Massingale provides a way through "decentralized" situations of competing moral-political viewpoints that do not entirely align and may even be in direct conflict. Probabilism reminds us that fluidity and uncertainty of particular discernments do not necessarily preclude constancy of basic values (of the Gospel and of justice), and that some outlooks and discernment outcomes can with a fair degree of certainty be identified as more "probable" than others—without claiming absoluteness.

It is well to remember (as Pope Francis seems to do) that, at the end of the day, no matter how authentic ecclesial or political impulses are to the Gospel, they will never completely defeat resurgent powers of violence and domination. As Theodora Hawksley rightly discerns, Christian politics carries on amid "realities of risk and ambiguity, tragedy, and setback, costliness, conflict, resistance and struggle, and the sheer magnitude of the call to transformation."[71] The Church and its members, too, come under the power of sin.[72] They must embody love, reconciliation, mercy, and peace as faithfully as they can, while negotiating conflicts as compassionately and prudently as possible.

Pope Francis's collaborative mode of Christian discernment has the potential to overcome the marginalization of less powerful stakeholders and correct for limited perspectives and biases, though only if traditional lines of power are rebalanced, and dynamic ecclesial unity is sustained.[73] Collaboration could add epistemological security to situations where no easy or direct application of a general rule brings a clear and definitive resolution. Christian collaborative discernment should be guided by Luke's parable of the Good Samaritan, Matthew's parable of judgment, and Paul's commitment to the unity of culturally different churches. Decentralized and collaborative moral-political discernment could nourish mutual respect, humility, solidarity, faithfulness, and hope—all virtues for the truth in action that is moral truth.

NOTES

1. Catholic News Agency, "Cardinal Sarah Says the Christian Family Counters Both Islamic, Western Extremism," October 14, 2015, www.catholicnewsagency.com/news/32817/cardinal-sarah-says-the-christian-family-counters-both-islamic-western-extremism.
2. See Second Vatican Council, *Gaudium et spes*, December 7, 1965, no. 51, www.vatican.va/archive/hist_councils/ii_vatican_council/documents/vat-ii_const_19651207_gaudium-et-spes_en.html; Second Vatican Council, *Optatum totius*, October 28, 1965, no. 16, www.vatican.va/archive/hist_councils/ii_vatican_council/documents/vat-ii_decree_19651028_optatam-totius_en.html; and *Gaudium et spes*, no. 1, respectively. These texts are treated further below.
3. The term "social justice" appears early in the Catholic social tradition, with the second modern papal social encyclical *Quadragesimo anno*. For the first of nine mentions, see Pius XI, *Quadragesimo anno*, May 15, 1931, no. 57, www.vatican.va/content/pius-xi/en/encyclicals/documents/hf_p-xi_enc_19310515_quadragesimo-anno.html.
4. Pius XI, *Gaudium et spes*, no. 51.
5. Linda Bordoni, "Pope Francis: 'Mercy Is the True Face of Love,'" Vatican News, July 14, 2019, www.vaticannews.va/en/pope/news/2019-07/pope-angelus-catechesis-good-samaritan-mercy.html. This article reports on Pope Francis's Sunday Angelus reflection for July 14, 2019.
6. *Optatam totius*, no. 16.
7. *Gaudium et spes*, no. 1.
8. This is the translation by Richard A. McCormick, "Notes on Moral Theology: 1981," *Theological Studies* 43, no. 1 (March 1982): 69. While the official English translation still has "his acts," the original Latin provided by McCormick is "*objectivis criteriis ex personae ejusdemque actuum natura desumptis.*"

9. *Schema constitutionis pasatoralis de ecclesia in mundo huuis temporis: Expensio modorum partis secondae* (Rome: Vatican Press, 1965), 37–38; as cited by McCormick, "Notes," 69.
10. McCormick.
11. Richard A. McCormick, *The Critical Calling: Reflections on Moral Dilemmas Since Vatican II* (Washington, DC: Georgetown University Press, 1989), 339–40; originally published as "Ethical Considerations of the New Reproductive Technologies," *Fertility and Sterility* 46 (1986), Supplement 1.
12. McCormick, "Notes," 69. McCormick cites Louis Janssens, "Artificial Insemination: Ethics Considerations," *Louvain Studies* 8 (1980) 3–29.
13. See Bernard Hoose, *Proportionalism: The American Debate and Its European Roots* (Washington, DC: Georgetown University Press, 1987).
14. John Paul II, *Veritatis splendor*, August 6, 1993, no. 76, www.vatican.va/content/john-paul-ii/en/encyclicals/documents/hf_jp-ii_enc_06081993_veritatis-splendor.html.
15. Aline Kalbian, "Where Have All the Proportionalists Gone?" *Journal of Religious Ethics* 30, no. 1 (Spring 2002): 3–22.
16. Richard A. McCormick, "Moral Theology Since Vatican II: Clarity or Chaos," *Cross Currents* 29, no. 1 (1979): 24.
17. Thomas Aquinas, *Summa Theologiae* (hereafter *ST*), trans. Fathers of the English Dominican Province, 2nd ed. (Denver: New Advent, 2017), www.newadvent.org/summa, I-II.Q 91.a 2.
18. Aquinas, *ST*, I-II.Q 91.a 2.
19. Aquinas, *ST*, I-II.Q 94.a 2.
20. Aquinas, *ST*, I-II.Q 94.a 2.
21. Francis, *Evangelii gaudium*, November 24, 2013, no. 125, www.vatican.va/content/francesco/en/apost_exhortations/documents/papa-francesco_esortazione-ap_20131124_evangelii-gaudium.html.
22. Aquinas, *ST*, I-II.Q94.a4. See Francis, *Amoris laetitia*, March 19, 2016, no. 304, www.vatican.va/content/dam/francesco/pdf/apost_exhortations/documents/papa-francesco_esortazione-ap_20160319_amoris-laetitia_en.pdf. See also Thomas Aquinas, *Questiones quodlibetales*; some actions that involve a "disorder" can be "made right by reason of particular circumstances." This text is cited by McCormick, "Clarity or Chaos," and is debated by Mark Johnson, "Proportionalism and a Text of the Young Aquinas: Quodlibetum IX, Q. 7, A. 2," *Theological Studies* 53, no. 4 (December 1992): 683–99; and Germain Grisez, *The Way of the Lord Jesus: Christian Moral Principles* (Chicago: Franciscan Herald Press, 1983), chap. 6, Question D, www.twotlj.org/G-1-6-D.html.
23. Francis, *Amoris laetitia*, no. 300.
24. Francis, no. 301.
25. Francis, no. 304. Here Francis draws on Aquinas, *ST*, I-II.Q 94.a 4.
26. Francis, no. 305n348.
27. Francis, no. 301. See Aquinas, *ST*, I-II.Q65.a3.ad3; cf ad2. Aquinas himself attributes these difficulties to previously formed vices that have not yet been overcome, preventing the acts appropriate to the infused (graced) moral virtues. Pope Francis seems to envision that the difficulty could owe to circumstances beyond the agent's control or that are impossible to remedy satisfactorily.
28. See Warren Sazama, SJ, "Some Ignatian Principles for Making Prayerful Decisions," *Faith at Marquette*, www.marquette.edu/faith/ignatian-principles-for-making-decisions.php; accessed January 4, 2023. Sazama cites "Draw Me into Your Friendship: The Spiritual Exercises, A Literal Translation and a Contemporary Reading," by David Fleming, SJ,

5, 16, 24–26, 149–55, 169. He notes that the "numbers [here] refer to the paragraph numbers of the Ignatian text. All quotations from *The Spiritual Exercises* in this booklet are taken from Fleming's contemporary reading of the *Spiritual Exercises*."
29. Sazama, citing *Spiritual Exercises*, nos. 175–87.
30. For an astute reflection on the relation between natural law, conscience, and pastoral flexibility in challenging family situations, and on the related perspectives of Pope Francis, see Johan Bonny, "The Synod on the Family: A Bishop's Expectations," *The Furrow* 65, no. 10 (October 2014): 455–64.
31. Pius XI sees justice as dependent on "social charity"; *Quadragesimo Anno*, nos. 88, 126. However, his concern is not so much loving discernment of context-specific moral truth in what could be termed "individual" decisions, especially not in sexual or marital morality, but rather the need for Christians to convey charity as a social force to uplift the pursuit of justice. See Christine Firer Hinze, "Commentary on *Quadragesimo anno* (On Reconstructing the Social Order)," in *Modern Catholic Social Teaching: Commentaries and Interpretations*, 2nd ed., ed. Kenneth R. Himes (Washington, DC: Georgetown University Press, 2018), 160, 179; and Anna Rowlands, *Towards a Politics of Communion: Catholic Social Teaching in Dark Times* (New York: T&T Clark, 2021), 249.
32. This is how solidarity is defined in John Paul II, *Sollicitudo rei socialis*, December 30, 1987, nos. 38–39, www.vatican.va/content/john-paul-ii/en/encyclicals/documents/hf_jp-ii_enc_30121987_sollicitudo-rei-socialis.html.
33. Francis, *Evangelii gaudium*, nos. 124–25.
34. John Paul II says that it is "possible to identify many points of contact between solidarity and charity, which is the distinguishing mark of Christ's disciples (cf. Jn. 13:35). In the light of faith, solidarity seeks to go beyond itself, to take on the specifically Christian dimension of total gratuity, forgiveness and reconciliation" (*Sollicitudo rei socialis*, no. 40). Following on the Vatican II document *Nostra aetate*, the Congregation for the Doctrine of the Faith, in 2000, released *Dominus Iesus*, which confirmed that the saving grace of God is present to members of all religions and to religious nonbelievers. Congregation for the Doctrine of the Faith, *Dominus Iesus*, August 6, 2000, www.vatican.va/roman_curia/congregations/cfaith/documents/rc_con_cfaith_doc_20000806_dominus-iesus_en.html.
35. Francis, *Amoris laetitia*, nos. 43–49.
36. Francis, no. 304.
37. Francis, no. 79.
38. Francis, no. 305.
39. Cathleen Kaveny, "A Companion, Not a Judge," *Commonweal* 150, no. 1 (January 2023): 30.
40. Bernard Häring, *Das Gesetz Christi* (Freiburg: Verlag Wewel, 1954); Bernard Häring, *La Legge di Cristo, I. Morale Generale* (Brescia: Morcelliana, 1959); Bernard Häring, *The Law of Christ* (Paramus, NJ: Newman Press, 1961).
41. Charles E. Curran, "Take and Read: The Law of Christ," *National Catholic Reporter*, February 1, 2016, www.ncronline.org/blogs/take-and-read-law-christ.
42. Curran.
43. James F. Keenan, "Bernard Häring's Influence on American Catholic Moral Theology," *Journal of Moral Theology* 1, no. 1 (2012): 23, citing Thomas Slater, an early twentieth-century English manualist.
44. Keenan.

45. *Optatum totius*, no. 16.
46. Francis, *Amoris laetitia*, no. 306; see also no. 311.
47. Francis, no. 38.
48. Francis, no. 297.
49. Inés San Martín, "Pope Says Walk with Trans Persons, but Fight Gender Theory" (citing interview with reporters, return flight from Georgia, October 1, 2016), *Crux*, October 2, 2016, available at: https://cruxnow.com/global-church/2016/10/pope-says-walk-trans-persons-fight-gender-theory. See the very similar statement by Francis, *Amoris laetitia*, no. 312.
50. See Francis DeBernardo, "Lessons to Be Learned from Pope's Meeting with Transgender Man," New Ways Ministry, February 11, 2015; www.newwaysministry.org/2015/02/11/lessons-to-be-learned-from-popes-meeting-with-transgender-man/. See also James Martin, "Pope Francis Is Making Space for LGBT People in the Church—and It's a Huge Step Forward," *America*, September 23, 2021, www.americamagazine.org/faith/2021/09/23/james-martin-pope-francis-lgbt-241483; and Linda Bordoni, "Pope to LGBT Catholics: God Is Father Who Does Not Disown Any of His Children," Vatican News, May 9, 2022, www.vaticannews.va/en/pope/news/2022-05/pope-letter-fr-martin-lgtb-outreach-questions.html.
51. E.g., in *Amoris laetitia*, no. 251, the pope seems to distance himself from the idea that there are "absolutely no grounds" for considering same-sex marriage to be "even remotely analogous" to Christian marriage and family, by stating simply that "the Synod Fathers observed" that such is the case. In contrast, in no. 297, we have Pope Francis's personal endorsement of the idea that there is "grace in the lives" of divorced Catholics in a civil marriage: "the Synod Fathers reached a general consensus, which I support." This is a remarkable shift in pontifical teaching style and exercise of authority.
52. See chapter 4 in this volume, by Elyse Raby.
53. Anne Arabome, SS, *Why Do You Trouble This Woman? Women and the Spiritual Exercises of St. Ignatius of Loyola* (Mahwah, NJ: Paulist Press, 2022), 127.
54. Arabome, 126, citing *Spiritual Exercises*, 325, 326.
55. E.g., *Sollicitudo rei socialis*, nos. 39, 42.
56. See Massimo Borghesi, *The Mind of Pope Francis: Jorge Mario Bergoglio's Intellectual Journey* (Collegeville, MN: Liturgical Press, 2017); Rafael Luciani, *The Theology of Pope Francis* (Maryknoll, NY: Orbis Books, 2017); and Juan Carlos Scannone, "Pope Francis and the Theology of the People," *Theological Studies* 77, no. 1 (March 2016) 118–35. Chapter 6 in this volume, by M. T. Davila, also explores Francis's contributions on this topic.
57. Scannone, "Pope Francis," 118–19.
58. Scannone, 122.
59. Akasha (Gloria T.) Hull et al., eds., *But Some of Us Are Brave: All the Women Are White, All the Blacks Are Men; Black Women's Studies* (New York: Feminist Press at the City University of New York, 1993).
60. Francis, *Querida Amazonia*, February 2, 2020, no. 31, www.vatican.va/content/francesco/en/apost_exhortations/documents/papa-francesco_esortazione-ap_20200202_querida-amazonia.html.
61. Francis, *Laudato si'*, May 24, 2015, no. 169, www.vatican.va/content/francesco/en/apost_exhortations/documents/papa-francesco_esortazione-ap_20200202_querida-amazonia.html.

62. One commentator, Christine Gudorf, has called *Octogesima anno* and its recognition of popular authority a "dead letter" to the subsequent magisterium, Christine E. Gudorf, "*Octogesima adveniens*: A Call to Action on the Eightieth Anniversary of *Rerum Novarum*," in *Modern Catholic Social Teaching*, ed. Himes, 341.
63. Francis, *Fratelli tutti*, October 3, 2020, chap. 5, esp. nos. 159, 161, www.vatican.va /content/francesco/en/encyclicals/documents/papa-francesco_20201003_ enciclica-fratelli-tutti.html. See also Julio L. Martinez, "La Revitalización comunitarista del Bien Común en el Magisterio del Papa Francisco," in *Teología con Alma Bíblica: Miscelánea Homenaje al Prof. Dr. José Ramón Busto Saiz*, ed. Pablo Alonso Vicente and Jesús Santiago Madrigal Terrazas (Madrid: Comillas Pontifical University, 2021), 397.
64. Francis, *Laudato si'*, no. 169.
65. Francis, no. 179.
66. Francis, "Participation at the Second World Meeting of Popular Movements," Bolivia, 2015, no. 1, www.vatican.va/content/francesco/en/speeches/2015/july /documents/papa-francesco_20150709_bolivia-movimenti-popolari.html.
67. Francis, *Querida Amazonia*, no. 42: "The wisdom of the original peoples of the Amazon region . . . inspires care and respect for creation, with a clear consciousness of its limits, and prohibits its abuse."
68. Amazonian Synod preparatory document, "Amazonia: New Paths for the Church and for an Integral Ecology," June 17, 2019, nos. 4, 6, www.sinodoamazonico.va /content/sinodoamazonico/en/documents/preparatory-document-for-the-synod-for -the-amazon.html. On controversies, see Austen Ivereigh, "When the Amazon Meets the Tiber: What to Expect from the First 'Territorial' Synod," *Commonweal*, October 9, 2019, www.commonwealmagazine.org/when-amazon-meets-tiber.
69. Francis, *Querida Amazonia*, no. 103.
70. See the Public Religion Research Institute's 2022 *American Values Survey* (repeated annually),www.prri.org/research/challenges-in-moving-toward-a-more-inclusive-democracy -findings-from-the-2022-american-values-survey/.
71. Theodora Hawksley, *Peacebuilding and Catholic Social Teaching* (Notre Dame, IN: University of Notre Dame Press, 2022), 210.
72. Hawksley, 210, 231.
73. See Massimo Faggioli, "From Collegiality to Synodality: Promise and Limits of Francis's 'Listening Primacy'" *Irish Theological Quarterly* 85, no. 4 (November 2020): 352–69.

2

RESPONSIVE LISTENING

Giving Recognition and Empowering the Voices of Those Long Ignored

James F. Keenan, SJ

The pontificates of John Paul II and Benedict XVI were known for instructing and demanding assent to their teachings on matters regarding beginning-of-life and end-of-life issues as well as on matters of sexuality. Recognizing the cultures of death and relativity, they explicated teachings they saw as essential for Catholics to resist these harmful cultures. Though, rightly, Thomas Massaro's, Megan McCabe's, and Andrea Vicini's chapters in this volume (respectively, chapters 5, 10, and 11) each highlight the ways Pope Francis has contributed to matters of social ethics, sexuality, and bioethics, respectively, Pope Francis still seems much less interested than his predecessors in keeping the tradition up to date or better defined. And while he does label our world as a "throwaway culture,"[1] and advocates for greater attention to climate change and in particular to those who are forced to migrate as both Kristin Heyer and Daniel DiLeo argue in this volume (in chapters 7 and 13, respectively), he spends far less time than his predecessors in critiquing culture and in proposing strategies of resistance. He seems less interested in "othering" culture; rather than resisting, he seeks to promote encounters. Above all, he seems more interested in empowering agency for a new recognition of persons. Pope Francis wants to change not what we know about the tradition, but whether we recognize that the world is at risk and that those most endangered are at once those closest to the social impact of these threats *and* farthest from having any "control" over them. He wants us to recognize them, listen to them, learn from them, and then accompany them. He wants to waken us to their situation and to keep us vigilant to their needs. He wants us to be, above all, responsive.

He wants us to see those whom he sees: the poor and working classes living in a progressively precarious world. Whether the matter is economic justice, public health, migration, or climate change, these people are the ones in increasingly challenging situations in each instance. So as to respond rightly, he wants us to be attentive to their voices. Thus, he speaks not only to us but to them as well, so as to solicit their voices, to make the world alert to what they have to say.

He is not convinced that we understand the lament of others. For instance, in *Amoris laetitia,* he prophetically depicts the challenges of contemporary marital and family relations; he raises the context of the families who face these challenges so that we become attentive to and understand what they say. He tries to prompt Church leaders to restrain the clerical habit of directing the laity; rather, he insists that clerics and other ministers must listen to those whom they serve. As Elyse Raby notes in chapter 4 of this book, Francis wants a ministry much more motivated by mercy. Still, many in the hierarchy fail to heed his admonitions and have passively declined to receive his promptings.[2]

Finally, so as to keep open the possibility of recognition, listening, and dialogue with those in need, the pope rarely countenances censorship, a practice that his predecessors frequently invoked.[3] He seems more interested in keeping communications open than in silencing those who speak and think otherwise.[4]

In this chapter, I begin with the salutary work of Pope Francis in starting the World Meetings of Popular Movements. This work is emblematic of the inclusive listening of his pontificate to those still not yet adequately recognized. I invoke indications from *Evangelii gaudium* and the Amazonian synod that complement and support this project. Then I turn to synodality and *Amoris laetitia,* which first highlight the need to get a diversity of voices to have a culture of inclusive listening and, second, provide a vision for a ministry of accompaniment that recognizes and heeds their voices and agency. The conclusion turns to his appointment of cardinals as a practice of empowering the voices of the peripheries and notes the reforms of *Praedicate Evangelium* so as to highlight how in reforming and restructuring the curia, Francis is animating the Church to institutionally develop an acumen for diversity in order to listen to voices long alienated and recognize the agency of forgotten neighbors.

THE WORLD MEETINGS OF POPULAR MOVEMENTS

Since October 2014, Pope Francis has been convening the "World Meetings of Popular Movements." In Rome, the pope launched his first meeting with these popular movements to address what he called in *Evangelii gaudium* the "economy of exclusion and inequality."[5] With representatives from over one hundred such movements, the pope articulates a recurring motif of linking three Spanish terms—*tierra, techo, trabajo*—which he calls the "3 Ts," and which are translated into English as the 3 Ls (land, lodging, and labor). This motif is frequently invoked by the pope in a multitude of contexts.[6] Yet at this meeting, as Mathew Whelan argues, "Francis has invited the peripheries to the ecclesial center."[7] The second meeting was held in Bolivia, in July 2015; and the third was again held in Rome, in November 2016.

After the third meeting, the popular movements moved into a mode of preparing for the Amazonian synod, which was held in October 2019. Later, in his Easter letter to Popular Movements on April 12, 2020, the pope resumed the specific global discussions with the popular movements.[8] Subsequently, the popular movements met again virtually on October 24 to present their document, "The Economy of Francis,"[9] as a contribution to the larger initiative, "The Economy of Francesco," that was held in Rome on November 19–22.[10] These encounters set the stage for the fourth formal meeting in 2021.

Michael Cardinal Czerny and Paolo Foglizzo detail this fourth meeting, which was held in two stages on July 9 and October 16, 2021. They note that the four major meetings together are one of the "most innovative characteristics" of Pope Francis's pontificate, the result of "a strategic choice, rooted in his teaching and at the same time nourishing it. The fact that his speeches at the World Meeting of Popular Movements are cited seven times in the encyclical *Fratelli tutti* is evidence for this."[11]

At the core of all these meetings is giving recognition to these workers who lack such acknowledgment. The commentators help us to see how we are not familiar with the workers' conditions, precisely because we do not yet recognize the workers themselves. They are missing from our horizons. Powerfully, they urge us to recognize those whom we overlook:

> These workers are statistically invisible, and they risk remaining hidden from public opinion, from the Church, from the political world and from those who design economic, social and welfare policies. Proof of this is the remarkable lack of coverage of the effects of the pandemic and lockdown with which they had to deal in every part of the world, in contrast with those who work in the formal sector. Yet we are not talking about a marginal or residual phenomenon: at the global level, the International Labour Organization estimates that 60% of workers and 80% of businesses operate in the informal sector, although there are many differences between countries. For example, while informality affects 20% of US workers, in the Democratic Republic of Congo the figure is over 90%.[12]

Their "informal" work is not recognized; nor are they. As such, we do not hear them.

At the first stage of the fourth meeting, held on July 9, 2021, the popular movements discussed the impact of the COVID-19 pandemic and generated a document titled *Let's Save Humanity and the Planet*.[13] By this point in the meetings, the movements had articulated a game plan. They are not only objects to be heard, but are also subjects leading reform. This document served as the foundation for the second meeting, on October 16, which highlighted a documentary, *La Fuerza del Nosotros (The Power of We)*,[14] and then the pope's reply, a video message that invoked the apostolic exhortation *Evangelii gaudium*'s famous paragraph 198:

> This is why I want a Church which is poor and for the poor. They have much to teach us. Not only do they share in the *sensus fidei*, but in their difficulties they know the suffering Christ. We need to let ourselves be evangelized by them. The new evangelization is an invitation to acknowledge the saving power at work in their lives and to put them at the centre of the Church's pilgrim way. We are called to find Christ in them, to lend our voice to their causes, but also to be their friends, to listen to them, to speak for them and to embrace the mysterious wisdom which God wishes to share with us through them.[15]

Czerny and Foglizzo use the language of recognition to explain the pope's reply:

> From the very first lines, the pope's affection for the popular movements shines through with great force. It is a deep bond, based on respect and devoid of any condescension. It is as a friend, an equal, that Francis speaks. For this reason, he offers what every person needs to become aware of and exercise their dignity: recognition. Being recognised, as citizens and as workers, is moreover a demand that popular movements explicitly formulate, even in the documentary *La fuerza del nosotros*.[16]

Philosophers like Charles Taylor, Paul Ricouer, Paddy McQueen, Axel Honneth, Nancy Fraser, and Michael Sohn have argued that recognition entails an awakening from a tendency to overlook or ignore to an acknowledgment of the rightful dignity of others.[17] They propose that we respond through an encounter of mutual vulnerability to the dignity of others who have not yet been given their socially due recognition. A recent contribution by Honneth makes the significance of recognition all the more palpable.[18] Here we must acknowledge the human need for recognition and note how, when recognition is given, the long-overlooked respond.

Rightfully, Czerny and Foglizzo's commentatary highlights how Pope Francis provides this deep form of recognition to the world's long-overlooked workers in his message to the World Meeting of Popular Movements:

> Above all, he highlights how well they have been able to care for the common good during the pandemic: many "essential" workers, who could not stop working during the lockdown and indeed faced a higher risk of contagion, belong precisely to the informal sector: "Like the doctors, nurses, and health workers in the trenches of healthcare, you have taken your place in the trenches of marginalized neighbourhoods." In summary, Pope Francis recognizes a twofold identity of those belonging to popular movements: that of victims of an unjust system, and that of protagonists of their own liberation and the building of alternatives.[19]

Throughout these meetings, the recognition of these movements becomes the centerpiece of his pontificate. It is not a condescending recognition; it is recognition of their capacity to teach and instruct about the world in which we all live.

Recognition is key to understanding Francis's inclusive, responsive listening. He recognizes first that the participants in these movements have been long ignored and then, second, that we could learn better from them what we need to understand about our world. Here we see that he is interested in the social location of the speakers, a theme that Lisa Sowle Cahill highlights in chapter 1 of this volume. Francis seeks to ensure that those coming from the borders are not simply token representatives but rather constitute an expansive, inclusive, and diverse mass that can represent as many of those who have been overlooked as possible. These are the voices from whom he wants us to learn.

Finally, in the pope's video at the Fourth Meeting, we hear him identify the biases that cause the lack of recognition of others. Breaking down these biases by guaranteeing the voices of the poor is his agenda for a Church and world that genuinely dreams together:

> Let us build bridges of love so that the voices of the periphery with their weeping, but also with their singing and joy, provoke not fear but empathy in the rest of society. And so, I persist in my pestering. It is necessary to confront together the populist discourses of intolerance, xenophobia, and *aporophobia*, which is hatred of the poor. Like everything that leads us to indifference, meritocracy and individualism, these narratives only serve to divide our peoples, and to undermine and nullify our poetic capacity, the capacity to dream together.[20]

In *Let Us Dream: The Path to a Better Future*, Pope Francis instructs us to go to the peripheries: "to return the dignity of the people we need to go to the margins of society. Hidden there are ways of looking at the world that can give us all a fresh start. We cannot dream of the future while continuing to ignore the lives of practically a third of the world's population rather than seeing them as a resource."[21] Abandoning the margins is an abandonment of ourselves. Our dignity is tied to their dignity. He adds, "The health of a society can be judged by its periphery. A periphery that is abandoned, sidelined, despised, and neglected shows an unstable, unhealthy society that cannot survive without major reforms. . . . By opening to the margin, to the people's organizations, we unleash change. . . . To embrace the margins is to expand our horizons, for we see more clearly and broadly from the edges of society."[22]

SYNODALITY AND *AMORIS LAETITIA*

On the fiftieth anniversary of the Synod of Bishops, Pope Francis stated emphatically: "The journey of synodality is the journey that God wants from his Church in the third millennium. . . . A synodal Church is a listening Church, aware that listening is more than hearing. It is a reciprocal listening in which each one has something to learn."[23]

When we think of the pope giving voice to the margins, we need to think of the synod as an institutional event that promotes not only newer or more diverse voices, but also a plethora of them. There we will hear critical masses of voices long excluded. To avoid privileging a few who could become reductively instructive, the pope continues to exhort that we open ourselves to hearing from more.

These synodal practices are not Francis's inventions but rather integral to the development of the tradition of the Church. Francis wants us to learn more. He creates space and conditions that generate the pathways for learning what we do not yet know. Interested in making progress, he sees that through synodality we could learn from those long overlooked who can teach that we need to hear and heed.

The paradigm or original model of such moral discernment is found in the Church's first synod, the Council of Jerusalem, as described in Acts 15.[24] The account is very much foundational for any understanding of the synodal gatherings that exercise moral discernment. Acts 15 begins with a problem: people from Judea are teaching "Unless you are circumcised according to Mosaic custom you cannot be saved" (Acts 15:1). But the Gentiles are asking, "Is this really necessary for salvation?" How does the Church resolve this? Fundamentally, it listens to the witnessing of Peter and then to Paul and Barnabas, who narrate from the peripheries the acts of God through the Holy Spirit. They witness to "the signs and wonders God had done with them" (Acts 15:12).

This chapter cannot address all the intricacies of the Council of Jerusalem, but by that "synod," the Church in Jerusalem was led to the discernment by and through the Holy Spirit. Engaging missionary testimonies, all in the context of prayer, the discernment is completed effectively when the decision is promulgated and received. Thus, just as the missionaries brought their questions and insights before the apostles at Jerusalem, the cardinals brought to the recent synods their local questions on marriage, divorce, and remarriage.

We should remember that the Apostolic Exhortation *Amoris laetitia* was born of two synods. The exhortation is the pope's response to this reinstituted practice of the church. He also proposes the ministry of accompaniment that emerges from Acts 15 and, therefore, from synodal practice. Through the synods' search for an answer from the Spirit, the Church hears in Pope Francis's exhortation a call to move ahead together, listening and ministering through accompaniment.

Accompaniment requires recognizing the conscience of the one speaking. We discover this in two key comments in *Amoris*. The first is the famous remark "We have been called to form consciences, not to replace them."[25] This comment reminds the reader to respect and not ignore the conscience of the other. The second comment insists that we ought to listen not to correct but rather to understand what constitutes the attainable. Here the pope suggests that in our ministry, we must temper the Catholic tendency to dismiss the other's positions when they do not square with actual teachings. Rather, he wants us to recognize the utterance long overlooked: "I am doing the best I possibly can." The pope proposes the ministerial recognition of another's own generous efforts to progress as a worthy form of accompaniment. He writes:

> Conscience can do more than recognize that a given situation does not correspond objectively to the overall demands of the Gospel. It can also recognize with sincerity and honesty what for now is the most generous response which can be given to God, and come to see with a certain moral security that it is what God himself is asking amid the concrete complexity of one's limits, while yet not fully the objective ideal. In any event, let us recall that this discernment is dynamic; it must remain ever open to new stages of growth and to new decisions which can enable the ideal to be more fully realized.[26]

As history helped us to see that synods are well rooted in early pastoral practices, history helps again in understanding moral discernment and accompaniment as, in fact, an ancient practice. A study of the originality of the Irish practice of confessing sin from the sixth century notes that in the beginning these "confessions were usually made to a spiritual guide known as an *anamchara*, an Irish word which literally means soul-friend. The soul-friend was esteemed within the monastic system. An ancient Irish saying comments that 'anyone without a soul-friend is like a body without a head.' Every monk was expected to have an *anamchara* to whom he could make manifest his conscience (*manifestation conscientiae*)."[27]

The practice spread. The role of the soul-friend was not just to discern or judge for the other; rather, the *anamchara* was a guide to accompany the individual through the trials of life. The encounter between the soul-friend and the individual aimed at a dialogue that "was neither contractual nor constraining but which bore testimony, instead to a God who was always willing to forgive." The dialogue therefore was a "healing" one.[28] For this reason, the *anamchara* was to be hospitable, welcoming the weary penitent on their journey so that the individual could manifest their conscience. Thus, the *anamchara* is a fellow pilgrim on the "same pilgrim path."[29] The hospitality that the *anamchara* offered was solidarity, so that the pilgrim maintained the journey. In many ways, the *anamchara* was a person who knew suffering, who "comes through the fire of real suffering and self-sacrifice while at the same time, growing ever more open to the saving forgiving grace of Christ, and one who always reserves in his heart, a sincere hospitality for the stranger, the fellow-pilgrim, the fellow-sufferer."[30]

A humble conscience needs a good listener who is more interlocutor than judge. Married couples can find in the Church their own *anamchara*. It seems we will need more and more *anamchara* to accompany our members as they in conscience begin to think anew of how they are called to be disciples with one another in a Church that is not fearful of gathering in synods.

This type of ministry is also instructive for theological ethicists. For instance, Conor Kelly argues that the role of the ethicist was now significantly changed by the exhortation.[31] His argument concerns how the matter of discernment affects not only the reception of a teaching and its ministry but also the teachers of the Church who, in articulating or interpreting the tradition, must discern reality as it is before they articulate their own assessments. Kelly's position is held by others who argue that the models of listening and accompaniment are prompting a paradigm shift in pastoral theology and in theological ethics. The titles of each of these collections tells the story: From Belgium, Thomas Knieps's *A Point of No Return? "Amoris Laetitia" on Marriage, Divorce and Remarriage*;[32] from Italy, Antonio Autiero's *For a New Pastoral Culture: The Contribution of* Amoris Laetitia;[33] from Germany, Stephan Goertz and Caroline Witting's Amoris Laetitia: *A Turning Point in Moral Theology?*;[34] from India, Shaji George Kochuthara's Amoris Laetitia: *Transforming Pastoral Theology and Transforming the Church*;[35] from Nigeria, Stan Chu Ilo's *Love, Joy, and Sex: African Conversations on* Amoris Laetitia *and Gospel of Family in a Divided World*;[36] and from the United States, Thomas

Rausch and Roberto Dell'Oro's *Pope Francis on the Joy of Love: Theological and Pastoral Reflections on* Amoris Laetitia.[37] In order to make progress, we need to see what we are actually learning about the world in which we live.

REMAKING THE COLLEGE OF CARDINALS

The pope's aim to get the voices of the peripheries heard is, as we have seen, the cornerstone of *Evangelii gaudium* made manifest in the World Meetings of Popular Movements. Antonio Spadaro and Mauricio López Oropeza distinguish the peripheries from the center in their essay on synodality in *La Civiltà Cattolica*:

> Francis, in his discernment as universal pastor of the Church and as a moral leader with a global impact, speaks to us of a process in which the periphery illuminates the center without pretending to take its place, but contributing to transforming, purifying and renewing it. That is to say, the periphery contributes to the conversion of this center, which has lost in a certain sense some of its capacity to listen and be amazed at the ever new and renewed voice of the Spirit. And the periphery can contribute to the transformation of the center to the extent that it does not lose its identity. It is from that marginal existence that Christ made his way and continues to do so today in our world with all its tensions and contrasts in order to redeem it.[38]

Using their insights, we can see that as Paul and Barnabas brought their witness from the peripheries to the center in Jerusalem; it was Jerusalem that in listening was able to discern how to progress. The injunction of Francis to do this needs to be recognized here. He perpetually calls us to make progress. The peripheries and the center come together in the exhortation to follow the lead of the Spirit.

The call to forge ahead has long been regarded as part of the tradition. Gregory the Great wrote: "Certainly, in this world, the human spirit is like a boat foolishly fighting against the river's rush: one is never allowed to stay still, because unless one forges ahead, one will slide back downstream."[39] Bernard of Clairvaux too emphasized how idleness cannot not be a disciple's stance, by writing: "To not progress on the way of Life is to regress."[40] Thomas Aquinas conflated their insights into a motto: "To stand on the way of God is to withdraw."[41] Disciples are always called to progress, so as not to lose sight of the one who summons us. Indeed, I had the privilege at a papal audience on May 13, 2022, to hear Pope Francis echo these sentiments as he urged us to progress, noting the contemporary tendency that "does so much harm to the Church," of wanting to "'turn back,' either out of fear or because of a lack of ingenuity or a lack of courage."[42]

Still, the distinction on the peripheries and the center must not be misunderstood when examining the consistories appointing cardinals. Andrea Tornielli noted at the announcement of the fifth consistory in August 2022: "Once again, the Pope has chosen to associate the College of Cardinals with bishops from all over the world, preferring the peripheries and overlooking those sees that were once traditionally considered '*cardinalitial*.'"[43] Was the center overlooked?

As he reported the same news, the American journalist John Allen reminded readers that "In his first consistory in February 2014, Pope Francis created new cardinals from Nicaragua, Ivory Coast [Côte d'Ivoire], South Korea, Burkina Faso, and Haiti, all of whom were prelates without any detailed profile on the global Catholic stage."[44] Yet here, Allen notes not only are the new cardinals for 2022 not known on the global scene; they do not seem to know one another either. Allen subsequently wrote that Francis will "solidify his reputation as the 'Pope of the Peripheries,' featuring first-ever cardinals from Paraguay, East Timor, Singapore and Mongolia."[45] But in that essay, after naming the four countries in the first paragraph, Allen spends another twenty paragraphs on how the pope has overlooked potential cardinals from Southern Italy. Clearly, if one looks at the upcoming consistory, then it seems that Spadaro's center is not holding.

I found the best journalistic assessment of the 2022 announcement came from Claire Giangravé of Religion News Service. Regarding the bishop of San Diego being elevated when the archbishop of Los Angeles was not, she noted the pattern repeated itself over the past ten years, of the pope recognizing a particularly dedicated bishop, while overlooking "*cardinalitial*" territories. Thus, she noted, "His choice to deny Milan while making Bishop Oscar Cantoni of Como, Italy, a cardinal was greeted with shock and indignation from Italian news outlets but was understood as a twin expression of concern for migrants and scorn for careerism in the Church."[46]

Still, she emphasized his predilection for getting representatives of overlooked places as more important than whether they were cut from the same cloth as Francis. She explained, "geography—pulling from all corners of the globe—trumped ideology in this round of appointments."[47] Lest anyone still think that the pope is stacking the college to secure a successor in his image, Giangravé reminded us that in the 2022 consistory, Archbishop Fernando Vérgez Alzaga, who oversees the management of the Vatican City State, was to become the first cardinal from the Legionaries of Christ.

Finally, Francis giving voice to the peripheries is a constant, in all the commentaries. Still there is a major "periphery" missed in his planning for each of the consistories. Giangravé notes that "in 2015, he appointed the Reverend Ernest Simoni, an ordinary priest he had met in Albania the year before, overriding the requirement that only bishops be made cardinals."[48] If the pope can appoint men who are not bishops, a violation of canon law, he is but a small step away from appointing a woman, who whether from the peripiheries or not, would be a voice never before heard in the college of cardinals.[49]

PRAEDICATE EVANGELIUM

Austen Ivereigh provides us a hermeneutical key to the relatively new constitution for the Curia, *Praedicate Evangelium*.[50] He explains: "The constitution consolidates and deepens the reform that Francis has been carrying out these past nine years. It is a reform aimed at nothing less than a conversion of the way power is exercised in and from Rome, and by extension in the global Catholic Church." That curial power exists, as the subtitle of the constitution states, for "its service to the Church in the world."[51]

From the very beginning of the constitution, the Church is defined as composed of "missionary disciples." Fundamental among its general principles is the possibility that everyone—including the lay faithful—can be appointed to roles of government in the Roman Curia by virtue of the vicarious power of the Successor of Peter.[52]

A key statement within the constitution emerges: "Each Christian, by virtue of baptism, is a missionary disciple 'to the extent that he or she has encountered the love of God in Christ Jesus.' This must necessarily be taken into account in the reform of the Curia, which should consequently make provision for the involvement of lay women and men, also in roles of government and responsibility."[53]

Ivereigh warns against seeing this as primarily a breakthrough for "lay empowerment." Instead, he argues, this promotes "a Church in which leadership is tied to charisms and ministries, rather than bound up with the clerical state and ecclesiastical careerism. What this implies is a synodal Church in which communion is the fruit of a mutual listening, in which people of faith, bishops, the Bishop of Rome are each listening to the other, and all listening to the Holy Spirit."[54] I tend to think of a missionary disciple as a descendant of both those who left Jerusalem after Acts 15 and later those who were known as *anamchara*.

Ivereigh refers us to Pope Francis's earlier use of the missionary disciples in *Evangelii gaudium*, where in commenting on *Lumen gentium*, Francis writes, "In all the baptized, from first to last, the sanctifying power of the Spirit is at work, impelling us to evangelization. The people of God is holy thanks to this anointing, which makes it infallible *in credendo*. This means that it does not err in faith, even though it may not find words to explain that faith. The Spirit guides it in truth and leads it to salvation."[55] Now, nearly nine years later, the term helps the pope explain how a synodal Church that accompanies is called to inclusive listening for the sake of itself and for the world.[56]

Still, Ivereigh, who points us back to *Evangelii gaudium* so as to understand *Praedicate Evangelium*, points us back further still to *Aparecida* in order to understand the apostolic letter. As Ivereigh notes, the question of the synod on the new evangelization that Benedict XVI convened was the question that the Church faces: "How to propose the Gospel in a secular, liquid world?" Ivereigh directs us to Francis's first foray into the topic: "*Aparecida* is essential to understand the evangelizing vision of the Francis pontificate."[57]

Ivereigh notes that in 2007 it was Bergoglio who "masterfully and patiently reconciled different groups, fashioning a final draft from thousands of amendments."[58] Ivereigh adds that in his first months as pope, it was the *Aparecida* document that Francis handed to heads of state so as to give them an idea of his upcoming agenda. He told a delegation of Latin American bishops that as pope he would be "doing nothing else but apply *Aparecida*." Massimo Borghesi, Ivereigh notes, called *Aparecida* Francis's "manifesto."[59]

It was through listening to the margins that Francis brought *Aparecida* to fruition to set an evangelizing agenda for a continent whose Church leaders had effectively lost their way for how to proceed. In his address to El Consejo Episcopal Latinoamericano y Caribeño (the Latin American and Caribbean Episcopal Council) in 2017, Francis said that *Aparecida* "was the effort to put Jesus' mission at the very heart of the Church, making it the yardstick for measuring the effectiveness of her structures, the results of her labors, the fruitfulness of her ministers and the joy they awaken—for without joy, we attract no one."[60]

Eloquently, Ivereigh explains *Aparecida*'s genius and affords us a summary presentation of the genesis of the papal call to inclusive listening:

> Rather than accommodating to modernity—whether through acceptance or rejection—*Aparecida* called for an alternative modernity, built from the ground up, from the periphery, from those left behind. Rather than lamenting secularization, *Aparecida* saw Christianity's loss of cultural and political power as an opportunity to recover the gratuity of God's grace. Rather than defining itself as antiglobalization, it sought a globalization of solidarity. Rather than seeking to bolster the power and the prestige of the Church's beleaguered institutions, it offered a paradox: that precisely those bodies of people that are weak in resources yet rich in mercy and witness are the most capable of evangelizing in a liquid world, and can give God's Kingdom a new birth in our time.[61]

An inclusive, responsive listening, particularly to those on the furthest margins, reconciles us to one another and to our shared mission of discipleship. This became Bergoglio's lesson and is now ours.[62] By accompanying and listening to one another, we begin to recognize yet again the Spirit who leads us.

NOTES

1. Charles M. A. Clark and Helen Alford, "The Throwaway Culture in the Economy of Exclusion: Pope Francis and Economists on Waste," *American Journal of Economic Sociology* 78, no. 4 (September 2019): 973–1008, https://doi.org/10.1111/ajes.12295.
2. James F. Keenan, "Regarding *Amoris Laetitia*: Its Language, Its Reception, Some Challenges, and the Agnosticism of Some of the Hierarchy," *Perspectiva Teológica* 53, no. 1 (2021): 41–60, www.faje.edu.br/periodicos/index.php/perspectiva/article/view/4675/4605; Antonio Autiero, "Resistances to *Amoris Laetitia*: A Critical Approach," *Journal of Moral Theology* 11, no. 2 (2022): 1–14, http://doi.org/10.55476/001c.37339.
3. See chapter 9 in this volume, by Bryan N. Massingale.
4. Austen Ivereigh, "Pope Francis' Reforms Make the Heresy-Hunting Vatican of John Paul II Barely Recognizable," *National Catholic Reporter*, June 7, 2022, www.ncronline.org/news/opinion/pope-francis-reforms-make-heresy-hunting-vatican-john-paul-ii-barely-recognizable.
5. Francis, *Evangelii gaudium*, November 24, 2013, no. 53, www.vatican.va/content/francesco/en/apost_exhortations/documents/papa-francesco_esortazione-ap_20131124_evangelii-gaudium.html.
6. Michael Czerny and Paolo Foglizzo, "The Strength of the Excluded: World Meeting of Popular Movements at the Vatican," *Thinking Faith*, January 29, 2015, www.thinkingfaith.org/articles/strength-excluded-world-meeting-popular-movements-vatican.
7. Matthew Whelan, *Blood in the Fields: Oscar Romero, Catholic Social Teaching, and Land Reform* (Washington, DC: Catholic University of America Press, 2020), 305–12, at 307.
8. Francis, "Letter of his Holiness Pope Francis to the Popular Movements," April 12, 2020, www.vatican.va/content/francesco/en/letters/2020/documents/papa-francesco_20200412_lettera-movimentipopolari.html.
9. Inés San Martín, "Popular Movements Meeting Supported by Pope Francis Presents Proposals for New Economic System," *The Tablet*, October 26, 2020, https://thetablet.org/popular-movements-meeting-supported-by-pope-francis-presents-proposals-for-new-economic-system/. The document can be found online at https://movpop.org/wp-content/uploads/2020/10/ENG-DF_PPMM_EconomyFrancis.pdf.
10. "The Economy of Francesco," Economy of Communion, www.edc-online.org/en/eventi-e-news/the-economy-of-francesco.html.
11. Michael Czerny and Paolo Foglizzo, "The World Can Be Seen More Clearly from the Peripheries: The Fourth World Meeting of Popular Movements," *Thinking Faith*, June 1, 2022, www.thinkingfaith.org/articles/world-can-be-seen-more-clearly-peripheries-fourth-world-meeting-popular-movements.
12. Czerny and Foglizzo.

13. Fourth World Meeting of Popular Movements, *Let's Save Humanity and the Planet* (Summary Document), October 16, 2021, https://drive.google.com/file/d/1i-bBxYQEX3XRVMpBu0d-aES3cIfkphav/view.
14. "La fuerza de nosotros," *Encuentro Mundial de Movimientos Populares*, https://movpop.org/2021/10/la-fuerza-del-nosotros/.
15. Francis, *Evangelii gaudium*, November 24, 2013, no. 198, www.vatican.va/content/francesco/en/apost_exhortations/documents/papa-francesco_esortazione-ap_20131124_evangelii-gaudium.html.
16. Czerny and Foglizzo, "World Can Be Seen." For the video and the text of the pope's speech, see "Message of the Holy Father Francis on the Occasion of the Fourth Meeting of Popular Movements," World Movement of Christian Workers, October 16, 2021, https://mmtc-infor.com/en/noticias-4/noticias-del-mmtc/504-message-of-the-holy-father-francis-on-the-occasion-of-the-fourth-world-meeting-of-popular-movements.
17. Charles Taylor, "The Politics of Recognition," in *Multiculturalism: Examining the Politics of Recognition*, ed. Amy Gutmann (Princeton, NJ: Princeton University Press, 1994), 25–74; David Pellauer and Paul Ricoeur, *The Course of Recognition* (Cambridge, MA: Harvard University Press, 2007); Axel Honneth, *The Struggle for Recognition: The Moral Grammar of Social Conflicts* (Cambridge, MA: Polity Press, 1995); Nancy Fraser and Axel Honneth, eds., *Redistribution or Recognition: A Political-Philosophical Exchange* (London: Verso Books, 2003); Paddy McQueen, "Social and Political Recognition: The Internet Encyclopedia of Philosophy," www.iep.utm.edu/recog_sp/. I have found very helpful Michael Sohn, *The Good of Recognition: Phenomenology, Ethics, and Religion in the Thought of Lévinas and Ricœur* (Waco, TX: Baylor University Press, 2014).
18. Axel Honneth, *Recognition: A Chapter in the History of European Ideas* (New York: Cambridge University Press, 2020).
19. Czerny and Foglizzo, "World Can Be Seen."
20. "Message of the Holy Father Francis."
21. Pope Francis and Austen Ivereigh, *Let Us Dream: The Path to a Better Future* (New York: Simon & Schuster, 2020), 119.
22. Francis and Ivereigh, *Let Us Dream*, 126.
23. Quoted by Cindy Wooden, "Pope Calls for 'Synodal' Church that Listens, Learns, Shares Mission," *National Catholic Reporter*, October 17, 2015, www.ncronline.org/news/vatican/pope-calls-synodal-church-listens-learns-shares-mission.
24. James F. Keenan, "Moral Discernment in History," *Theological Studies* 79, no. 3 (September 2018): 668–79.
25. Francis, *Amoris laetitia*, March 19, 2016, no. 37, www.vatican.va/content/dam/francesco/pdf/apost_exhortations/documents/papa-francesco_esortazione-ap_20160319_amoris-laetitia_en.pdf.
26. Francis, no. 303.
27. Hugh Connolly, *The Irish Penitentials and Their Significance for the Sacrament of Penance Today* (Dublin: Four Courts Press, 1995), 14.
28. Connolly, 15, 16.
29. Connolly, 178.
30. Connolly, 181. For more on the penitentials, see James F. Keenan, *A History of Catholic Theological Ethics* (Mahwah, NJ: Paulist Press, 2022), 84–93.
31. Conor M. Kelly, "The Role of the Moral Theologian in the Church: A Proposal in Light of *Amoris Laetitia*," *Theological Studies* 77, no. 4 (December 2016): 922–48, https://journals.sagepub.com/doi/full/10.1177/0040563916666824.

32. Thomas Knieps-Port Le Roi, ed., *A Point of No Return? "Amoris Laetitia" on Marriage, Divorce, and Remarriage* (Münster: LIT Verlag, 2017).
33. Antonio Autiero, ed., *Per una nuova Cultura Pastorale: Il Contributo di Amoris Laetitia* (Milan: San Paolo, 2019).
34. Stephan Goertz and Caroline Witting, ed., *Amoris Laetitia: Wendepunkt in der Moraltheologie?* (Freiburg: Herder, 2016).
35. Shaji George Kochuthara, ed., *Amoris Laetitia: Transforming Pastoral Theology and Transforming the Church* (Bangalore: Dharmaram, 2021).
36. Stan Chu Ilo, ed., *Love, Joy, and Sex: African Conversations on Amoris Laetitia and Gospel of Family in a Divided World* (Eugene, OR: Cascade Books, 2019).
37. Thomas Rausch and Roberto Dell'Oro, ed., *Pope Francis on the Joy of Love: Theological and Pastoral Reflections on Amoris Laetitia* (Mahwah, NJ: Paulist Press, 2018). See also James Martin, "Top Ten Takeaways from *Amoris Laetitia*," *America*, April 8, 2018, http://americamagazine.org/issue/top-ten-takeaways-amoris-laetitia; Kevin Ahern, "The Listening Pope," *America*, April 8, 2018, http://americamagazine.org/issue/listening-pope; and Meghan J. Clark, "Look to the Margins," *America*, April 8, 2018, www.americamagazine.org/issue/look-margins; and Megan McCabe, "Francis, Family, and Feminism," *America*, April 8, 2018, www.americamagazine.org/issue/article/francis-family-and-feminism.
38. Antonio Spadaro and Mauricio López Oropeza, "Four Criteria to Interpret the Amazon Synod," *La Civiltà Cattolica*, October 15, 2019, www.laciviltacattolica.com/four-criteria-to-interpret-the-amazon-synod-2/.
39. "In hoc quippe mundo humana anima quasi more navis est contra ictum fluminis conscendentis: uno in loco nequaquam stare permittitur, quia ad ima relabitur, nisi ad summa conetur"; Gregory, Reg. Past., p. III. c. 34: ML 77, 118c.
40. "In via vitae non progredi regredi est"; Bernard, Serm II in festo. Purif., n. 3: ML 183, 369 C.
41. "In via Dei stare retrocedere est." Thomas attributes the quotation to Bernard in III Sen d29, a8, qla2, la, and to Gregory in *ST*, II-II,24,6 ob3.
42. Quoted by Carol Glatz, "Pope Francis: Christians Wanting to Go Backward 'Does So Much Harm to the Church,'" *America*, May 13, 2022, www.americamagazine.org/faith/2022/05/13/pope-francis-amoris-laetitia-conference-242986.
43. Andrea Tornielli, "An End-of-Summer Consistory That Looks to the World," *Vatican News*, May 29, 2022, www.vaticannews.va/en/vatican-city/news/2022-05/an-end-of-summer-consistory-that-looks-to-the-world.html.
44. John Allen, "August Consistory May be Among Most Fateful Moments of Francis Papacy," *Angelus News*, June 6, 2022, https://angelusnews.com/voices/august-consistory-may-be-among-most-fateful-moments-of-francis-papacy/.
45. John Allen, "Pope Honors World's Peripheries with New Cardinals, but Not His Own Backyard," *Crux*, June 17, 2022, https://cruxnow.com/news-analysis/2022/06/pope-honors-worlds-peripheries-with-new-cardinals-but-not-his-own-backyard.
46. Claire Giangravé, "Pope Francis Disrupts Tradition While Drawing Firm Lines in New Cardinal Picks," Religion News Service, June 13, 2022, https://religionnews.com/2022/06/13/pope-francis-disrupts-tradition-while-drawing-firm-lines-in-new-cardinal-picks/.
47. Giangravé.
48. Giangravé.

49. James Keenan, "The Church Needs Women Cardinals: Ordination Does Not Equal Competency for Leadership," *National Catholic Reporter*, July 28, 2020, www.ncronline.org/news/opinion/church-needs-women-cardinals.
50. Francis, *Praedicate Evangelium*, March 19, 2022, www.vatican.va/content/francesco/en/apost_constitutions/documents/20220319-costituzione-ap-praedicate-evangelium.html.
51. Ivereigh, "Pope Francis' Reforms."
52. Andrea Tornielli and Sergio Centofanti, "Pope Francis Promulgates Apostolic Constitution on Roman Curia 'Praedicate Evangelium,'" *Vatican News*, March 19, 2022, www.vaticannews.va/en/pope/news/2022-03/pope-francis-promulgates-constitution-praedicate-evangelium.html.
53. Francis, *Praedicate Evangelium*, no. 10.
54. Ivereigh, "Pope Francis' Reforms."
55. Francis, *Evangelii gaudium*, no. 119.
56. In preparation for this chapter, I interviewed Ivereigh, who argued that the drafting of *Aparecida* gave Francis the first opportunity to develop his own vision of what it meant to propose the Gospel today to a world in need.
57. Austen Ivereigh, *The Wounded Shepherd* (New York: Henry Holt, 2019), 153.
58. Ivereigh, 159.
59. Ivereigh.
60. Ivereigh, 158, citing Pope Francis, "Address to Executive Committee of CELAM," September 7, 2017, www.vatican.va/content/francesco/en/speeches/2017/september/documents/papa-francesco_20170907_viaggioapostolico-colombia-celam.html.
61. Ivereigh, *Wounded Shepherd*, 154.
62. I wish to thank Austen Ivereigh for the guidance he provided to me, particularly in conversations we had on June 15–16, 2022, at Campion Hall, Oxford.

3

POPE FRANCIS

Virtue Ethicist?

Conor M. Kelly

One distinctive feature of Pope Francis's approach to moral matters is his reluctance to engage moral theology as a discrete element of the tradition he shepherds as the Successor of Peter. This reluctance sets Francis apart from his predecessors. For instance, Pope Benedict XVI, while still Joseph Ratzinger, made direct contributions to some of the most contentious debates in moral theology when he was an academic in Germany.[1] These views are frequently used to illuminate his practical engagement with moral issues as pope.[2] Pope John Paul II, meanwhile, produced an entire encyclical on moral theology, elucidating an explicit moral methodology.[3] The moral vision of Pope Francis, however, is much more loosely defined, built less with the prefabricated "bricks" of established philosophical schools that shape the formal discourse of fundamental moral theology and more with the *bricolage* of a pastor who is intent on using whatever means are available to respond to the needs of his flock. Indeed, Jeffrey Stout's presentation of the moral *bricoleur* as someone who "start[s] off by taking stock of problems that need solving and available conceptual resources for solving them" aptly applies to Francis, who—as Lisa Cahill points out in chapter 1 of this volume—eschews a top-down approach that attempts to impose abstract universals on particular situations and instead begins always with the concrete.[4]

Cognizant of these traits, one must tread lightly around the idea that Francis has a singular approach to moral theology, for he admittedly does not have the kind of systematic method characteristic of his immediate predecessors, to say nothing of the regimented consistency of moral theology's academic schools.[5] Nevertheless, there is something useful to be gained by asking how Francis's unique approach to moral matters aligns with (or departs from) the traditional categories found in moral theology, even if a healthy dose of epistemic humility is required in pursuing the analysis. Given the overarching emphases of Francis's forays into practical ethics, the most fruitful way of posing this question is to ask to what extent Francis can be characterized as a virtue ethicist, because although he clearly has not committed himself to one moral methodology in isolation, his practical judgments in ethics share the same concerns for personal character, discernment, and everyday moral growth that define the field of virtue ethics. By mining these overlaps, Catholics can more clearly identify the fresh elements that Pope Francis has injected into the magisterial trajectory of moral theology, allowing the faithful to engage his vision for the Church more fully. At the same time, the benefits of this comparison also extend to the field of moral theology, where the gaps between Francis and more traditional virtue ethicists reveal potential avenues for growth in the discipline.

To achieve these aims, the chapter proceeds in three sections. The first section describes an emphasis on personal character, a space for discernment in context, and an orientation to growth in the moral life as central features of virtue ethics and demonstrates Francis's own commitment to these priorities, revealing ways he acts like a virtue ethicist. Noting that Francis's use of these concepts is not in perfect alignment with the way virtue ethicists traditionally employ them, the second section identifies areas where Francis's work calls for further development in Catholic virtue ethics and also specifies spaces where Francis's own moral reflections might benefit from a more explicit engagement with virtue ethics. Finally, the third section describes the novelty of Francis's partial embrace of virtue ethics and offers a plausible explanation for this magisterial development based on his background and formation as a Jesuit priest. The end result is a coherent justification for a classic Catholic both/and response to the question that drives this chapter, allowing that Pope Francis is a virtue ethicist but maintaining that he is neither exclusively nor completely committed to virtue as a moral methodology. This caveat is important, for while others have argued that Francis has a fairly clear and consistent alignment with virtue ethics, I believe the inconsistencies in his use of virtue ethics are just as informative of his moral vision as the obvious parallels.[6]

FRANCIS'S PARTIAL ALIGNMENTS WITH VIRTUE ETHICS

While a virtue-based approach to ethics has roots that trace back to at least the time of Plato and Aristotle, the idea of virtue ethics as an identifiable school of thought emerged only recently in the Catholic moral tradition.[7] As a result, the precise features that define virtue ethics within Catholic moral theology remain diffuse and open to interpretation. Nevertheless, there are some common features, and among these are three emphases that not only represent the least common denominator of virtue ethics for Catholic moral theology but also feature prominently in Pope Francis's approach to moral questions. This first section of the chapter therefore explores the shared emphases on character, discernment, and growth that unite Pope Francis and virtue ethicists, highlighting the alignments so that the next section can examine the areas where he is implicitly pushing the field to expand its understanding of the proper implications of these concerns.

Character

To begin, an emphasis on character is the sine qua non of virtue ethics, not just in Catholic moral theology but also across moral philosophy. The chief rationale motivating the twentieth-century appeal to virtue was a desire to account for the moral goodness of the agent and not simply the rightness or wrongness of an agent's actions.[8] This, of course, is not to say that moral actions do not matter in virtue ethics. Quite the opposite is true, for virtue ethicists stress the impact of the actions an agent chooses to pursue, either because they see specific actions as necessary for the acquisition of the virtues that will define the agent's character—as in the strand of Catholic virtue ethics that traces its lineage to Thomas Aquinas and his reliance on Aristotle—or because they maintain that proper actions are the most important way for an agent to actualize their virtues and reveal their true character.[9] This latter claim is often expressed using the Latin adage *agere sequitur esse*, or "action follows being," which explains why character is central to virtue ethics, because the expectation is that good actions will follow from good human beings. The emphasis on character is thus the virtue ethicist's attempt to orient ethics to the root of the problem, so that people spend less time dwelling on the eventual actions of an agent in isolation and more time attending to the nature and dispositions of the agent that determine the actions in the first place.

Although Pope Francis has not, to my knowledge, quoted the dictum *agere sequitur esse*, he has regularly embodied this first emphasis of virtue ethics in his reflections on moral matters. Consider his repeated calls for the church to return to "the heart of the message of Jesus Christ."[10] He employs this as a criticism of the way "the Church has sometimes locked itself up in small things, in small-minded rules," and by way of contrast maintains, "we must always consider the person."[11] While he rarely portrays this shift in focus as a matter of reprioritizing an agent's character, that is the de facto consequence of his appeal. Significantly, his rationale for championing this transformed analysis nicely mirrors the case for attending to dispositions in virtue ethics—namely, that the act flows from the essence of the person and therefore that any hope of reforming actions must begin with the conversion of the actor. While Francis has been most explicit on this point in relation to his vision for the Catholic Church as a whole, insisting that "the structural and organizational reforms are secondary—that is, they must come afterward. The first reform must be the attitude," he has not limited this insight to institutional agents.[12] As he explained in *Laudato si'*, "the existence of laws and regulations is insufficient in the long run to curb bad conduct.... If the laws are to bring about significant, long-lasting effects, the majority of the members of society must be adequately motivated to accept them, *and personally transformed to respond*" (emphasis added).[13] Hence, he thinks much like a virtue ethicist when he asserts that interior conversion is the unavoidable prerequisite to lasting moral change.

Notably, in *Amoris laetitia*, Francis is even more explicit about the links between his emphasis on personal disposition and the traditional concerns of virtue ethics. For instance, he adopts the virtue ethicist's conviction that "doing what is right means more than 'judging what seems best' or knowing clearly what needs to be done," a claim that scholars describe as the catalyst that led Aristotle to depart from Plato and create an ethical system centered around the cultivation of virtue.[14] Francis places himself squarely on the Aristotelian side of this debate when he adds, "good habits need to be developed.... Mere desire, or attraction to a certain value, is not enough to instill a virtue in the absence of those properly motivated acts," a point that ultimately segues into the need to cultivate virtue in order to realize the full potential of human freedom in moral choices.[15] Francis thus not only recognizes the primacy of character like a virtue ethicist but he also speaks about the need for virtue to form that character.

The extent to which Francis's emphasis on the formation of character is indeed indicative of a broader attentiveness to virtue can be seen in the way he articulates the major obstacles Christians face along the path of discipleship. Rather than categorizing and condemning specific sinful acts, as has been typical of the papal "strand" of moral theology in the last two hundred years, Francis instead denounces the attitudes and dispositions—one could say vices—of a malformed character.[16] Thus, in *Laudato si'*, although there are specific behaviors that Francis links to the crisis facing our common home, he pinpoints the roots of the environmental crisis in a deeper malaise that strikes at the very core of our being. While not discounting the ways excessive consumption and extractive practices are threatening the planet, Francis insists that these behaviors have an earlier origin in an attitude of "compulsive consumerism," which he then traces to the vice of selfishness.[17] Meanwhile, in *Fratelli tutti*, Francis argues that the Parable of the Good Samaritan "warns us about the attitude of those who think only of themselves and fail to shoulder the inevitable responsibilities of life as it is."[18] Lest we lose sight of the ways in which this primary concern for flawed attitudes first and flawed behaviors second matches the ordering of priorities in virtue ethics, Francis goes on to insist that "the people walking by [the wounded man] did not heed their interior summons to act as neighbours; they were concerned with their duties, their social status, their professional position within society," thereby asserting that we find failure in the moral life when we invert the order and emphasize duty over interiority.[19] Moreover, the spirit of "fraternity," which he encourages throughout the encyclical as the ideal corrective, is subsequently identified as an "essential human quality" that is expressly reliant upon the cardinal virtues to achieve its proper ends.[20] In both his positive vision for ethics and his negative warnings about the dangers that lurk in our way, Francis thus thinks like a virtue ethicist and places the accent heavily on the agent more than the *agere*.

Discernment

Similar overlaps can be found in Francis's concern for discernment, which aligns with the second emphasis of virtue ethics, where a focus on discernment is a logical extension of the field's shift from act to agent. As Lisa Fullam explains, "Since virtue ethics begins with questions about the moral agent, we gauge actions based on what sort of persons we will tend to become as a result."[21] This question is much more dynamic than a static application of an abstract rule to a concrete context and instead requires carefully identifying the most prudent course of action in a way that can account for the totality of one's immediate circumstances. Rather than simply following a set of preordained rules, the virtuous person is virtuous precisely because they are able to discern both which rules to apply and how to act virtuously even in situations where no existing rules fit the question at hand. Relatedly, virtue ethics also calls for discernment as a means of recognizing that moral agents "can only become morally excellent persons by being themselves," a claim that reflects the idea that virtue perfects the person in the concrete particularities of their lives and not in the abstract.[22] The art of discernment is thus key to the shifts that virtue ethics seeks to incorporate into moral theology.

Pope Francis, of course, has made the promotion of discernment one of the hallmarks of his pontificate. In his first major solely authored text as pope, *Evangelii gaudium*, Francis famously rejected the idea "that the papal magisterium should be expected to offer a definitive or complete word on every question which affects the Church and the world" and expressed his sincere hope that by refraining from doing so, he would encourage greater discernment at the local level, a strategy that has had significant consequences in applied fields, as Bryan Massingale's chapter in this volume demonstrates.[23] Later, in *Amoris laetitia*, Francis indicated that this expectation extended to the faithful at the personal level when he argued that ministers of the church "have been called to form consciences, not replace them" because "the faithful . . . very often respond as best they can to the Gospel amid their limitations, and are capable of carrying out their own discernment in complex situations."[24] Significantly, his calls to maximize ordinary Catholics' space for discernment closely match the virtue ethicists' own insistence on discernment as an outgrowth of their emphasis on character, for the aim, in Francis's account, is likewise to "encourag[e] the responsible use of freedom to face issues with good sense and intelligence. It involves *forming persons* who readily understand . . . their own lives" (emphasis added).[25] Or, as Christoph Cardinal Schönborn put it, the goal of discernment for Francis is "personal maturity: not forming automatons, externally conditioned and remote-controlled, but people who have matured in their friendship with Christ."[26] It is hard to imagine a more agent-centered, and thus virtue-ethics-aligned, approach to discernment than the one expressed in these ambitions.

In the realm of discernment, however, the points of contact between Pope Francis and virtue ethicists extend beyond a set of common goals. His emphasis on the need for discernment also stems from a similar constellation of presuppositions. Specifically, Francis articulates the necessity of discernment in relation to two central ideas found in virtue ethics. First, he appeals to the notion that general rules will not be sufficient for the complexity of the moral life. "It is reductive simply to consider whether or not an individual's actions correspond to a general law or rule," Francis cautions, "because that is not enough to discern and ensure full fidelity to God in the concrete life of a human being."[27] One can see a similar motivation in the virtue ethicists' claim that their system can provide "the kind of moral discernment that leaves us better able to respond to new kinds of ethical questions," because the implication is that a virtue-based discernment process is essential to address the concrete situations in which the usual rules do not apply as neatly or as clearly as other systems might assume.[28] Second, Francis argues that discernment is particularly incumbent "when some novelty presents itself in our lives, . . . [and] we have to decide whether it is new wine brought by God or an illusion created by the spirit of this world or the spirit of the devil."[29] With this rationale, he echoes the classic virtue ethics assertion that virtue operates as a mean that avoids the two extremes of "excess and deficiency."[30] Typically, these extremes manifest as two primary vices, one that is a vice of opposition (think courage correcting cowardliness) and another that is a vice of deceptive semblance (as foolhardiness is connected to courage).[31] Francis's presentation of discernment as a tool to help us avoid deceptive illusions recalls this split and shows an additional alignment with virtue ethics.

Growth

The third emphasis of virtue ethics that resonates with Francis's approach to moral theology is the stress virtue ethics places on growth. Much like discernment, this third emphasis emerges from and complements the field's focus on moral character, for a person's central disposition is not a static trait but a dynamic feature that changes as one develops. As the Jesuit theological ethicist and biblical scholar Lúcás Chan has observed, from the virtue ethicist's perspective, "our choices and actions help form our tendencies and dispositions, which in turn help inform and direct our subsequent choices and actions."[32] Consequently, virtue ethics presents the moral life as a process of becoming, because our actions are always forming and reforming our existing dispositions, making us progressively more or less virtuous depending on whether we act in accordance with or in opposition to the virtues.[33] For virtue ethicists, this dynamism is constitutive of the system, because there is a degree of circularity involved in the Aristotelian account of the acquisition of virtue: In order to become more prudent, I must act prudently, but I only know how to act prudently if I am prudent. The solution to this circular feedback loop is to claim that agents begin with a general sense of what the virtuous life entails and then refine that understanding as they cultivate virtue, yielding "a continuing dialectic of telos [i.e., end goal] and the current state of virtue in the soul, each shaping the other."[34] One can therefore rightly describe growth as the very nature of the moral life from a virtue ethics perspective.

Ultimately, Pope Francis's vision for the moral life makes a similar claim. Growth is central to his account of the lives Christians are called to lead, a point he highlights in two interrelated ways. First, Francis places considerable weight on the impact of growth, even when measured in small increments, as an indicative marker of a person's upright moral standing before God. As he explained in *Evangelii gaudium*, "A small step, in the midst of great human limitations, can be more pleasing to God than a life which appears outwardly in order but moves through the day without confronting great difficulties."[35] From this first perspective, Francis employs growth as a critique of the assumption that the call of discipleship equates to a life of moral perfection. Thus, in *Amoris laetitia*, he connected growth with the need for discernment and cautioned that "by thinking that everything is black and white, we sometimes close off the way of grace and of growth, and discourage paths of sanctification which give glory to God."[36] Francis thus uses the notion of growth to remind everyone that no matter where they are, they are still capable of moving closer to God, which they do through growth in virtue.[37] By presenting growth as a way to accept imperfection, then, Francis encourages the kind of ongoing personal development that virtue ethicists describe as essential to the moral life.

Second, Francis discusses moral growth as an invitation to maturity in moral matters. For instance, in *Fratelli tutti*, when Francis defined love as the heart of the Christian's calling, he went on to add, "by its very nature, love calls for growth in openness and the ability to accept others as part of a continuing adventure."[38] Elsewhere, he characterized the Christian moral life in terms of the universal call to holiness and insisted, "This holiness to which the Lord calls you will grow through small gestures," a point that nicely aligns with the virtue ethicist's assertion that moral growth happens through the daily choices that allow one to practice—and thus refine—the virtues.[39] Francis's clearest connection between growth and moral maturity, however, appeared in *Amoris laetitia*, when he dramatically proclaimed that conscience could affirm an agent's decision to act in a way that was "not yet fully the objective ideal" found in the church's teachings, provided one "recall[ed] that this discernment is dynamic; it must remain ever open to new stages of growth and to new decisions which can enable the ideal to be more fully realized."[40] Here his message is the same as the virtue ethicist's: success in the moral life requires a rejection of complacency and a determination to continue on the journey at all times.

As these overlaps show, Francis shares the virtue ethicist's familiarity with character, discernment, and growth, and similarly places each at the heart of his ethical framework. At the broad level of what a moral theologian might call the pope's "fundamental moral theology," then, Francis behaves much like a virtue ethicist, prioritizing the same themes and characterizing the work of ethics in the same vein. Lest all these overlaps should lead to the overly simplified conclusion that Francis is a full-fledged virtue ethicist, however, one must also acknowledge that Francis's thinking fails to embody all the conventions normally found in virtue ethics. In fact, he has some significant departures that deserve attention for what they reveal about how the field might develop further in light of Francis's papal interventions and also how the insights of virtue ethics might be of greater service to Francis's own moral project.

IMPLICIT EXPANSIONS FROM FRANCIS'S PARTIAL ALIGNMENTS

There are, unsurprisingly, multiple points of tension between Francis's unsystematic approach to moral theology and the more carefully delineated method embraced by committed virtue ethicists. Some of these reflect a degree of inconsistency in Francis's thought, and so are not especially useful for a dialogue with virtue ethicists. One point of departure, however, represents a more substantive disagreement and merits a brief discussion to illustrate what Francis can add to Catholic virtue ethics if one engages him as a virtue ethicist (of sorts).

The simplest way to capture this substantive departure is to say that across the major themes of character, discernment, and growth, virtue ethicists are oriented more immediately to an idea—one or more of the virtues—while Francis is oriented to a personal encounter with the relational God revealed in Christ.[41] To be clear, this observation is not meant to suggest that Catholic virtue ethicists ignore God in their conception of the moral life. It is simply intended to acknowledge a difference in emphasis that has two consequential implications.

First, Francis's stress on the relational character of Christian morality amplifies his attention to discernment and growth, creating a difference in degree rather than kind when comparing his approach with that of more traditional virtue ethicists. Recall his cautionary comments about an overreliance on rules when he championed more space for discernment in *Amoris laetitia*. The chief concern was that a narrow application of norms, "thinking that everything is black and white," prevents people from living in fidelity to the God whom the Christian tradition professes is infinite mystery.[42] In this way, Francis's promotion of discernment and his insistence on the centrality of growth reveal a vision of the Christian life not as a summons to follow a certain rulebook, but as an invitation to an ongoing relationship with a personal God whose love for us entails greater plans than we could ever imagine alone. Francis's alignment with virtue thus stems from his engagement with the doctrine of God, for Francis resolutely avers that "God infinitely transcends us; he is full of surprises" and concludes, by extension, that "we cannot claim that our understanding of [God's] truth authorizes us to exercise a strict supervision over others' lives."[43] If this is who God is, then the moral life must be dynamic and open to personal variation, for anything less would deny the mystery and freedom of the divine. With his unique perspective, Francis demonstrates the value of discernment and growth in ethics and suggests that virtue ethics might still mine the depths of these concepts as its influence in Catholic moral theology expands.

Second, Francis's ready focus on the divine–human interaction in ethics opens another avenue for growth in Catholic ethicists' presentation of the agency involved in the acquisition of virtue. Heavily reliant on the Aristotelian understanding of virtue, Catholic virtue ethicists tend to stress the human capacity for acquiring virtue through practices as a way of encouraging the process of growth and discernment that they describe at the heart of the moral life.[44] While this emphasis is certainly not incompatible with a theologically rich account of humanity's moral responsibilities, it has nevertheless been criticized for its potential to overstate the power of human agency as a corrective to sin.[45] The charge of Pelagianism is not unheard of, particularly from other (non-Catholic) Christian ethicists.[46] Although this criticism is not entirely fair to the Catholic understanding of habituation and the divine roots of human agency, the critique raises a legitimate concern for the Catholic virtue ethicist who must be certain not to elevate virtue in a way that overshadows grace.

Helpfully, Francis's theological impulses and his partial alignments with virtue ethics show how Catholic virtue ethicists might better blunt this critique. Specifically, he criticizes any Pelagian impulse in the Church, whereby "those who ultimately trust only in their own powers . . . feel superior to others because they observe certain rules or remain intransigently faithful to a particular Catholic style from the past."[47] Calling instead for "a heartfelt and prayerful acknowledgment of our limitations," Francis explains that the Christian moral life depends on God's grace to help us overcome our concupiscence, which he reminds the faithful is a "flaw" that "has been present from the beginning of humanity."[48] With his reassertion of these traditional categories, Francis shows how the pursuit of growth and the work of discernment in the realm of virtue can be identified and articulated as manifestations of God's grace rather than misinterpreted as illustrations of human hubris, potentially opening a new ecumenical dialogue around virtue in theological ethics.[49]

Although Francis's distinctive emphases can thus make meaningful contributions to the field of virtue ethics, the process of expansion should not be understood as a one-way street. The insights of virtue ethics can also aid Francis's own articulation of the course he intends to chart for the Church in moral theology, even if he refrains from a complete adoption of virtue ethics as a consistent methodology. The most meaningful contribution would be a fuller presentation of the specific virtues that should guide the moral agent in the life of discipleship. Francis has shown a willingness to identify individual virtues in order to make a point about how to respond to discrete circumstances, variously highlighting tenderness, humility, hospitality, and solidarity as explicit virtues that aid Christians in their growth toward holiness.[50] He has not, however, clearly stated the complete constellation of virtues that would yield the formation of character for freedom in discernment and a sustained pursuit of growth that constitute his vision for the moral life as a whole. This type of specification is particularly important given Francis's invocation of Thomas Aquinas's "'hierarchy,' in the virtues and in the acts which proceed from them," for this understanding indicates not only that there are multiple virtues for the formation of character in the Christian moral life (as any good virtue ethicist would maintain), but also that there is a proper relationship between these virtues.[51] By more directly engaging existing efforts in the field of virtue ethics that wrestle with the unity of the virtues and the interrelationship between primary and subsidiary virtues, Francis might be able to provide even more concrete guidance for the kind of growth, discernment, and formation he asserts all Christians should pursue.

As this discussion of the nuanced overlaps and departures found in Francis's partial alignment with virtue ethicists reveals, an examination of the parallels between the moral vision of Pope Francis and the central priorities of this emerging field in moral theology can be mutually illuminating. For those virtue ethicists willing to mine the connections, Francis's work provides some potential pathways to strengthen the theological orientation of the ongoing efforts to transform what was originally a philosophical school into a resource for Catholic theological ethics. At the same time, the work of virtue ethicists engaged in this endeavor could fruitfully support Francis's stated goals for a renewed form of moral theology built around a "special care . . . shown to emphasize and encourage the highest and most central values of the Gospel."[52] If either of these benefits is going to be realized, however, scholars will need a deeper appreciation of the novelty Francis is injecting into Catholic moral theology, especially at the papal level. To facilitate this deeper awareness, the final section of this chapter highlights some of the differences between Francis and his predecessors and proposes that there are significant reasons he has been the one to introduce these shifts.

THE NOVELTY OF FRANCIS'S APPROACH AND ITS IGNATIAN ROOTS

Francis's quiet embrace of the central tenets of virtue ethics represents a genuine development in the papal tradition of moral theology. To make the point just briefly, consider the contrast that emerges from a comparison of Francis's and John Paul II's incorporation of the natural law into their reflections on moral matters. In *Veritatis splendor*, John Paul II appealed to the Thomistic tradition and stressed the *"universality* and *immutability"* of the natural law (emphasis in the original), arguing that these were the traits that made the natural law such a valuable guide for Christians in an otherwise relativistic world.[53] Francis has similarly grounded his discussions of the natural law in Thomistic thought, but he has emphasized a different strand of that tradition, explicitly citing the section from Aquinas's treatise on law in which the scholastic theologian averred, "in matters of action, truth or practical rectitude is not the same for all, as to matters of detail, but only as to the general principles . . . [because] the principle will be found to fail according as we descend further into detail."[54] While not denying the universality of the natural law, Francis has chosen to highlight the room for variation it nevertheless permits, openly commending the International Theological Commission's conclusion that "natural law could not be presented as an already established set of rules that impose themselves *a priori* on the moral subject; rather, it is a source of objective inspiration for the deeply personal process of making decisions."[55] This interpretation of the natural law puts its resources at the service of discernment and personal growth, using the emphases of virtue ethics to usher in an *aggiornamento* in moral theology at the papal level.

As much as it would be interesting to explore other examples of Francis's "development of doctrine" in the papal strand of moral theology, the idea that there would be a contrast with the thought of his predecessors on particular moral questions is hardly a shocking claim at this point. The more interesting question, then, is not whether such a development has happened but why, and here Francis's unique position as the first Jesuit pope is especially relevant. Specifically, there are several key themes in Saint Ignatius's *Spiritual Exercises*—one of the defining texts of Jesuit formation—that provide a clear foundation for an approach to the moral life that would prioritize character, discernment, and growth.

The most obvious point of contact between the *Spiritual Exercises* and Francis's partial alignments with virtue ethics is the idea of discernment itself, which is literally at the center of Ignatius's text. As Antonio Spadaro observed in his interview with Pope Francis, "Discernment is therefore a pillar of the spirituality of Pope Francis. It expresses in a particular manner his Jesuit identity."[56] It is hard to imagine any Jesuit, to say nothing of this Jesuit, writing about moral matters in a way that did not prioritize discernment and thus open a bridge to virtue ethics. Francis has strengthened this bridge by championing discernment in a decidedly Ignatian key, as his vision for the flexibility of discernment can only be sustained by accepting Ignatius's originally controversial claim "that God can deal with people directly."[57]

Other aspects of Francis's overlaps with virtue can also be linked back to this feature of the doctrine of God found in Ignatian spirituality and the anthropological claims it logically entails. The emphasis on character formation, for instance, reflects the conviction that the moral life is oriented not so much to yielding specific behaviors but to the transformation of our very being, so that "you will become what the Father had in mind when he created you, and you will be faithful to your deepest self."[58] The goal is not to achieve some abstract idea of virtue, but to live into the personal and particularized plan God has for this individual moral agent as a unique human being. The orientation to growth, meanwhile, can be understood as a natural extension of the *Spiritual Exercises*' emphasis on the merciful nature of God. At the heart of the *Exercises*' First Week is a recognition of one's own sinfulness not to inculcate shame but rather to heighten one's appreciation of God's mercy. This twofold recognition of the depth of one's sinfulness and the breadth of God's mercy creates the proper justification for envisioning the moral life as a process of growth, for as Francis explains in *Gaudete et exsultate*, "the lack of a heartfelt and prayerful acknowledgment of our limitations prevents grace from working more effectively within us, for no room is left for bringing about the potential good that is part of a sincere and genuine journey of growth."[59] Without the theological anthropology of the *Exercises* and the doctrine of God that informs it, it would not make sense for Francis to speak about growth in the moral life, character, or discernment. With them, however, a plausible rationale for the priority of these three tenets of virtue ethics in the current papal magisterium emerges.

CONCLUSION

Returning to the question at the heart of this chapter, I want to offer that Pope Francis is a virtue ethicist. Sort of. He certainly shares the same concern for character, discernment, and moral growth that distinguishes virtue ethics from other moral methodologies, and he seems to have particularly Ignatian reasons for doing so. His alignment with more traditional virtue ethicists is partial, however, even on these central claims. He ties the formation of character, the need for discernment, and the orientation to moral growth to a much more personalist understanding of God's direct role in the moral life, yielding areas where Catholic theological ethicists might benefit further from engaging his work as a form of virtue ethics. At the same time, he does not articulate his vision for the moral life consistently enough or thoroughly enough in the key of virtue, reinforcing the idea that he is not a virtue ethicist in the most traditional sense. Clearly, though, Francis is doing something different than his predecessors did, and while these differences can plausibly be rooted in his background and formation as a Jesuit, they can also be best understood through the priorities found in virtue ethics.

Ultimately, there is something fruitful about asking the question of whether Francis is a virtue ethicist, even when the answer must remain contingent and partial at best. While this ambiguity may strike some as a cop out, I would maintain that it is an appropriate application of the virtue of humility that allows us to appreciate what Francis is doing without overstating any claims. Such nuance is required because "we fail to do justice to an instance of creative moral thinking or writing when we force it into the mold of some other moral trope."[60] If we are truly going to respect the novelty Francis is trying to introduce into the Church in the realm of moral theology, then we must be careful not to get overly prescriptive. Still, Francis is more of a virtue ethicist than any of his predecessors, and we ought not lose sight of that development as we seek to expand the reception of his teaching into moral matters.

NOTES

1. See, e.g., Joseph Ratzinger, "The Church's Teaching Authority—Faith—Morals," in *Principles of a Christian Morality*, ed. Heinz Schürmann, Joseph Ratzinger, and Hans Urs von Balthasar (San Francisco: Ignatius Press, 1986), 45–74.
2. E.g., Tracey Rowland, *Ratzinger's Faith: The Theology of Benedict XVI* (Oxford: Oxford University Press, 2008), 66–83.
3. John Paul II, *Veritatis splendor*, August 6, 1993, www.vatican.va/content/john-paul-ii/en/encyclicals/documents/hf_jp-ii_enc_06081993_veritatis-splendor.html.
4. Jeffrey Stout, *Ethics after Babel: The Languages of Morals and Their Discontents* (Princeton, NJ: Princeton University Press, 2001), 75.
5. Notably, this remains a relative claim, for the systematic method of John Paul II or Benedict XVI must not be overstated, as they too had their nuances and inconsistencies. For a discussion of the variations involved in John Paul II's moral methodology, see Charles E. Curran, *The Moral Theology of Pope John Paul II* (Washington, DC: Georgetown University Press, 2005), 103–4.
6. For one interpretation of a close alignment between Francis and virtue ethics, see Daniel J. Daly, *The Structures of Virtue and Vice* (Washington, DC: Georgetown University Press, 2021), 108–15.
7. James F. Keenan, *A History of Catholic Moral Theology in the Twentieth Century: From Confessing Sins to Liberating Consciences* (New York: Continuum, 2010), 76.
8. James F. Keenan, "Proposing Cardinal Virtues," *Theological Studies* 56, no. 4 (December 1995): 709–29, at 709–10.
9. Lisa Fullam has a detailed explanation of these Aristotelian and Thomistic presuppositions in her argument for a greater integration of virtue in the field of sexual ethics. Lisa Fullam, "Sex in 3-D: A Telos for a Virtue Ethics of Sexuality," *Journal of the Society of Christian Ethics* 27, no. 2 (Fall–Winter 2007): 151–70, at 157–62.
10. Quoted by Antonio Spadaro, "A Big Heart Open to God: The Exclusive Interview with Pope Francis," *America*, September 30, 2013, 15–38, at 26. See also Francis, *Evangelii gaudium*, November 24, 2013, no. 34, www.vatican.va/content/francesco/en/apost_exhortations/documents/papa-francesco_esortazione-ap_20131124_evangelii-gaudium.html.

11. Quoted by Spadaro, "Big Heart," 24, 26.
12. Quoted by Spadaro, 24.
13. Francis, *Laudato si'*, May 24, 2015, no. 211, www.vatican.va/content/francesco/en/encyclicals/documents/papa-francesco_20150524_enciclica-laudato-si.html.
14. Francis, *Amoris laetitia*, March 19, 2016, no. 265, www.vatican.va/content/dam/francesco/pdf/apost_exhortations/documents/papa-francesco_esortazione-ap_20160319_amoris-laetitia_en.pdf. For the parallels to Plato and Aristotle, see David Carr, "Knowledge and Truth in Virtuous Deliberation," *Philosophia* 48 (2020): 1381–96, at 1382.
15. Francis, *Amoris laetitia*, no. 266; see also no. 267.
16. Historically, the papal magisterium's tendency to pronounce on the licitness or illicitness of particular behaviors was not simply a reflection of the Vatican's understanding of the purpose of the papal teaching office but also an extension of the fact that starting in the nineteenth century, bishops frequently sought a Roman ruling on disputed moral questions and thus put the pope in a position to make moral pronouncements in act-oriented terms. See Charles E. Curran, *The Development of Moral Theology: Five Strands* (Washington, DC: Georgetown University Press, 2013), 186–99.
17. Francis, *Laudato si'*, nos. 203–4.
18. Francis, *Fratelli tutti*, no. 67.
19. Francis, no. 101.
20. Francis, "Message of His Holiness Francis for the Celebration of the World Day of Peace 1 January 2014," December 8, 2013, www.vatican.va/content/francesco/en/messages/peace/documents/papa-francesco_20131208_messaggio-xlvii-giornata-mondiale-pace-2014.html.
21. Lisa Fullam, "Virtue for Genomics: Curiosity and Skepticism in Genetic Research," *Irish Theological Quarterly* 68 (2003): 307–23, at 309.
22. Keenan, "Proposing Cardinal Virtues," 713.
23. Francis, *Evangelii gaudium*, no. 16.
24. Francis, *Amoris laetitia*, no. 37.
25. Francis, no. 262.
26. Quoted by Gerard O'Connell, "'Amoris Laetitia' Represents an Organic Development of Doctrine, 'Not a Rupture,'" *America*, April 8, 2016, http://americamagazine.org/content/dispatches/pope-francis-exhortation-family-organic-development-doctrine.
27. Francis, *Amoris laetitia*, no. 304.
28. Fullam, "Virtue for Genomics," 311.
29. Francis, *Gaudete et exsultate*, March 19, 2018, no. 168, www.vatican.va/content/francesco/en/apost_exhortations/documents/papa-francesco_esortazione-ap_20180319_gaudete-et-exsultate.html.
30. Thomas Aquinas, *Summa Theologiae*, I-II.64.1 c.
31. Rebecca Konyndyk DeYoung, *Glittering Vices: A New Look at the Seven Deadly Sins and Their Remedies* (Grand Rapids: Brazos Press, 2009), 36.
32. Yiu Sing Lúcás Chan, *The Ten Commandments and the Beatitudes: Biblical Studies and Ethics for Real Life* (Lanham, MD: Sheed & Ward, 2012), 11.
33. Keenan, "Proposing Cardinal Virtues," 711.
34. Fullam, "Sex in 3-D," 153.
35. Francis, *Evangelii gaudium*, no. 44.
36. Francis, *Amoris laetitia*, no. 305.
37. Francis, *Evangelii gaudium*, no. 161.
38. Francis, *Fratelli tutti*, no. 95; see also no. 92.

39. Francis, *Gaudete et exsultate*, no. 16.
40. Francis, *Amoris laetitia*, no. 303.
41. Daly, e.g., has described Francis's ethics as part of a larger magisterial "trajectory toward a more theocentric ethics." Daly, *Structures*, 100.
42. Francis, *Amoris laetitia*, quotation at no. 305; see also no. 304.
43. Francis, *Gaudete et exsultate*, nos. 41, 42.
44. Lúcás Chan, *Biblical Ethics in the 21st Century: Developments, Emerging Consensus, and Future Directions* (Mahwah, NJ: Paulist Press, 2013), 86–88.
45. Aquinas's own system of virtue ethics, for instance, is richly theological and also gives a prominent role to the acquisition of virtue, albeit with important nuances due to his concept of "infused virtue." See Thomas Aquinas, *Summa Theologiae*, I-II.55.4 c; see also I-II.63.
46. See Jennifer A. Herdt, *Putting on Virtue: The Legacy of the Splendid Vices* (Chicago: University of Chicago Press, 2008), 113–14, 131.
47. Francis, *Evangelii gaudium*, no. 94.
48. Francis, *Gaudete et exsultate*, no. 50; Francis, *Fratelli tutti*, no. 166.
49. For the role of divine action in discernment, see Francis, *Amoris laetitia*, no. 300. The potential ecumenical impact of engaging virtue in relation to divine and human agency can be seen in the focus on this question in the Protestant development of virtue ethics. Elizabeth Agnew Cochran, *Protestant Virtue and Stoic Ethics* (London: T&T Clark, 2018).
50. See Francis, *Amoris laetitia*, no. 28; Francis, "Homily of His Holiness Pope Francis Holy Mass and Canonization of the Blesseds: Vincenzo Grossi, Mary of the Immaculate Conception, Ludovico Martin and Maria Azelia Guérin," October 18, 2015, www.vatican.va/content/francesco/en/homilies/2015/documents/papa-francesco_20151018_omelia-canonizzazioni.html; Francis, "Angelus," July 17, 2016, www.vatican.va/content/francesco/en/angelus/2016/documents/papa-francesco_angelus_20160717.html; and Francis, "Message of His Holiness Pope Francis for the Celebration of the XLIX World Day of Peace, 1 January 2016," December 8, 2015, 6, www.vatican.va/content/francesco/en/messages/peace/documents/papa-francesco_20151208_messaggio-xlix-giornata-mondiale-pace-2016.html. Daly also discusses specific virtues in Francis's ethics. Daly, *Structures*, 112–15.
51. Francis, *Evangelii gaudium*, no. 37; see also nos. 38–39.
52. Francis, *Amoris laetitia*, no. 311.
53. John Paul II, *Veritatis splendor*, no. 51; see also nos. 43–44, 52–53.
54. Francis, *Amoris laetitia*, no. 304, citing Aquinas, *Summa Theologiae*, I-II.94.4.
55. Francis, no. 305, citing International Theological Commission, *In Search of a Universal Ethic: A New Look at Natural Law* (Vatican City: International Theological Commission, 2009), 59.
56. Spadaro, "Big Heart," 18.
57. James Martin, "What Some Critics of 'Amoris Laetitia' Are Missing," April 13, 2016, http://americamagazine.org/content/all-things/what-some-critics-amoris-laetitia-are-missing.
58. Francis, *Gaudete et exsultate*, no. 32.
59. Francis, no. 50.
60. Stout, *Ethics*, 75–76.

4

POPE FRANCIS'S ECCLESIAL ETHICS

Mercy, Subsidiarity, Justice

Elyse J. Raby

In the first decade of his papacy, Pope Francis put forth a vision of the Church as missionary in its very nature. Rooted in the merciful love of God made incarnate in Jesus Christ, the Church, the pilgrim People of God, exists to proclaim God's tender love for the world in word and in deed. In order to more effectively proclaim the Gospel and more clearly be a sacrament of this love, the Church, especially but not exclusively in its ministry and governance, must be renewed and reformed so that all its members experience the incarnate love of God within its own walls. In short, the Church needs an ecclesial ethics.

Ecclesial ethics can be defined as the application of ethical norms or values to the Church's organizational or institutional life—to the formation and function of Church structures and laws, as well as to the actors (clergy or laity, individual or collective) therein.[1] It parallels other forms of professional ethics that seek to guide the moral reflection, the identity, and the behavior of organizations and their members. Efforts at developing an explicit ecclesial ethics in the United States began in the wake of the sexual abuse revelations in 2002 and have tended to focus on governance of the Church and on the moral formation and training in professional ethics for Church ministers.[2] As part of this movement, some theologians, canon and civil lawyers, and sociologists have called on the US Church to develop a code of ethics for clergy and lay ministers and have offered detailed proposals for how the Church might go about envisioning, writing, and enforcing such a code.[3]

Although such a nationwide code of ethics has not yet materialized, Francis's papacy is a rich resource for thinking anew about the ethics of being the Church. The Jesuit pope has never, to my knowledge, used the phrase "ecclesial ethics" or called for a code of ethics to be developed. He has, however, spoken at length about his desires for the Church and has initiated cultural, structural, and canonical changes that promote a more ethical Church. In this chapter, I argue that Francis's papacy proposes an ecclesial ethics marked by three interrelated virtues or principles: mercy, subsidiarity, and justice.[4] These three keys are expressed in, and shape, Francis's vision of ministry, his reforms of Church governance, his exercise of the papal magisterium, and his response to the ongoing clergy sexual abuse crisis.[5] Moreover, they are reflective of his life in the Society of Jesus, with its emphases on discernment, consultative governance, and the promotion of justice. I conclude by indicating ways in which the Church in the United States might take up Francis's vision of becoming a more merciful, subsidiary, and just Church.

MERCY: THE PRIMACY OF THE PASTORAL

Mercy is the touchstone and motto of Bergoglio/Francis's episcopacy, and is "the very foundation of the Church's life.[6] All of her pastoral activity should be caught up in the tenderness she makes present to believers; nothing in her preaching and in her witness to the world can be lacking in mercy."[7] In Francis's thought, mercy has a twofold meaning. First, God's mercy is the unending offer of love and forgiveness in spite of our sinfulness. It is "the divine attitude which embraces" and is "God's identity card."[8] Second, mercy is the visceral response of compassion and healing that Jesus enacts whenever he encounters the poor, sick, suffering, and excluded. Mercy "means opening one's heart to wretchedness."[9] While an ecclesial commitment to mercy may be interpreted by some as paternalistic (for the one who chooses to be merciful is also one who could choose to wield power and judgment), for Francis, the Church must show mercy because it is nothing more—and nothing less—than a sacrament of God's love for God's people.

As an ecclesial virtue, mercy resists abstract dogmatism and rigid legalism, and it embraces humility, discernment, and pastoral sensitivity. It is a "style" of being Church—an attitude or disposition of listening, solidarity, and accompaniment. It fosters a "culture of encounter" rather than a culture of condemnation. A merciful Church does not seek security in doctrinal formulations or laws, but rather seeks the grace and will of God even amid "irregular situations." It acknowledges context and complexity and celebrates any small step, even imperfect ones, toward greater closeness to Christ.[10]

Yet mercy is not a capitulation to relativism, the diminishment of doctrine, or the watering-down of the Gospel. Quite the opposite—Francis has reminded us of the fundamental "pastorality of doctrine" that was retrieved at Vatican II.[11] Mercy is the fullness of justice and truth, and it is the very heart of the Gospel.

Though Francis never puts forth a kind of "professional ethics" for ministers, he does insist that God's mercy must be reflected in the Church's pastors, especially in their preaching and the administration of the sacraments. Preaching, like all missionary evangelization, must not be "obsessed with the disjointed transmission of a multitude of doctrines to be insistently imposed," but rather should focus on "the essentials, on what is most beautiful, most grand, most appealing and at the same time most necessary," in order to communicate the joy of the Gospel.[12] Francis also reminds priests "that the confessional must not be a torture chamber but rather an encounter with the Lord's mercy which spurs us on to do our best."[13] The importance of pastoral discernment and mercy amid complexity is expressed most strongly in *Amoris laetitia*. Attentive to the wide variety of concrete circumstances and "irregular situations" in which couples and families find themselves, *Amoris laetitia* refrains from issuing new general canonical norms regarding divorced and remarried Catholics and instead puts forth "a renewed encouragement to undertake a responsible personal and pastoral discernment of particular cases," with the goal of helping couples and families integrate more fully into the community and advance in grace.[14] Here we feel the influence of the Jesuit identity of this pope. When asked how his life as a Jesuit influences his exercise of the papacy, Francis said "discernment."[15]

In its second meaning, mercy as an ecclesial virtue demands that the entire people of God are to "go out to others, seek those who have fallen away, stand at the crossroads and welcome the outcast. Such a community has an endless desire to show mercy."[16] All baptized disciples, not only priests, are to be evangelizers who "take on the 'smell of the sheep.'"[17] A merciful Church actively includes the poor and vulnerable and "says no" to an economy of exclusion, the idolatry of money, oppressive financial systems, inequality, and violence.[18] It seeks a full inculturation of the Gospel in every place and people. It promotes the inclusion of the poor, marginalized, and vulnerable within society and within the Church, affirming the inviolable dignity of the human person. In other words, mercy has a "social character," which requires that all the baptized "contribute actively and selflessly to making justice and a dignified life not simply clichés."[19] Francis has embodied the affective proximity of mercy as pope—dining with the staff at Santa Marta, embracing the poor and sick gathered in Saint Peter's Square, washing the feet of women and prisoners on Holy Thursday, and welcoming Muslim refugees into Vatican City.

When asked, he stated clearly that he has never denied the Eucharist to anyone. In words and in deeply symbolic actions, Francis models a Church that shows mercy in the face of human need, limitations, and suffering.

Finally, an ethical Church must not only offer mercy but also ask for mercy and forgiveness for itself. In continuity with the papal apologies of John Paul II and Benedict XVI, Francis has publicly apologized on behalf of the Church for the sins and crimes of sexual abuse and other violations of human dignity. In response to the August 2018 Pennsylvania Grand Jury Report detailing the abuse of over a thousand children, he wrote, "with shame and repentance, we acknowledge as an ecclesial community that we were not where we should have been, that we did not act in a timely manner; . . . we showed no care for the little ones; we abandoned them."[20] In July 2022, he traveled to Canada on a "Penitential Pilgrimage," where he expressed deep sorrow for residential school abuses—not only for the physical and spiritual abuse of children, but for the "colonizing mentality" that systematically oppressed indigenous peoples, destroyed their cultures and languages, and forced assimilation.[21] This statement echoed his 2015 apology for the "grave sins" and crimes in the colonial conquest of the Americas.[22] His apology on Canadian soil is only the first step toward justice and healing, he noted, and will be followed by a formal investigation into the residential schools and efforts to assist survivors.

An ecclesial ethics of mercy, especially one that rejects dogmatism and legalism and strives for discernment amidst concrete particulars, cannot be manifest in a Church that governs unilaterally and from a distance. An ethics of mercy requires, therefore, an ethics of subsidiarity. If mercy is the foundation of the Church's life and the fullness of justice, subsidiarity is the organizational scaffolding that allows mercy and justice to actually manifest in the lives of individual ministers and believers.

SUBSIDIARITY: "A SOUND 'DECENTRALIZATION'"

The second key that marks Francis's ecclesial ethics is subsidiarity—the principle that higher-level institutions or social groups are to provide help to lower-level institutions without usurping their power, responsibility, and primary role in society.[23] At the heart of the principle of subsidiarity is the firm belief that all societies exist for the person—not the other way around— in order to help individuals "in their free but obligatory assumption of responsibility for their own self-realization."[24] The role of the state, and of other higher-level social institutions, is in "directing, watching, stimulating, and restraining" the initiatives of smaller groups.[25] It is important to note that subsidiarity is not simply "decentralization" or a shift of all authority to lower rungs of a hierarchy or to the local level; rather, it encourages power to operate (and cooperate) at many levels, depending on circumstances and competencies, in order to promote the common good and the participation of individuals in society.

Though the Catholic Church has a strong tradition of advocating subsidiarity within the civil realm, its applicability to the life of the Church has been contested in recent decades.[26] It is perhaps for this reason that Pope Francis does not explicitly invoke the principle of subsidiarity in his ecclesial reforms, preferring the language of a "healthy decentralization." Nevertheless, his reforms, and the vision behind them, are clear applications of the principle. We see subsidiarity manifest in Francis's use and reforms of the synodal process, his attention to episcopal conferences, and his expansion of lay ministries—but also through a few more "centralizing" reforms.

Synods and Synodality

Although Francis has not convened *more* synods than his predecessors, he has significantly reshaped their way of proceeding and given them a central role in the exercise of the papal magisterium. He enacted more consultative procedures for the Synods on the Family, the Synod on Young People, and the Synod on the Amazon. In *Episcopalis communio*, he mandated a three-phrase consultative process for the Synod of Bishops: a preparatory phase of widespread consultation, a discussion phase at the synodal assembly, and an implementation phase. These new procedures of consultation are being put to the test in the 2021–24 Synod on Synodality and are, at least in theory, the kinds of participation in ecclesial life by individuals and small groups, and coordination by higher levels, that subsidiarity encourages. Moreover, Francis's postsynodal apostolic exhortations often draw deeply from the reports developed *during* the synod process—in other words, these are not written in advance of synods and merely given a stamp of approval after the fact, but are the result of genuine listening to the *sensus fidei*. Finally, in a significant move affirming the importance of synodal processes, the final document of a synod can carry papal authority if a pope so wishes.[27]

Francis's vision for the Church goes beyond these procedural reforms. He desires a truly synodal Church, one "which listens, which realizes that listening 'is more than simply hearing.' It is a mutual listening in which everyone has something to learn. The faithful people, the college of bishops, the bishop of Rome: all listening to each other, all listening to the Holy Spirit, the 'Spirit of truth' in order to know what he 'says to the Churches.'"[28] Francis's desire for a synodal Church reflects the Ignatian "way of proceeding," in which decision-making within the society involves processes of personal and communal discernment as well as dialogue and consultation between superiors and members.[29] But reciprocal listening can only occur, I would point out, if there is *regular* participation and inclusion of all the faithful at all levels of the Church, not just during the consultation phase of a synod. In other words, synodality requires subsidiarity.

Of course, synodality is not a panacea for all the Church's ills. As Vincent Miller has pointed out, the exercise of synodality is constrained by neoliberalism and colonialism.[30] The hope for a more synodal Church also faces the reality of increasing political polarization that affects not just the civil sphere but the Church as well.[31] Moreover, synodality is a practice of consultation, not necessarily deliberation; a synodal Church does not *necessarily* ensure self-determination at lower levels. And the methods of consultation will almost assuredly fail to reach former or disaffected Catholics, who have much to teach the Church.[32] Nevertheless, Francis's call for a more fully synodal Church invites renewed reflection on subsidiarity as a principle that ought to apply to the Church's own life.

Episcopal Conferences, Local Churches, and Individual Bishops

Francis has also created a more subsidiary Church by affirming the fundamental importance of local churches. First, he has given greater authority back to episcopal conferences—a structure that was deeply valued at Vatican II and mandated by Paul VI, but was gradually denied authority and significance in subsequent decades.[33] With the *motu proprio Magnum principium*, Francis modified canon law such that episcopal conferences once again have the authority to translate and approve liturgical texts; the role of the Apostolic See is to "confirm" and "recognize" these approved adaptations. He also reordered the relationship between episcopal conferences and the Apostolic See on other procedures. Whereas formerly, the Vatican would "approve" items such as the national program of priestly formation and the publication of regional catechism, the Vatican now simply "confirms" those actions that were *already* approved by the episcopal conference.[34] Both these examples can be seen as expressions of subsidiarity—episcopal conferences, the "lower" levels, have the competency, for example, to translate the liturgical texts in a way that is faithful to both the Latin text and the vernacular in order to promote the full participation of the laity in the liturgy; the Apostolic See, the "higher" level, has the competency to review the various adaptations and ratify their prior approval "in order to safeguard the substantial unity of the Roman Rite."[35] Such "decentralizing" reforms affirm the dignity, autonomy, and diversity of local churches and enable the full inculturation of the Gospel in each time, place, and culture.

The new constitution on the Curia reflects the principle of subsidiarity as well. It "leave[s] to the competence of Bishops the authority to resolve, in the exercise of 'their proper task as teachers' and pastors, those issues with which they are familiar and that do not affect the Church's unity of doctrine, discipline, and communion." At the same time, the coordinating function of higher bodies is also clearly expressed. Lifting up the diversity of the Church and the "immense store of successful experiences regarding evangelization," the Curia "is in a position to draw upon and process" this wealth of experience and initiatives and share them with other particular churches and episcopal conferences.[36] These reforms reflect Francis's oft-quoted statement in *Evangelii gaudium* that the papal magisterium should not "be expected to offer a definitive or complete word on every question which affects the Church and the world. It is not advisable for the Pope to take the place of local Bishops in the discernment of every issue which arises in their territory."[37] In other words, "decentralization is not just administrative but also magisterial."[38]

"Centralization"

We must not forget that subsidiarity is not simply "decentralization"; it also recognizes that higher levels are necessary to coordinate the lower levels and ensure the good of the whole. Francis applies the principle of subsidiarity in this regard as well. He has increased authority at higher levels or instituted new practices of oversight to ensure the common good of the Church, especially with regard to sexual abuse and Church finances. With *Vos estis lux mundi*, he made it mandatory for clergy and religious to report sexual abuse to Church authorities. This document also established the "metropolitan model," whereby the local metropolitan has the responsibility of receiving and investigating reports of abuse, or its cover-up, by bishops or heads of religious orders in his province. Even if imperfect, the metropolitan model is an example of the use of higher levels of authority to ensure the common good of the Church. Francis has also expanded the authority of "higher" levels in the Church in some of his financial reforms. He has centralized procurement procedures in order to combat financial corruption and increase transparency,[39] and has created a new committee to oversee and control all Vatican investments.[40] These reforms ensure financial, legal, and moral accountability "upward and outward," so to speak.

Francis's "centralizing" reforms are also concerned with unity in the Church, particularly in response to ideological polarization and resistance to the liturgical reforms of Vatican II. For example, *Authenticam charismatis* requires that bishops obtain prior written permission from the Vatican (formerly, just prior consultation) in order to establish religious communities of diocesan rite. This new policy is aimed, in part, at ensuring the authenticity and ecclesial character of a charism. Perhaps more significant is *Traditionis custodes*, which greatly restricted the celebration of the Mass in Latin according to the 1962 *Roman Missal*. Individual priests no longer have the freedom to celebrate according to earlier liturgical forms as they wish; rather, the bishop alone has the right and responsibility to authorize the use of the 1962 *Missal* in his diocese (and on occasion, only after consulting the Apostolic See). The bishop is also charged with ensuring that those celebrating in this form maintain a sense of ecclesial communion and "do not deny the validity and legitimacy of the liturgical reform dictated by Vatican Council II."[41] While empowering different levels of authority—one papal, one episcopal—both *Authenticam charismatis* and *Traditionis custodes* are examples of giving greater oversight and authority to a higher institution or body within the Church for the sake of the good and unity of the whole. This is not a contradiction of Francis's other calls for a "healthy decentralization," but is once again subsidiarity in practice.

A more subsidiary Church promotes missionary evangelization by allowing for deeper inculturation of the Gospel, while still striving for unity. It also enables fuller participation of the entire people of God in the whole life of the Church and facilitates oversight in order to correct injustice. In other words, an ethics of subsidiarity cultivates a more just Church.

JUSTICE: ECCLESIAL RIGHT RELATIONSHIPS

Finally, Francis's papacy suggests that an ecclesial ethics should foreground justice, especially for the poor and vulnerable, for survivors of clergy sexual abuse, and for the laity. His commitment to justice is reflective of the mission of the Jesuits, which is "the promotion of faith and the service of justice," as articulated by the Thirty-Second General Congregation. An ethical Church is one that strives for right relationships between its members and gives each their due.

Justice for the Poor and Vulnerable

As novice master and rector of the Jesuit community at the Colegio Máximo in Buenos Aires, Jorge Bergoglio made sure the formation for young Jesuits included "an option for the poor expressed in manual labor, hands-on pastoral care, and a deep respect for popular culture and values, especially a religiosity of pilgrimages, shrines, and devotions."[42] He insisted that seminarians spend time with the poor, even checking their shoes for dust and dirt, evidence that they had spent time in the barrios.[43] Now, as bishop of Rome, Francis wants the whole Church to get its shoes dirty. Just as he insists that mercy be the animating spirit of evangelization, he also insists that the "social character" of mercy be manifest in the Church's advocacy for social justice and the inclusion of the poor and vulnerable in Church and in society. Francis has institutionalized this concern for the poor in his reforms of Vatican finances, mentioned above. He has also mandated that all investments of Vatican finances must align with Catholic social teaching, especially those pertaining to care for the environment, peacemaking, and poverty relief.[44]

Yet, for Francis, justice for the poor is not simply about alleviating suffering or changing the economic and political systems that create conditions of poverty. It also entails the inclusion of the poor and marginalized in the Church at all levels and a closeness to the poor that recognizes their dignity, experience of life, and faith. Francis has advanced inclusion of the marginalized in several ways. As James Keenan shows in chapter 2, Francis has created structures of recognizing and listening to the voice on the margins through the World Meetings of Popular Movements. The Synod on the Amazon centered indigenous voices and traditions that are marginalized both within the Church and within South American societies and economies. His encyclicals and apostolic exhortations draw deeply from documents from episcopal conferences around the world, such that he "realigns the canon of the sources of papal teaching with a more universal and less Europe-centered canon."[45] Francis has also greatly increased the number of cardinals from outside Europe, and has chosen cardinals who represent minorities even within their own countries.[46] The new constitution on the Curia states that its officials should be "selected, as far as possible, from various regions of the world, so that the Curia may reflect the universal character of the Church."[47] His travels, beginning with his trip to the island of Lampedusa, are often to "peripheral but symbolically important places rather than big cities."[48] Francis's Church is a Church of and for "the poor" not simply in the sense of all those left behind by neoliberalism and globalization but also those peoples and places rendered valueless by cultural and academic elites and by centuries of ecclesial Eurocentrism.

Justice for Sexual Abuse Survivors

Without doubt, the Catholic Church must also be committed to justice for survivors of sexual abuse and their families. In addition to his formal apologies for sexual abuse within the Church, Francis has undertaken a number of reforms aimed at preventing abuse and holding bishops accountable. As a result of the February 2019 global summit on the protection of minors, Francis made it mandatory for clerics and religious to report sexual abuse and established the metropolitan model. He also abolished the pontifical secret, which had held under the highest level of confidentiality all information pertaining to sexual abuse allegations, trials, and decisions, and he raised the age limit for the definition of child pornography from fourteen to eighteen. Finally, Francis promulgated a newly revised Book VI of the Code of Canon Law on penal sanctions (begun under Benedict XVI) that penalizes not just sexual abuse but also the failure to report sexual abuse. While none of these actions, in themselves or collectively, fully heal the wounds of sexual abuse or repair the harms done by the Church, they are necessary steps toward justice for survivors and their families—steps that must be continued in local churches around the world, including in the United States.

Justice for the Laity

A just Church must also strive to give the laity their due. Pope Francis has decried the culture of clericalism within the Church not just because it is a cause of the sexual abuse crisis but also because it inhibits the full realization by the laity of the grace and responsibility of their baptism.[49] Although Francis does not use the language of justice in these contexts, he has instituted several reforms that contribute to setting right the relationships between laity and clergy. With the reform of the Roman Curia, laypeople can now head curial dicasteries, an advance that has been noted as one of the most significant developments in ecclesiology and Church structure since Vatican II.[50] During the Synod on Synodality, Francis included lay men and women as full voting members of a synod of bishops for the first time. These reforms, together with the structures of subsidiarity described above, are means toward greater justice for laity within the Church by advancing their full participation at all levels. At the same time, justice for the laity must go beyond these nevertheless-important reforms that allow a privileged few laypersons entrance into the halls of the Curia. It also requires a cultural shift such that the term "Church" no longer is seen as synonymous with "the ordained" or "the hierarchy" but with *the people*. Francis has led the way once again, with his insistence that all the baptized are missionary disciples called to the task of evangelization, that popular piety and the faith of the poor is a privileged *locus theologicus* and expression of the *sensus fidei*, and that baptism is more significant than ordination.

Francis's record on ecclesial justice for women in particular, however, is mixed. On one hand, he has increased women's opportunities for ministry and governance in the Church. He formally opened the instituted ministry of lector and acolyte to women; he created the new instituted ministry of catechist, also open to both women and men; and he has reopened the conversation about readmitting women to the diaconate.[51] Moreover, he has appointed women to key leadership positions in the Vatican, including to the dicastery that advises on the selection of bishops. Although only one of these positions is held by a nonreligious woman thus far, their appointments by Francis remain symbolically and canonically significant.[52] Finally, he requested that half the nonbishop members of the Synod on Synodality be women (both religious and nonreligious), and thereby granted voting rights in a synod to women for the first time. On the other hand, Francis retains a framework of gender complementarity, often saying that women are needed in such ministerial and advisory positions because of their sensitivity and distinctive Marian nature, rather than for their theological acumen or as a matter of justice. As Megan McCabe suggests in chapter 10, such a mindset falls short of full equality for women in the Church.

CONCLUSION: ECCLESIAL ETHICS FOR THE CHURCH IN THE UNITED STATES

The ecclesial ethics implicit in Francis's papacy invites the US Church, its parishes, and its ordained ministers to growth and reform, although there are notable challenges to becoming a more ethical Church as well. Yet reforms are necessary, for only an ethical Church can be an effective public witness to the incarnate love of God.

First and foremost, mercy, subsidiarity, and justice must be manifest at the parish level. For example, precisely because Francis avoids issuing new norms in *Amoris laetitia*, focusing instead on the need to exercise pastoral discernment and form mature consciences, the actual experience of mercy—or in contrast, of rigidity or condemnation—will occur between individuals and their pastors and faith community. It is imperative, then, that seminaries admit and form persons who have a capacity for nuance and complexity and who remain close to the ordinary lives of lay Catholics. In particular, theological education and pastoral training must communicate the "pastorality of doctrine" that is at the heart of Francis's vision of ministry.[53] Unfortunately, the fact that most seminary formation in the United States is physically and ecclesially isolated—seminarians rarely study alongside or live among laypeople and are typically sheltered from the demands of household management—impedes the kind of closeness and solidarity that is necessary for the praxis of mercy.

Of course, a parish is more than its pastor. Subsidiarity urges parishes and dioceses to see lay participation in the liturgy and in parish and diocesan governance not as a kind of "special concession" to the modern era or a democratic society but as necessary for being a just Church. An ecclesial ethics of subsidiarity calls the laity to be protagonists in their local church and urges priests and bishops to ask what roles belong to the laity by virtue of their baptism; how they can encourage the freedom, responsibility, and self-realization of lay Catholics and the flourishing of lay associations; and how they can advance the inculturation of liturgy amidst the many diverse cultures within the United States. Moreover, more subsidiary structures at the parish and diocesan levels may advance the full inclusion of the vulnerable and marginalized that Francis envisions—which must entail the full inclusion of women and LGBTQ persons in all forms of ministry, leadership, and governance as well. Finally, the principle of subsidiarity in its "centralizing" dimension (e.g., Francis's restrictions on the celebration of the Mass in Latin) holds out hope for tempering ideological polarization in the US Church.

Unfortunately, both dimensions of subsidiarity face challenges in the US context. On one hand, a number of US bishops have resisted Francis's reforms toward a more synodal, subsidiary, and participatory Church. Some bishops have been slow to embrace the consultative phase of synods; for example, during the Synod on the Family, only a third of US dioceses made the questionnaire available within six months after Francis called for this to happen "immediately and as widely as possible."[54] During the Synod on Synodality, many bishops were skeptical of or outright resistant to the idea of synodality and to hosting listening sessions.[55] On the other hand, subsidiarity poses a challenge to the laity as well, perhaps especially to more liberal individuals and groups. For "the individual and small group must be open to the assistance that a larger society can offer," and "those who support decentralization . . . must at least be open to the positive function of higher ecclesiastical authority and the fact that there will be situations when the positive function will need to be invoked."[56] In a Church wounded by decades of sexual abuse and cover-ups, it may be understandably difficult for some to be open, even simply in theory, to the positive and necessary function of a bishop.

There is much room for growth in the US Church's commitment to justice as well. The US bishops must continue to work for justice for survivors of clergy sexual abuse by transparently instituting Francis's procedural reforms, of course, but also by confronting the structures and culture of clericalism, so visible in the case of Theodore Cardinal McCarrick, that have enabled abuse and its cover-up. Francis's ecclesial ethics also challenges the Church to embrace a more holistic commitment to care for the vulnerable—not only the unborn but also the poor and marginalized, migrants and refugees, and the Earth itself. In this regard, the US episcopate's focus on abortion as the preeminent moral issue threatens the church's commitment and witness to justice more broadly; as Daniel DiLeo shows in chapter 13 of this volume, they have largely failed to act or to teach on climate issues.[57] The tendency toward single-issue politics and the increasing political and ideological polarization in the US Church is both an impediment to becoming a more ethical Church and is exacerbated by the lack of a broader commitment to justice by the nation's bishops.

A Church whose structures, culture, and leaders are more merciful, just, and subsidiary can advance these virtues beyond its own bounds as well. If the US Church can take a cue from Francis and strive to be more merciful, encountering others with tenderness across difference, then our Church might begin to heal the polarization that pains the Church and all of civil society in the United States today. A Church that seeks justice, inclusion, and right relationship for its own members can be a stronger witness to the preferential option for the poor and the obligation of society to create structures of inclusion and participation. Likewise, a more subsidiary and just Church can press Catholic civic leaders to a more complete and accurate consideration of subsidiarity, in both its "decentralizing" and "centralizing" dimensions, in the public sphere. (Recall that during the Obama administration, the Catholic congressman Paul Ryan invoked a rather partial view of subsidiarity to justify budget and tax cuts in the name of Catholic social thought.[58]) Such a Church is a stronger witness to civil society that economic justice will, at times, require coordinated action at higher levels of government. Finally, a Church that is more fully committed to a broad range of justice issues (e.g., a commitment to reducing emissions, as DiLeo argues) not only concretely advances justice throughout the world but may also inspire other organizations, groups, and governments to do the same.

Mercy, subsidiarity, and justice certainly are not the only virtues or principles necessary for an ecclesial ethics. We would do well to consider the importance of humility, its relation to mercy, and the need for ongoing reform and conversion in the Church, for example, or the virtue of prudence in relation to pastoral discernment or the means by which ecclesial reform is undertaken. Francis's papacy gives us a starting point, one that invites further development. The Church is, after all, the *pilgrim* people of God, ever on the way.

NOTES

1. My usage is distinct from other uses of the term "ecclesial ethics." E.g., William Cavanaugh uses it to mean a Gospel-inspired ethics applied to the public sphere; William Cavanaugh, "Ecclesial Ethics and the Gospel *Sine Glossa*: Sacramental Politics and the Love of the World," *Modern Theology* 36, no. 3 (July 2020): 501–23. Sigrid Müller uses it to mean ethics or moral theology as done by the pope or other magisterial figures; Sigrid Müller, "'A Lantern on the Way': Pope Francis's Signposts for Ecclesial Ethics," *Ecclesiology* 17 (2021): 213–37. My use is in line with that of the Margaret Beaufort Institute of Theology's Centre for Ecclesial Ethics (www.mbit.cam.ac.uk/centre-for-ecclesial-ethics/).
2. Stephen J. Pope, ed., *Common Calling: The Laity and Governance of the Catholic Church* (Washington, DC: Georgetown University Press, 2004); Richard M. Gula, *Just Ministry: Professional Ethics for Pastoral Ministers* (New York: Paulist Press, 2010).
3. Jean Bartunek, Mary Ann Hinsdale, and James F. Keenan, eds., *Church Ethics and Its Organizational Context: Learning from the Sex Abuse Scandal in the Catholic Church* (Lanham, MD: Rowman & Littlefield, 2006).
4. My framework here resonates with Conor Kelly's chapter in this volume, in which he demonstrates that Pope Francis is, in some ways, a virtue ethicist.
5. I am indebted to Richard Gaillardetz for sharing with me his personal document tracking the many reforms and documents, and their significance, of Francis's pontificate, which greatly facilitated the writing of this chapter.
6. *Miserando atque eligiendo*, translated by Austen Ivereigh as "He saw him through the eyes of mercy and chose him" (in reference to Jesus calling the tax collector Matthew); Austen Ivereigh, *The Great Reformer: Francis and the Making of a Radical Pope* (New York: Picador, 2014), 12.
7. Francis, *Misericordiae vultus*, April 11, 2015, nos. 10, 12. All the papal documents cited herein can be accessed online at www.vatican.va.
8. Francis, *The Name of God Is Mercy*, trans. Oonagh Stravinsky (New York: Random House, 2016), 8–9.
9. Francis.
10. Francis, *Evangelii gaudium*, November 24, 2013, no. 44; see also Francis, *Amoris laetitia*, March 19, 2016, no. 305.
11. John O'Malley, "Reconciling Doctrine, Theology, Spirituality, and Pastorality," in *Pope Francis: A Voice for Mercy, Justice, Love, and Care for the Earth*, ed. Barbara Wall and Massimo Faggioli (Maryknoll, NY: Orbis Books, 2019), 10–22.
12. Francis, *Evangelii gaudium*, nos. 35, 39.
13. Francis, no. 44.
14. Francis, *Amoris laetitia*, no. 300.
15. Antonio Spadaro, "A Big Heart Open to God," interview with Francis, September 30, 2013, www.americamagazine.org/faith/2013/09/30/big-heart-open-god-interview-pope-francis.
16. Francis, *Evangelii gaudium*, no. 24.
17. Francis.
18. Francis, chap. 2.
19. Francis, *Misericordia et misera*, November 20, 2016, 19.
20. Francis, "Letter to the People of God," August 20, 2018, no. 1.

21. Francis, "Address to Indigenous Peoples: First Nations, Métis and Inuit," July 25, 2022.
22. Francis, "Address at the Second World Meeting of Popular Movements," July 9, 2015.
23. Francis, *Evangelii gaudium*, no. 16.
24. Joseph A. Komonchak, "Subsidiarity in the Church: The State of the Question," *The Jurist* 48, no. 1 (1988): 298–349, at 301.
25. Pius XI, *Quadragesimo anno*, May 15, 1931, no. 80.
26. See Komonchak, "Subsidiarity"; and John J. Burkhard, "The Interpretation and Application of Subsidiarity in Ecclesiology: An Overview of the Theological and Canonical Literature," *The Jurist* 58, no. 2 (1998): 279–342.
27. Francis, *Episcopalis communio*, September 15, 2018, art. 18.
28. Francis, "Address Commemorating the 50th Anniversary of the Institution of the Synod of Bishops," October 17, 2015.
29. See the constitutions and complementary norms on the vow of obedience, community life, and the governance of society in *"Our Way of Proceeding,"* by William A. Barry, SJ (Saint Louis: Institute of Jesuit Sources, 1997), 78, 160–64, 168–72.
30. Vincent J. Miller, "Synodality and the Sacramental Mission of the Church: The Struggle for Communion in a World Divided by Colonialism and Neoliberal Globalization," *Theological Studies* 83, no. 1 (March 2022): 8–24.
31. Richard Gaillardetz, "Reflections on Impediments to Synodality: Polarization and the Escalation of Conflict," *Worship* 96, January 2022, 4–12.
32. Patrick Hornbeck, "Synodality and/with Disaffiliated Catholics," paper delivered at the 2022 convention of the Catholic Theological Society of America.
33. Francis A. Sullivan, "The Teaching Authority of Episcopal Conferences," *Theological Studies* 63, no. 3 (September 2002): 472–93.
34. Francis, *Competentias quasdam decernere*, February 11, 2022.
35. Comment on the *motu proprio* by the secretary of the Congregation for Divine Worship and the Discipline of the Sacraments, September 9, 2017.
36. Francis, *Praedicate Evangelium*, II.3 and II.4; article 21.
37. Francis, *Evangelii gaudium*, no. 16.
38. Massimo Faggioli, *The Liminal Papacy of Pope Francis: Moving Toward Global Catholicity* (Maryknoll, NY: Orbis Books, 2020), 143.
39. John L. Allen Jr., "Pope Enacts New Procurement Law to Combat Deficits, Corruption," *Crux*, June 1, 2020, https://cruxnow.com/vatican/2020/06/pope-enacts-new-procurement-law-to-combat-deficits-corruption.
40. Christopher Lamb, "Pope Francis Launches New Finance and Investment Overhaul," *The Tablet*, July 19, 2022, www.thetablet.co.uk/news/15678/pope-francis-launches-new-finance-and-investment-overhaul.
41. Francis, *Traditiones custodes*, July 16, 2021, article 3, no. 1.
42. Ivereigh, *Great Reformer*, 173, 177–90.
43. Ivereigh, 182.
44. Junno Arocho Esteves, "Vatican Investments Must Follow Catholic Social Teaching, New Policy Says," Catholic News Service, July 19, 2022, available at www.ncronline.org.
45. Faggioli, *Liminal Papacy*, 10.
46. Gerard O'Connell, *Inside the Vatican* podcast, June 3, 2022, at www.americamagazine.org. The cardinals represent 69 countries as of August 2022, compared with 48 at the 1978 conclave that elected John Paul II and 52 at the conclave of 2005; Faggioli, *Liminal Papacy*, 148.

47. *Praedicate Evangelium*, no. 14.3.
48. Faggioli, *Liminal Papacy*, 73.
49. Francis, "Letter to the People of God," 2.
50. Austen Ivereigh, "Mission First: Pope Francis Reforms the Roman Curia," *Commonweal*, May 2022, 10–13; Paul Lakeland, "Ministry and Governance: What Might *Praedicate Evangelium* Have Started?" *Commonweal*, May 6, 2022, www.commonwealmagazine.org/ministry-governance.
51. Francis, *Spiritus Domino*, January 15, 2021; Francis, *Antiquum ministerium*, May 10, 2021.
52. Sr. Nathalie Becquart to the Synod of Bishops; Sr. Alexandra Smerilli to the Dicastery for Integral Human Development; Sr. Rafaella Petrini as Secretary General of the Governorate of Vatican City State as well as the Dicastery of Bishops; Sr. Yvonne Reungoat and nonreligious (but consecrated virgin) Maria Lia Zervino to the Dicastery for Bishops.
53. The latest edition of the *Program for Priestly Formation* (2022) is moving in this direction, though its impact likely will not be seen for some time.
54. Michael O'Loughlin, "Some US Dioceses Report Results of Questionnaire," *National Catholic Reporter*, March 11, 2014, www.ncronline.org/news/accountability/some-us-dioceses-report-results-questionnaire.
55. Brian Fraga, "Synod Phase for Local Listening Gets an Uneven Start in US Dioceses," *National Catholic Reporter*, December 14, 2021, www.ncronline.org/news/parish/synod-phase-local-listening-gets-uneven-start-us-dioceses; Oscar Cantú, "As Bishop, I Was Skeptical about Synodality; the Latin American Church Changed That," *National Catholic Reporter*, February 3, 2022, www.ncronline.org/news/opinion/bishop-i-was-skeptical-about-synodality-latin-american-church-changed.
56. Burkhard, "Interpretation," 333.
57. Even the Congregation for the Doctrine of the Faith suggested as much. In 2021, as the US Conference of Catholic Bishops considered a national policy of denying Communion to politicians who support legal abortion, a letter from the prefect of the Congregation for the Doctrine of the Faith discouraged such a policy, for two reasons: first, it would mislead people into thinking "that abortion and euthanasia alone constitute the only grave matters of Catholic moral and social teaching that demand the fullest level of accountability on the part of Catholics"; and second, it would deny the authority of each bishop to administer the sacraments within his diocese (i.e., it would be a failure of pastoral discernment and subsidiarity). See "Cardinal Ladaria to US Bishops: Debate on Communion and Abortion Should Not Lead to Division," May 12, 2021, www.vaticannews.va/en/vatican-city/news/2021-05/vatican-letter-ladaria-bishops-us-communion-politics-abortion.html.
58. David Gibson, "Analysis: Paul Ryan's Not-Very-Catholic Catholic Budget," Religion News Service, April 26, 2012, https://religionnews.com/2012/04/26/news-analysis-paul-ryans-not-very-catholic-catholic-budget/.

5

POPE FRANCIS'S SOCIAL ETHICS

Advocacy for Economic Justice and Equity

Thomas Massaro, SJ

Social ethics explores normative dimensions of all manner of human relations. Because this volume contains illuminating chapters on so many topics within social ethics (e.g., gender, race, migration, peacebuilding, the environment), this chapter focuses on what Pope Francis has done and said regarding economic ethics, including his advocacy for labor justice and equitable distribution of material goods in society.

Of this chapter's four sections, the first documents the renewal of Catholic social teaching under Francis, examining how his economic teachings at once stand in continuity with previous Church teachings, while also incorporating substantially innovative dimensions. The second section describes the influence of Ignatian spirituality upon Francis's approach to economic life. As the first Jesuit pope, Francis displays a set of social concerns and "ways of proceeding" that have distinguished the Society of Jesus throughout its nearly five-hundred-year history. The third section examines several key texts where Francis offers a sharp critique of the exploitive contemporary economy, documenting his deep concerns regarding spiraling inequality, violations of worker justice, and global maldistribution of goods and resources. The fourth section contextualizes Francis's commentary on economic justice in two ways: specifically, within the US Catholic community, and then as part of his larger agenda of promoting Gospel values, affirming the social mission of the Church, and extending solidarity to all.

CONTINUITY AND RENEWAL IN CATHOLIC SOCIAL TEACHING

Francis's first major teaching document, the apostolic exhortation *Evangelii gaudium*, contains the most extensive treatment of economic ethics in his entire corpus, rivaled only by the encyclical *Fratelli tutti*. Interestingly, Francis was quite insistent that his commentary on economic issues within *Evangelii gaudium* contained nothing new that was not already present in previous Catholic social teachings. Less than a month after the document's publication, he granted an interview to the Italian daily publication *La Stampa* in which he disavowed introducing any new social teachings. His words on that occasion were: "In the exhortation, I did not say anything that is not already in the teachings of the social doctrine of the church."[1] A similar claim is asserted in no. 184 of *Evangelii gaudium* itself, which steers the reader in search of guidance on economic analysis to a 2004 Vatican-produced reference work on Catholic social teaching, *Compendium of the Social Doctrine of the Church*. Here, Francis calls this resource "a most suitable tool . . . whose use and study I heartily recommend."

Three observations seem most pertinent in assessing this demurral on the part of Francis. First, Vatican watchers readily recognize Francis as echoing in this instance a common papal trope; popes habitually couch many innovations they introduce in a mantle of utter continuity with their own "esteemed predecessors of happy memory." Although scholars of theology are generally comfortable with speaking of doctrinal development, popes display a marked preference for describing their contributions as simply building upon earlier doctrines, or perhaps making explicit what may have been previously obscure in received teachings. The facetious quip runs that when even the most momentous of Church policy or teaching reversals is announced, the official papal proclamation will begin: "As we have always taught, . . ." Even the most adventuresome popes display a marked aversion to appearing at all critical of what has preceded them. In short, ample reason can be found for not quite taking Francis at his word in this particular instance. He is perpetuating the papal proclivity for downplaying any innovations in the exercise of his teaching office.

A second inescapable observation is that there is indeed much that is new (or, at the very least, quite "fresh") in Francis's social teachings. No objective observer would reach the conclusion that all Francis has said or done regarding social justice is merely "more of the same," merely repeating the contents of the one-hundred-thirty-year tradition of modern Catholic social teachings. Even in advance of the close analysis of Francis's key texts on economic justice provided in the third section of this chapter, it is not hard to identify novel directions that Francis brings to these topics. No previous pope has so consistently applied the categories of inclusion and exclusion to the workings of the global economy, nor spoken so directly about the tragic outcomes of accelerating concentrations of wealth and power that produce spiraling inequality, nor denounced trickle-down approaches to economic growth with such urgency and acuity. When Francis pulls these threads together, with his noteworthy cry in *Evangelii gaudium*, no. 53, "Such an economy kills," he is articulating a new interpretation on the part of the official Church regarding the reality of economic exploitation, victimization, oppression and inequity.

A third observation that advances our understanding of these matters involves the familiar distinction between style and substance in exercising any type of leadership, but especially for those exercising religious authority. Both the "how" and the "what" must be considered in any assessment of leadership, especially when judging the enactment of consequential changes. Unlike most secular organizations, religious institutions (e.g., the Roman Catholic Church) are constructed on a foundation of revered traditions that can in no way be overturned or cavalierly disregarded. As noted above, this situation tends to render leaders and authoritative teachers markedly averse to announcing sweeping changes. Successive leaders do manage to place their own preferred "spin" on teachings and management practices. Each pope who has contributed to the development of modern Catholic social teaching has followed this pattern, and the Church has surely benefited from this progression of leaders sporting their own styles. In the end, it would indeed be more accurate to speak of "an interplay" between style and substance than a simple "distinction" between them in dealing with the complexities of religious teachings regarding the economy. The medium and the message by which Catholic moral teachings proceed are bound to be deeply entangled.

To be more explicit, then, about the points of continuity between Francis and his predecessors, we need only review a list of the major concepts and claims of Catholic social teaching to detect enduring through-lines. Notions of economic justice within this long tradition have always been grounded in the dignity of the individual (often expressed approvingly in the language of human rights), which is of course always realized in the context of a community of persons, to which members of society hold solemn duties. Catholic teachings tend to measure the justice of any economic system by how well it respects the balance between the two poles of the personal and the collective. The freedoms available to the individual must be reconciled with the promotion of the common good within wider social relations.

In his teachings on economic justice, Pope Francis consistently relies on precisely this framework, namely, the interconnected networks of rights and duties that promote the well-being of individuals and collectivities as well, and that protect both from harm. In so many places where he comments on economic justice, including solemnly authoritative teaching documents (see especially chapters 3 to 6 of the encyclical *Fratelli tutti*) and in occasional addresses (consider his "Messages for World Day of Peace" and "World Day of the Poor"), Francis hastens to reaffirm these patterns of Catholic social thought. When he speaks of basic social institutions, from private property to the voluntary associations of civil society to government itself, Francis reflects the intellectual heritage that recognizes such polestars of Catholic social theory as the universal destination of created goods, subsidiarity, and the rights to participation and free association—the entire intellectual framework developed by his predecessor popes. After all, Francis himself was formed in this tradition of thought, so it naturally shapes how he perceives the world, identifies injustices, and recommends solutions to problems that threaten the core economic values identified by earlier popes in their social teachings.

In many highly perceptive writings on the papacy of Francis, the theologian Massimo Faggioli provides valuable reminders of the many factors that shaped the man who would become the 266th pontiff. One set of these influences relates to his generational status. Francis is the first pope to enter the priesthood after the Second Vatican Council; ordained in 1969, the seminarian Jorge Mario Bergoglio would have read with great interest the newly available documents of Vatican II, as required material in his graduate courses in theology. The portrayal of the Church as the gathered "people of God" in *Lumen gentium* ("Dogmatic Constitution on the Church"), the universal call to holiness in *Apostolicam actuositatem* ("Decree on the Apostolate of the Laity"), the recognition of "the legitimate autonomy of the secular" that ushers in a new style of public engagement appropriate for a pluralistic society in *Gaudium et spes* ("Pastoral Constitution on the Church in the Modern World")—all these themes shaped the impressionable young Jesuit and his later actions as a Church leader. Indeed, Faggioli characterizes Francis as the first pope displaying an "unproblematic relationship with both the council and the postconciliar period."[2]

If we may venture that these rich ecclesial themes informed the eventual stance of Francis on economic matters, even if somewhat indirectly, then we can claim with greater confidence the more direct influence on the future pope of John XXIII's stated intention for the (still upcoming) council to usher in "a Church of the poor." Indeed, no single Vatican II–related utterance seems to have exerted greater influence on the future Francis (who was a Jesuit novice when Pope John announced his intention to convene the council). Just three days after his election, Francis, in his first media interview, echoed those words from over a half century earlier: "How I would love a church that is poor and for the poor."[3] A Church that identifies with the poor, and is demonstrably on the side of the poor, will reach a markedly different set of judgments on economic justice than a Church identified with the affluent and influential. A new ethos, a new set of allies, and a new matrix of relationships accompany a new social location.

Turning (as Francis himself often does) to that word *location*, in both its literal geographical and metaphorical senses, Faggioli comments further not only on *when* the future Francis came along but also *where* he came from. He makes much of the social location of the man Bergoglio himself, shedding further light on the distinctiveness of his perspective on global economic realities—from the effects of accelerating globalization to the persistent economic distortions that are legacies of European colonialism. Starting with the most overarching observation, Faggioli reminds us of Karl Rahner's description of the Second Vatican Council as the first gathering of a truly "world Church," one fully conscious of its global reach and identity. There is no turning back; a definitive break had occurred from the legacy of medieval European Christendom and the assumed cultural dominance of a "center" over a "periphery." Never again can the Catholic Church be satisfied to reflect a Eurocentric bias; rather, it must take up with utter seriousness the full global inculturation of the Gospel message, however complex an agenda this turns out to entail. A corollary of this portrayal of the overdue de-Europeanization of the Catholic Church is Faggioli's assertion that "the pontificate of Pope Francis is the first pontificate of a bishop from the world Church."[4]

A more specific facet of the social location occupied by Francis throughout his life is his identity as an Argentinian. Other observers of Francis, including Lisa Cahill in chapter 1 of this volume, offer thorough analyses of the many ways in which the pope's national identity influences his ecclesiology, his pastoral approach, and (in particular, for present purposes) his approach to economic life.[5] Suffice it to say that it does indeed make an enormous difference that a native of a formerly colonized nation has ascended to the papacy and is able to place his mark on Catholic social teaching. The perspective of a man who openly embraces his identity as coming to Rome "from the ends of the Earth" is one shaped by an acute awareness of global economic structures and how they disadvantage much of the world's population.[6]

Admittedly, Argentina is not an archetypal "periphery country"; as one of the most economically advanced nations of Latin America, its national experience is far from typical of the world's underdeveloped nations. Still, a citizen of that land who lived through the Great Depression (which ruined the Bergoglio family business during Jorge's early boyhood), two turbulent reigns of Juan Perón, the brutal "Dirty War" of the military junta of the 1970s and 1980s, and disastrous economic instability at the beginning of the new millennium—such a man will naturally harbor deep distrust of a neoliberal economic order that has subjected his homeland to so much suffering. The first pope from the Global South (and from the Western Hemisphere) brings to the Vatican firsthand knowledge of economic dysfunction and vulnerability that are markedly different from the perceptions of any recent pope—all Europeans as they have been.

Faggioli contributes further to our appreciation of the economic ethic of Francis in highlighting one final aspect of the geography of Bergoglio's Argentina. He makes the indisputable observation that Francis is the first pope to reside in the geographical confines of a massive megalopolis, one of the sprawling metropolitan areas that have become home to an ever-increasing proportion of the global population.[7] Indeed, Bergoglio spent the great majority of his life in the megacity of Buenos Aires, a port city and multicultural capital of great diversity that has long been a magnet for new immigrants from all over Latin America and beyond. As a youngster growing up in the modest middle-class neighborhood of Flores, he lived in close proximity both to extremely affluent districts and to precincts populated by the desperately poor.[8] As a seminarian, then as a Jesuit superior, and even as cardinal archbishop of Buenos Aires, Bergoglio frequented the *villas miseria* (the large urban slums, or shantytowns, referred to in other parts of Latin America as *barrios* or *favelas*). Many at the time referred to him as *un obispo callero* ("a bishop of the streets"), while Faggioli labels him unabashedly "an advocate for the urban poor."[9]

Although such pastoral work was never his main assignment, Bergoglio was well known for making frequent impromptu visits to the ramshackle homes of the poor and offering in-person encouragement to the "slum priests" who were permanent residents, living a lifestyle of voluntary poverty in solidarity with the suffering poor who comprise the majority of the population. Such intense and frequent contact with the impoverished naturally fosters acute awareness of the unjust burdens that fall on the marginalized. Is it any wonder that Francis was eager to inspire a renewal of Church social teachings regarding economic justice and poverty? Almost every chapter of Austen Ivereigh's definitive biography of Francis makes some mention of this aspect of the long ministerial life of Bergoglio, arguing that a perduring commitment to accompanying underserved communities has been a key marker of the pastoral vision of the pope.[10] The next section of this chapter examines another key marker and source of this vision of Francis: his identity as a member of the Society of Jesus.

THE INFLUENCE UPON FRANCIS OF IGNATIAN SPIRITUALITY AND JESUIT IDENTITY

By his own account, no single influence on Francis (whether in his approach to economic justice or any other topic) is more important than the Society of Jesus. His long years of formation, his occupying multiple positions of authority, his exemplary mastery of spiritual practices, his decades of life in Jesuit communities—all suggest that the Jesuit "way of proceeding" has left its fingerprints all over Francis. Even though he has not actually lived or worked closely with other Jesuits since he became auxiliary bishop of Buenos Aires in 1992, the Jesuit DNA of the pope perdures in ways that mark his social teachings and inspire his advocacy for economic justice.

The Jesuit charism, rooted in the *Spiritual Exercises* of Saint Ignatius Loyola and developed through an impressive array of diverse apostolic involvements of the Society of Jesus for nearly five hundred years, contains numerous elements that predispose practitioners to the pursuit of social justice. The vision of Ignatius includes dimensions that are both vertical (featuring God-directed religious devotion) and horizontal (featuring genuine concern for neighbor) in nature. Those touched by Ignatian spirituality are called to be "men and women for others," who ceaselessly strive for the *magis*, or ever greater service to God and neighbor. This spiritual tradition displays a genius for bridging the transcendent and the immanent, allowing its adherents to readily combine attention to the needs of the body and the soul in a holistic approach that inspires efforts for inner-worldly transformation and redressing injustices, both individual and social in nature. Note the pattern by which interior conversion within an individual practitioner manifests itself in a commitment to ameliorate conditions in the exterior world of social relations. The temptation to "spiritualize away" concerns about the material conditions of any members of the human family has simply not been a characteristic of the Jesuit charism. Though realistic about the costs of the struggle for social justice, the practitioner of Ignatian spirituality is confident in the possibility of forging a better world, rejecting the fatalism or despair that might hinder potential agents of transformation.

Even the casual observer of Francis will detect in his words and actions numerous further elements of Ignatian spirituality and long Jesuit practice: the practice of careful discernment, the prudent combination of reason and emotions in shaping responses to challenges, and an orientation favoring merciful application of moral laws and utmost respect for the individual conscience—to name just a few items with relevance to moral theology and social ethics.[11] Other chapters in this volume amplify these points, especially that of Conor Kelly in chapter 3, discussing the role of careful discernment and the virtue of mercy. All these legacies of this well-developed spiritual tradition work together to make the first Jesuit pope one who is not only dedicated to shaping an energetic pastoral strategy that advances social justice and the well-being of all but who is also particularly empathetic toward those on the margins and eager to commit the Church to making a preferential option for the poor, as documented in chapter 6 of this volume by M. T. Dávila. While none of these directions are unique to Jesuit spirituality or the apostolic involvements of the Society of Jesus, certain related dimensions of Jesuit experience and practice in recent decades illuminate the approach of Pope Francis to economic realities along these very lines, as the remainder of this section describes.

In Catholic circles worldwide, the twentieth century witnessed a growing consciousness of three closely related intellectual developments within social ethics: (1) the imperative to supplement the long-standing "charity alone orientation" with a "charity-and-justice orientation," to account for new institutional realities in the political and economic spheres; (2) the power of social sin, or structural injustices that urgently require redress at the level of root causes; and (3) the value of probing social and cultural analysis in order to study and reveal the deepest causal roots of social injustices. All three developments can be observed flowering in successive documents of official Catholic social teaching. Major breakthroughs along these lines occurred with Paul VI's 1967 social encyclical *Populorum progressio*, with *Justitia in Mundo* (the teaching document of the 1971 Worldwide Synod of Bishops highlighting the reality of social sin and encouraging structural analysis of global economic injustices), and with John Paul II's 1987 encyclical *Sollicitudo rei socialis* (which, on a dozen occasions, alludes to "structures of sin" or related concepts). By the close of the millennium, the Catholic Church's teaching magisterium had confirmed its commitment to conducting deep structural analysis in pursuit of social justice.

These documents and developments, coming so soon after Vatican II's call for the renewal of the charisms of all religious orders, prompted the Society of Jesus to update its understanding of its global mission, inspiring a renewed orientation toward social justice in all Jesuit ministries and sponsored works, including its educational institutions. The ardent desire to meet these challenges inspired Superior General Pedro Arrupe to call the momentous Thirty-Second General Congregation (1974–75), which identified "the service of faith and the promotion of justice" as at the core of all Jesuit ministries.[12] Bergoglio represented the Jesuit Province of Argentina at this congregation in Rome and further applauded his hero Arrupe for the 1980 founding of the Jesuit Refugee Service, a particularly bold initiative that manifested the Jesuit commitment to serve the world's most vulnerable people through accompaniment, service, and advocacy.

It is practically impossible to miss the parallels on display here. The outstanding efforts of Pope Francis to advocate for the needs of refugees and displaced persons are of a piece with these episodes in recent Jesuit history. Francis's constant advocacy for worker rights (e.g., in his convening the World Meetings of Popular Movements) is of a piece with previous initiatives of the Society of Jesus on behalf of labor justice, such as the founding of dozens of "labor schools" by US Jesuits in the early twentieth century. Francis's extravagant efforts to offer direct assistance to the poor of Rome (greatly expanding the office of the almoner of the Holy See, and sometimes hosting meals himself with the homeless) is of a piece with constant efforts of Jesuits (starting with Ignatius himself) to distribute alms to relieve urgent needs. Francis's pursuit of peacebuilding in so many global hotspots is of a piece with the long Jesuit tradition of prioritizing peacebuilding and social reconciliation wherever Jesuits are positioned to play a constructive role as arbitrators and negotiators.

Behind all these faces of social concern lies a penchant for social analysis that has become a hallmark of the Society of Jesus in recent decades. Though not always the earliest of adopters, Jesuit apostolates often found themselves at the forefront of this movement. The curricula of Jesuit-sponsored universities around the world include courses in social analysis and research programs employing this methodology. In many parts of the world, and especially in Latin America, Jesuits have founded and continue to sponsor social research centers, which conduct probing social analysis of local political and economic realities; a very prominent center in Venezuela was long led by Superior General Arturo Sosa. Providing resources and central coordination for these efforts is the Social Justice and Ecology Secretariat (SJES) in Rome, an important component of the Jesuit Curia. Close observers of the work of this Jesuit office will discover remarkable similarities between the occasional reports it publishes and the contents of papal documents promulgated by Francis. For example, a detailed 2011 report of the Task Force on Ecology of the SJES bears remarkable similarities to the overall message of *Laudato si'*, the 2015 papal encyclical on the environment.[13] Other documents and initiatives of Francis reflect the analysis of 2016's "Special Report on Justice in the Global Economy: Building Sustainable and Inclusive Communities," produced by the Task Force on the Economy of the SJES.[14] Further practical initiatives associated with his papacy, such as the "Economy of Francesco" project and the *Laudato si'* Action Platform, similarly bear the marks of Jesuit inspiration.

Once again, through its spirituality as well as its apostolic practice and accustomed "way of proceeding," the Society of Jesus provides valuable resources for the first Jesuit pope. From his Jesuit roots, Francis has inherited a "structural eye" that includes an appreciation of the expanding role of large institutions in human society and that enables him to probe the root causes of the many threats to peace and social justice. These tools enable Francis (or any observer) to identify structures of sin, to develop accurate diagnoses of social and economic problems, and then to propose prescriptions for changes that will address the dysfunctions and ameliorate the social and economic order. Nowhere in his teaching documents is Francis clearer about his own appropriation of these insights than in *Evangelii gaudium*, no. 59, when he acknowledges the pernicious effects of "an evil imbedded in the structures of society, . . . [which] is an evil crystalized in unjust social structures."

By successfully applying this "structural lens" and leveraging a systemic analysis of what has gone wrong, we can identify and apply remedies for such economic injustices as accelerating inequality and exploitation of workers, not to mention momentous problems such as climate change, widespread violence, and human trafficking. As pope, Francis has joined his efforts to those of the religious order that formed him and has pioneered these tools in pursuit of social justice.

KEY TEXTS AND MESSAGES OF FRANCIS ON ECONOMIC JUSTICE

By now, the overarching message of Francis regarding the economy should be clear: a global economy that exploits the labor of disadvantaged workers, that accelerates unbearable inequality, and that allows a harmful maldistribution of resources is intolerable and urgently demands reform. A key motif within Francis's critique of the contemporary neoliberal economy is exclusion—a root error of all systemic injustices, including racial discrimination, gender bias, and toxic nationalism. To exclude anyone from economic opportunities, indeed from meaningful participation in political and social life in general, is the gravest of offenses against the very humanity of the other. Francis devotes an early segment of *Evangelii gaudium* (nos. 52–60) to outlining his diagnosis of current economic dysfunctions. Here, he crystalizes his judgments regarding unacceptable economic practices in four dramatic section titles: "No to an Economy of Exclusion," "No to the New Idolatry of Money," "No to a Financial System Which Rules Rather Than Serves," and "No to the Inequality Which Spawns Violence."

In the course of these seminal paragraphs, Francis denounces the "'throwaway' culture" that relegates so much of the world's population to the status of "outcast, the 'leftovers,'" capable of being discarded entirely while others thrive on accumulated wealth (no. 53). He has particularly harsh words for "trickle-down theories" of the economy, which he paints as "an opinion that has never been confirmed by the facts" (no. 54). He even connects this aspect of neoliberal economic theory to social Darwinism, citing its cruelty to those who fall behind in economic competition. These judgments emerge as elucidations of the summary verdict he had shared in the previous paragraph—the sentence that became a favorite soundbite in press coverage of the release of this programmatic inaugural teaching document of Francis: "Such an economy kills" (no. 53).

It goes without saying that neither *Evangelii gaudium* nor any writing of Francis functions as a free-standing treatise on economic justice. Indeed, Francis folds these reflections on economics into the longer section titled "Some Challenges of Today's World," which in turn is lodged in an entire chapter titled "Amid the Crisis of Communal Commitment." His ultimate goal is not to score points for any particular theory or interpretation of economic phenomena, but rather to contribute to the comprehensive agenda of evangelization. Of course, the task of spreading the Gospel benefits from any advance in the Church's teachings on morality and the education of Catholics on contemporary ethical challenges.

Although Francis ventures this foray into critiquing such economic structures as the global trade and financial systems, his deeper agenda involves moral attitudes and behavior. He issues heartfelt appeals to avoid the idolatry of money and to overcome attitudes like selfishness—imperatives that apply as much to the level of individual morality as they do to the collective and institutional. Near the end of this section (no. 58), he offers a papal direct address (a rare literary device in such a formal document), issuing this appeal: "I exhort you to generous solidarity." He thus leverages this opportunity to jump start a process of attitudinal conversion, which he hopes will inspire many to turn away from high-consumption lifestyles (no. 54) and toward deep and concrete solidarity with the poor. He is primarily after our hearts, and only secondarily interested in educating us about economics. This gentle pastor of souls invites us to accompany and embrace the poor, as he has long done in Buenos Aires and on the streets of Rome, not merely to embrace superior economic theories, as important as that continues to be.

These insights into the overall agenda of Francis also hold explanatory power regarding a later section of *Evangelii gaudium*. In the entirety of this 288-paragraph document, the only occasion when the pope returns to matters of economic justice is in nos. 186–216, the section titled "The Inclusion of the Poor in Society," situated in the chapter titled "The Social Dimension of Evangelization." Near the center point of this section is another attention-grabbing soundbite within the economic analysis offered in *Evangelii gaudium*: "Inequality is the root of social ills" (no. 202). Like no. 59 (as noted above), this section explicitly engages in structural analysis, endorsing deep reforms in society that will enact the solidarity to which we are summoned throughout salvation history. Here, Francis commits the Church to doing its part in "working to eliminate the structural causes of poverty" (no. 188), specifically by fostering the "convictions and habits of solidarity [which], when they are put into practice, open the way to other structural transformations and make them possible" (no. 189).

Notice how Francis, displaying a nuanced view of proper Church–world relations, as honed by the Second Vatican Council, hastens to recognize the practical limits of the Church's agenda. Though religion plays a crucial role in forming people dedicated to values and possessing virtues such as solidarity,[15] such social change will obviously be put into effect by actors beyond the Church, including government authorities that enact enlightened public policies. Francis proceeds to identify specific institutional sectors—such as education, health care, and labor—where favorable institutional arrangements (labor unions and just wages receive attention here) are crucial to protecting the "temporal welfare and prosperity ... and dignity" of the vulnerable (no. 192). In no. 205, Francis appeals to "politicians, government leaders and financial leaders [to] take heed and broaden their horizons, working to ensure that all citizens have dignified work, education and health care." Notably, Francis identifies business as "a noble vocation" oriented (just as surely as politics) to "serve the common good by striving to increase the goods of this world and to make them more accessible to all" (no. 203).

The economic proposals of Francis benefit not only from his appreciation of the proper division of functions between the Church and temporal institutions but also from appropriate applications of the notions of charity and justice, which need to be distinguished in the workings of the social order. In these particular paragraphs, Francis is endorsing not simple charity (the act of distributing material goods to the needy) but social justice, which requires overcoming the structural causes of inequality and exclusion, and for which charity is not an adequate substitute. Later in the section, he indeed goes on to recognize the value of "welfare projects which meet urgent needs [but] should be considered merely temporary responses" (no. 202). While there is still a place for "a welfare mentality" (no. 204) that involves eliciting voluntary charitable responses to dire human needs, the most consequential challenge is securing for all people "adequate access to all the other goods which are destined for our common use" (no. 192).

Francis elucidates and extends these insights and lines of economic analysis in two encyclicals: *Laudato si'* and *Fratelli tutti*. The first, the (globally) well-received environmental encyclical of 2015, issues this set of instructions related to the foregoing social ethics concerns: "Politics must not be subject to the economy.... Today, in view of the common good, there is urgent need for politics and economics to enter into a frank dialogue in the service of life, especially human life" (no. 189). In keeping with the overall tone and content of this encyclical, Francis proceeds to explain the urgency of protecting the natural environment as well, as Daniel DiLeo shows in chapter 13 of this volume, calling upon his audience to modify the wasteful, high-consumption lifestyles and destructive systems of economic production that destroy the global environment, our common home that cannot be replaced.

Fratelli tutti devotes considerable attention (especially in its fifth chapter, "A Better Kind of Politics") to spelling out precisely how political life constitutes a key arena where the human community rightly pursues the common good and directs the economy to its proper ends. In this 2020 document that synthesizes many themes from throughout his earlier papal teachings, Francis offers an inspiring encomium to the virtue of solidarity. He contrasts solidarity to the regnant neoliberal model of economics and politics that feeds indifference to suffering, divides people and fragments society just as surely as global pandemics (including the one that occasioned the writing of the encyclical), and separates and isolates people from one another. Early in the document, he laments: "In today's world, a sense of belonging to a single human family is fading, and the dream of working together for justice and peace seems an outdated utopia" (no. 30).

In chapter 7 of this volume, as well as in an essay on the many contributions of this encyclical, Kristin Heyer describes well how Francis employs structural analyses, particularly by unveiling "interconnected dimensions of social sin," to shed light on societal dysfunctions.[16] In an encyclical that acknowledges the pivotal concept of power far more frankly than is customary in Catholic social teaching, Francis highlights a range of structural forces that constitute threats to solidarity. He thus offers an insightful analysis that helps explain the vicissitudes of this virtue in our historical moment of divisive populism, bitter extremism, and virulent nationalism.

While the diagnosis may sound grim, with his characteristic cheery hopefulness, Francis proposes a number of promising prescriptions for overcoming human divisions: simple human kindness, forgiveness, and a commitment to a culture of encounter. In keeping with its title, *Fratelli tutti* contains an unabashed appeal to social charity and political love (see the sections bearing that phrase in their titles, in nos. 180–92) that hold the promise of motivating exceptional acts of sacrifice to benefit the marginalized. The contributions offered here to social ethics are obvious; even if they do not provide significant new content to our judgments about economic justice, these words of Francis brilliantly frame the challenges facing economic relations at all levels of society.

FRANCIS'S SOCIAL JUSTICE ADVOCACY IN THE CONTEXT OF THE CHURCH'S EVANGELIZING MISSION

It bears repeating that the economic commentary offered by Pope Francis must be understood in the context of his ardent desire to renew the mission of the Church to spread the Gospel. Indeed, his economic teachings are consistently presented within this frame, as the previous section documents. Francis advocates for social justice as part of his overall pastoral program to advance the social mission of the Church, not as a plank of any ideological agenda based on abstractions. This is the pope, after all, who repeatedly affirms the axiom, "Realities are more important than ideas."[17] Whether we attribute this brand of pragmatism to his Latin American roots or his Jesuit background or other particular intellectual influences, there is no reason to doubt his contention that the concrete needs of people take precedence in the priorities that guide his papacy.

Needless to say, these qualities and commitments do not win Francis universal acclaim. His detractors have been heard to complain that his aversion to ideology makes him a poor ally in the supposedly escalating conflict between Catholicism and the decadent secular culture. He has claimed victory in this attempted war of words, largely by a strategy of silence—freezing out his harshest critics by refusing to engage or respond. In all fairness, his critics never really had a chance of ushering this churchman, one with the heart of a pastor above all, into the camp of the culture warriors. Faggioli detected this dynamic at play early during Francis's papacy, when he acknowledged that "Francis is trying to disengage Catholicism from the 'culture wars.'"[18]

This observation is particularly relevant in the field of social ethics, where ideologues have long attempted to "steal" Catholic social teaching for their preferred position on the political spectrum. Nowhere has this game been played with more bluster and disingenuousness than in the United States, especially in several episodes when political conservatives (and even libertarians) have repeatedly mounted campaigns attempting to persuade the general public that their own favored economic approaches and free market policies represent the truest interpretation of the Catholic faith and its social teachings.

For example, shortly after Benedict XVI published the judicious 2009 social encyclical *Caritas in veritate,* the conservative columnist George Weigel ventured the implausible theory that only a fraction of the document (sections that required no serious reform of neoliberal economic practices) should be considered genuine and reliably orthodox. Presumably, Weigel alone possessed the skill to identify the deviations from what Pope Benedict really meant to say.

This was by no means the first episode of resistance to genuine Catholic social teaching in the US context. Before the 1986 publication of the US bishops' pastoral letter "Economic Justice for All," several prominent members of the Catholic laity (led by Michael Novak and William Simon) issued a counterletter (called "Toward the Future"), taking the bishops to task for supposedly excessively left-leaning or even socialist-inspired critiques of the American economy. Indeed, the US bishops have themselves been accused of turning their courageous document into something of a dead letter by failing to consistently promote the reforms it advocated; oddly, successive anniversaries of its publication have been virtually ignored, even in church circles. Given the fierce resistance in US culture to Church-based calls for economic reform, it perhaps came as no surprise when the release of *Evangelii gaudium* prompted sharp criticism from US conservative voices, from Rush Limbaugh to Sarah Palin to the editorial board of *Forbes* magazine—all of whom accused Pope Francis of promoting his allegedly Marxist perspective by challenging greed and inequality.

As much as he surely desires a warmer reception for his economic teachings, this is simply not a game that Pope Francis is willing to play. He has arguably been quite successful in sidestepping such disedifying charades entirely through the carefully crafted messaging that is found within his teachings on economics. One shining example appears near the end (at no. 208) of *Evangelii gaudium,* and it merits full citation. After proposing the adoption of economic policies that are much more favorable to the poor majority than those presently pursued by ascendant economic systems, Francis offers:

> If anyone feels offended by my words, I would respond that I speak them with affection and with the best of intentions, quite apart from any personal interest or political ideology. My words are not those of a foe or an opponent. I am interested only in helping those who are in thrall to an individualistic, indifferent, and self-centered mentality to be freed from those unworthy chains and to attain a new way of living and thinking which is more humane, noble, and fruitful, and which will bring dignity to their presence on this Earth.

How hard it would be for darkness of any variety or political stripe to drive out the kindness and light found in such a magnanimous expression of social concern. As so often, Francis here models an open hand extended in greeting, rather than the clenched fist we too commonly see in US culture. With this humble appeal to receive a fair hearing for his proposals for a more humane economy, Francis is offering us a further glimpse of the spiritual well from which he drinks so deeply. In no. 22 in the *Spiritual Exercises*, Saint Ignatius of Loyola offers a piece of advice (labeled the "Presupposition" in the English translation) that is especially valuable for guiding relations in a contentious Church (whether in his era of the Spanish Inquisition or in ours today). This Ignatian principle affirms the prudent and irenic practice of placing the most favorable interpretation on the utterance of another (whether in spiritual conversation or in larger venues), and then working out through dialogue the precise way that the other intends any statement that may initially offend.

This is very much in line with the anticipated legacy of Pope Francis to Catholic social ethics, and indeed to the entire social mission of the Church. While his teachings stand in solid continuity with those of his predecessors, Francis has introduced a new tone and idiom into Catholic moral life—indeed, a new grammar of deep social concern. It features renewed prominence for such terms as mercy, dialogue, welcoming, relationships, culture, values, conversion, commitments, and inclusion. All these terms show up frequently in his contributions to social ethics; together, they supply a fresh approach to social justice capable of inspiring a more Gospel-infused life.

NOTES

1. An English translation of the transcribed interview appears as the final chapter in *This Economy Kills: Pope Francis on Capitalism and Social Justice*, by Andrea Tornielli and Giacomo Galeazzi (Collegeville, MN: Liturgical Press, 2015). This quotation appears on p. 151.
2. Massimo Faggioli, *The Liminal Papacy of Pope Francis: Moving Toward Global Catholicity* (Maryknoll, NY: Orbis Books, 2020), 8.
3. These words of Francis also appear in *Evangelii gaudium*, no. 198. Faggioli not only notes the parallels of these two pontiffs' references to "a Church of the poor" but devotes half a chapter to drawing parallels between the careers and personalities of John XXIII and Francis. See Faggioli, *Liminal Papacy*, 29–41.
4. Massimo Faggioli, *Pope Francis: Tradition in Transition* (Mahwah, NJ: Paulist Press, 2013), 61.
5. Two informative sources of reliable information about the significance of the national background of Francis for his social, political, and economic thought are Thomas R. Rourke, *The Roots of Pope Francis's Social and Political Thought: From Argentina to the Vatican* (Lanham, MD: Rowman & Littlefield, 2016); and Austen Ivereigh, *The Great Reformer: Francis and the Making of a Radical Pope* (New York: Henry Holt, 2014).
6. Francis, "First Greeting of the Holy Father Pope Francis: Apostolic Blessing 'Urbi et Orbi,'" March 13, 2013, www.vatican.va/content/francesco/en/speeches/2013/march/documents/papa-francesco_20130313_benedizione-urbi-et-orbi.html.

7. Faggioli, *Liminal Papacy*, 157.
8. For revealing analysis of the influence of his original Buenos Aires neighborhood on the future Pope Francis, see Noga Tarnopolsky, "The Immigrant Neighborhood—and Interfaith Friendships—That Made Pope Francis," *America Magazine*, March 25, 2022, www.americamagazine.org/faith/2022/03/25/flores-argentina-neighborhood-friends-pope-francis-jorge-bergoglio-242576?utm.
9. Faggioli, *Liminal Papacy*, 37.
10. Ivereigh, *Great Reformer*.
11. See the writings of William A. Barry, SJ, which treat all these themes, particularly the affective dimensions of Ignatian spirituality. E.g., see William A. Barry, SJ, *Changed Heart, Changed World: The Transforming Freedom of Friendship with God* (Chicago: Loyola University Press, 2011); and William A. Barry, SJ, *Letting God Come Close: An Approach to the Ignatian Spiritual Exercises* (Chicago: Loyola University Press, 2001).
12. The quoted phrase constitutes the subtitle of Decree 4 ("Our Mission Today") of General Congregation 32, promulgated May 8, 1975; in *Documents of the 31st and 32nd General Congregations of the Society of Jesus* (Saint Louis: Institute of Jesuit Sources, 1977), 411–38.
13. Task Force on Ecology of the Social Justice and Ecology Secretariat of the Society of Jesus, "Special Report on Ecology: Healing a Broken World," *Promotio Justitia* 106 (2011):1-67.
14. Task Force on the Economy of the Social Justice and Ecology Secretariat of the Society of Jesus, "Special Report on Justice in the Global Economy: Building Sustainable and Inclusive Communities," *Promotio Justitia* 121 (2016): 1–35.
15. Not coincidentally, this section of *Evangelii Gaudium* contains perhaps the clearest statement of Francis (no. 198) on the preferential option for the poor and the role it plays in a Christian social ethic of solidarity.
16. Kristin Heyer, "Walls in the Heart: Social Sin in *Fratelli Tutti*," *Journal of Catholic Social Thought* 19, no. 1 (2022): 25–40, at 25.
17. It appears (among other places) in *Evangelii gaudium*, no. 233, as one of four related axioms that guide his approach to social action.
18. Faggioli, *Pope Francis*, 81.

6

THE PREFERENTIAL OPTION FOR THE POOR

Incarnational Theology in the US Context

M. T. Dávila

Pope Francis's gestures give us concrete representations of his understanding of the option for the poor. These gestures are the intentional, prayerful, humble, and solidary movement toward the impoverished—the migrant, the sick, the religious other, the imprisoned, the gang member, the unhoused.[1] The first images from Francis's papacy—washing the feet of imprisoned youth during his first Holy Thursday service (March 2013), visiting migrants on the island of Lampedusa (July 2013), installing showers for the unhoused in Saint Peter's Square (November 2014)—speak the language of gesture and encounter characteristic of Francis's approach. The Argentinian ethicist Pablo Blanco González calls this a pastoral theology with an incarnational expression, or what Emilce Cuda identifies as a middle way between the theology of the people (*teología del pueblo*) and liberation theology.[2] "Don't forget the poor," Carlos Cardinal Hummes of Brazil told the newly elected Jorge Mario Bergoglio. This reminder informs Francis's vision for the Church: "How I would like a Church which is poor and for the poor!"[3]

Throughout the papacies of John Paul II, Benedict XVI, and now Francis, the preferential option for the poor has developed as a central principle of Catholic social teaching.[4] This key insight from Latin American liberation theology, present in essence at the Second Meeting of Latin American Bishops in Medellín (1968) and outlined in their Third Meeting in Puebla (1979), can be considered "the most important event in the Christian churches since the Protestant Reformation of the 16th century."[5]

Pope Francis brings the option for the poor to the fore as constitutive of who we are as a Church. Under Francis's papacy, the faithful must wrestle with this teaching.

This chapter examines Francis's use of the option for the poor throughout his papacy. First, it asks whether there are now two (or more) traditions of understanding and reflection on the option for the poor—one developed by the magisterium in Rome, and one developed by liberationist thought globally. Second, does Francis align more with one over the other, or is he developing a distinct tradition of interpretation on the option for the poor? Next, the chapter presents specific challenges of Francis's development of the option for the poor for the Church in the United States. The pastoral and missional priorities of the US Catholic bishops fail to acknowledge the centrality of the option for the poor in Catholic social teaching and in Francis's papacy. Since its articulation in Latin American liberation theology in the 1970s, the option for the poor has raised profound suspicions among US Christians due to its contrasts with values considered constitutive for the US project of industry and progress, economic and otherwise. In addition, as the commentator John Gehring highlights, the US Catholic Church's emphasis on the culture wars prevents it from engaging the fullness of Catholic social teaching in their context.[6] More specifically, Francis's additions to the corpus of Catholic social teaching in the areas of political thought and ecological ethics directly challenge the dominant ethos in US society that privileges individual agency over community, profit over sustainability, and expediency over encounter and connection. These contrasts force US Catholics to come to terms with Francis's critique of the "throwaway culture," those traits that condemn certain sectors of society and the environment to suffer the violence of our individualism and greed.[7] Finally, this chapter hopes to propose specific areas of study, reflection, and action, with particular applicability to the US context, but in a way that models for other contexts the kind of historical and social consciousness and real encounter with the poor that Francis extols.[8]

Pope Francis affirms that "the text of Matthew 25:35–46 is 'not a simple invitation to charity: it is a page of Christology which sheds a ray of light on the mystery of Christ.' In this call to recognize him in the poor and the suffering, we see revealed the very heart of Christ, his deepest feelings and choices."[9] Gustavo Gutiérrez calls the option for the poor a "theocentric" option, that is, a reflection of how God acts in history based on the biblical witness of who God is.[10] Francis's understanding of the option for the poor, while in line with Catholic social teaching, does provide points of contact with the concerns and directions of contemporary liberation theology.

FRANCIS AND THE OPTION FOR THE POOR

Before becoming pope, Jorge María Bergoglio was a strident voice against the sin of greed and its impact on the impoverished: "Some might say that I am speaking against this government [of Nestor Kirchner]. That is not the case. We have been struggling with this for the last 20 years. This is not a political problem. It is a problem of sin. . . . When I say that we are living in scandalous situations of poverty, I am saying that those responsible for this are all of us!"[11] These words from Bergoglio are echoed throughout his leadership of the Church in Buenos Aires.[12] Of note is his video address to Caritas Argentina on the occasion of its annual meeting in 2009. Here, the future pope calls out the immorality of holding lavish feasts as part of the work of Caritas:

> If you want to share in Caritas' mission of solidarity with the poor, your habits must change accordingly. You cannot afford certain luxuries that you used to enjoy before your conversion. You may say, "Father, you are a Communist!" Maybe, but I don't think so! I only interpret what the church asks of each one of us. To work with Caritas means to renounce to something. It requires spiritual poverty. Solidarity has to take you to the visible gesture of spiritual poverty.[13]

Having witnessed the profound impact on the poor in Argentina of the structural adjustment programs by international financial organisms and the neoliberal policies of various administrations, Bergoglio took a firm stand for the impoverished, labeling as sinful the injustices that led to their suffering.[14] Once elected pope, Francis continued to decry the throwaway culture and unbridled capitalism, pronouncing that "such an economy kills."[15]

Centering the Poor in Evangelization and Discipleship

Francis's papacy was launched with a clear agenda spelled out in the apostolic exhortation *Evangelii guadium*: "A Church which goes forth [*en salida*]," "a Church which is poor and for the poor," is a Church "called to be an instrument of God for the liberation and promotion of the poor, and for enabling them to be fully a part of society."[16] *Evangelii gaudium* picks up on the theme of evangelization beyond the doors of church buildings. Centering the poor, Francis rehearses Catholic social teaching with respect to solidarity and the universal destination of created goods.[17] But Francis takes the option for the poor further than his two immediate predecessors by linking it directly to the imitation of Christ: "For the Church, the option for the poor is primarily a theological category rather than a cultural, sociological, political or philosophical one. God shows the poor 'his first mercy.' This divine preference has consequences for the faith life of all Christians, since we are called to have 'this mind, ... which was in Jesus Christ' (Phil. 2:5)."[18]

In *Evangelii gaudium*, Francis makes declarative statements on the current state of the world economy. This includes denouncing the "throwaway culture,"[19] and establishing a set of denunciations or categorical "NO!"s that the Church and the faithful must pronounce against economic dynamics that do violence to the human family.[20] Francis uses this moment to highlight once again the social dimension of evangelization that Pope Paul VI had previously laid out in his exhortation *Evangelii nuntiandi* (1975). Following Christ and proclaiming the Gospel leads one "to desire, seek and protect the good of others."[21]

Francis's messages on the World Day of Migrants and Refugees, World Youth Day, and the World Gathering of Popular Movements demonstrate the centrality of the option for the poor in his theological style.[22] He explains how God's incarnation into human reality provides an invitation to encounter others in love.[23] Encounter, therefore, is one of the most prominent marks of the Christian life for Francis. It brings one closer to the realities experienced by others, especially the impoverished and suffering, and calls us to transformative relationships of solidarity.[24] The concept of encounters with others as reflections of Christ brings to light two distinct influences on Francis's thought. First, Francis's attention to the historical reality of the people is attributed to the influence of the Argentinian priests Lucio Gera and Rafael Tello, who, along with the theologian Juan Carlos Scannone, had already developed a theology that centered people's concrete struggles throughout their histories, accounting for their way of making sense of liberation and salvation within their particular realities.[25] Second, Francis's Ignatian spirituality brings not just a level of comfort with engaging reality but also a requirement to consider the reality of suffering closely, because the experience of suffering provides the locus for encountering Christ through the Passion. This latter influence asks that the faithful consider all that is revealed in suffering, even when doing so confronts us with "ambiguity, contradiction, uncertainty, and paradox."[26] The Jesuit liberation theologian Ignacio Ellacuría calls this "the 'theologal' character of all things, and especially the theologal character of humanity and history."[27]

Throughout Francis's papacy, encounter with people and their reality has become the lens that shapes his social teaching. It has also become a hallmark of his use of papal authority, as outlined in chapter 4 of this book, by Elyse Raby. Thus, three of the four apostolic exhortations that followed *Evangelii gaudium* (2016's *Amoris laetitia*, 2019's *Christus vivit*, and 2020's *Querida Amazonia*) were the result of synodal listening and consultation processes.

As Lisa Sowle Cahill and James Keenan, SJ, explain, respectively, in chapters 1 and 2 of this volume, this consultative approach has been crucial for Francis's examination of moral questions, yielding a distinctive style that is dedicated to engaging the realities and contexts of people in order to accompany them in their struggles for peace and justice. Notably, this process brought the experiences and voices of the poor to the center of the conversation, resulting in documents that present the injustice of poverty in its many forms as key challenges not only for human dignity but also for life in community and to the role of the Church as a pastoral and social agent.

Centering the Poor in Magisterial Teaching

Francis's two social encyclicals, *Laudato si'* (2015) and *Fratelli tutti* (2020), formalize his attention to the option for the poor. While in *Evangelii gaudium* Francis had already signaled the environment as one of the "vulnerable,"[28] *Laudato si'* speaks about "our Sister, Mother Earth," who "cries out to us because of the harm we have inflicted by our irresponsible use and abuse of the goods with which God has endowed her."[29] In this encyclical, Francis connects the fate of the Earth with the fate of the poor, and draws direct causal lines between the sin of indifference, the throwaway culture, and the environmental crisis.[30]

Laudato si' includes numerous illustrations of Francis's centering of the option for the poor in his reflections. For example, his identification of climate change as a challenge to human dignity is done from the perspective of those most directly affected by it. Francis notes that impoverished and marginalized communities are the first to suffer from climate change's impact on access to water, open spaces, air quality, biodiversity, and fertile soil. This judgment implicates policymakers, corporations, and consumers whose practices and attitudes toward the environment reflect not only a lack of concern for the fate of the world's most vulnerable and the environment but also a direct causal impact on that fate.

In framing his critique this way, Francis aligns more closely than any of his predecessors with the development of the option for the poor in liberation theology, which emphasizes the concrete needs of the impoverished, including the need for land, housing, and work. Thus, in *Laudato si'*, Francis expands concern for the poor to include the way that behaviors and attitudes endemic to developed countries make a direct impact on the life of the poor, their livelihoods, their access to food and water, their considerations to migrate, and their experience of conflict.[31] While John Paul II and Benedict XVI similarly advocated for the poor, they also set methodological and practical boundaries around the option for the poor, preferring to identify the poor as the recipient of a special form of Christian charity or love.[32] Their constraints trace back to then–Cardinal Ratzinger's time as the prefect of the Congregation for the Doctrine of the Faith, when he oversaw two responses to liberation theology. In one, "Instruction on Certain Aspects of a Theology of Liberation," the congregation critiqued a perceived error of liberation theology that read history through the lens of class struggle. It judged this to be against Christian truth because it made conflict in history a dominant lens through which to understand the destiny of humanity.[33] Francis, however, engages the liberation theologians' claims about conflict more readily. In *Laudato si'*, for instance, he accepts liberation theology's assertion that conflict in history is a result of sin and thereby is inherently linked not only to Jesus's unjust death on the cross but also to the unjust deaths of so many throughout history who suffer the impact of sinful structures shaped by greed and indifference. He thus recognizes that the option for the poor in liberation theology does not center conflict as inevitable. Rather, as an act of solidarity, and through a close examination of the realities of oppression experienced by so many, the option for the poor requires "honesty with the real," which includes the grappling with the reality of conflict.[34] This genuine engagement with reality in its totality is both essential to Ignatian spirituality and key to Francis's practice of encounter.

Also aligning Francis's understanding of the option for the poor with that of liberation theology is his insistence on the active role that impoverished and marginalized communities must have in determining their destiny and in transforming structures of injustice. Gustavo Gutiérrez, for example, speaks about "the irruption of the poor in history," that moment when the voices of the most marginalized surface as they claim their destinies amid a history marked by abuse and oppression.[35] This theme appears frequently in Francis's message to the World Meeting of Popular Movements:

> You are not satisfied with empty promises, with alibis or excuses. Nor do you wait with arms crossed for NGOs to help, for welfare schemes or paternalistic solutions that never arrive; . . . You want to be protagonists. You get organized, study, work, issue demands and, above all, practice that very special solidarity that exists among those who suffer, among the poor, and that our civilization seems to have forgotten or would strongly prefer to forget.[36]

In *Laudato si'*, Francis emphasizes the role of local communities embedded in their histories and particularities, working together toward concrete solutions. He is especially concerned about acknowledging the work of indigenous groups whose members often most directly suffer the impact of various human-made climate catastrophes.[37]

The theme of empowerment, which is central to Francis's papacy in the ways detailed by James Keenan in chapter 2 of this volume, is explicitly expanded to include local movements of impoverished and marginalized peoples (what Francis often refers to as "the peripheries") in his proposals for political life in *Fratelli tutti*. Quoting from *Evangelii gaudium* (no. 205), Francis affirms "a renewed appreciation of politics as 'a lofty vocation and one of the highest forms of charity, inasmuch as it seeks the common good.'"[38] "Political love" seeks to organize society around common goals, especially those that build and promote more just structures and networks.[39] Previously, John Paul II had raised the need for structural transformation by acknowledging structural sin as a subversion of God's will, making an impact on the lives of many.[40] Francis adds to this diagnosis by more directly linking political action with the fate of the impoverished: "It is an act of charity to assist someone who is suffering, but it is also an act of charity, even if we do not know that person, to work to change the social conditions that caused his or her suffering."[41] Specifically, Francis calls for

> a model of social, political and economic participation "that can include popular movements and invigorate local, national and international governing structures with that torrent of moral energy that springs from including the excluded in the building of a common destiny," while also ensuring that "these experiences of solidarity which grow up from below, from the subsoil of the planet—can come together, be more coordinated, keep on meeting one another." ... In that sense, such movements are "social poets" that, in their own way, work, propose, promote and liberate. They help make possible an integral human development that goes beyond the idea of social policies being a policy *for* the poor, but never *with* the poor and never *of* the poor, much less part of a project that reunites people.[42]

Admittedly, Francis's treatment of the option for the poor in *Laudato si'* and *Fratelli tutti* remains more in line with that of John Paul II and Benedict XVI. However, these encyclicals carefully quote and reference Francis's messages and exhortations, where a closer alignment with liberation theology remains. Specifically, *Evangelii gaudium* and various messages to the World Meeting of Popular Movements are heavily cited to support the Church's obligation to focus on and move toward, and then forward with, the impoverished in order to address today's most pressing challenges. In *Laudato si'*, meanwhile, Francis makes extensive use of the work of various conferences of bishops, both acknowledging local voices and empowering them to address the needs of the marginalized in their regions.[43] The result is that prominent themes from liberation theology's conception of the option for the poor come through, even when the primary language of the encyclicals appears to preserve the interpretations of Francis's immediate predecessors.

Is Francis a Liberation Theologian?

Ultimately, Francis's rapprochement with Gustavo Gutiérrez and other key figures in the development of the option for the poor signals a deeper commitment to a liberationist reading of the option previously not present in the work of his predecessors.[44] Francis's approach to the option for the poor emphasizes its theocentric nature, underscoring its essential importance for Christian discipleship. But there is still ambiguity in Francis's use of the concept, as he sometimes ascribes a more socially transformative nature to its practice. His message to the World Meeting of Popular Movements in 2021, for example, included a detailed call to global corporate actors, such as pharmaceutical companies and media conglomerates, to transform their ways of operating in the world, which cause so much harm to the marginalized and the environment.[45] This directly reflects the understanding of poverty as solidarity in the option for the poor that initially appeared in the documents from the Latin American bishops at Medellín and in the earliest works of liberation theology: solidarity with the poor takes on some of their suffering as we struggle alongside them for justice and a transformation of history. But at other times, Francis presents the option as a tool for reflection and conversion, as in the call for ecological conversion embedded in *Laudato si'*.[46] And, yet, at every moment, the framing of the option for the poor is done in the context of listening and accompaniment, emphasizing the synodal encounter with the peripheries, from which "the world can be seen more clearly."[47] Francis's ambiguity in his use of the option for the poor allows for its broad appeal and application. On one hand, it profoundly challenges current systems and our participation in such systems, as it highlights their impact on real communities. On the other hand, Francis's articulation of the option for the poor also demands that the impoverished be heard and become the protagonists of efforts to restructure political life toward greater justice. Significantly, he does all this while sustaining the theocentric character of the option, demonstrating that it ought to shape the character of Christian discipleship.[48]

THE UPHILL BATTLE FOR THE OPTION FOR THE POOR IN THE UNITED STATES

Promptly after releasing the exhortation *Evangelii gaudium*, "the pope was rudely called a Marxist with little understanding of economics—and only because he does not worship the absolute autonomy of markets."[49] As Andrea Tornielli and Giacomo Galeazzi carefully explain, this is not a surprising development in the United States, given the Catholic right's relationship with the magisterium's social teaching on economic matters. During the time of John Paul II's attack on socialist materialism, figures like Michael Novak, Richard John Neuhaus, and George Weigel expressed rousing support for the pope's position in *Centesimus annus* and other encyclicals. Especially important for these figures on the right was the magisterium's seeming admission that capitalism as it had developed in the early 1990s represented the most Christian form of economic arrangement for respecting personal freedoms and promoting the common good.[50] When Benedict XVI published *Caritas in veritate*, however, Novak suggested that "Benedict XVI's text . . . is too reticent. It fails to recognize . . . the importance of capitalism for the advancement of the poor."[51] Benedict's insistence on the Church's defense of the right to unionize and Catholic social teaching's promotion of solidarity and subsidiarity were seen as betrayals of what Novak and others felt was the Church's blanket and uncritical support for modern capitalism.

Resistance to *Laudato si'* mirrored these concerns, focusing on Francis's critique of markets that serve the idolatry of money and that are shaped by technocratic ideologies. The climate analyst David Montgomery, for example, critiqued the "flawed economics" of the encyclical by claiming that Francis places blame for the consumption and environmental exploitation that adds to the suffering of the poor on the very market economies that, in Montgomery's estimation, have materially improved the lives of the poor.[52] The commentator R. R. Reno critiqued *Laudato si'* as theologically weak because it failed to frame principles of Catholic social teaching in the deep well of Christian truth. Instead, he suggested, it proposed climate change "talking points" prepared to engage the broadest of audiences possible—a hallmark of liberal ideology.[53] Specifically, Reno mentioned a tension within the encyclical that subjugates the right to private property (as he understands this particular teaching) to the social and universal use of the goods of creation.[54]

Criticism of *Fratelli tutti* similarly targeted Francis's critique of market capitalism as a topic that was beyond his field of expertise. Charles Russo, for example, considered that Pope Francis "is out of his depth when commenting on economics . . . because he offers one-sided criticisms without recognizing the good that capitalism has done for untold millions, if not billions, of people."[55] Much of the criticism of Francis in the United States stems from the interpretation that he has moved dramatically away from commentators' own misperceptions of John Paul II's social teaching, which they believed contained an unconditional defense of the right to private property and an unqualified embrace of market capitalism as the only option for a truly Christian economy. Such interpretations, however, reflect US cultural values far more than actual Catholic moral analyses.

The ethicist David Lantigua highlights how the argument for private property in the Americas was championed by those who privileged the civil right to the land over the natural rights of the indigenous. The colonizer understood himself as "productive" and "industrious," laboring the land, taming and subduing it to be more productive, in opposition to the indigenous, whose communal use for basic necessities was seen as backward and immoral.[56] This primacy of private property as a right of the individual, and the enlightened individualism necessary to exercise and promote it, became hallmarks of US political and social culture.[57] Religious traditions were then greatly shaped by these values, which required turning a blind eye to the "necessary evils" of militarism and slavery/racism.[58] The result is a contemporary US Church in which turning the gaze toward the impoverished and suffering, let alone acknowledging complicity with the various systems that produce it, becomes an impossibility. In this moral landscape, compromised by the sacralization of market capitalism and individual rights, many Catholics, including a number of US bishops, resist Francis's message.[59]

Perhaps the most salient source of tension between the US Church and Francis is his failure to embrace the culture wars. Francis moves away from the divisive stance of the culture wars, going as far as to critique the poison of gossip and vitriol of so much Catholic media dedicated to fanning the flames of divisiveness around culture war issues, such as same-sex-marriage and abortion.[60] Francis does not just reject participation in the culture wars; he also considers the culture wars inhospitable to the true calling of discipleship in "a poor Church of the poor."[61] The US Church, already inordinately entangled in the ethos exalting the right to private property, the benefits of market capitalism, and the myth of individual prosperity, finds itself held captive by the political and social dynamics of the culture wars. As such, it cannot make room for a robust appreciation of the option for the poor as embraced by Pope Francis. By framing elements of the culture wars as "nonnegotiable" issues (e.g., abortion and opposition to same-sex marriage), the US Church has set a limited agenda in the public square, one that greatly benefits the economic and social status quo.

What Does a "Poor Church for the Poor" mean for the US Church?

To become a Church that takes seriously the option for the poor as central to Catholic social teaching, the US Catholic Church must critically examine itself in light of Francis's critique of the idolatry of money and the ideologies of the culture wars. It must put into practice the ways of encounter, accompaniment, conversion, transformation, justice seeking, sharing in each other's destinies, and consciousness of our particular and shared histories that Francis expresses in his messages and makes concrete in his actions.

In light of the Synod on Synodality (2022–24), the US Church ought to expand its own openness to lay listening and empowerment. One way to do this is through close engagement with popular movements such as Black Lives Matter, ideally by establishing spaces and projects for direct encounters and collaboration between diocesan structures and diverse movements for justice.[62] Synodality as a practice and stance toward the world allows for disagreement on certain issues, opening the possibility for collaboration and friendships across differences, including political and religious differences, but always toward the goal of protecting or enhancing the common good and alleviating unjust suffering. In *Fratelli tutti*, Pope Francis lays out a map for how cooperation across different histories and particularities is not only possible, but the hallmark of a political process truly committed to shared projects and dreams.[63]

For the Church in the United States to embrace the option for the poor, it must acknowledge the racial and colonial dynamics of Christianity in the Americas. Pope Francis's Synod on the Amazonia (2019) and the resulting document *Querida Amazonia* serve as a model for the kinds of processes US bishops could embrace to work toward racial justice in the nation.[64] During this synod, Francis paid close attention to the voices of the most marginalized communities in the Amazonia region, the indigenous whose land and livelihood are continually threatened due to corporate greed. His postsynodal exhortation acknowledges that colonialism is one of the main reasons why the powerful find it so easy to abuse these peoples and their lands, often silencing them, in pursuit of the goal of selfish enrichment.[65] This level of historical consciousness is also promoted in *Fratelli tutti*, where Francis suggests that new political pathways must begin from historical truth, engaging a "penitential memory" that "honour[s] the memory of victims."[66] In the United States, this might look like further engaging the truth behind Church-sponsored boarding schools, where countless indigenous children were taken after being forcefully removed from their families.[67] Once again, *Fratelli tutti* offers some guidance: "Nowadays it's easy to be tempted to turn the page, to say that all these things happened long ago and we should look to the future. For God's sake, No! We can never move forward without remembering the past; we do not progress without an honest and unclouded memory."[68] For the US Church to take seriously the option for the poor, it must come to terms with a history of the intentional fracturing of the human family in the shape of the genocide of indigenous communities for their land and natural resources, and the trafficking of human beings for slave labor, all done for the economic development of a few. The US Church must wrestle with the ongoing impact of these past evil practices on marginalized communities today, both in the nation and abroad.

Equally important will be a rejection of the culture wars and their stranglehold on the Church's public witness. Francis's preferred practices for implementing the option for the poor—synodality/listening and encounter—can be understood as the antidote to the culture wars insofar as they invite Catholics to be Church for each other in the public square. As the US Catholic Church sees a post-*Roe* political landscape, it is perhaps most urgent to declare solidarity with the poor, especially women and young families, through concrete acts of accompaniment and support. Truly breaking out of the culture wars, however, will require the Church to deeply reflect and consider what solidarity looks like in the context of other ongoing divisions about issues of racial, migrant, and environmental justice.

CONCLUSION: WHICH OPTION FOR THE POOR?

Adoption of the option for the poor into Catholic social teaching cannot be separated from its roots in Latin American liberation theology and the meetings of the Latin American bishops in Medellín, Puebla, and Aparecida. It is the only principle of social teaching whose articulation comes to the magisterium from outside ecclesial and clerical boundaries. It surfaces as a concept via a fourfold dynamic dialogue that begins with the reality of the suffering of impoverished peoples, is interpreted by theologians, and is subsequently integrated and amplified by the magisterium, all while attending to the signs of the times. It is possible that the integration of this concept into the Church's official social teaching tames its essence. It is possible that the option for the poor is no longer understood as stepping into the world of the impoverished and marginalized and working alongside them in their struggles for justice. A pressing question then becomes: what does Francis's vision for the option empower and enable us, the faithful, to do?

One possible answer can be found in Doing Theology from the Existential Peripheries, a research project carried out under the auspices of the Migrants and Refugees Section of the Dicastery for Promoting Integral Human Development. This project sought to incorporate the most marginalized of the world's communities into the synodal process, to be counted in the Synod on Synodality, and to help the members of the Church dream together. Lay and religious men and women were tasked with listening for what communities of migrants in detention centers at the United States / Mexico border, women street workers in Nigeria, indigenous communities in Oceania, street children in Chile, women who volunteer for the Church in the Philippines, and many more had to say about their visions and hopes for the Church.[69] The project provides another illustration of the ways Pope Francis's use of the option for the poor moves the Church in directions not seen during the papacies of John Paul II and Benedict XVI, and it suggests a model for a richer engagement of the option for the poor in the US Catholic Church.[70]

Ultimately, the option for the poor is not simply a command embedded in Catholic social teaching. It is a much deeper understanding of our reality and commitment to transforming all forms of unjust suffering.[71] As Gustavo Gutiérrez reminds us, "The vision of Christian life manifested in this statement and in the practice of this commitment is, in fact, the most substantial part of the contribution from the life and theological reflection of the Church in Latin America to the universal Church."[72] The option for the poor is an integral part of following Jesus and understanding faith in terms of a hermeneutics of hope.[73] In this way, Francis's use of the option for the poor coincides with its use among first-generation liberation theologians.

We must not forget, however, that the option for the poor requires resistance, social analysis, and a questioning of the structures that harm vulnerable communities, both historically and in the present. A newer generation of liberation theologians brings this into relief. Joseph Drexler-Dreis, for example, argues that "the intuition that prompted Latin American liberation theologians to articulate the option for the poor can be retrieved and deepened by pushing liberation theology toward a decolonial option."[74] His insights align with *Fratelli tutti*'s depiction of political transformation as a special form of charity grounded in the option for the poor. Francis and this new generation of liberation theologians seem equally open to the possibility that the option for the poor serves as a moral imperative for developing a much-needed postcolonial historical consciousness.

The US Church is in a unique position to respond to the challenge of Francis's development of the option for the poor. Far more than any other country, the United States was complicit in the very history of oppressive regimes in Latin America that occasioned the option for the poor, posing a distinctive challenge for US Catholics. The continued impact of colonial and racist systems, in which we currently participate and which we sustain at home and abroad, means that we must wrestle deeply with the calls for transformation issued by Pope Francis, a transformation centered on an option for the poor articulated anew for a poor Church of the poor, a Church that goes forth, *en salida*.

NOTES

1. Although the theological and moral weight of the expression "the preferential option for the poor" hangs on the trifold meaning of the word "poor," more recently I have moved to using the descriptor "impoverished" and "marginalized." This move more conscientiously impresses the ethical reality that the social and economic status of various peoples and communities are the result of our participation in various forms of structural injustice, not natural or God-ordained.
2. Pablo A. Blanco González, "Gesto, Palabras y Praxis Pastoral de Francisco," *Revista Criterio* no. 2462 (2019), www.revistacriterio.com.ar/bloginst_new/2019/09/15/gestos-palabras-y-praxis-pastoral-de-francisco/; Emilce Cuda, "Teología y Política en el Discurso del Papa Francisco. ¿Dónde está el Pueblo?" *Nueva Sociedad*, no. 248 (December 2013), https://nuso.org/articulo/teologia-y-politica-en-el-discurso-del-papa-francisco-donde-esta-el-pueblo/.
3. Francis, "Address to Representatives of the Communications Media," March 16, 2013, www.vatican.va/content/francesco/en/speeches/2013/march/documents/papa-francesco_20130316_rappresentanti-media.html.
4. Pontifical Council for Justice and Peace, *Compendium of the Social Doctrine of the Church* (Vatican City: Libreria Editrice Vaticana, 2005), nos. 182–84, www.vatican.va/roman_curia/pontifical_councils/justpeace/documents/rc_pc_justpeace_doc_20060526_compendio-dott-soc_en.html.
5. José María Vigil, "Presentación," in *Sobre la Opción por los Pobres*, ed. José María Vigil (Quito: Ediciones Abya-Yala, 1999), 7. Gerhard Ludwig Cardinal Müller, former prefect of the Congregation for the Doctrine of the Faith, goes so far as to call liberation theology "one of the most significant currents of Catholic theology in the twentieth century." Gustavo Gutiérrez and Gerhard Ludwig Müller, *On the Side of the Poor: The Theology of Liberation* (Maryknoll, NY: Orbis Books, 2015), 11.
6. John Gehring, *The Francis Effect: A Radical Pope's Challenge to the American Catholic Church* (Lanham, MD: Rowman & Littlefield, 2015).
7. Francis, *Evangelii gaudium*, November 24, 2013, no. 53, www.vatican.va/content/francesco/en/apost_exhortations/documents/papa-francesco_esortazione-ap_20131124_evangelii-gaudium.html.
8. Francis, "Paths of Renewed Encounter," chap. 7 in *Fratelli tutti*, October 3, 2020, www.vatican.va/content/francesco/en/encyclicals/documents/papa-francesco_20201003_enciclica-fratelli-tutti.html.
9. Francis, *Gaudete et exultate*, March 19, 2018, no. 96, quoting John Paul II, *Novo Millennio ineunte*, 2001, no. 49.
10. Gustavo Gutiérrez, "Option for the Poor," in *Mysterium Liberationis: Fundamental Concepts of Liberation Theology*, edited by Ignacio Ellacuría, SJ, and Jon Sobrino, SJ (Maryknoll, NY: Orbis Books, 1993), 239–41.
11. Silvina Premat, "Duro Mensaje de Bergoglio en la Celebración de San Cayetano," *La Nación*, August 8, 2009, https://farodelautopia.webcindario.com/portal/Bergogliopobreza.htm.
12. Aldo Marcelo Cáceres, "J. M. Bergoglio: Claves de su Pensamiento Social antes de Ser Elegido Pontífice," *Moralia* 36 (2013): 117–35.
13. English translation by Andrea Tornielli and Giocomo Galeazzi, *This Economy Kills: Pope Francis on Capitalism and Social Justice*, trans. Demetrio S. Yocum (Collegeville, MN: Liturgical Press, 2015), 14. The video message in Spanish can be seen at https://youtu.be/OcZpKXA9KYk.

14. Tornielli and Galeazzi, *This Economy Kills*, 8–9.
15. Francis, *Evangelii gaudium*, no. 53.
16. Francis, nos. 20, 198, 187.
17. Francis, no. 189.
18. Francis, no. 198.
19. Francis's coining of the phrase "throwaway culture" echoes John Paul II's "culture of death" (*Evangelium vitae*, no. 12), but expands it to include broader sectors of cultural, social, and economic interactions that treat entire segments of the human family as disposable.
20. Francis, *Evangelii gaudium*, nos. 53–60.
21. Francis, no. 178.
22. Other chapters in this volume discuss these messages more specifically. See chapter 7 on Pope Francis and migrant justice by Kristin Heyer, and chapter 13 on climate change and ecological justice by Daniel DiLeo.
23. González, "Gestos."
24. See, e.g., Francis, "Address of Pope Francis to the Participants in the World Meeting of Popular Movements," October 20, 2014, www.vatican.va/content/francesco/en/speeches/2014/october/documents/papa-francesco_20141028_incontro-mondiale-movimenti-popolari.html.
25. Thomas R. Rourke, *The Roots of Pope Francis's Social and Political Thought* (Lanham, MD: Rowman & Littlefield, 2016), 71–79.
26. Mary Jo Meadow, "Personal Growth and the Ignatian Spiritual Exercises," *The Way* Supplement 76 (1993): 22.
27. Ignacio Ellacuría, "The Historicity of Christian Salvation," in *Mysterium Liberationis: Fundamental Concepts of Liberation Theology*, ed. Ignacio Ellacuría and Jon Sobrino (Maryknoll, NY: Orbis Books, 1993), 277.
28. Francis, *Evangelii gaudium*, no. 56.
29. Francis, *Laudato si'*, May 24, 2015, no. 2, www.vatican.va/content/francesco/en/encyclicals/documents/papa-francesco_20150524_enciclica-laudato-si.html.
30. Francis, no. 25.
31. Francis, nos. 51, 55, 138, 161.
32. John Paul II, *Solicitudo rei socialis*, December 30, 1987, no. 42, www.vatican.va/content/john-paul-ii/en/encyclicals/documents/hf_jp-ii_enc_30121987_sollicitudo-rei-socialis.html.
33. Congregation for the Doctrine of the Faith, *Instruction on Certain Aspects of the Theology of Liberation*, August 6, 1984, www.vatican.va/roman_curia/congregations/cfaith/documents/rc_con_cfaith_doc_19840806_theology-liberation_en.html.
34. O. Ernesto Valiente, "From Conflict to Reconciliation: Discipleship in the Theology of John Sobrino," *Theological Studies* 74, no. 3 (2013), https://go.gale.com/ps/i.do?id=Gale%7CA341818863&sid=googleScholar&v=2.1&it=r&linkaccess=abs&issn=00405639&p=AONE&sw=w&userGroupName=mlin_oweb&isGeoAuthType=true.
35. Gustavo Gutiérrez, *The Power of the Poor in History* (Maryknoll, NY: Orbis Books, 1983); Gustavo Gutiérrez, *A Theology of Liberation: History, Politics, and Salvation* (Maryknoll, NY: Orbis Books, 1988), x, xxix.
36. Francis, "Address of Pope Francis to the Participants in the World Meeting of Popular Movements," October 28, 2014, www.vatican.va/content/francesco/en/speeches/2014/october/documents/papa-francesco_20141028_incontro-mondiale-movimenti-popolari.html.

37. Francis, *Laudato si'*, nos. 144–46.
38. Francis, *Fratelli tutti*, no. 180.
39. Francis, no. 186.
40. John Paul II, *Solicitudo rei socialis*, nos. 36–40.
41. Francis, *Fratelli tutti*, no. 186.
42. Francis, no. 169.
43. For a discussion on the role and authority of local bishops conferences in the teaching of the magisterium, see María Teresa Dávila, "The Option for the Poor in Catholic Social Teaching," in *The Grace of Medellín: History, Theology, and Legacy—Reflections on the Significance of Medellín on the Church in the United States*, ed. Margaret Guider, Felix Palazzi, and Ernesto Valiente (Miami: Convivium Press, 2018), 412–19.
44. Joshua McElwee, "Pope Meets with Liberation Theology Pioneer," *National Catholic Reporter*, September 25, 2013, www.ncronline.org/news/theology/pope-meets-liberation-theology-pioneer. See also Ole Jakob Løland, "The Solved Conflict: Pope Francis and Liberation Theology," *International Journal of Latin American Religions* 5 (2021): 287–314.
45. Francis, "Video Message of the Holy Father Francis on the Occasion of the Fourth World Meeting of Popular Movements," October 16, 2021, www.vatican.va/content/francesco/en/messages/pont-messages/2021/documents/20211016-videomessaggio-movimentipopolari.html.
46. Francis, *Laudato si'*, nos. 216–21. See also María Teresa Dávila, "The Option for the Poor in *Laudato Si'*: Connecting Care of Creation with Care for the Poor," in *The Theological and Ecological Vision of* Laudato Si': *Everything Is Connected*, ed. Vincent Miller (New York: T&T Clark, 2017).
47. Michael Czerny, SJ, and Paolo Foglizzo, "The World Can Be Seen More Clearly from the Peripheries: The Fourth World Meeting of Popular Movements," *Thinking Faith*, June 1, 2022, www.thinkingfaith.org/articles/world-can-be-seen-more-clearly-peripheries-fourth-world-meeting-popular-movements.
48. Rafael Luciani and Félix Palazzi, "Pope Francis' 'Option for the Poor' Means Living and Thinking with the People," *America*, November 13, 2015, www.americamagazine.org/issue/peoples-church.
49. Tornielli and Galeazzi, *This Economy Kills*, 43.
50. Tornielli and Galeazzi, 55, 83. The authors note, however, that the same commentators often failed to notice that John Paul II's attack on socialist materialism was always accompanied by a critique of the ideologies of consumption and individualism characteristic of capitalist societies.
51. Tornielli and Galeazzi, 84.
52. W. David Montgomery, "The Flawed Economics of *Laudato Si'*," *New Atlantis*, Fall 2015, www.thenewatlantis.com/publications/the-flawed-economics-of-laudato-si.
53. R.R. Reno, "The Weakness of *Laudato Si*," *First Things*, July 1, 2015, www.firstthings.com/web-exclusives/2015/07/the-weakness-of-laudato-si.
54. Reno.
55. Charles J. Russo, "Reflections on *Fratelli Tutti*: Something Old, Something New, Much Ado About Not too Much," *Canopy Forum*, November 25, 2020, https://canopyforum.org/2020/11/25/reflections-on-fratelli-tutti-something-old-something-new-much-ado-about-not-too-much/.
56. David Lantigua, "Liberal Domination, Individual Rights and the Theological Option for the Poor in History," *Journal of the Society of Christian Ethics* 38, no. 2 (Fall–Winter 2018): 175–77.

57. Robert Bellah et al., *Habits of the Heart: Individualism and Commitment in American Life* (Berkeley: University of California Press, 2007).
58. On this topic, see contributions by Kelly Brown Douglas, *Stand Your Ground: Black Bodies and the Justice of God* (Maryknoll, NY: Orbis Books, 2015); Anthea Butler, *White Evangelical Racism: The Politics of Morality in America* (Chapel Hill: University of North Carolina Press, 2021); and Bryan Massingale, *Racial Justice and the Catholic Church* (Maryknoll, NY: Orbis Books, 2010).
59. Even while the US Catholic bishops had released a pastoral letter on the economy, *Economic Justice for All* (1986), experts lament the impossibility of there being an anniversary or follow-up document on economic justice. Mark Pattison, "Church Not as Committed to Economic Pastoral 35 Years Later, Say Panelists," CatholicPhilly.com, November 29, 2021, https://catholicphilly.com/2021/11/news/national-news/church-not-as-committed-to-economic-pastoral-35-years-later-say-panelists/.
60. Francis, *Fratelli tutti*, no. 46; also see "Pope Francis Asks Catholic Media to Combat 'Toxicity, Hate Speech, and Fake News,'" *America*, July 18, 2022, www.americamagazine.org/politics-society/2022/07/18/pope-francis-signis-toxic-media-243373.
61. John Gehring, *The Francis Effect: A Radical Pope's Challenge to the American Catholic Church* (New York: Rowman & Littlefield, 2015).
62. Olga Segura, "Why a Catholic Journalist Is Urging the Church to Engage Black Lives Matters," *National Catholic Reporter*, March 3, 2021, www.ncronline.org/news/why-catholic-journalist-urging-church-engage-black-lives-matter; US Conference of Catholic Bishops, "Reflections on the Movement for Black Lives (BLM)," www.usccb.org/reflections-movement-black-lives-blm.
63. Francis, *Fratelli tutti*, no. 157, 162.
64. Francis, *Querida Amazonia*, February 2, 2020, www.vatican.va/content/francesco/en/apost_exhortations/documents/papa-francesco_esortazione-ap_20200202_querida-amazonia.html.
65. Francis, nos. 9, 12, 33, 42.
66. Francis, *Fratelli tutti*, no. 226.
67. Editors, "The Catholic Church Must Come Clean—Completely—About What It Did to Native Americans," *America*, June 30, 2021, www.americamagazine.org/politics-society/2021/06/30/native-american-boarding-schools-catholic-church-investigation-240950.
68. Francis, *Fratelli tutti*, no. 249.
69. Reports from the various regions as well as study aids and other documentation can be found at "Doing Theology from the Peripheries," https://migrants-refugees.va/theology-from-the-peripheries/.
70. Rohan Curnow, "Which Preferential Option for the Poor? A History of the Doctrine's Bifurcation," *Modern Theology* 31 (January 1, 2015): 43–44.
71. Curnow, 48.
72. Gustavo Gutiérrez, "The Option for the Poor Arises from Faith in Christ," *Theological Studies* 70, no. 2 (June 2009): 318.
73. Gutiérrez, 317.
74. Joseph Drexler-Dreis, "The Option for the Poor as a Decolonial Option: Latin American Liberation Theology in Conversation with Teología India and Womanist Theology," *Political Theology* 18, no. 3 (2017): 270.

PART II
APPLICATIONS

7

AN EVER WIDER WE
Pope Francis's Migration Ethics
Kristin E. Heyer

For the 107th World Day of Migrants in 2021, Pope Francis adopted the theme "Towards an Ever Wider 'We.'"[1] Given his approach to pastoral and social concerns alike, a dynamically more inclusive community provides an apt symbol for his migration ethic. In the 2021 message, the pope traces the history of our common origin and destiny, highlighting how we are redeemed as a people, not as individuals, "that all might be one" (Jn. 17:21). He links this social salvation history to the present time in which that "we" willed by God has become wounded and fragmented: "Our 'we,' both in the wider world and within the Church, is crumbling and cracking due to myopic and aggressive forms of nationalism and radical individualism.[2] And the highest price is being paid by those who most easily become viewed as *others*: foreigners, migrants, the marginalized, those living on the existential peripheries."[3]

Leo Guardado points out that, in Spanish, "the play on words of '*nos*' and '*otros*' that make up '*nosotros*' grammatically illustrates the point that 'we' is the communion of 'us' and 'others.'"[4] In this message, Francis "transcends the distinction between us and them, leaving us only with a '*nosotros*,' a 'we.'"[5] The pope invokes the prophet Joel, pointing to a future without fear or division and the power of the Holy Spirit to build community in diversity, as on the day of the Church's baptism at Pentecost. Fellow Jesuit Gregory Boyle similarly frames his accompaniment of "outsiders," in his case former gang members, in terms of God's dream that no daylight separates "them" from "us." He regularly characterizes the broader Christian call as creating "a community of kinship such that God might recognize it."[6]

Pope Francis's social framing of migration is also evident in his diagnoses of its root causes, abetting factors, and barriers to just responses.

He frequently highlights forces that make an impact on people on the move, expanding the migration question to consider currents like populist discourse and virulent individualism. This emphasis on the structural and cultural dimensions of social sin widens the scope of migration ethics beyond dominant "crisis management" approaches. His attention to structures of injustice that propel and harm migrants and to the affective dimensions of conversion are reflective of his Ignatian influences and help illuminate a path forward. This chapter traces Pope Francis's written work on migration and related institutional moves to indicate the ways in which he has productively shifted the standard migration ethics paradigm. It concludes by suggesting practical implications for the US context, in light of Francis's Ignatian attentiveness to structure, affect, and encounter.

CURA MIGRANTIUM AMONG IDOLS OF INDIFFERENCE

The story of the Jewish and Christian pilgrim communities is one of migration, diaspora, and the call to live accordingly. Indeed, after the commandment to worship one God, no moral imperative is repeated more frequently in the Hebrew Scriptures than the command to care for the stranger.[7] For Israel's own experience of displacement grounded its ethic of compassion toward outsiders: "You shall not wrong or oppress a resident alien, for you were aliens in the land of Egypt (Ex. 22:21)."[8] When Joseph, Mary, and Jesus flee to Egypt, the émigré Holy Family becomes the archetype for every refugee family.[9] In Matthew's Gospel, "Jesus begins his early journey as a migrant and a displaced person—Jesus who in this same Gospel would radically identify with the 'least' and make hospitality to the stranger a criterion of judgment (Mt. 25:35)."[10]

Scripture and Christian history reflect an ambivalent approach to strangers, however. Susanna Snyder's work has shown how an isolating ecology of fear conditions responses to migration "crises" in virtually every world capital, illuminating the dynamic via strands in the biblical tradition rooted in ecologies of fear and of faith.[11] Throughout history churches have both developed sanctuary provision and supported white Christian supremacist politics targeting migrants.[12] Significant Catholic social teaching treating migration includes *Exsul familia* (1952), shaped by a postwar European context, and *Erga migrantes caritas Christi* (2004), which attends to the changing nature of migrant flows and the need for a new economic order that would reduce the need for survival migration.[13] Persons' right to remain is central to a Catholic migration ethics, grounded in inherent human dignity and universal human rights. Whereas the Catholic social tradition recognizes the right of sovereign nations to control their borders, this right is not understood to be absolute. In the case of blatant human rights violations, the right to state sovereignty is relativized by the tradition's primary commitment to protecting human dignity. The encyclicals issued by John Paul II and Benedict XVI expand the social and theological analysis of migration, both refusing to isolate migration from broader factors abetting movement, from economic to governance issues.[14]

Francis's papacy has witnessed an intensification in global migration, both in numbers of displaced persons and the issue's increased politicization.[15] Addressing each has become a central priority, as evidenced through his "unprecedented volume of teaching on the subjects through homilies, addresses and public statements" and frequent pastoral visits to borders and detention facilities.[16] Anna Rowlands notes that Francis has rebalanced his predecessor's emphasis on global political actors by "positioning the Church as itself a critical social actor,"[17] and offering "a more place-based vision of migrant response," stressing the relationship of the local to the global.[18] The central message repeated throughout his many addresses remains "migrants and refugees are human beings, precious in the eyes of God; they are our brothers and sisters; they are worthy of respect; what we do for them, we do directly for Christ."[19] This attentiveness to concrete migrants and their precious value reflects the Jesuit value of *cura personalis*. For example, at a border mass in Ciudad Juárez, Pope Francis bade listeners to measure the impact of forced migration not in numbers or statistics but with concrete names and stories, evoking a counternarrative to those dominating the airwaves: "Injustice is radicalized in the young; they are 'cannon fodder,' persecuted and threatened when they try to flee the spiral of violence and the hell of drugs, not to mention the tragic predicament of the many women whose lives have been unjustly taken."[20]

The pope grounds his concern in scriptural texts, some reflective of the tradition he inherited, like the Exodus story, the Holy Family's flight, the parable of the Good Samaritan and the Final Judgment summons; he also incorporates less familiar applications, whether of Jonah and the Ninevites or the ideal of the new Jerusalem. Beyond the annual messages for the World Day of Migrants and Refugees and other regular addresses on migration, Pope Francis has used social media to draw attention to the plight of displaced persons.[21] In 2017 he established a new Vatican office to oversee the Church's response to migrants and refugees: the Dicastery for Promoting Integral Human Development. He personally directs its Migrants and Refugee Section.[22] The office provides pastoral and policy resources, and migrant profiles, and it frames its work in terms of one human family, brothers and sisters all. Through his teachings and appointments, resource allocations, and new reporting structures, Francis has repeatedly signaled "his strong support and personal interest in the success of this newly reorganized Vatican office for refugees and migrants."[23]

Pope Francis's gestures of solidarity with migrants have also been central to his papacy, as well, from his repentance on Lampedusa to his lived example, returning from Lesbos with refugee families. During his first official trip outside Rome after his election, he celebrated Mass on Lampedusa, the Italian island that has become a safe haven for migrants seeking passage from North Africa to Europe. Before making any public statement, he made the sign of the cross and tossed a wreath of flowers into the sea, commemorating the estimated 20,000 African immigrants who had died over the previous twenty-five years trying to reach a new life in Europe. The pope celebrated mass within sight of the "graveyard of wrecks," where fishing boats carrying migrants and asylum seekers end up after they drift ashore.

Other reminders that Lampedusa is synonymous with dangerous attempts to reach Europe abounded: the altar was built over a small boat; the pastoral staff, the lectern, and even the chalice were carved from the wood of shipwrecked boats.[24] He lamented in his homily our disorientation in sin and indifference to the plight of these vulnerable brothers and sisters: recalling immemorial temptations to power and its consequences: "Adam, where are you?" and then "Cain, where is your brother?" These are questions addressed to each of us, "How many times do those who seek [a better place for their families] not find understanding, . . . not find welcome, . . . not find solidarity!" He concluded by petitioning the Lord for the grace to weep over our indifference, to weep over the cruelty in the world, in ourselves, and even in those who anonymously make socioeconomic decisions that open the way to tragedies like this.[25] Admitting to his own disorientation, Francis did not merely condemn "the world" for this indifference and its consequences, but instead repented: "Forgive us Lord!" whether for being closed in on our own well-being in a way that leads to anesthesia of the heart, or for making global decisions creating situations that lead to these tragedies.[26] Since Lampedusa, he has continually connected harmful idolatries with a summons to remember our fundamental relatedness. In a 2021 homily he lamented that the Mediterranean, once a cradle of civilizations that connected people, continues to become "a grim cemetery without tombstones." Echoing earlier pleas to counteract the apathy and amnesia that foster such shipwrecks, he adds, "Let us not permit this 'sea of memories' to be transformed into a 'sea of forgetfulness.'"[27]

In the US context, it is worth noting the pope's historic address to Congress in 2015, in which he summoned listeners to apply the Golden Rule with respect to migration policy. Identifying as a fellow descendant of immigrants from a shared continent of immigrants, he asked the nation through its representatives to identify with the needs and dreams propelling those traveling north in search of a better life for themselves and for their loved ones, asking, "Is this not what we want for our own children?" He pleaded with lawmakers to resist the temptation to discard them as troublesome or to fear and dehumanize them due to their numbers. With characteristic directness and clarity he concluded, "In a word, if we want security, let us give security; if we want life, let us give life; if we want opportunities, let us provide opportunities. The yardstick we use for others will be the yardstick which time will use for us."[28] In an inflight interview with reporters the following year, in response to a question about Donald Trump's campaign promise to build a border wall, he responded, "A person who thinks only about building walls, wherever they may be, and not building bridges, is not Christian. This is not the Gospel."[29] By the end of its four years, the Trump administration had accomplished more than four hundred immigration-related policy changes, "effectively ending asylum at the southern border."[30] That administration's policies and rhetoric stand in sharp contrast to the pope's emphases on migrants' dignity and just modes of reception. The hopes of immigrant rights advocates have not been fully realized by the subsequent Biden administration, either. The pope's 2020 encyclical on social friendship analyzes the impact of populist tendencies like Trump's and offers more sustained insight into social approaches to migration dynamics.

FRATELLI TUTTI: MIGRATIONS IN CONTEXT

Fratelli tutti offers an extended example of how Pope Francis draws attention to structural and cultural forces impacting people who are on the move today.[31] Here he expands the migration question to consider the impact of neoliberal economics and virulent individualism. This scope offers a welcome reorientation to rhetoric and analyses that often focus on states' rights or on border crossers alone. When addressing migration directly, Pope Francis revisits longstanding commitments to the right to remain, duties of reception, and the humanity of migrants and the gifts they bring. He identifies chief causes of displacement as armed conflict and social violence, economic exploitation, climate vulnerability, and political corruption.[32] He decries the perils facing migrants from unscrupulous traffickers, to fragmented communities of origin, to physical and psychological abuse on the journey (no. 38), and he helpfully underscores the threats posed by the political exploitation of fear and xenophobia (nos. 39, 86).

He revisits themes of welcome, protection, promotion, and integration, even as he neglects tasks of adjudicating conflicting claims or offering a blueprint for just entry policies. Pope Francis first introduced these four central verbs in a 2017 address to participants in an international forum on migration and peace. They offer organizing principles for his subsequent addresses (and work of the dicastery section), where he regularly suggests that "conjugating these verbs, in the first person singular and the first person plural" is a "duty of justice, civility, and solidarity."[33] For Francis, *welcome* entails offering broader options for migrants to safely and legally reach destination countries; *protect* involves defending the human rights and dignity of those on the move regardless of their legal status; *promote* summons the empowerment of newcomers' participation in areas of work, religious expression, family integrity and active citizenship; and *integrate* refers to efforts at mutual intercultural enrichment, not the mere assimilation of newcomers.[34]

The encyclical's broader emphases reveal how barriers to reception and humane policy are not limited to matters of border fortification and refugee policies alone, but also include pervasive tendencies toward isolationism and populist ideologies. The encyclical's illuminating analyses of such tendencies contest individualistic approaches in light of its fundamentally social vision. Francis's treatment of the Christian tradition's social anthropology, implicit understanding of social sin, and tempering of sovereignty rights with a commitment to the universal destination of created goods reorient responsibility for forced migrants. Persons' inherently social nature and fulfillment figure prominently, with compelling reminders of how fundamentally we belong to one another and how this recovery can serve as an antidote to the individualism, isolation, and indifference that harm persons on the move. In contrast to standard communitarian and cosmopolitan models that primarily address rights to individual freedom of movement or the self-determination of political communities, these relational emphases contextualize the individual acts of migrants and underscore social dimensions of justice and sinful complicity alike. He is calling readers throughout to retrieve an "ever wider we."

The pope's discussion of the universal destination of created goods similarly accents social understandings of what belongs to those in need and constraints on market freedom (nos. 119, 122–24). Understanding each country as "also belong[ing] to the foreigner" (no. 124) offers a strikingly countercultural vision to entrenched nationalism and opportunistic forms of interdependence—even though a focus on generous welcome alone invites further nuance and development with respect to sovereignty rights. Exploitative economic structures have been an ongoing concern for Pope Francis more broadly. Warning that our "economy of exclusion and inequality kills," he has long challenged not only the reductive market ethos dominating trade and migration policies but also its desensitizing effects.[35] In *Fratelli tutti*, he critiques markets rooted in reductive anthropologies that make individuals either consumers or bystanders, strengthening more powerful regions and diminishing weaker ones (nos. 12, 22). Bringing a structural analysis to causes of inequality and reiterating the core understanding of justice in the Catholic social tradition as meaningful participation, the pope has regularly lambasted the impact of economies of exclusion.[36]

Neoliberal globalization's operative priorities are often internalized in ways that shape perceptions and actions. Whether in fatalistic understandings of the "price of progress" or the "neutrality" of the market system, these more ideological currents of globalization configure coordinates for what becomes conceivable.[37] As he notes subsequently in *Let Us Dream*, "the laissez-faire market-centered approach confuses ends and means."[38] These dynamics directly impact economic migrants, and their risk is magnified, as "an uprooted person is very easy to dominate."[39]

Francis's analyses of inequality and migration are explicitly structural, attending to the effects of engrained social patterns and root causes.[40] Thomas Massaro rightly argues that Pope Francis takes his predecessors' awareness of structural evil to a new level, "applying a structural perspective to the reality of economic exclusion in an original and comprehensive way . . . and a style of prophetic denunciation that no pope had previously employed."[41] He also notes how the pope's Latin American context has contributed to his sensitivity to patterns of social injustice affected by legacies of colonialism and consequences of economic exclusion.[42] Massaro characterizes this structural approach as characteristic of Francis's approach to many issues (e.g., peacemaking, the environment) and as particularly Ignatian:

> Similarly for the Society of Jesus, the pursuit of justice must involve preventing great inequities from developing due to skewed political and social systems and economic structures that generate massive inequality and maldistribution. Both Francis and his fellow Jesuits display a "structural eye" when they identify the role of large social institutions in the struggle for a just social order. Once again the first Jesuit pope reflects the DNA of his spiritual heritage, as the work of the Society of Jesus has for decades reflected structuralist perspectives in its analysis of global realities and its adoption of pastoral planning efforts to support urgent reform in light of gospel values.[43]

As Massaro likewise underscores in chapter 5 of this volume, these foundational structural emphases ground the pope's analyses of forces pushing and pulling migrants across borders like "pawns on a chessboard," whether exploitative economic models, colonial patterns, or myopic nationalisms.[44]

IDEOLOGICAL THREATS AND AFFECTIVE CONVERSION

These emphases on structural causes of inequality and migration and more ideological barriers to an "ever wider we" reflect Francis's employment of social sin in ways and degrees distinct from his predecessors. The Christian category of social sin connects these structural relationships with their harmful consequences and abetting ideologies.[45] In its broadest sense social sin encompasses the unjust structures, distorted consciousness, and collective actions that facilitate dehumanization. Popes and theologians have differed on the precise scope of social sin, from limiting it to the effects or embodiment of personal sin, to an expansive sense of all sin as primarily social, with personal sins as mere manifestations of social sin.[46] An expansive understanding of social sin is evident in Francis's critiques of histories of unequal relationships between countries, extreme wealth and power concentrations (*Fratelli tutti*, no. 171), and harmful ideologies like xenophobia.

This attention to more cultural and affective elements also reflects Ignatian insights, evident in the discernment of spirits in the *Spiritual Exercises*, for example. His focus on the gift of mercy indicates his skepticism about the ability of intellectual ideas alone to lead to holiness or initiate just outcomes.[47] His signature culture of encounter elevates contact over concepts. If previous magisterial understandings of social sin remained primarily personal or interpersonal, Francis seems more disposed to a transpersonal sense of sin that understands our collective sin as greater than the sum of individual sins.[48] This nonvoluntary dimension of social sin, which reflects the impact of El Consejo Episcopal Latinoamericano y Caribeño (the Latin American and Caribbean Episcopal Council) at Medellín, may also be understood in terms of false consciousness. So beyond identifying structural forces demanding institutional solidarity, Francis interrogates more ideological dimensions of social sin that harden resistance to justice and hospitality. His incorporation of insights from liberation theology regarding these nonvoluntary dimensions of sin allows him to unmask the forces facilitating pervasive rights violations and callous indifference. He repeatedly targets the roots of nonvoluntary indifference rather than individual vices or unjust structures alone: cynicism, media pathologies, narcissism, and entitlement.

Recent years have witnessed a rise in nativist populism fueled, in part, by anxieties about the economic and cultural impact of globalization. Politicians running on populist platforms have capitalized on fears of demographic shifts, terrorist activities, and chaotic border scenes—increasingly disseminated through unvetted new media platforms—asserting that they alone are willing to control borders and restore law and order. In the US context, the

Trump administration's rhetoric, travel bans, misconstrued "national border emergency" and "zero tolerance policy" forcibly separating thousands of migrant children from their parents reflect such tendencies, for example.[49] *Fratelli tutti*'s analyses of how resentful nationalism creates "new forms of selfishness" under the guise of defending a country's interests uncover forces that are inimical to migrants today (no. 11) and also recall "America First" withdrawals from international agreements. Francis's encyclical critiques neoliberalism and populism alike for their "disdain for human frailty and vulnerability."[50]

In response to such fear-stoking isolationism, Francis has called on communications media to counter stereotypes that feed attitudes of defensiveness, indifference, and marginalization in favor of shaping attitudes "based on a culture of encounter, the only culture capable of building a better, more just and fraternal world."[51] His 2019 World Day of Migrants message centers on the harmful role of fear, lamenting the way fears of newcomers "condition our thinking" and engender intolerance and racism, calling us to instead take courage and foster encounter.[52] Pope Francis's deepened attention to the effects of fear and indifference urges a recognition of our fundamental relatedness in light of the harm that borders wreak. Hence *Fratelli tutti*'s charge to develop "antibodies" of social friendship in response exemplifies the relational focus of his migration ethic in the face of infectious forces that serve to exclude, exploit, and isolate.[53]

Related to this concern for nonvoluntary social sins is Francis's Ignatian engagement of affective motivation.[54] As Bernard Brady notes, "Francis offers a development in the tradition's description of persons as moral agents that stresses more deeply the emotive roots of action for justice within an interconnected rather than ordered world, and the related experience of others, not as objects of moral responsibility or impersonal holders of abstract dignity, but as brothers and sisters."[55] Throughout his papacy, Francis has underscored affective dimensions of metanoia and social transformation. As we have seen on Lampedusa, he laments the pervasive idolatry that not only facilitates migrants' deaths but also robs us of the ability to weep, a theme he revisited in Manila and then in Juárez, insisting that "only eyes cleansed by tears can see clearly."[56] The tears "sensitize our gaze and our attitude hardened and especially dormant in the face of another's suffering," priming us for conversion.[57] As he insists in *Evangelli gaudium*, "changing structures without generating new convictions and attitudes will only ensure that those same structures will become, sooner or later, corrupt, oppressive and ineffectual" (no. 189).

In *Fratelli tutti*, Francis shows how self-absorption fuels both apathy and hardened insulation or group preservation across a variety of contexts. He elaborates how a culture of consumerist comfort, abetted by social media distractions, incubates false ideologies that can manipulate consciences and insulate them from different perspectives (no. 45). This welcome attention to how indifference and a sense of invulnerability facilitate injustice is captured neither by political and economic considerations alone nor purely cognitive accounts of culpability. In his 2015 Lenten message summoning listeners to "become islands of mercy in a sea of indifference," Pope Francis signals how challenging economic inequalities must extend beyond meeting needs and crafting policies to healing these harmful mind-sets.[58] In a related way, Bryan Massingale has long framed white supremacy (which directly exacerbates xenophobia and ethnonationalism) in terms of cultural sin, illuminating how a culture of racism shapes our identities, frames our meaning-making, and malforms our conscience.[59] This pope seems similarly troubled by "soul sickness."[60]

Hence Francis helpfully attends to our formation by disvalues (anesthetizing consumerism, a cheerful recklessness) and the ways they shape loyalties, frame questions, and prevent us from even hearing the cry of forced migrants, or, as Daniel DiLeo indicates in chapter 13, the cry of the Earth. Francis's approach to these pervasive temptations to build a culture of walls "in the heart" and "on the land" employs structural analyses but also elevates ideologies abetting such harms, signaling a development in the use of social sin and relevant barriers to a culture of encounter.

This consistent identification and indictment of structural injustices and the ideologies that legitimate them constitute a key contribution to a migration ethics and Catholic social thought more broadly. Entrenched, intertwined patterns of social sin require repentance from idolatries that marginalize and disempower those beyond our immediate spheres of concern and borders. From repentance Francis calls Christians to conversion toward interdependence in solidarity. Such metanoia can occur through personal encounters and relationships that encourage new perspectives and receptivity, particularly if isolation and indifference are at the root of the problem. At the broader systemic level, nations must understand themselves as collectively responsible for the shared challenges forced migration poses.

CULTIVATING AN EVER WIDER WE

Francis's social contextualization of the causes of forced migration demands responses that attend to the abetting structures and attitudes he rightly underscores. On a geopolitical level, the scale of migration today demands systematic "cooperation between states and international organizations [that] can be capable of regulating and managing such movements effectively."[61]

Illustrating this approach, the Holy See consulted on and supported the 2018 Global Compact for Safe, Orderly, and Regular Migration and the Global Compact on Refugees. Throughout his papacy, Francis has also modeled practical dialogue across difference, insisting that "what saves us is not an idea but an encounter."[62] His own engagement with various existential extremities provides an apt orientation for the culture of encounter he promotes, calling others to ongoing accompaniment of (and conversion by) those at various borders.[63]

In the US context, where comprehensive legislative reform remains long overdue and politicization of the issue misleads, framing migration as a matter of justice rather than mercy or mere hospitality is warranted by Francis's structural emphases. Blaming border crossers alone eclipses transnational actors responsible for violent conflict, economic instability, or climate change from view, much less blame. Steps toward contextualizing migration patterns in light of an honest appraisal of the history of US interventions in sending countries and destabilizing international practices could move the nation toward a more just policy framework.

Whereas the US bishops have engaged in advocacy and individual witness in certain cases, as a body their conference has not elevated the matter among its public priorities, nor has preaching on the question been consistently widespread.[64] Episcopal leaders should be unafraid to condemn destructive policies and practices when they harm children, separate families, demonize migrants, and roll back historic protections. For example, Bishop Mark Seitz explicitly decries white supremacy, xenophobia, and the deadly function of the southern border wall, calling it an "open wound through our sister cities" and "a monument to hate" in his welcome pastoral letter, "Night Will Be No More."[65] Preaching and advocacy should identify citizens' complicity in generating migration flows rather than treating migrant and refugee arrivals as an unexpected "crisis" or "invasion." For example, pastoral leaders can expose ways in which consumers directly benefit from underpaying for goods and services and politicians benefit from unfounded scapegoating. In drawing attention to relevant history and complicity in this way, we can appropriately frame a response to migrants and refugees in terms of human rights and reparative justice, not optional largesse. The legislative priorities of the Justice for Immigrants campaign over the years have been welcome, but the Church's position on the need for comprehensive reform has not been advanced with the urgency of other priorities. In terms of the dynamic conversion the pope summons, parish-based outreach programs, testimony sharing, and educational programming can widen communities' self-understanding.

Catholic parishes minister to people on all sides of the immigration issue, so in terms of fostering encounters across divides, they would do well to guard against xenophobic rhetoric, scapegoating, and conspiracy theorizing; help counteract myths about immigrants and refugees while remembering that our own "deep stories" can tempt us to select facts, too; and remain mindful that migrants may be in particular need of allies to amplify their voices amid climates of increased fear and intimidation. Convening honest dialogues across difference can help break through insulating echo chambers. Whereas Francis's use of the "culture of encounter" remains more evocative than precise, meeting across differences, both within and across communities, offers a point of departure. Churches are well poised not only to defend the rights and meet the needs of immigrants, but also to name and counteract the abetting forces Francis identifies.

Although Francis's attention to such forces and to affect are welcome, attention must also be paid to connecting encounter and indictment with policy change. Structural diagnoses require comparable solutions rather than individualistic or palliative ones. The binational Kino Border Initiative's integration of humanitarian outreach, pastoral formation, and legislative advocacy offers a helpful example in this vein. The initiative is marked by "mutual evangelization" in ways that safeguard against casting migrants as welcome but not one of "us," as well.[66] The annual Ignatian Family Teach-In for Justice offers thousands of students at Jesuit secondary schools and universities the opportunity to move from "consciousness-raising" in moving plenaries and workshops to visits to representatives on Capitol Hill, providing another model of bridging the gap between micro-level encounter and macro-level change.[67]

On the 105th World Migrant and Refugee Day in 2019, the magnificent *Angels Unawares* sculpture was installed in Saint Peter's Square. The piece was commissioned by Michael Cardinal Czerny, prefect of the Dicastery for Promoting Integral Human Development, and produced by Timothy Schmalz. It features immigrants from across time and locations forging ahead on a common ship, incorporating Muslims escaping Syria beside Jews escaping Nazi Germany beside an Irish boy escaping the potato famine. One figure could easily be an Eritrean attempting to reach Lampedusa. The bronze and clay of *Angels Unawares* can help counter the collective delusion that we are not responsible and remind us that in our acts of welcome and widening we may be "entertain[ing] angels" (Heb. 13:2). When I took my students to see a replica of the sculpture that visited our campus, many instantly recognized their own family histories, their very identities. Like art, religious practices, narratives, and symbols hold potential to (re)shape moral imagination. This Jesuit pope has called attention to the urgency of this formation task, from Lampedusa to *Angels Unawares*. His uses of scripture, appeal to affect, and encounters across differences illuminate a path to the work for conversion and structural justice. These approaches spring from and move us toward an "ever wider we."

NOTES

1. Francis, "Towards an Ever Wider 'We,'" Message for 107th World Day of Migrants, September 27, 2021, www.vatican.va/content/francesco/en/messages/migration/documents/papa-francesco_20210503_world-migrants-day-2021.html. I am grateful to Emma McDonald for her research assistance supporting this chapter. Elyse Raby and Joshua Snyder offered valuable input on an earlier draft.
2. Francis, *Fratelli tutti*, October 3, 2020, nos. 11, 105, www.vatican.va/content/francesco/en/encyclicals/documents/papa-francesco_20201003_enciclica-fratelli-tutti.html.
3. Francis, "Towards an Ever Wider We."
4. Leo Guardado, panel presentation, "Evaluating the Churches' Teaching on Migration Ethics," Migration Ethics interest group, Society of Christian Ethics Annual Meeting, January 10, 2022, Zoom.
5. Guardado.
6. Gregory Boyle, *Tattoos on the Heart: The Power of Boundless Compassion* (New York: Free Press, 2011), 188, 190.
7. William O'Neill, "Rights of Passage: The Ethics of Forced Displacement," *Journal of the Society of Christian Ethics* 127, no. 1 (Spring–Summer 2007): 113–35.
8. Ched Myers and Matthew Colwell, *Our God Is Undocumented* (Maryknoll, NY: Orbis Books, 2012), 15.
9. Pius XII, *Exsul familia* (On the Spiritual Care to Migrants), September 30, 1952, in *The Church's Magna Charta for Migrants*, ed. Rev. Giulivo Tessarolo (Staten Island: Saint Charles Seminary, 1962), "Introduction."
10. Donald Senior, "'Beloved Aliens and Exiles:' New Testament Perspectives on Migration," in *A Promised Land, a Perilous Journey: Theological Perspectives in Migration*, ed. Daniel G. Groody and Gioacchino Campese (Notre Dame, IN: University of Notre Dame Press, 2008), 23.
11. Susanna Snyder, *Asylum-Seeking, Migration and Church* (Farnham, UK: Ashgate, 2012), 85–87, chap. 7.
12. Anna Rowlands, *Toward a Politics of Communion: Catholic Social Teaching in Dark Times* (London: T&T Clarke, 2021), 75.
13. Rowlands, 77. Pius XII, *Exsul familia*; Pontifical Council for the Pastoral Care of Migrants and Itinerant People, *Erga migrantes caritas Christi*, May 1, 2004, www.vatican.va/roman_curia/pontifical_councils/migrants/documents/rc_pc_migrants_doc_20040514_erga-migrantes-caritas-christi_en.html.
14. Rowlands, *Toward a Politics of Communion*, 80–81. See John Paul II, *Sollicitudo rei socialis*, December 30, 1987, www.vatican.va/content/john-paul-ii/en/encyclicals/documents/hf_jp-ii_enc_30121987_sollicitudo-rei-socialis.html; Benedict XVI, *Caritas in veritate*, June 29, 2009, www.vatican.va/content/benedict-xvi/en/encyclicals/documents/hf_ben-xvi_enc_20090629_caritas-in-veritate.html.
15. Rowlands, *Toward a Politics of Communion*, 84.

16. Rowlands, 84. Austen Ivereigh notes that Pope Francis has not needed to write an encyclical on migration, given that it "runs through all of his teaching documents," citing *Evangelii gaudium*, *Laudato si'*, *Amoris laetitia*, and *Gaudete et exultate*. Ivereigh, "From Strangers to Siblings," *Commonweal*, March 2023, 20–24, at 21.
17. Rowlands, *Toward a Politics of Communion*, 85.
18. Rowlands, 87.
19. Robert Ellsberg, introduction to *I Was a Stranger and You Welcomed Me: A Call to Mercy and Solidarity with Migrants and Refugees*, by Francis (Maryknoll, NY: Orbis Books, 2018), xvii–xxiv, at xviii.
20. Francis, "No Border Can Stop Us from Being One Family," Vatican Radio, February 18, 2016, http://en.radiovaticana.va/news/2016/02/18/pope_francis__%E2%80%98no_border_can_stop_us_from_being_one_family%E2%80%99/1209507.
21. Thomas Massaro, *Mercy in Action: The Social Teachings of Pope Francis* (Lanham, MD: Rowman & Littlefield, 2018), 131.
22. David Hollenbach, "Welcoming Refugees and Migrants: Catholic Narratives and the Challenge of Inclusion," *Annals APPS* 690, July 2020, 160. See Francis, "Statutes of the Dicastery for Promoting Integral Human Development," www.vatican.va/content/francesco/en/motu_proprio/documents/papa-francesco_20160817_statuto-dicastero-servizio-sviluppo-umano-integrale.html.
23. Massaro, *Mercy in Action*, 124.
24. For a theological reflection on Eucharist and migration in light of this liturgy on Lampedusa, see Daniel G. Groody, "Cup of Suffering, Chalice of Salvation: Refugees, Lampedusa and the Eucharist," *Theological Studies* 78, no. 4 (December 2017): 96087.
25. Cindy Wooden, "Pope Calls for Repentance over Treatment of Migrants," Catholic News Service, July 8, 2013, www.catholicnews.com/services/ englishnews/2013/pope-calls-for-repentance-over-treatment-of-migrants.cfm.
26. Francis, "Visit to Lampedusa: Homily of Holy Father Francis, 'Arena' Sports Camp, Salina Quarter," July 8, 2013, www.vatican.va/content/francesco/en/homilies/2013/documents/papa-francesco_20130708_omelia-lampedusa.html.
27. Pope Francis, "Homily at a Migrant Reception Facility in Mytilene, on Lesbos," December 5, 2021, available via Francis, "Pope Francis in Lesbos: The Root Causes of the Migration Crisis 'Should be Attacked,' Not Migrants," *America*, December 5, 2021, www.americamagazine.org/faith/2021/12/05/pope-francis-lesbos-greece-migration-refugees-speech-241969.
28. Address of Pope Francis to the Joint Session of the US Congress, September 25, 2015; transcript at www.washingtonpost.com/local/social-issues/transcript-pope-franciss-speech-to-congress/2015/09/24/6d7d7ac8-62bf-11e5-8e9e-dce8a2a2a679_story.html.
29. Lindsey Bever, "Pope Francis—Not Naming Names—Makes Appeal Not to Create Walls but Build Bridges," *Washington Post*, February 8, 2017.
30. Sarah Pierce, Jessica Bolter, and Andrew Selee, *Trump's First Year on Immigration Policy: Rhetoric vs. Reality* (Washington, DC: Migration Policy Institute, 2018), 1, 4–5. For a moral analysis of these developments, see Kristin E. Heyer, "Christian Responses to Migration Along the US-Mexican Border," in *Oxford Handbook of Religion and Contemporary Migration*, ed. Anna Rowlands and Elena Fiddian-Qasmiyeh (Oxford: Oxford University Press, 2024).
31. Francis, *Fratelli tutti*, October 3, 2020, www.vatican.va/content/francesco/en/encyclicals/documents/papa-francesco_20201003_enciclica-fratelli-tutti.html. Portions of this section and the next draw from Heyer, "Walls in the Heart: Social Sin in *Fratelli Tutti*," *Journal of Catholic Social Thought* 19, no. 1 (Winter 2022): 25–40.

32. Rowlands, *Toward a Politics of Communion*, 89.
33. Francis, "Justice, Civility, and Solidarity: Address to Participants in the International Forum on 'Migration and Peace,'" February 21, 2017, cited by Francis, *I Was a Stranger*, 64.
34. Francis, *I Was a Stranger*, 61–64.
35. E.g., Francis, *Evangelii gaudium*, November 24, 2013, no. 53, www.vatican.va/content/francesco/en/apost_exhortations/documents/papa-francesco_esortazione-ap_20131124_evangelii-gaudium.html.
36. Francis, no. 202.
37. Timothy Jarvis Gorringe, "Invoking: Globalization and Power," in *The Blackwell Companion to Christian Ethics*, ed. Stanley Hauerwas and Samuel Wells (Malden, MA: Blackwell, 2004), 346–59, at 353.
38. Francis and Austen Ivereigh, *Let Us Dream: The Path to a Better Future* (New York: Simon & Schuster, 2020), 109.
39. Francis and Ivereigh.
40. Massaro, *Mercy in Action*, 28–29.
41. Massaro, 31.
42. Massaro, 31–32.
43. Thomas Massaro, "The Peace Advocacy of Pope Francis: Jesuit Perspectives," *Journal of Jesuit Studies* 8, no. 4 (2021): 543.
44. Francis, "Message of His Holiness Pope Francis for the World Day of Migrants and Refugees (2014)," August 5, 2013, www.vatican.va/content/francesco/en/messages/migration/documents/papa-francesco_20130805_world-migrants-day.html.
45. Francis understands ideology as "an idea, theory, or program that is developed and championed by an elitist group and posited as a reliable and totalizing . . . truth. Ideology operates as an intellectually pure, rigorist, or gnostic hermeneutic of reality, developed and wielded by power elites over and against less powerful audiences including the poor, the vulnerable, and the marginalized. . . . He speaks of certain economic positions ('market-based, consumerist'), cultural viewpoints ('throwaway culture'), and gender theories as ideologies." Bradford E. Hinze, "The Ecclesiology of Pope Francis and the Future of the Church in Africa," *Journal of Global Catholicism* 2, no. 1 (2017): 24. Here I am using "ideology" more broadly to capture the harmful mind-sets Francis targets in *Fratelli tutti* and elsewhere.
46. For an overview of this range of understandings, see Conor Kelly, "The Nature and Operation of Structural Sin: Insights from Theology and Moral Psychology," *Theological Studies* 80, no. 2 (June 2019): 293–327.
47. Daniel Amiri, "Ignatius: A Brief Introduction to the Theology of Pope Francis," in *Where Peter Is, There Is the Church*, February 13, 2019, https://wherepeteris.com/ignatius-a-brief-introduction-to-the-theology-of-pope-francis/. As J. Matthew Ashley puts it, Francis does not find ideas unimportant, but believes we "should prioritize reality and the ways that ideas are rooted in realities, and prove their value by how they enable us to engage those realities creatively." J. Matthew Ashley, *Renewing Theology: Ignatian Spirituality and Karl Rahner, Ignacio Ellacuría, and Pope Francis* (Notre Dame, IN: University of Notre Dame Press, 2022), 262.
48. Kenneth R. Himes, "Human Failing: The Meanings and Metaphors of Sin," in *Moral Theology: New Directions and Fundamental Issues: Festschrift for James P. Hannigan*, ed. James Keating (New York: Paulist Press, 2004), 145–61, at 158.
49. For analyses of the Trump administration's rhetoric and policies in light of Catholic migration ethics, see Kristin E. Heyer, "Migration, Social Responsibility and Moral Imagination: Resources from Christian Ethics," in *Christianity and the Law of Migration: An Introduction*, ed. Silas W. Allard, Kristin Heyer, and Raj Nadella (New York: Routledge, 2021).

50. Meghan J. Clark and Anna Rowlands, "*Fratelli Tutti*: Reading the Social Magisterium of Pope Francis," *Journal of Catholic Social Thought* 19, no.1 (Winter 2022): 14.
51. Francis, "Migrants and Refugees: Toward a Better World—2014 World Day of Migrants and Refugees Message," in *I Was a Stranger*, by Francis, 97.
52. Francis, "105th World Day of Migrants and Refugees Message," April 30, 2019, www.vaticanva/content/francesco/en/messages/migration/documents/papa-francesco_20190527_world-migrants-day-2019.html.
53. Clark and Rowlands specify that for Francis, "social dialogue and social friendship emerge from securing patterns of distribution of wealth, work, status, and so forth that enable survival, rootedness, stability of life, and nonenforced movement of peoples." Clark and Rowlands, "*Fratelli Tutti*," 15.
54. Bernard Brady, "From Catholic Social Thought to Catholic Social Living: A Narrative of the Tradition," *Journal of Catholic Social Thought* 15, no. 2 (Summer 2018): 318.
55. Brady, 318.
56. Francis, "Homily of His Holiness Pope Francis, Cuidad Juárez Fair Grounds," February 17, 2016, www.vatican.va/content/francesco/en/homilies/2016/documents/papa-francesco_20160217_omelia-messico-ciudad-jaurez.html.
57. Francis.
58. Francis, "Message of His Holiness Pope Francis for Lent 2015: 'Make Your Hears Firm' (Jas. 5:8)," October 4, 2014, www.vatican.va/content/francesco/en/messages/lent/documents/papa-francesco_20141004_messaggio-quaresima2015.html.
59. For a recent example, see Bryan Massingale, "Toward a Spirituality for Racial Justice: The Transformation of Consciousness and the 'Souls of White Folks,'" in *Desire, Darkness, and Hope: Theology in a Time of Impasse*, ed. Laurie Cassidy and M. Shawn Copeland (Collegeville, MN: Liturgical Press, 2021), 325–45.
60. Massingale, 334.
61. Francis, "Church without Frontiers, Mother to All," 101st World Day of Migrants Address 2015, September 3, 2014, www.vatican.va/content/francesco/en/messages/migration/documents/papa-francesco_20140903_world-migrants-day-2015.htmlDrawing on *Caritas in Veritate* 62.
62. Francis and Ivereigh, *Let Us Dream*, 107.
63. Ashley highlights Francis's summons to the peripheries in his profile of how Ignatian spirituality has affected the pope's theology and leadership in *Renewing Theology*, chapter 6.
64. One exception I would note is the online resource Catholic Women Preach, where connections between the week's Scriptures and implications for immigration are made with regularity (see catholicwomenpreach.org).
65. Mark Joseph Seitz, bishop of El Paso, "Night Will Be No More," October 13, 2019, www.hopeborder.org/nightwillbenomore-eng.
66. For an elaboration of the Kino Border Initiative's ministries and their ecclesiological and ethical implications, see Kristin Heyer, "The Promise of a Pilgrim Church: Ecclesiological Reflections on the Praxis of Kinship with Migrants," in *Church in the Age of Migration: A Moving Body*, ed. Susanna Snyder, Agnes Brazal, and Joshua Ralston (New York: Palgrave Macmillan, 2015), 83–98. I am grateful to Federico Cinnoca for underscoring the importance of such mutuality.
67. Information about the Ignatian Family Teach-in for Justice may be found at https://ignatiansolidarity.net/iftj/. I am grateful to Barbara Anne Kozee for this suggestion.

8

POPE FRANCIS, ANTIRACIST?

Revealing the Heart in a Time of Racial Reckoning

Maureen H. O'Connell

On June 3, 2020, amid roiling tensions in the United States around the murder of George Floyd at the hands of three Minneapolis police officers, Pope Francis unequivocally reminded the nation's 70 million Catholics that "we cannot tolerate or turn a blind eye to racism and exclusion in any form and yet claim to defend the sacredness of every human life."[1] Francis said Floyd's name twice, once in naming his death as "tragic" and then again to invite Americans to pray for the repose of his soul, "and of all those others who have lost their lives as a result of the sin of racism." In his brief statement, Francis also aligned himself with a particular context attempting to deal with both the pattern of racism as a cause of death for peoples of color and a "self-destructive and self-defeating" violent response to it. He did so by "join[ing] the Church of Minneapolis, and the entire United States," in praying for victims of police-involved shootings and their families and imploring "a national reconciliation and peace for which we all yearn" and by invoking the intercession of Our Lady of Guadalupe, patroness of the Americas, in guiding efforts toward peace and justice.

Just days earlier, a representative group of seven members of the Conference of US Catholic Bishops issued their own statement about Floyd's death.[2] They, too, acknowledged a pattern to these "killings" and their racist natures, invoked prayers for victims and their families, and called for an end to violent protests. They, too, insisted that "this deadly treatment is antithetical to the Gospel of Life" and stated "unequivocally" that "racism is a life issue." Distinctive points of emphasis in Francis's address, however, suggest that even though he has not explicitly uttered the phrase "antiracism," Catholics engaged in racial justice work can find in him helpful resources to move intentionally toward a horizon where racial belonging rooted in racial equity increasingly becomes a reality, especially in our own Catholic institutions and cultures, where we are only just beginning to acknowledge our role in making, sanctifying, and perpetuating white supremacy.[3]

For example, while both the US bishops and the bishop of Rome describe Floyd's death as tragic, Francis calls the racism that caused it a sin. Whereas the US bishops couch the problem of and solution to racism in largely individualistic ways—whether in terms of personal indifference to the plight of others or the need for personal conversion through meaningful encounters among individuals who are different—Francis calls for "national reconciliation," which suggests a more collective sense of responsibility. Moreover, where the US bishops call for peace, in part through the intercession of the Spirit of Truth to "come down on our criminal justice and law enforcement systems," Francis seeks the assistance of an inculturated Mary—who appeared as an indigenous woman to an indigenous man with the purpose of decentering a colonizing Church—for "all those who work for peace *and* justice."[4]

In that eight-sentence address in June 2020—as well as in other elements of Francis's witness to the harm of racism and the possibility of racial justice—we can find a praxis for antiracism that is at once rooted in the Catholic social tradition where racial justice is concerned while enlarging it at the same time. His is a praxis that is at once deeply personal and emotionally attuned to the depth and pain of this problem. And yet it also reflects an awareness of structural realities, including ecclesial structures, that undergird personal bias and interpersonal discrimination, and even violence, and require more than personal conversation in order to undo. Finally, Francis's method illuminates spiritual resources latent in local traditions that can assist us in working together toward justice. In Francis's praxis of naming, wondering, and integrating, we find tools for collective response that can be characterized as antiracist: actively resisting and dismantling cultures, structures, and systems of white body supremacy.

NAMING: FRANCIS ACKNOWLEDGES RACISM

Francis has acknowledged the reality of racism—its history, structures, and interplay with culture—far more than his predecessors. For example, two months after a spring 2022 audience with Indigenous peoples affected by the abuse of Catholic residential schools across Canada, Francis made a "Penitential Pilgrimage" there and offered a public apology, where he acknowledged, with shame, that "many Christians supported the colonizing mentality of the powers that oppressed the Indigenous peoples"; and asked, "in particular," forgiveness "for the ways in which many members of the Church and of religious communities cooperated, not least through their indifference, in projects of cultural destruction and forced assimilation promoted by the governments of that time, which culminated in the system of residential schools."[5] In terms of addressing the structural reality of racism, consider his 2022 appointment of Archbishop Anthony Poola of Hyderabad as the first cardinal to come from the Dalit population, the lowest in India's caste system.[6] Finally, in his reflection on what we might learn from the global pandemic, *Let Us Dream*, Francis reveals racism as a culture of amnesia in which we "armor-plate" ourselves by turning ideas into ideologies and "[amputate] history." He notes: "History is what was, not what we want to it to have been, and when we try to throw an ideological blanket over it, we make it so much harder to see what in our present needs to change in order to move toward a better future."[7]

Many committed to racial justice identify truth telling about our histories as a critical first step on that lifelong path, since doing so forces us to contend with competing and conflictual narratives and frameworks of understanding. For example, Bryan Massingale contends, "Facing history and ourselves, telling the truth of our situation, acknowledging our responsibility and complicity, and declaring who profited and how from these [racial] estrangements are essential to healing the wounds of racism."[8] In a way that intones a polyhedric complexity of the interrelatedness of our human and natural realities that informs Francis's approach to other social problems, such as climate change or violent conflict, Francis similarly names the history of racism and moves us beyond the limited understandings of it as interpersonal interactions in the present moment or as the choices of bad actors at some point in the distant past. Instead, he helps us see racism as a far more morally complicated reality, a reality that belies neat chronological categories of past, present, and future or moral assessments of guilt and innocence. For example, equipped with an awareness of history, Francis names racism as "a virus that quickly mutates and, instead of disappearing, goes into hiding, and lurks in waiting";[9] as a kind of amnesia that allows us to be easily manipulated;[10] or as an intergenerational dynamic of denying history and multiculturalism.[11]

In addition, Francis focuses on power. He notes that contemporary populist politics, rife with racialized nationalism, seeks to create a "power over society," as opposed to building up power among the people within it, and as such breeds and exploits anxieties that divide.[12] A common denominator here is Francis's awareness of racism as an expression of power over others exercised collectively in and through cultures—whether that of consumerist capitalism that reduces interactions among people to mere transactions, the "hyperinflation of the individual" that reinforces a white male Christian default, or the "technological paradigm" that demands assimilation—which then shape self-understandings, both individual and collective, as well as modes of relationship and access to the common good.[13] To that extent, he addresses a significant concern about Catholic social teaching where racism is concerned: an awareness of the connection between racial identity and power in the US context. "Color differences are not the problem," explains Massingale. "It is the meaning and value assigned to these differences—the use of color differences to advance or circumscribe, enhance or impeded, the life changes and opportunities of a human group—that is problematic and socially divisive."[14]

Francis also signals an awareness of the "othering" impulse at the heart of racism and the impact othering has, both on the subject and recipient of this impulse. In a 2019 address to students in Milan, which he referenced in *Fratelli tutti*, the pope named a "culture of walls" erected for the self-preservation of some, which relegate those on the other side to "other" and preclude meaningful encounters with differences. Harm arises on both sides. "Those who raise walls will end up as slaves within the very walls they have built. They are left without horizons, for they lack this interchange with others."[15] He speaks of closed rooms of fear and shame, where we cut ourselves off from the mercy of God and as such become ill in stank air.[16] This harkens to ideas of racism as a form of social asphyxiation in light of its deleterious impact on individual and collective capacities for empathy.[17]

In his image of the "isolated conscience," Francis implicitly engages with James Baldwin's idea that the driving cause of racism is whites' inability for self-love.[18] "The bad-spirit temptation to withdraw spiritually from the body to which I belong, closes us in on our own interests and viewpoints by means of suspicion and supposition," Francis explains in unapologetically Ignatian language.[19] The resulting rigidity of the isolated conscience in the long run is unhealthy in that it "[clings] to something that feeds the ego" and, likewise, to my mind, the unattainable and yet idolatrous pursuit of white supremacy through "power, influence, freedom, security, status, money, property, or some combination of these."[20] Massingale provides evidence of how racism fuels and distorts isolated consciences, rendering people who operate with them a liability for racial justice work.[21] These ideas also invoke Robin DiAngelo's insights about how racism ultimately festers within white people a fragility or inability to engage with the stress of racial incidents or encounters with difference or with truths we (white people) would rather not face.[22] "The growing verbal violence reflects a fragility of self-hood," Francis observes in *Let Us Dream*, "a loss of roots, in which security is found in discrediting others through narratives that let us feel righteous and give us reasons for silencing others."[23]

Racism as power gives rise to cultures that impede the common good. In *Fratelli tutti*, for example, Francis presents racism in terms of a "periphery" with a power to separate us or to keep us from caring for "those I do not naturally consider a part of [our] circle of interests."[24] To this extent, Francis echoes scholars like Elijah Anderson, who understand racism in terms of the power to create conditions of belonging and alienation, particularly in spaces where we gather in order to create the common good.[25] Moreover, Francis suggests that racism's peripheries are not merely incidents, or even patterned incidents of personal bias or prejudices, but are socially constructed whenever people in need are "abandoned or ignored by the society in which [we] live."[26] He names as racism the power to change the status of persons in the context of their communities, rendering even "citizens with full rights" a "foreigner" status.[27]

In all this, Francis advances the Catholic social tradition in the critical ways named by Catholic scholars attempting to use the tradition for racial justice work. Consider Massingale's critique of the contributions of the US Catholic bishops. He notes that episcopal teaching on racism is not timely and is reactive rather than proactive; it is overshadowed by other priorities and lacks pastoral passion; it is not informed by social analysis and downplays structural realities; it lacks ethical and theological reflection, particularly such reflection informed by the people closest to the pain of racism; and it is overly optimistic about what change demands.[28] While hardly flawless, in naming racism, Francis does attend to some of these concerns. He brings a structural lens, offers theological and ethical grounds for contending with racism, insists that it lies at the heart of other social problems, and acknowledges that it presents a daunting challenge for Christian discipleship.

WONDERING: FRANCIS ENCOUNTERS RACISM

Part of what makes it possible for Francis to do this acknowledging is the role that wonder plays in his moral method. In *Laudato si'*, he notes that wonder is an approach that can interrupt our attitude of "masters, consumers, ruthless exploiters, unable to set limits on their immediate needs."[29] Instead, wonder helps us "feel intimately united with all that exists," which in turn can spark a deep sense of care.[30] Encounters with others, especially those closest to the pain of injustices, spark wonder for Francis. He models what those kinds of encounters, moments when we might step out of constricting spaces and ideological stances of judgment, can look like in the context of racism. For example, on the last day of his 2015 visit to the United States, a trip that included an address to the US Congress and culminated with a Mass for more than 100,000 people on Benjamin Franklin Parkway in Philadelphia, Francis visited ninety-five incarcerated men in one of Philadelphia's correctional facilities. In his translated remarks, shared from a wooden chair several of the men had made for him for the occasion, he indicated, "I am here as a pastor, but above all as a brother to share your situation and make it my own."[31] While he never mentioned the word racism, Francis literally spoke from inside of the most egregious drivers of racism in American culture, the prison industrial complex, which has been the neocapitalist answer to a variety of problems arising from racial inequality—lack of health care for addiction or mental illness, adverse childhood experiences caused by poverty, lack of funding for public education, stagnant minimum wages.[32] "Any society, any family, which cannot share or take seriously the pain of its children, and views that pain as something normal or to be expected, is a society 'condemned' to remain a hostage to itself, prey to the very things which cause that pain."[33] In the case of the racist prison system in the United States, Francis implied that viewing racism as normal means we shall continue to be held hostage by it. He intones the Christian theologian and antiracist educator Joseph Barndt's understanding of racism as sin of collective captivity rather than intentional and individual choice. While the latter requires repentance, then the former can only be redressed through liberation from the very cultures and systems of imprisonment we created in the first place, through the "isolation, separation, hostility and mistrust" that racism perpetuates.[34]

In some ways, Francis's choices about where he goes with his body are intended to elicit insight from people most affected by the injustice his presence seeks to acknowledge rather than only provide a platform for his own Eurocentric, masculine, and clerical perspectives. As he says in *Laudato si'*, approaches to justice have to be social, by which he means rooted in "insight gained from encounters with others."[35] These encounters can help resist the temptations that many people often experience when confronted with their own racism, which he implicitly names: the temptation either to "wrap ourselves in the banner of one side or the other, exacerbating the conflict" or to "avoid engaging in conflict all together, denying the tension involved and washing our hands of it."[36] As such, wonder is an important tool for interrupting white supremacy as it has the power to decenter us from positions of rigid certainty to more flexible and malleable curiosity, empathy, and self-reflection. Francis also names this sensibility in terms of "self-accusation" or lowering ourselves to be more dependent on God and others; an antidote to a "spirit of self-sufficiency and superiority."[37] The key is to hold space for disagreement and to allow that disagreement to generate breakthroughs—an "overflow" that "breaks the banks that confined our thinking"—rather than something that sends us to our separate corners.[38]

Wonder is at the heart of Francis's fascination with cultures of dialogue, which can dismantle cultures of white body supremacy. For example, where white body supremacy demands perfection and immutability, cultures of dialogue do not require participants to be blameless and acknowledge that people are capable of change, particularly through the transformative processes of "pain and conflict."[39] Where white body supremacy shuns vulnerability and intimacy by maintaining superficiality, cultures of dialogue move beyond "good manners that mask reality" in order to "speak from the stark and clear truth," helping participants to "cultivate penitential memory" that "can accept the past in order not to cloud the future with their own regrets, problems and plans."[40] Francis insists that dialogue is different from ideological debate and even conversation, and as such can move us beyond the race relations framework for understanding racial justice. For example, more than mere "conversations about racism," Francis proposes cultures of dialogue that require a far more rigorous commitment to creating "processes of encounter" that " build a people that can accept differences."[41] "Integrating differences is a much more difficult and slow process" than "superficial and fragile" arrangements that "keep freedom and differences in check with cleverness and a few resources" or "[ignore] social demands or [quell] disturbances."[42] In this way, cultures of dialogue create social peace, which is different from the mere absence of racial prejudice or even of interpersonal racism.

To that end, Francis encourages us to consider collective discernment or communal wondering as a second step in the praxis of Catholic social thought where racial justice is concerned. In fact, he implicitly deemphasizes judging, which can reinscribe righteous isolated consciences. "Ideas are debated," he says in *Let Us Dream*, but "reality is discerned."[43] Discernment protects us against fundamentalism, which Francis claims closes us off and shuts us down, "shelter[ing] people from destabilizing situations in exchange for a kind of existential quietism" and fueling an anxiety that needs certainty.[44] Discernment opens us up to greater understanding. "Discerning what is and what is not of God," Francis says, "we begin to see where and how to act. When we find God's mercy is waiting to overflow, we can open the gates and work with all people of goodwill to bring out the necessary changes."[45]

We can learn from Francis's modeling of what wonder looks like: get curious, draw close, risk ceding control to another, listen with the heart and not simply the head. Olga Segura implicitly recommends that the US bishops do some wondering in order to address racism within the Church: "to change our Church, there must be ongoing dialogue between bishops and Black Americans."[46] To her mind, the bishops need to listen to "Black women and men who are leading the efforts toward a more liberated and Christ-like world."[47] Francis implicitly endorses this approach through his prioritizing a relational role for local bishops, particularly in a polarized political and ecclesial context. "What interests me is the relationship of the bishop with the people, which is sacramental," he said in response to a question from the editorial staff of *America* about the polarizing impact of the US Conference of Catholic Bishops' prioritizing antiabortion policies above other moral issues: "Obviously, each bishop must seek fraternity with the other bishops, that is important. But what is essential is the relationship with his people."[48] Bishop Mark Seitz of El Paso offers an example of insight and courage that comes from privileging that sacramental relationship between bishops and the faithful. He incarnates much of Francis's own praxis in his pastoral letter "Night Will Be No More," written in the wake of a 2019 mass shooting that killed twenty-two in a Walmart in his diocese. Seitz starts with prayer and "speaking with the People of God in the Church of El Paso," names "racism and white supremacy" as the cause of "evil" that killed the people of his flock, and then indicates the need for a communal response: "Together we are called to discern the new paths of justice and mercy required of us and to rediscover our reasons for hope."[49]

Ultimately, wonder is expression of humility and openness to learn, something that Segura demands of all white people: "start by learning from me and the women who shaped me, including the Black women who have taught a generation of young Catholics how to think, learn and fight for the most marginalized people in our communities."[50] Karen Teel offers pedagogical recommendations, informed by womanist understandings of racism, for practicing wonder in all kinds of teaching and learning contexts. We can find many of them in Francis's own witness: stay mindful to our contexts, resist the idea of a racial neutrality; perform rather than preach or trade in propaganda; leave outcomes of learning open; avoid getting derailed by discomfort; remember, especially for white people, our limitations.[51]

INTEGRATING: FRANCIS AND BELONGING

In some ways, Francis echoes the long-standing refrain of the US bishops that racism is ultimately a matter individual hearts in need of conversion. After all, from the midst of the global COVID-19 pandemic, he himself noted that polarization, which is crippling the moral imagination of so many in our species, is "born of the heart."[52] And yet, Francis also recognizes that resolving racial inequity cannot simply remain in the realm of the personal and interpersonal. The point of any conversion experience is to compel us to move beyond ourselves and into missionary discipleship, which is characterized by a deep sense of interdependent belonging to others and the planet. To that end, he implicitly models for us that becoming antiracist is an ongoing process of internal transformation and collective action that continuously forms us for belonging. "Just as what separates me from my brother and sister is my (and their) spirit of self-sufficiency and superiority, so what unites us in our shared insufficiency, our mutual dependence on God and each other," he explains. "We are no longer rivals, but members of the same family.... We do not think the same, but we are part of the same Body moving together."[53] Abiding with our neighbors in this way has the potential to "decenter" and reveal ways toward mutual belonging that our captive imaginations, to use Barndt's phrase for the sin of racism, cannot conjure.[54]

Ultimately, as he did in *Laudato si'*, Francis invites us to shift our focus toward culture, both to properly diagnose what is going on and to implement solutions we might create *together*. What he says about the ecological crisis holds true for the racial one: "There needs to be a distinctive way of looking at things, a way of thinking, policies, an educational programme, a lifestyle and a spirituality which together generate resistance to the assault of the technocratic paradigm," or in this case the white supremacist paradigm.[55] This effort is simultaneously deeply personal and urgently collective. "Social problems must be addressed by community networks and not simply by the sum of individual good deeds."[56]

Francis has explicitly named the work of those engaged in social movements as offering directions in which we could move toward racial justice. While he decried violent protest after the Floyd killing as "self-destructive" and "self-defeating," he did not discourage protests against injustice. More than a year later, in an address to the World Gathering of Popular Movements, Francis in fact named those engaged in the protests as "collective Samaritans," in light of the fact that "this movement did not pass by on the other side of the road when it saw the injury to human dignity caused by an abuse of power."[57] Francis calls us into this work by cultivating shared senses of urgency and care, rather than guilt or shame. The care generates a sense of belonging to each other and shared responsibility while guilt often catalyzes charity that can reinforce already racialized boundaries.

Francis also recognizes that power is not necessarily something to be avoided. In fact, it can and should be claimed when done in deep relationship with others, especially those from the centers of power in our society and especially in our Church. It is worth wondering if Francis's invitation for lay people to become protagonists in the Church through the unfolding Synod on Communion, Participation, and Mission is fundamentally an attempt to resist "power over" cultures by cultivating cultures of encounter, dialogue, and communal discernment instead. In his homily to open the synod in October 2021, Francis notes that participating in synod "means discovering with amazement that the Holy Spirit always surprises us, to suggest fresh paths and new ways of speaking. It is a slow and perhaps tiring exercise, this learning to listen to one another—bishops, priests, religious, and laity, all the baptized—and to avoid artificial and shallow and prepackaged responses." A critical task is to "not soundproof our hearts" and "not remain barricaded in our certainties."[58]

As a global ecclesial movement characterized by encounter, active listening, dialogue, and communal discernment, the "Synod on Synodality" has the potential to affirm people wounded by racism and to privilege their wisdom for healing and reconstructing ecclesial structures and cultures. At diocesan, national, and global levels, the synod process has created opportunities for dialogical encounters and, given what the people of God around the world shared with each other, it highlighted racism within the world—and the Church—as in need of transformation through new cultures of dialogical encounter. In their national synthesis report, the US bishops cite a report from the New England region of the United States: "The sinfulness of racism fueled by events in our country in recent years must also remain an ever-present concern and be acknowledged by our Church. As we do so, we must continue to listen. Providing forums for conversations on race, immigration, and loving openness to others is critical in allowing individuals to be heard and understood."[59] "The wounds of the Church are intimately connected to those of the world," states the global synthesis document, "Enlarge the Space in Your Tent." "The reports speak of the challenges of tribalism, sectarianism, racism, poverty, and gender inequality within the life of the Church, as well as the world."[60] The kind of protagonism—or exercise of collective power anchored in dialogue and oriented toward those on the margins—required to become a synodal Church might also help us in becoming an antiracist one in the process. The conspiring—breathing together—that synodality is calling forth can form us for the hard personal and structural work of racial justice: reconciliation and reparations.

Finally, Francis orients us toward what he calls the "horizon of possibility," which is part of his very definition of fraternity, our central "organizing principle" to combat individualism: "a sense of belonging to each other and working together against a shared horizon of possibility."[61] Organizers do not underestimate the creative freedom that comes with even the possibility of a possibility. Possibility keeps people motivated, connected, hopeful, awake, committed. "If we wake up, we are in a place where we can create so much history and so much change," says the antiracist teacher, activist, and organizer adrienne maree brown. "Everything is falling apart, but also, new things are possible. . . . And we can be mindful about that. That's exciting."[62] Francis practically echoes her. "This is what makes for the excitement and drama of human history, in which freedom, growth, salvation and love can blossom, or lead towards decadence and mutual destruction," he notes in *Laudato si'*. "The Spirit of God has filled the universe with possibilities and therefore, from the very heart of things, something new can always emerge."[63] In a way that calls for grassroots responses that flow around the obstacles often presented by those at the tops of our racial hierarchies, Francis urges persistence in a mature faith that works towards the justice in which it hopes. "We should not expect everything from those who govern us, for that would be childish," he says in *Fratelli tutti*. "We have the space we need for co-responsibility in creating and putting into place new processes and changes. Let us take an active part in renewing and supporting our troubled societies."[64]

POSSIBILITIES FOR GROWTH

Francis's journey in and toward racial justice, like that of most of the work of antiracism, is still emerging. As such, there are places where scholars and activists are deepening and refashioning his witness to increase its efficacy in our only increasingly racialized contexts. For example, I have been curious about the dynamics of racism in Jorge Borgolio's story, given that he is the son of Italian immigrants to Argentina, a country with its own painful racial caste system.[65] Segura encourages a more accurate historical consciousness in her discussion of ways in which the Catholic social tradition's critique of capitalism, including Francis's own critique, fails to acknowledge racial capitalism.[66] Likewise, there is work to be done to bring an intersectional awareness to Francis's framework. Just as feminist theologians expressed concern about the lack of awareness of patriarchy and misogyny in *Laudato si'*, primarily in the encyclical's insufficient acknowledgment of how climate change disproportionately burdens women and its lack of recognition of women leading efforts for climate justice at local and international levels, there is room to explore the emerging concept of "misogynoir" in Francis's approach to racism.[67]

In addition, the necessarily choreographed nature of Francis's encounters always opens him up to the danger of performance or moral signaling when attempting to encounter people closest to pain, which can preclude the kind of decentering that is necessary to imagine new ways forward and can give rise to a lack of specificity in what still needs to come next. Reactions to his 2022 "Penitential Pilgrimage" to Canada to meet with survivors of Catholic-run residential schools note as much.[68] One cannot help but wonder if his behind-the-scenes support of Bishop Seitz in the midst of the racial tumult in the United States in the summer of 2020 was not an effective way to avoid a spectacle while using his power to support a brother bishop in claiming his own power.[69] But certainly, Francis's own warnings against superficiality, especially in the context of digital encounters, suggest that he may be attuned to this liability in encounters across the color line.[70]

That said, if not paired with meaningful action, all statements and bodily encounters run the risk of being merely performative and suggesting that statements are all that are required of Catholics to engage in the work of antiracism. Francis could better support the handful of US bishops who are publicly committed to racial justice by taking concrete action steps of his own. For example, Douglas Cremer encourages Francis and his fellow bishops to develop a theological anthropology of "integral humanism" that rejects the very idea of "race," given that it was and continues to be the primary tool by which racism functions, and that names racism as among the primary threats to human dignity.[71] Given the way in which race was a tool of the colonialism that the Church at best colluded with and at worst catalyzed in the name of evangelization, some suggest an encyclical on racism is not unwarranted.[72] Follow-through on the terms of those closest to the pain is also critical. Doing so can illuminate the limits of Catholic social teaching in some of the particularly neuralgic areas of racism in the United States. Moreover, following the lead of those closest to the pain of racism in the United States calls into question Francis's recommendation that we embrace the "contraposition" in conflict in order to tap a creative tension that can open us to new ways forward by "[preserving] what is good and valid in both in a new perspective."[73] A "good people on both sides" strategy will not work in light of the violent history of white supremacy in the US context.

CONCLUSION

"Racism is an intolerable sin against God," Francis said in 2022 to the editors of *America* in answer to a question about the challenges facing Black Catholics in the United States. "The Church, the pastors and lay people must continue fighting to eradicate it and for a more just world." Again, we see a pope who does not hesitate to name racism as a sin, to link its removal to justice, and to place responsibility for this effort on all the People of God. In that same interview, he suggests that "a mature pastoral development" as a possible response—"be it of the bishops or of the laity."[74] Francis's own name, wonder, and integrative praxis provide a method we might employ in order to become an antiracist Church committed to racial justice in a time of reckoning.

NOTES

1. Gerard O'Connell, "Pope Francis on the Death of George Floyd: We Cannot Tolerate Racism and Claim to Defend Life," *America*, June 3, 2020, www.americamagazine.org/faith/2020/06/03/pope-francis-death-george-floyd-we-cannot-tolerate-racism-and-claim-defend-life?gclid=CjwKCAiAqaWdBhAvEiwAGAQltr5JU5rXxu5nDtkH_ISwk5Q4AUQkfWtSt0kytNLpdB8adJDLtavPcBoCsKcQAvD_BwE.
2. US Conference of Catholic Bishops, "Statement of US Bishops Chairmen in Wake of George Floyd's Death and National Protests," May 29, 2020, www.usccb.org/news/2020/statement-us-bishop-chairmen-wake-death-george-floyd-and-national-protests.
3. I propose the subtle distinctions between antiracism and racial justice. I see antiracism as an evolving internal disposition, which, echoing Ibram Kendi's definition in *How to Be an Anti-Racist* (New York: One World, 2019), refuses to accept the racist idea that there is something wrong with Black people. Racial justice, conversely, is the collective work to redress systems and cultures that perpetuate this idea, by implementing and, in some cases, enlarging resources for social change in secular and faith-based frameworks. For a bibliography of Catholic sources on both, see College Theology Society, "Resources for Anti-Racism in Theological Education," www.collegetheology.org/CTS-compiled-Resources-For-Anti-Racism-in-Theological-Education; and a similar curation: Catholic Theological Ethics in the World Church, "Resources for Countering White Supremacy and Racism," https://catholicethics.com/resources/publications-by-topic/countering-racism/. Karen Teel offers a comprehensive overview of what has been done in the still predominantly white Catholic academy on white supremacy, even as she names the work to be done: Karen Teel, "Can We Hear Him Now? James Cone's Enduring Challenge to White Theologians," *Theological Studies* 81, no. 3 (September 2020): 582–604. See also the annotated overview by Bryan Massingale, "Has the Silence Been Broken? Catholic Theological Ethics and Racial Justice," *Theological Studies* 75, no. 1 (March 2014): 133–55.
4. See Olga Segura's assessment of a subsequent summer 2020 statement from three of the US bishops on police reform: Olga Segura, *Birth of a Movement: Black Lives Matter and the Church* (Maryknoll, NY: Orbis Books, 2021), 45–52. For an interpretation of the Guadalupian narrative with an eye for building a Church oriented toward encounter, dialogue, and collective discernment, see "An Intercontinental Synodal Encounter," prepared by Discerning Deacons and the Women and Ministeriality Thematic Core Group of the Ecclesial Conference of the Amazon, December 12, 2022, https://discerningdeacons.org/pilgrimage-2022/.
5. See the full text of Francis's July 25, 2022, apology in *America Magazine*, July 25, 2022, www.americamagazine.org/faith/2022/07/25/pope-francis-apology-canada-243411.
6. See Deborah Castellano Lubov, "First Dalit Cardinal: My Mission, Help as Many Poor Children as Possible," *Vatican News*, June 8, 2022, www.vaticannews.va/en/church/news/2022-06/dalit-india-consistory-cardinal-anthony-poola-interview.html.
7. Francis and Austen Iverleigh, *Let Us Dream: The Path to a Better Future* (New York: Simon & Schuster, 2020), 27–30.
8. Bryan Massingale, *Racial Justice and the Catholic Church* (Maryknoll, NY: Orbis Books, 2010), 100.
9. Francis, *Fratelli tutti*, no. 97.
10. Francis, no. 20.

11. Francis, no. 13.
12. Francis and Iverleigh, *Let Us Dream*, 69.
13. Francis and Iverleigh, 46; Francis, *Laudato si'*, no. 108.
14. Massingale, *Racial Justice*, 90.
15. Francis, *Fratelli tutti*, no. 27.
16. Francis, *The Church of Mercy* (Chicago: Loyola University Press, 2014), 19.
17. George Yancy, *Black Bodies, White Gazes: The Continuing Significance of Race in America* (Lanham, MD: Rowman & Littlefield, 2017), 7.
18. James Baldwin, "Letter from a Region in My Mind," *New Yorker*, November 9, 1962, www.newyorker.com/magazine/1962/11/17/letter-from-a-region-in-my-mind.
19. Francis and Iverleigh, *Let Us Dream*, 69.
20. Francis and Iverleigh.
21. Massingale, "Has the Silence Been Broken?"
22. Robin DiAngelo, *White Fragility: Why It's So Hard for White People to Talk about Racism* (Boston: Beacon Press, 2018).
23. Francis and Iverleigh, *Let Us Dream*, 76.
24. Francis, *Fratelli tutti*, no. 97.
25. Elijah Anderson, *Black in White Space: The Enduring Impact of Color in Everyday Life* (Chicago: University of Chicago Press, 2022).
26. Francis, *Fratelli tutti*, no. 97.
27. Francis.
28. Massingale, *Racial Justice*, 75–78.
29. Francis, *Laudato si'*, no. 11.
30. Francis.
31. Francis, "Visit to Detainees at Curran Fromhold Correctional Facility," September 27, 2015.
32. See Michelle Alexander, *The New Jim Crow: Mass Incarceration in an Age of Colorblindness* (New York: New Press, 2012); and Bryan Stevenson, *Just Mercy: A Story of Justice and Redemption* (New York: One World, 2015).
33. Francis, "Visit to Detainees."
34. Joseph Barndt, *Becoming an Anti-Racist Church: Journeying Toward Wholeness* (Minneapolis: Fortress Press, 2011), 108–9.
35. Francis, *Laudato si'*, no. 49.
36. Francis and Iverleigh, *Let Us Dream*, 80.
37. Francis and Iverleigh, 75.
38. Francis and Iverleigh, 80.
39. *Fratelli tutti*, nos. 217, 226.
40. Francis, no. 226.
41. Francis, no 217.
42. Francis, no. 217.
43. Francis and Iverleigh, *Let Us Dream*, 54.
44. Francis and Iverleigh, 55.
45. Francis and Iverleigh, 61.
46. Segura, *Birth*, 79–80.
47. Segura, 80.
48. Matt Malone, Sam Sawyer, Kerry Weber, Gerard O'Connell, and Gloria Purvis, "Exclusive: Pope Francis Discusses Ukraine, US Bishops and More," *America*, November 28, 2022, www.americamagazine.org/faith/2022/11/28/pope-francis-interview-america-244225.

49. Mark J. Seitz, "Night Will Be No More," August 3, 2019, www.hopeborder.org/nightwillbenomore-eng.
50. Segura, *Birth*, 22.
51. Karen Teel, "Getting Out of the Left Lane: The Possibility of White Antiracist Pedagogy," *Teaching Theology and Religion* 17, no. 1 (January 2014): 3–26.
52. Francis and Iverleigh, *Let Us Dream*, 77.
53. Francis and Iverleigh, 75.
54. Francis and Iverleigh, 137.
55. Francis, *Laudato si'*, no. 111.
56. Francis, no. 219.
57. Nate Turner, "In Conference Address Pope Francis praises George Floyd Protesters as 'Collective Samaritans,'" *Black Catholic Messenger*, October 17, 2021, www.blackcatholicmessenger.com/pope-francis-george-floyd-wmpm/; see also "Pope to Popular Movements: You Create Hope and Forge Unity," *Vatican News*, October 16, 2021, www.vaticannews.va/en/pope/news/2021-10/pope-popular-movements-poets-solidarity-subsidiarity-hope.html.
58. Francis, "Opening of the Synodal Path," October 10, 2021, www.vatican.va/content/francesco/en/homilies/2021/documents/20211010-omelia-sinodo-vescovi.html.
59. US Conference of Catholic Bishops, "National Synthesis of the People of God in the United States of America for the Diocesan Phase of the 2021–2023 Synod," 9, www.usccb.org/resources/US%20National%20Synthesis%202021-2023%20Synod.pdf.
60. "Enlarge the Space in Your Tent," document for the Continental Stage of the Global Synod, no. 44, www.synod.va/content/dam/synod/common/phases/continental-stage/dcs/Documento-Tappa-Continentale-EN.pdf.
61. Francis and Iverleigh, *Let Us Dream*, 68.
62. adrienne maree brown, "We are in a Time of New Suns," *OnBeing* podcast, June 23, 2022, https://onbeing.org/programs/adrienne-maree-brown-we-are-in-a-time-of-new-suns/.
63. Francis, *Laudato si'*, nos. 79–80.
64. Francis, *Fratelli tutti*, no. 77.
65. Maureen O'Connell, "Taking on the 'Smell of the Sheep': Racial Justice in the Missionary Key of *Evangelii Gaudium*," in *Pope Francis and the Future of Catholicism: Evangelli Gaudium and the Papal Agenda*, ed. Gerald Manion (New York: Cambridge University Press), 143–61.
66. Segura, *Birth*, 61.
67. For feminist critiques of *Laudato si'*, see Lisa Sowle Cahill, "Social Justice and the Common Good: Improving the Catholic Social teaching Framework," in *Ethical Challenges in Global Public Health: Climate Change, Pollution, and the Health of the Poor*, ed. Philip Landrigan and Andrea Vicini, Global Theological Ethics 1 (Eugene, OR: Pickwick Publications, by Wipf and Stock, 2021), 106–17, at 113–14. For more on misogynoir, see Moya Bailey, *Misogynoir Transformed: Black Women's Digital Resistance* (New York: New York University Press, 2021).
68. Reactions to the Penitential Pilgrimage note lack of specificity—about the sexual abuse of children; about deaths; about the sterilization of women; about other Catholic institutions beyond schools where this happened, such as hospitals; and about plans for healing that incorporate reparations. See, e.g., Charnel Anderson, "'The Real Work Begins Now': Three Indigenous Leaders on the Pope's Apology," *TVO Today*, July 27, 2022, www.tvo.org/article/the-real-work-begins-now-three-indigenous-leaders-on-the-popes-apology?gclid=Cj0KCQjwrs2XBhDjARIsAHVymmQM4km-fqVQ7u5_EgSKjcc8-ry_bCgW4WbBfrjAYeGpc7-k5ZfRkZ9EaAjBvEALw_wcB.

69. Catholic News Agency, "Pope Called El Paso Bishop After Prayerful Demonstration," June 4, 2020, www.catholicnewsagency.com/news/44742/pope-francis-called-el-paso-bishop-after-prayerful-demonstration.
70. See Francis, *Fratelli tutti*, no. 43: "[Digital campaigns] lack the physical gestures, facial expressions, moments of silence, body language and even the smells, the trembling of hands, the blushes and perspiration that speak to us and are a part of human communication. Digital relationships, which do not demand the slow and gradual cultivation of friendships, stable interaction or the building of a consensus that matures over time, have the appearance of sociability."
71. Douglas Cremer, "Toward an Anti-Racist Theology: American Racism and Catholic Social Thought," MA thesis, Loyola Marymount University, Spring 2020, 48–50.
72. Cremer, 50. See also Alex Mikulich, *Unlearning White Supremacy: A Spiritual of Racial Liberation* (Maryknoll, NY: Orbis Books, 2022).
73. Francis, *Laudato si'*, no. 80.
74. Malone et al., "Exclusive."

9

THE TWILIGHT OF DISSENT
Pope Francis and LGBTQ Persons and Morality

Bryan N. Massingale

Many on the "left" criticize Pope Francis for not changing official teaching on sexual morality in general, and on LGBTQ issues in particular. This chapter examines how something more subtle, but no less significant, has occurred in his papacy, namely, a shifting of alternate proposals on sexual morality out of the category of "dissent"—a paradigm that has dominated Catholic moral discourse for the past forty-plus years. Pope Francis has allowed, through the encouragement of *parrhesia,* or bold and forthright discourse in the Church and even among the bishops, the magisterium's plurality on issues of sexual morality to emerge. It is now obvious that "dissenting" opinions are no longer confined to "disloyal" or "unorthodox" theologians. Rather, so-called dissenting opinions are now found even among the official teachers (e.g., the Church's bishops). That the official teachers are allowed and encouraged to voice and adopt alternative theological views and pastoral approaches concerning LGBTQ Catholics means that these can no longer be considered "dissenting." This constitutes a true doctrinal development.

Thus, this chapter argues that Pope Francis's actions and the developments of the synods that he has convened now encourage, perhaps unwittingly, a renewed appreciation for the tradition of probabilism for contemporary moral reflection. We are in a situation where ethical reflections on LGBTQ issues that differ from a previous magisterial consensus are now solidly "probable," that is, are seriously legitimate guides for conscience formation and moral action. This constitutes a real doctrinal development, and perhaps heralds an approach to ethical discourse better suited to a synodal Church.

POPE FRANCIS AND INTIMATIONS OF A DIFFERENT APPROACH

To appreciate the major shifts and tensions that mark Pope Francis's approach to LGBTQ persons and the Synods of Bishops,[1] we must recall the previous state of Catholic teaching on homosexual persons as it has developed since the 1980s.[2] Same-sex behaviors (usually left unspecified) are judged to be an objective intrinsic evil that cannot be made morally right under any circumstance; that is, they are presented as always morally wrong, although the individual's subjective culpability is to be judged with prudence. Moreover, unlike heterosexuality, homosexuality is not considered a true "sexual orientation." Rather, it is spoken of as an "inclination," a "condition," or a "tendency," which, because it orders a person to intrinsically moral evil acts, is judged to be an "objective disorder."[3] This does not mean that homosexual persons are incapable of moral rectitude outside their sexual activities; their sexual condition "does not mean that homosexual persons are not often generous and giving of themselves." Yet, "when they engage in homosexual activity, they confirm within themselves a disordered sexual inclination which is essentially self-indulgent."[4]

This moral assessment of same-sex *behaviors* has decisively conditioned the official response to gay and lesbian *persons* and social justice concerns in the Catholic Church. For example, the official documents speak of the human dignity of homosexual persons. They are to be welcomed sensitively and compassionately. (Note the third person address. With very few exceptions, magisterial documents speak *about* homosexual persons, but rarely *to* them or *with* them). Yet this dignity is highly qualified and conditional. All "unjust discrimination" against homosexual persons is condemned. But this phrasing allows for "just" or legitimate forms of discrimination. Indeed, it is explicit teaching that discrimination in the areas of housing, teaching, coaching, adoption or foster care, and military service is not only justifiable but indeed is at times mandatory.[5] This ostensibly is required to protect the unique status of heterosexual marital and familial love.[6]

Furthermore, "current" magisterial teaching, at least up until 2013, not only viewed homosexual *sex* as unconditionally morally illegitimate. It also judged homosexual *persons* as being civilly unequal, spiritually hobbled, and psychologically damaged. One is left with the impression that these are members of an unfortunate group of people with a tragic affliction. Never is it stated or suggested that they have a positive contribution to make to Church and society. At best, they merit the faith community's compassion and sympathy. Yet in the name of "truth," they cannot be extended a welcome on the basis of their sexuality.[7]

The implicit yet operative Christian anthropology and soteriology at work here is problematic, to say the least. Gay and lesbian persons are saved—after all, they are counseled to link their sufferings to the cross of Christ—but not in or through their sexuality; not as gay and lesbian persons.[8] Consequently, insofar as they are advocates for social equality and ecclesial acceptance, their presence is viewed with suspicion and their existence is seen with hostility. In their efforts at civil justice and recognition, they are deemed a threatening menace—as a dangerous "contagion" that needs to be contained and combated, if not eradicated.[9]

Against this backdrop, much has been made of Pope Francis's groundbreaking intervention given during a 2013 press conference: "If someone is gay, and searches for the Lord and has goodwill, who am I to judge? We shouldn't marginalize people for this. They must be integrated into society."[10] With this single, seemingly spontaneous comment, Pope Francis appeared to move official Catholic discourse on homosexuality away from what one high-ranking prelate had called "a theology of contempt" for gay persons.[11] The significance of this intervention lies in the recognition that LGBTQ people exist as *persons*, and not as "walking sex acts" or embodiments of a hostile ideology. Consider also that in a 2013 interview, Francis delivered this statement: "When God looks at a gay *person*, does he endorse the existence of the *person* with love, or reject and condemn the *person*? We must always consider the *person*. Here we enter into the mystery of the human being. In life, God accompanies *persons*, and we must accompany them, starting from their situation" (emphasis added).[12] This declaration, with its multiple repetitions, reveals the "revolution" at the heart of Francis's changed engagement with LGBTQ concerns. He puts the focus on LGBTQ *persons*, not their sexual *behaviors* or *conduct*.

Although the most emphatic illustrations of this new emphasis have been seen in Francis's own pastoral outreach to the LGBTQ community, rather than in any doctrinal changes, the impact of this focus on persons is potentially far-reaching.[13] For example, if LGBTQ persons exist as persons, then they become included in the realm of justice. "Acts" or "behaviors" do not have rights, but human persons do. As persons, even as same-gender loving persons, the Church's social justice teaching includes and applies to gay and lesbian persons fully and unambiguously. The Catholic ethicist David Hollenbach declares that the fundamental understanding of Catholic social justice is summarized in the right to participation—that is, the right to be included as a fully respected and contributing member of one's society.[14] LGBTQ persons thus have the right to full participation in society—and in their Church.

The right to fully participate in and contribute to one's society, as an expression of one's human dignity and personhood, means first that LGBTQ persons have the right to gainful employment and immunity from arbitrary or wrongful employment termination; the right to have their marriages and families respected by others in society; the right to enjoy safety and immunity from violence when associating in public; the right to nondiscrimination in housing—in short, the full range of human rights, immunities, and responsibilities that are granted to and incumbent upon all other members of society, and that the Church has been hesitant to affirm in an unambiguous fashion for LGBTQ persons.

Second, personhood also entails full participation in the life of the Church, in accord with one's dignity as a fully baptized member, equally redeemed by Christ, and radically loved by God. This demands access to participate in the full sacramental life of the Church, including the sacrament of baptism for one's children and the sacraments of marriage and ordination for those who are called to these states of life.[15]

Thus, we see the far-reaching implications of Pope Francis's 2013 statements regarding sexual minority personhood, his public acknowledgment of "gay" persons as a part of the Church, and his explicit desire that they be "integrated into society" and included in the life of the Church.

THE SYNODS ON THE FAMILY AND YOUNG PEOPLE: THE END OF MAGISTERIAL CONSENSUS

These papal actions are significant. And even more significant for theological ethics concerning LGBTQ issues, I argue, are the developments that Francis has allowed and even encouraged in the global assemblies of the bishops under his pontificate. Key to these developments has been the pope's *fostering a culture of ecclesial parrhesia.*

In the Acts of the Apostles, frankness in announcing the Gospel becomes the "courage" given by the Holy Spirit in situations of persecution: "They were all filled with the Holy Spirit and continued to speak the word of God with boldness (*meta parrhesias*)" (Acts 4:31). Some describe *parrhesia* as "the supreme apostolic virtue."[16] Such courageous speech and forthright truth-telling has received renewed attention in the Catholic Church in the pontificate of Pope Francis. In his opening address to the 2014 Synod of Bishops, Francis exhorted the gathered leaders to speak forthrightly, candidly, and boldly, even on neuralgic issues involving sexual morality: "One general and basic condition is this: speaking honestly. Let no one say: 'I cannot say this . . .' It is necessary to say with *parrhesia* all that one feels."[17] Notably, Francis's encouragement of *parrhesia* should not be surprising, given his background as a Jesuit, for one practical component of the vow of obedience in the

Society of Jesus is an annual "account of conscience," in which an individual Jesuit meets with his superior to candidly discuss "all that is happening in his soul."[18] This process makes a personal form of *parrhesia* an essential feature of the regular functioning of the Society of Jesus, undoubtedly giving this first Jesuit pope a clear view of the benefits of frank conversation for governance and spiritual growth.

One major effect of magisterial *parrhesia* is that the official positions on LGBTQ persons enunciated until 2013 now are known to no longer reflect the consensus beliefs of the magisterium. Let us consider this development by turning to the synodal discussions.

The Synods on the Family

Midway through the 2014 Synod, a public report was issued that summarized the discussions up to that time. What generated copious news coverage was the positive appreciation expressed for gay and lesbian Catholics and their committed relationships:

> Homosexuals have gifts and qualities to offer to the Christian community: are we capable of welcoming these people, guaranteeing to them a fraternal space in our communities? Often they wish to encounter a Church that offers them a welcoming home. Are our communities capable of providing that, accepting and valuing their sexual orientation, without compromising Catholic doctrine on the family and matrimony? Without denying the moral problems connected to homosexual unions, it has to be noted that there are cases in which mutual aid to the point of sacrifice constitutes a precious support in the life of the partners.[19]

While not the most felicitous of phrasing, the attitude of welcome, and the onus placed upon the faith community to provide such welcome, is striking given previous official teaching and further develops the openings indicated by Pope Francis's 2013 remarks. Even more, the Church is exhorted to "accept and value their sexual orientation." This is remarkable, given that the prior teaching was that homosexuality was not an "orientation" but a "condition" or "tendency" that constitutes an "affliction." Finally, there is a positive value attributed to same-sex committed relationships. Even though they have unspecified "moral problems," there is an implicit yet clear break with the previous teaching that same-sex acts are an "intrinsic evil," that is, behavior that has no conceivable justification regardless of the circumstances. For if the behaviors in such relationships provide "precious support" to the "partners," how can it follow that such sexual behaviors have no possible ethical justification (i.e., are intrinsically evil)? Rather, this midterm report maintains that such relationships can and ought to be received as occasions of grace.

This intervention received considerable pushback and impassioned opposition from more traditionally inclined participants, leading to the release of a new translation on the Vatican website that downplayed the Church's obligations to welcome LGBTQ persons and avoided the term "partner" (presumably to guard against recognizing that form of partnership as a kind of committed relationship analogous to heterosexual marriage).[20] Not coincidentally, the final document of the 2014 Synod also contained none of the more positive language found in the midterm report. Homosexual persons are treated in a section revealingly titled "Pastoral Care for Persons with Homosexual Tendencies," which emphasizes "pastoral attention . . . in accordance with Church teaching" and explicitly reiterated, "There are absolutely no grounds for considering homosexual unions to be in any way similar or even remotely analogous to God's plan for marriage and family."[21] The document thus includes a vigorous reassertion of the traditional moral doctrine, as well as a strong assertion that any outreach to those with "homosexual tendencies" is a pastoral move only that must not even appear to compromise traditional teachings on homosexual activity, the homosexual inclination, or heterosexual marriage. Gone is any suggestion that "homosexual unions" have even a "remote" positive significance or value.

Yet it is noteworthy that these paragraphs (as well as those dealing with the reception of Communion for the divorced and remarried) did not receive the two-thirds majority usually required for inclusion into a final synodal document. Many synod participants did not endorse these paragraphs, for they did not go far enough in developing new directions or perspectives. These paragraphs were included only at the insistence of Pope Francis, respecting his desire for total transparency in the synod's deliberations.[22]

Thus, the conservatives carried the day. Or did they? The fact that the issues of gay and lesbian persons, and the intimate committed loving bonds they form, generated such vigorous discussion and open disagreement over what was previously a closed issue indicates that the matter is far from settled. Indeed, the open discussions then and since the synod reveal deep tensions within the hierarchy over these matters. At the very least, the traditional teaching on same-sex morality does not reflect the "consensus" of the synod's participants and presumably of the global episcopate.

To put the matter theologically, the strong and forthright debates at the synod demonstrate that traditional magisterial teaching on these matters is no longer unqualifiedly "received," not only by many of the laity but also by a significant portion of the hierarchy. Of course, it is hardly "breaking news" that there is a rift or chasm between the official teachings on sexual morality and the convictions of the majority of Catholics, not only in the West but also globally. But the lasting significance of the synod may well lie in the fact that it gave bishops permission to engage in an already existing conversation and debate—a debate from which they had insulated and isolated themselves, and indeed one they had actively proscribed and condemned.[23]

The 2018 Synod on Youth and Young People

The lack of magisterial consensus concerning the traditional teaching on LGBTQ morality is also evident in the discussions at the Synod on Young People. For example, at the synod's conclusion, the gathered bishops reflected upon what they had experienced, including pleas from many young people for a more realistic sexual ethics that takes account of contemporary trends and expresses a greater acceptance of LGBTQ persons and their relationships. In their "Final Report," then, the prelates made this observation:

> *There are questions relating to the body, to affectivity and to sexuality that require a deeper anthropological, theological, and pastoral exploration, which should be done in the most appropriate way, whether on a global or local level . . .*
>
> Many Christian communities already offer journeys of accompaniment in faith for homosexual persons: the Synod recommends that such initiatives be supported. In these journeys, people are helped to read their own history; to adhere with freedom and responsibility to their baptismal calling; to recognize the desire to belong and contribute to the life of the community; to discern the best ways of realizing this. Thus, all young people, without exception, are helped to integrate the sexual dimension of their personality more and more fully, as they grow in the quality of their relationships and move towards the gift of self [emphasis added].[24]

This statement aroused great concern and unease among many in the Church, including from high-ranking and influential figures. Archbishop Charles Chaput, then the ordinary of the see of Philadelphia, was among those who realized that present in this call for deeper examination was an admission that the current teachings were somehow deficient or inadequate. Paraphrasing his concern: Why would you have to explore or examine teachings that are already clear and certain?

Others, including myself, agreed that this summons for deeper exploration clearly suggests that the synod reached a consensus that the current state of official Church teaching on human sexuality is, in fact, problematic. As I noted to Religion News Service at the time: "It is clear that the bishops know that something needs to change, but . . . it is equally clear that they are not sure "what that change would or should entail; that is, they are uncertain about what should be the new shape of Catholic teaching on sexuality."[25]

The pope's encouragement of *parrhesia* among the bishops revealed not only the divisions among them but also a consensus concerning the inadequacy of the "official" magisterial discourse on sexual morality in general and LGBTQ issues in particular.[26] The bishops recognized the need for a deeper engagement with new understandings of human sexuality. The current teachings are inadequate, yet the bishops are unsure about what such changes should be. We are living in an interim time, where previously closed issues are revealed to be far from settled.

The Controversy Over Blessing Same-Sex Unions

Finally, the fluidity in official discourse on same-sex morality and the lack of a consensus in the magisterium is evidenced in the reception of the Congregation for the Doctrine of the Faith's response to a question concerning the possibility of blessing same-sex couples in committed relationships. This is the significant passage in the explanatory note on that response:

> It is not licit to impart a blessing on relationships, or partnerships, even stable, that involve sexual activity outside of marriage (i.e., outside the indissoluble union of a man and a woman open in itself to the transmission of life), as is the case of the unions between persons of the same sex. The presence in such relationships of *positive elements*, which are in themselves to be *valued and appreciated*, cannot justify these relationships and render them legitimate objects of an ecclesial blessing, since the positive elements exist within the context of a union not ordered to the Creator's plan....
>
> The answer to the proposed dubium does not preclude the blessings given to individual persons with homosexual inclinations, who manifest the will to live in fidelity to the revealed plans of God as proposed by Church teaching. Rather, it declares illicit any form of blessing that tends to acknowledge their unions as such. The Church recalls that God Himself never ceases to bless each of His pilgrim children in this world, because for Him "we are more important to God than all of the sins that we can commit." But he does not and cannot bless sin [emphasis added].[27]

Three things are noteworthy about this passage. First, despite its negative conclusion, the Congregation for the Doctrine of the Faith acknowledges that same-sex unions have "positive elements" that must be "valued and appreciated." This is a significant and unprecedented statement of official recognition that same-sex relationships offer something of value to the persons. Second, despite this recognition, these relationships are judged to be sinful, that is, apart from the Creator's plan. Yet, how these two affirmations are reconciled or held together is not explained. If committed same-sex relationships have "positive elements," then it is difficult to see how they can be held to be "intrinsically evil" and totally without any moral legitimacy, as the 1986, 1991, and 2003 documents held. There is an inherent tension expressed in the discourse and thinking of the official arbiter of magisterial teaching.

Finally, the *parrhesia* encouraged by Pope Francis revealed that many bishops held a contrary opinion. For example, many German bishops not only encouraged their priests and pastoral ministers to bless same-sex couples but did so themselves. They also were highly critical of the reasoning of the Congregation for the Doctrine of the Faith, taking exception to the conclusion that stable and loving same-sex unions should be unqualifiedly dismissed as "sin." More recently, the Flemish bishops have issued a rite of liturgical blessing for same-sex couples, explicitly stating that they are acting in concert with the orientations given by Pope Francis himself.[28]

Summary

What can we conclude from this survey? The major conclusion is that the official teaching on same-sex morality, as enunciated in the *Catechism of the Catholic Church* and in the documents of the late twentieth and early twenty-first centuries, no longer reflects the consensus of the magisterium itself. During the pontificate of Pope Francis, with his encouragement of *parrhesia*, the official teaching has repeatedly failed to garner the support of two-thirds of the world's bishops in synodal gatherings. Moreover, the need for alternative positions on same-sex issues is now the effective consensus position. In addition, there is a growing recognition and gradual acknowledgment of grace in same-sex relationships, including a new acceptance that same-sex relationships have positive elements that contribute to the life of the partners, and even have a special witness to offer to the faith community. Finally, there is no consensus on what the new shape of magisterial teaching on LGBTQ issues should be. There is considerable division and plurality in the approaches and positions being advanced by various bishops and episcopal conferences on this matter. These are major developments in official moral teaching.

These developments need to be balanced by the frank acknowledgment of several contrary trends: the continued papal resistance to same-sex "marriage"; the Curia's refusal to engage "gender ideology" (or rather, the use of that imprecise phrase to indict efforts to more deeply rethink sexual and gender morality); the reissuance of a ban on gay men in seminaries; and most significantly, no change on the most neuralgic of issues, namely, the description of homosexuality as an "objective disorder." Francis's promotion of *parrhesia* allows these trends to persist, leaving a latent potential for real harm, even as the other trends noted above bring some degree of hope.

The major shift is that the more positive developments are not only "dissenting" but are *also* descriptive of official approaches to same-sex morality and persons. Matters considered previously closed are now seen as no longer "settled." There is a real possibility that "dissenting" opinions—for which theologians were censured—may become the official positions.[29] Alternatively, we may be moving to a new paradigm of a multiplicity or pluralism of official positions.

This leads to what I argue is the most significant development on LGBTQ issues under Pope Francis: the need for a retrieval and rehabilitation of the tradition of probabilism in Catholic ethical reflection and moral guidance.

FROM DISSENT TO PROBABILISM

In 1982, I wrote my master's in divinity thesis on "The Role of Dissent in the Life of the Church." This was a pressing issue for both the Church at large and theological ethicists in the aftermath of *Humanae vitae* and during the pontificates of John Paul II and Benedict XVI. Indeed, two giants in the field, Richard McCormick and Charles Curran, devoted significant scholarly energy to advocating the legitimacy of disagreement with noninfallibly taught teachings of the hierarchical magisterium.[30] I began by observing that dissent did not mark every contentious disagreement or opposition to magisterial teachings. I was careful (in line with McCormick and Curran) to distinguish dissent from "rebellion," disloyalty, or heresy. Rather, I insisted that dissent is characterized by respect for the official teachers and their office; aims to be constructive and productive; and flows from a concern for the Church's truth. In light of this, and after realizing that no standard or commonly accepted definition was in print, I offered this definition:

> Dissent in the Church means that a member of the Church disagrees with, takes exception to, or otherwise withholds or qualifies his or her assent to a noninfallible teaching or position of the Church, out of an informed conviction that the official teaching or position is lacking, inadequate, or erroneous, and maintains a different opinion or approach and seeks to establish its legitimacy to the authoritative teachers. This opposition is motivated by a loyalty and deep concern for the institution and tradition of the Church.[31]

What motivated such studies was the intellectual and pastoral need to let people know that the right to dissent "is rooted in our Catholic tradition of theology and practice," and thus the idea that "one may dissent from authoritative teaching in the Church and not be cut off from the Church is a responsible Catholic possibility."[32]

We are now in a very different place concerning sexual morality in general and same-sex morality in particular. The paradigm of "dissent" is neither adequate nor applicable. This is true not only because "dissenting" positions are present even among the official teachers, but most of all because the official sexual teachings no longer reflect a "consensus" of the magisterium itself. Whether acknowledged explicitly or not, real doubt characterizes the state of Catholic same-sex morality. The magisterium is in a practical, if undeclared, state of doubt. Yet people must live their lives while the faith community discerns its official posture on LGBTQ issues. This situation of doubt is precisely what the moral system known as probabilism was intended to address.

Space does not allow me to give a detailed presentation of the history of probabilism.[33] I grant that the term is infelicitous, for "probable" means something very different in English than its Latin cognate. Yet its insight is enduring, namely, that the magisterium cannot always have a definitive answer for every moral quandary that the faithful encounter. This is especially pressing when the faithful have to make decisions "in real time" on issues that are perhaps novel or new. The faithful cannot put their lives on hold until the magisterium has the time or wisdom to develop a definitive, binding teaching. Or to put this more positively, probabilism is crucial during the time when the magisterium is still developing insight into the mind of the Spirit and the consensus of the Church, whereby they can issue a teaching that can elicit assent because it is recognized as being reflective of the wisdom of the community, that is, the *consensus fidelium*.[34]

Given the rise of historical consciousness, the increasing recognition that we live in a global society; the reality of mass, indeed instant, communication; and the fact that sexuality—perhaps more than any other facet of human experience—is profoundly shaped by cultural experience; it is difficult to find sexual teachings that will be universally applicable in every situation for all time. The clarity and certainty of previous declarations of "intrinsic evil" in sexual matters will prove elusive.

Probabilism allows us to understand how, even in the midst of significant cultural change and ecclesial uncertainty, theologians and official teachers can put forth reasonable positions based on solid arguments that can serve as guides for moral reflection, analysis, decision-making, and action. Probabilism allows us to live with doubt, and to resist the temptation of premature closure. As well, it allows us to live without the rush to intraecclesial condemnations or ruptures of communion.

Julia Fleming expresses this masterfully: "Even when moral knowledge is incomplete, probabilism helps us to separate the reasonable from the unreasonable.... Without denying the possibility of eventual resolution, [probabilism] insists upon the value of provisional knowledge. These, it argues, are the reasonable conclusions, the reasonable courses of action, given what we know at the present time."[35]

Doubt need not be a negative reality in the life of the Church. To cite the "Majority Opinion" of the ill-fated yet prescient Pontifical Birth Control Commission: "Doubt and reconsideration are quite reasonable when proper reasons for doubt and reconsideration occur."[36]

In arguing for probabilism, I am not suggesting that the pope is a proportionalist—that is, that he is advocating for same-sex relationships as a permissible ontic or premoral evil that, though not ideal, is yet morally acceptable. I am saying that through the creation of forthright and courageous discourse in the Church, he has fostered an environment in which proportionalist arguments—and others as well—can be seen as reasonable positions and offered as responsible guides for moral discernment and action.[37]

Probabilism is also congruent with what it means to be a synodal Church, a faith community that "walks together" as it discerns the ways and summons of the Spirit. Probabilism presumes a community of responsible moral discourse, where people of goodwill offer their best analyses of the human situation and interpretations of the tradition, and submit these to open discussion. Probabilism is also consistent with the deep respect for conscience and individual discernment that is a hallmark of Pope Francis's moral theology.[38] It provides the faith community with a living laboratory, as people of goodwill adopt and live out various probable opinions as the basis for moral actions. The members of the community can then discern, based on their shared experiences, which of these lifestyles reflects the presence of the Spirit—the classic list given in Galatians 5—and thus merits becoming the normative stance and consensus view of the faithful. In the interim, the faithful need to live their lives, and there are responsible, reasonable positions that allow them to live lives of grace and fidelity, even as the community lives amid unresolved issues.

In short, previous *dissenting* positions are now—or can be—*probable* positions and, therefore, a legitimate basis for guiding Christian discernment and moral action. Rather than being a proportionalist, the pope has opened the door for a reappreciation of probabilism—which in turn opens the door to options (e.g., queer arguments) that are more far-reaching than a proportionalist such as Richard McCormick might allow.

This development means that theological ethicists need to recover a deeper appreciation for probabilism without the spurious casuistry that ultimately derailed it. At the least, we will need new terminology, such as "reasonable" or "solid" rather than "probable." We have resources in our tradition to help us understand what Pope Francis has unleashed in the Church and allow for more positive assessments of LGBTQ persons and their loving relationships and expressions of sexual identity. Probabilism allows us to understand both the novelty of Pope Francis's engagements with LGBTQ morality, especially as compared with those of his predecessors, and to appreciate his deep respect for our moral tradition. This is not so much a "revolution" but an evolution rooted in our tradition by retrieving something long underutilized.[39]

Notably, this uncertainty raises risks in two directions. First, some will fear a new relativism, as competing moral claims are permitted to coexist. Second, this very permission will also allow harmful attitudes toward LGBTQ persons to persist alongside more affirming probable opinions, a situation that can cause real damage to the LGBTQ community. The manualist tradition provides a potential response to both these risks through its notion of the *viri probati*, that is, those authorities of proven sound judgment whose views could be trusted as a basis for action. We have ways today of recognizing authorities whose opinions can be reliable bases for responsible ethical discernment and faithful moral action, such as identifying former presidents of learned Catholic societies, or winners of prestigious awards—people whose peers have recognized them as a *vir probatus* or *mulier probata*. In sum, probabilism is an avenue for understanding our new, perhaps uncomfortable and unusual, situation—what Pope Francis calls "a change of era"—as legibly "Catholic." Fleming once again says it best: "Probable opinion is not moral license. It is a tool for ensuring responsibility in the absence of ethical certainty."[40]

CONCLUSION

Bold and fearless speech regarding the lives, loves, trials, and faith of LGBTQ persons is an indispensable condition for the eradication of homophobia and transphobia in both Church and society. *Parrhesia* challenges the aura of unspeakability that for so long has veiled same-sex attractions and relationships, silencing those who bear the abuse and violence of society's stigma. Bold truth-telling is a condition for authentic doctrinal progress. As John Noonan has pointed out, changes in ethical doctrines are preceded by an empathic reception of and openness to new experience by the faith community.[41] A culture of *parrhesia* is a sine qua non for developing a genuine "culture of encounter" with sexual minorities that can lead to social transformations and ecclesial conversions. This, I believe, will be Pope Francis's signal and lasting contribution to Catholic ethical engagement with LGBTQ morality.

NOTES

1. This section incorporates insights that I developed at greater length in "Beyond 'Who Am I to Judge?' The *Sensus Fidelium*, LGBT Experience, and Truth-Telling in the Church," by Bryan N. Massingale, in *Learning from All the Faithful: A Contemporary Theology of the Sensus Fidei*, ed. Bradford E. Hinze and Peter C. Phan (Eugene, OR: Wipf and Stock, 2016), 170–83.
2. I use the term "homosexual persons" because it is the term used in most magisterial documents. The terminology, especially the avoidance and/or acceptance of the term "gay," is part of the shift outlined herein. Note also that the major documents do not speak extensively, if at all, about bisexual or trans persons. The preoccupation is with male same-sex behaviors and same-sex identities. The official teaching summarized here is found in the following documents: Congregation for the Doctrine of the Faith (CDF), "Letter to the Bishops of the Catholic Church on the Pastoral Care of Homosexual Persons," October 1, 1986, www.vatican.va/roman_curia/congregations/cfaith/documents/rc_con_cfaith_doc_19861001_ho mosexual-persons_en.html; CDF, "Some Considerations Concerning the Response to Legislative Proposals on Non-Discrimination of Homosexual Persons," July 24, 1992, www.vatican.va/roman_curia/congregations/cfaith/documents/rc_con_cfaith_doc_19920724_homosexual-persons_en.html; CDF, "Considerations Regarding Proposals to Give Legal Recognition to Unions between Homosexual Persons," July 31, 2003, www.vatican.va/roman_curia/congregations/cfaith/documents/rc_con_cfaith_doc_20030731_ho mosexual-unions_en.html; and Congregation for Catholic Education, "Instruction Concerning the Criteria for the Discernment of Vocations with Regard to Persons with Homosexual Tendencies in View of Their Admission to the Seminary and to Holy Orders," November 4, 2005, www.vatican.va/roman_curia/congregations/ccatheduc/documents/rc_con_ccatheduc_doc_20051 104_istruzione_en.html.
3. CDF, "Letter on Pastoral Care," no. 3. On the usage of "inclination" or "same-sex attraction," see US Conference of Catholic Bishops, Ministry to Persons with a Homosexual Inclination: Guidelines for Pastoral Care, 2006, www.usccb.org/about/doctrine/publications/upload/ministry-to-persons-of-homosexual-inclination.pdf.
4. CDF, "Letter on Pastoral Care," no. 7.
5. CDF, "Response to Legislative Proposals," nos. 11 and 12.
6. CDF, "Considerations," "foreword" and no. 15.
7. Congregation for Catholic Education, "Instruction," no. 2.
8. CDF, "Letter on Pastoral Care," no. 12.
9. CDF, "Considerations," no. 5.
10. Francis, "On Gay Priests, Pope Francis Asks, 'Who Am I to Judge?'" *New York Times*, July 29, 2013, www.nytimes.com/2013/07/30/world/europe/pope-francis-gay-priests.html.
11. Archbishop Emeritus Rembert G. Weakland, personal communication to the author, August 31, 2002: "On the gay issue, the level of fears is so high that the official teaching

of the church skates so very close to the edge of a new 'theology of contempt.' Why is it presupposed—and I can tell you from correspondence and some writings of late that it is—that gays have less sexual 'self-control' than heterosexuals and are thus dangerous?"

12. Antonio Spadaro, "A Big Heart Open to God: The Exclusive Interview with Pope Francis," *America*, September 30, 2013, 26.
13. E.g., Francis has publicly praised Jeannine Gramick, a pioneering advocate in Catholic LGBTQ ministry; restored "the power of the keys" to Father James Alison, a noted theologian who has publicly disagreed with magisterial teaching on same-sex morality; and praised the ministry of Father James Martin, SJ, who has championed greater inclusivity for LGBTQ Catholics. See Jim McDermott, "Pope Francis Praises Sr. Jeannine Gramick's 50 Years of LGBT Ministry in Handwritten Letter," *America*, January 7, 2022, www.americamagazine.org/faith/2022/01/07/sister-jeanine-gramick-letter-pope-francis-242157; James Alison, "This Is Pope Francis Calling . . . ," *The Tablet*, September 26, 2019, www.thetablet.co.uk/features/2/16788/-this-is-pope-francis-calling-; and Madeleine Davison, "Pope Praises James Martin's Work with LGBT Catholics: Reflects 'Closeness of God,'" *National Catholic Reporter*, June 28, 2021, www.ncronline.org/news/pope-praises-james-martins-work-lgbt-catholics-reflects-closeness-god.
14. David Hollenbach, *Claims in Conflict: Retrieving and Renewing the Catholic Human Rights Tradition* (Mahwah, NJ: Paulist Press, 1979).
15. If gay and lesbian persons are as equally redeemed by Christ and radically loved by God as heterosexual persons, then the operative questions for the Church's discernment should be: If marriage—the lifelong, loving, covenantal commitment between two human beings—is a symbol of Christ's love for the Church, then why does same-sex covenantal love not participate in or manifest Christ's love for God's people? Why cannot a gay person be an *alter Christus*—that is, "another Christ"—to and for the faith community, a mediator of Christ's grace for God's people?
16. Enrico Cattaneo, "Parrhesia: Freedom of Speech in Early Christianity," *La Civilta Catolica* 1707, October 2017, https://laciviltacattolica.com/parrhesia-freedom-of-speech-in-early-christianity/.
17. Pope Francis, "Greeting of Pope Francis to the Synod Fathers," October 6, 2014, http://w2.vatican.va/content/francesco/en/speeches/2014/october/documents/papa-francesco_20141006_padri-sinodali.html.
18. "Obediency in the Life of the Society of Jesus," General Congregation 35—Decree 4, https://jesuits-eum.org/gc-decrees/obediency-society-of-jesus/.
19. Synod 14: Eleventh General Assembly—"Relatio post disceptationem" of the General Rapporteur, Card. Péter Erdő, 13.10.2014. nos. 50 and 52, http://en.radiovaticana.va/news/2014/10/13/synod_on_family_midterm_report_presented,_2015_synod_announ/1108442.
20. Elizabeth Dias, "Vatican Changes Draft Report Translation about Welcoming Gays," *Time*, October 16, 2014, https://time.com/3513071/vatican-synod-bishops-homosexuality/.
21. Third General Assembly of the Synod of Bishops, "The Pastoral Challenges of the Family in the Context of Evangelization: *Relatio Synodi*," October 18, 2014, no. 55, www.vatican.va/roman_curia/synod/documents/rc_synod_doc_20141018_relatio-synodi-familia_en.html#Pastoral_Attention_towards_Persons_with_Homosexual_Tendencies.
22. See "For Cardinal Baldisseri, Consensus at the Synod of Bishops Remains Important," Catholic News Agency / EWTN News, October 10, 2014, www.catholicnewsagency.com/news/for-cardinal-baldisseri-consensus-at-the-synod-of-bishops-remains-important-51492/.

23. This is a significant point that merits further discussion. In the synods on the family, Pope Francis brought the magisterium—the bishops—up to speed on conversations about sexuality that the rest of the church (the 99 percent) has been having for the past forty-five years and more, but from which the magisterium, for the most part, had either absented and insulated themselves or attempted to suppress, censor, and derail. During that time, the magisterium did its best to censor and silence theologians or scholars who advanced differing approaches to human sexuality and were indeed mandated to do so; cf. John Paul II, *Veritatis splendor*, 1993, nos. 110, 116. This makes Francis's encouragement of open discussions and debates at the 2014 and 2015 synods all the more remarkable—and difficult, since the majority of those participating were appointed to the episcopacy ostensibly because they possessed aptitudes for curbing such discussions, not facilitating or engaging in them.
24. "Final Document of the Synod of Bishops on Young People, Faith, and Vocational Discernment," October 27, 2018, no. 150, http://secretariat.synod.va/content/synod2018/en/fede-discernimento-vocazione/final-document-of-the-synod-of-bishops-on-young-people--faith-an.html.
25. This account of the synodal summons and the subsequent debate was reported by Paul O'Donnell, "A Vatican Opening on Sexuality Worries Conservatives—and Cheers Reformers," Religion News Service, October 30, 2018, https://religionnews.com/2018/10/30/a-vatican-opening-on-sexuality-worries-conservatives-and-cheers-reformers/.
26. Significantly, paragraph no. 150 received the number needed to reflect the two-thirds consensus but attracted the highest number of negative votes (sixty-five) as well. Thus, while there is an official consensus about the inadequacy of the current state of magisterial teaching, significant division among the prelates persists. See "Final Document of the Synod of Bishops on Young People."
27. Congregation for the Doctrine of the Faith, *"Responsum* of the Congregation for the Doctrine of the Faith to a *Dubium* Regarding the Blessing of Unions of Persons of the Same Sex," February 22, 2021, www.vatican.va/roman_curia/congregations/cfaith/documents/rc_con_cfaith_doc_20210222_responsum-dubium-unioni_en.html.
28. Michael J. O'Loughlin, "Belgian Bishops Create Prayer Liturgy for Same-Sex Couples," *America*, September 20, 2022, www.americamagazine.org/politics-society/2022/09/20/belgium-bishops-lgbt-blessing-243817.
29. Consider the CDF's censure of Margaret Farley for, among other things, her arguments in *Just Love* that mirror some current bishops' reflections on same-sex relationships. CDF, "Notification on the Book *Just Love: A Framework for Christian Sexual Ethics*, by Sr. Margaret A. Farley, RSM," March 30, 2012, www.vatican.va/roman_curia/congregations/cfaith/documents/rc_con_cfaith_doc_20120330_nota-farley_en.html.
30. E.g., see Charles E. Curran and Richard McCormick, eds., *Readings in Moral Theology No. 6: Dissent in the Church* (Mahwah, NJ: Paulist Press, 1988); Charles E. Curran and Robert E. Hunt, et.al, *Dissent In and For the Church: Theologians and Humanae Vitae* (New York: Sheed & Ward, 1969); and Charles E. Currran, *Faithful Dissent* (Kansas City: Sheed & Ward, 1986).
31. Bryan N. Massingale, "The Role of Dissent in the Life of the Church," MDiv. thesis, Saint Francis Seminary School of Pastoral Ministry, Milwaukee, 1982.
32. Richard Gula, "The Right to Private and Public Dissent from Specific Pronouncements of the Ordinary Magisterium," *Eglise et Theologie* 9 (1978): 321.
33. Two works that have informed my thinking on this are Julia Fleming, *Defending Probabilism: The Moral Theology of Juan Caramuel* (Washington, DC: Georgetown University

Press, 2006); and Eric Marcelo O. Genilo, *John Cuthbert Ford, SJ: Moral Theologian at the End of the Manualist Era* (Washington, DC: Georgetown University Press, 2007). See also Albert Jonsen and Stephen Toulmin, *The Abuse of Casuistry: A History of Moral Reasoning* (Berkeley: University of California Press, 1988); the discussion of probabilism by Henry Davis, *Moral and Pastoral Theology, Vol. 1: Principles*, 7th Edition (New York: Sheed & Ward, 1958); and the brief discussions of equiprobabilism, probabiliorism, and probabilism by James F. Childress and John MacQuarrie, eds., *The Westminster Dictionary of Christian Ethics* (Philadelphia: Westminster Press, 1986).
34. *Lumen gentium*, no. 12.
35. Fleming, *Defending Probabilism*, 144–45.
36. Quoted by Julie Clague, "Moral Theology and Doctrinal Change," in *Moral Theology for the 21st Century: Essays in Honor of Kevin T. Kelly* (New York: T&T Clark, 2008), 74.
37. Proportionalism grants too much to the tradition's view of the the questionable legitimacy of committed same-sex relationships. Under the aegis of proportionalism, one must see these as suspect, less than ideal concessions to human weakness for those unable to live out the ideal of heterosexual procreative marriage. That is indeed one solidly probable—that is, a well-reasoned and responsible—position. There are other views that take a more positive evaluation of same-sex loves that are also solid, responsible, and thus "probable."
38. Blase Cupich, "Pope Francis' Revolution of Mercy: *Amoris Laetitia* as a New Paradigm of Catholicity," *La Stampa*, February 9, 2018, www.lastampa.it/vatican-insider/en/2018/02/09/news/pope-francis-revolution-of-mercy-amoris-laetitia-as-a-new-paradigm-of-catholicity-1.33978121/.
39. Space does not allow for a more extended discussion of what would constitute a probable opinion in same-sex morality. The manualists offered detailed discussions of the distinctions between "intrinsic" probabilism (where the argument is considered respectable on the basis of the coherence of its reasoning) and "extrinsic" probabilism (where the argument is considered "actionable" on the strength of the number and quality of those authorities that endorsed it).
40. Fleming, *Defending Probabilism*, 142.
41. John T. Noonan, *A Church That Can and Cannot Change: The Development of Catholic Moral Teaching* (Notre Dame, IN: University of Notre Dame Press, 2005), 211–15.

10

THE WORK OF THE SPIRIT, OR MACHISMO WITH A SKIRT?
Feminism, Gender, and Pope Francis
Megan K. McCabe

When Jorge Bergoglio was elected to the papacy in 2013, he inherited decades of teaching on gender from his two most recent predecessors, John Paul II and Benedict XVI. Both were strong proponents of gender complementarity, which shaped their approaches to the role of women and LGBTQ issues in the Church. For them, complementarity implied a rigid causal relationship between biological sex assigned at birth and gender. In a kind of gender dualism, maleness implies masculinity and femaleness implies femininity. This line of reasoning helps to ground official Catholic teaching on women's leadership in the Church, including the ordination of women, and on same-sex relationships and trans and nonbinary gender identities. This context shapes but does not define the assessment of Pope Francis's own perspectives on gender, evident primarily through his statements on topics related to women, family life and parenting, and LGBTQ persons. As a result, his assessment includes a subtle shift, which has the potential to begin to move the Catholic Church in a new direction. On one hand, he directly upholds and endorses theologies of gender complementarity. On the other hand, his pastoral approach, attentive to the joy and suffering in lived experience, leads him to a softening of the gendered categories maintained by John Paul II and Benedict XVI. This subtle, though significant, shift on the topic of gender reflects Francis's broader pastoral approach, noted by Lisa Cahill in chapter 1 of this book, in which the pope engages with lived experience rather than prioritizing abstract ideals.

COMPLEMENTARITY ACCORDING TO JOHN PAUL II AND BENEDICT XVI

Francis's own remarks on gender and the role of women are interpreted against the backdrop of the magisterial teachings and statements on gender and sex offered during the papacies of John Paul II and Benedict XVI. On measure, not much of Francis's writings and statements are dedicated to the topic of gender. In response, particularly early in his papacy, many people read between the lines, in light of his predecessors' thought, to try to interpret Francis's approach to gender, sexuality, and the role of women in the Church.

Both John Paul II and Benedict XVI advocated for a strict understanding of gender complementarity to describe the role of women in the Church and society as well as to ground their papacies' approaches to sexual ethics. John Paul II emphasized the language of gender complementarity and the "feminine genius," working to establish it as the "norm for understanding the roles of women and men in the family, Church and society" in magisterial teaching.[1] In his view, the sexed body symbolizes and makes possible a being-for-the-other and a capacity for self-gift that is also realized in the gendered characteristics of masculinity and femininity. In *Mulieris dignitatem*, John Paul II's Apostolic Exhortation "On the Dignity and Vocation of Women," he defined femininity as the capacity for self-gift made possible in motherhood. Though parenthood is shared, it "is realized much more fully in the woman."[2] By modeling the "woman," singular, on the Virgin Mary, John Paul II links motherhood and virginity, concluding that those women who are not parents also possess a kind of spiritual motherhood.[3] As Mary Ann Hinsdale explains, "According to this Marian-centered anthropology, femaleness is characterized by receptivity and maternal nurturing, while maleness consists of initiation."[4]

As prefect of the Congregation for the Doctrine of the Faith before his own election to the papacy as Benedict XVI, Joseph Ratzinger echoed John Paul II's definition of the "feminine genius" as a distinctive capacity for the other.[5] It is this feminine genius that makes a unique contribution not only to the family but also to society. He maintained that the balance of family and work are different for women compared with men. Consequently, Ratzinger advocated for work schedules that allow women to be present in family life and for greater respect for women who do not work outside the home. In contrast to men, women have a distinctive mission within the family that must always be valued by society and supported by employment policies.

Here, too, he promoted the previous teaching of John Paul II, who had also argued that "society must be structured in such a way that wives and mothers are not in practice compelled to work outside the home," despite having the same rights as men to do so.[6] The underlying presumption here is that women may exist in public life but that they more properly and more fully have a distinctive vocation within the family. Later, Benedict XVI linked acceptance of one's sexed body with respect for the rest of God's creation.[7] For both previous popes, women were defined and assessed in terms of the ideal of "woman," not through attention to lived experience. And it is this approach, according to Hinsdale, that is the "issue under the issues" when turning to sexual ethics and the roles of women and men.[8]

For both John Paul II and Benedict XVI, the promotion of gender essentialism in their teachings led to a significant suspicion of feminism. John Paul II cautioned that the dignity of women, particularly in light of increased attention to women's rights, must not be separated from "the specific diversity and personal originality of man and woman."[9] Granting that male domination over women is a mark of original sin, he warned that "women must not appropriate to themselves male characteristics contrary to their own feminine 'originality.'"[10] Doing so would not only fail to elevate the status of women in society; it would, in his view, also undermine the particularity of women's feminine dignity. Similarly, Ratzinger responded to feminist approaches with concern that they are in opposition to Church teaching, and that would be harmful to promoting women's well-being. Specifically, he identified the danger that an emphasis on women's subordination would lead women to be antagonistic adversaries of men. He was also critical of trends in thought that distinguish biological sex from gender in order to emphasize the fundamental equality of women and men. In his view, this approach failed to appreciate the givenness of human nature as informed by the sexed body.[11]

Francis's own comments on gender, feminism, and the status of women in Church and society both affirm and depart from the thought of his predecessors. For some, Francis's statements can be assumed, until demonstrated otherwise, to affirm previous teaching. In contexts when he advocates for a "theology of women" or uses the phrase "feminine genius" without spelling out what he means, some critics fill in the gaps with the teachings from John Paul II and Benedict XVI. However, not unlike Bryan Massingale's argument in chapter 9 of this volume, Francis's silences speak in their own way—particularly when viewed against the backdrop of his predecessors—of his own subtle departures from existing language of gender complementarity and approaches to family life and feminism.

POPE FRANCIS AND GENDER COMPLEMENTARITY

Francis's own statements upholding the teaching of gender complementarity are, perhaps, most direct in his warnings against gender ideology. He cautions against a gender ideology that denies sexual difference and denies the connection of biological sex, male and female, to personal identity. The consequence of this kind of thinking, he maintains, is that human identity is reduced to individual choice.[12] Here, Francis expresses a particular concern for a rigidity of thinking that is "absolute and unquestionable, even dictating how children should be raised."[13] He warns that teaching gender theory can be a form of indoctrination or "ideological colonization."[14] Even still, Francis prioritizes the encounter with persons over enforcing a strict orthodoxy on the topic of gender. Noting that while he did not want to be misinterpreted as challenging the Church's teaching, he recounted to reporters an experience of meeting with a Spanish trans man and his wife, whom he welcomed after receiving a letter. Here, as throughout much of his teaching on gender and LGBTQ issues, and as the volume's foundational chapters stress, he makes clear that the primary goal is to accompany rather than condemn people.

In all of Francis's discussions of gender and family life, his silences and omissions are also significant. Although, as noted above, Francis tends to affirm the masculinity of men and femininity of women, it is not always clear what the content of these gendered categories is exactly. Though he names men protecting their families and women having a maternal disposition in families, he specifically, as noted above, rejects rigid gendered roles within family life and society. And, critically, he does not describe femininity as inherently maternal and self-giving, and he conspicuously avoids the language of "feminine receptivity." Similarly, although he identifies distinctiveness between motherhood and fatherhood, these characteristics do not get applied to *all* aspects of femininity and masculinity. In this way, he departs again from the thought of John Paul II, who characterized femininity as a maternal, self-giving nature. And in *Let us Dream*, Francis moves away from linking environmental domination to a rejection of gender essentialism, which was typical in the earlier writings of his papacy, including *Laudato si'*, and also in the writings of his predecessors.[15]

In his direct statements about the meaning of gender, however, Francis maintains previous teaching upholding gender complementarity. In *Amoris laetitia*, he draws on statements from John Paul II, affirming the inseparability of biological sex, male and female, from gender, masculinity, and femininity.[16] It is these gendered differences that make expressions of love possible, "'in which the human person becomes a gift.'"[17] And Francis seems to affirm inherent differences between the sexes when he claims that "men and women ... communicate differently. They speak different languages and they act in different ways."[18] He further promotes a form of sex education that would encourage young people to accept their sexed bodies as created by God, rather than be tempted "into thinking that we enjoy absolute power over creation."[19] Similarly, in *Laudato si'*, he draws from Benedict XVI, who connected a rejection of gender complementarity, and all that follows from it regarding expressions of gender and sexuality, to environmental degradation. Just as we ought to respect and honor the gifts of the natural world, so too we must respect and honor the masculine and feminine givenness of our sexed bodies.[20] As he writes, "The acceptance of our [sexed] bodies as God's gift is vital for welcoming and accepting the entire world as a gift from the Father and our common home, whereas thinking that we enjoy absolute power over our own bodies turns, often subtly, into thinking that we enjoy absolute power over creation."[21] In both *Amoris laetitia* and *Laudato si'*, Francis offers a critique of technocratic domination over God's creation in matters related to gender.[22] This critique would seem to extend to transgender and nonbinary gender identities, same-sex relationships, and forms of feminist thought that critique essentialist complementarian views. These statements suggest that Francis explicitly affirms and continues the magisterial approaches to gender found in two previous papacies.

Francis's affirmations of gender complementarity are also evident in his discussions of family life. He maintains that men play a critical role in family life, "particularly with regard to the protection and support of their wives and children."[23] Awareness of their role in marriage and family life leads men to "live their masculinity accordingly."[24] In contrast, mothers are described as "the strongest antidote to the spread of self-centered individualism,"[25] which points to an understanding of motherhood as inherently self-giving. Motherhood is also characterized by tenderness and compassion, which is contrasted with fatherhood's responsibility to guide children "to perceive the limits of life, to be open to the challenges of the wider world, and to see the need for hard work and strenuous effort."[26] Francis also talks of children whose mothers are not present in some way, such as when working outside the home or pursuing other interests, as being affected by "the sense of being orphaned" because of an unmet need for their mothers' presence.[27] However, while John Paul II seemed to put a distinctive emphasis on maternal presence in the home, Francis also expresses concern for the absence of fathers, who "are often so caught up in themselves and their work, and at times in their own self-fulfillment that they neglect their families."[28] The paternal presence is further defined by Francis's clarification that it ought to be understood as distinct from being controlling, and instead should offer guidance to children when they come "home with their problems."[29] And Francis maintains that these two gendered ways of parenting are the ideal context for raising children.[30]

At the same time, Francis softens the teaching on complementarity in comparison with both John Paul II and Benedict XVI, for he clarifies that complementarity does not require specific roles within a marriage associated with female and male identities. In remarks to a colloquium on the topic of complementarity organized by the Congregation for the Doctrine of the Faith (now the Dicastery for the Doctrine of the Faith), Francis noted that a complementary marriage is not characterized by specific, static gendered roles. Rather, persons are marked by the individual particularity they bring to marriage and family life.[31] Additionally, despite defining masculinity and femininity as part of God's creative work, *Amoris laetitia* notes that human ways of being in the world are not determined by biological sex alone. Instead, persons are shaped by "multiple elements having to do with temperament, family history, culture, experience, education, the influence of friends, family members and respected persons, as well as other formative situations."[32] He even notes that rigid gender categories can fail to appreciate the particular interests and abilities of individual persons, including a man's love of the arts or a woman's leadership. Further, rigid categories have the potential to inhibit the "legitimate freedom and hamper the authentic development of children's specific identity and potential."[33] Consistent with the Ignatian presupposition, explored in chapter 3 of this book by Conor Kelly, that God communicates directly with the soul, this framing shows a greater emphasis on the particularity of individual persons, who are shaped by the variety of contexts and relationships in which they live rather than insisting on talking about persons' gender expression in light of idealized categories. This approach reflects a shift from the discussions of gender that preceded Francis. But importantly, it demonstrates a consistent pastoral approach that has characterized Francis's papacy, one of listening and concern for the on-the-ground realities that mark the life of the Church.

Granted, in these reflections, Francis assumes that family life is rooted in heterosexual marriage, marked by complementarity. But he emphasizes the particularity of specific persons as constituting the complementary relationship, rather than the masculinity and femininity of the spouses. He also recognizes that the particularity of family situations requires "a certain flexibility of roles and responsibilities."[34] He is critical of overly rigid ways of thinking, and this framing gets applied to the meaning of gender. Thus, despite maintaining masculinity and femininity as essential, he argues that they cannot be held in a rigid way. For example, he notes "that a husband's way of being masculine can be flexibly adapted to the wife's work schedule. Taking on domestic chores or some aspects of raising children does not make him any less masculine or imply failure, irresponsibility or cause for shame."[35] Though it is not said directly, Francis here demonstrates understanding and respect for the nondomestic work, including public leadership roles, of women in the world, which cannot be simply put under the umbrella of the maternal or compassionate. He also supports a form of masculinity, not thoroughly explained, that is able to share domestic labor and parenting, with an awareness that such a model of masculinity is an important witness to children. He notes that a rigid approach would not appropriately "help children and young people to appreciate the genuine reciprocity incarnate in the real conditions of matrimony."[36] This sense of genuine reciprocity and mutual support for the work of one's spouse is not a simple capitulation to the values of a world transformed by feminist goals. Rather, it is a model of family life endorsed by feminist ideals but not realized as the norm, including in the United States, where women continue to take on the majority of household and parenting labor.[37]

This rejection of specific gender roles is a departure from the thought of John Paul II, whose influence is otherwise evident in the ongoing magisterial teaching of gender complementarity. Specifically, as noted above, John Paul II's *Familiaris consortio* endorsed a model of family life in which the home was more appropriately the sphere of femininity, and leadership in the world was appropriate to masculinity. Like Francis, John Paul II called for the presence of fathers, but his perspective on the concrete contribution of fathers to their children was decidedly less nurturing than the vision articulated in *Amoris laetitia*. And he offered no language to suggest that husbands should be flexible with shared household responsibilities in order to accommodate the nondomestic work of their wives.[38] Francis's shift regarding women within families allows for and is shaped by an expanded sense of the contributions women can and should make to public life.

CONSIDERING THE ROLE OF WOMEN IN CHURCH AND SOCIETY

Through both his specific actions regarding women's leadership in the institutional Church and his writings and statements, Francis's complicated, perhaps inconsistent, perspective on gender continues to emerge. He advocates for increased recognition and respect for the rights of women, demonstrating practical concern for the on-the-ground suffering that women disproportionately experience worldwide.[39] However, in his articulation, women are not only relevant to social life as victims of oppression; women also exercise leadership. His articulation of women's leadership is both shaped by and a challenge to his own affirmation of gender complementarity.

Francis's approach to the role of women in the Church is marked by the same push and pull that characterizes his thinking about gender more broadly.

On one hand, he acknowledges the contributions that women make to the Church, leading to new developments for women's roles within ecclesial structures. On the other hand, this acknowledgment remains somewhat tethered to complementarian notions of the "feminine genius," and he has been unwilling to make concrete moves toward ordaining women to the diaconate or priesthood, which results in women remaining out of formal leadership within the Church.[40]

Querida Amazonia, Francis's apostolic exhortation after the Amazonian Synod, demonstrates this tension. He notes that in communities that have not had access to priests for decades, the faith has been preserved and handed on largely because of the work of women. He says that they were "undoubtedly called and prompted by the Holy Spirit, [and] baptized, catechized, prayed and acted as missionaries," even to the point of "[keeping] the Church alive."[41] As he argues, this witness should lead the Church to find new ways to benefit from the "service and charisms that are proper to women" and that are specific to local context.[42] This language echoes the gender essentialism taught by John Paul II and Benedict XVI. And, like them, Francis's statement that "women make their contribution to the Church in a way that is properly theirs" justifies his ongoing unwillingness to consider the ordination of women to the priesthood.[43] He goes on to assert that the male priest stands *in persona Christi* in the Eucharist, echoing *Inter insigniores* and *Ordinatio sacerdoltalis*. Moreover, he warns that ordaining women would run the risk of "clericalizing them," which suggests an idealized view of femininity that aligns with a complementarian understanding.[44] This link is confirmed by his thoughts on the role of women in the Church in a long 2013 interview given to the Jesuit journals around the world. He noted that whatever role is discerned for women in the Church will emerge from a "profound theology of the woman" because "the feminine genius is needed wherever we make important decisions."[45] Though he makes clear that he wants to find places where women can exercise authority, he also makes clear that such authority is one that is distinctive to women and not, therefore, a matter of ordaining women. Echoing John Paul II, Francis deems the exclusion of women from the priesthood as a definitively answered issue. As such, despite the inroads he makes to foster women's place within the Church, the institutional structures fail to incorporate women's voices and decision-making.

However, unlike his predecessors, Francis has moved toward more formal recognition of women's contribution to the Church. He suggests that women should have "access to positions, including ecclesial services . . . that can better signify the role that is theirs," that would also "entail stability, public recognition and a commission from the bishop."[46] Francis is here speaking about Amazonian communities, in light of their particularities. But it also offers the possibility that communities in other contexts could take similar approaches to meet the needs of their own local realities. Doing so would not only formally recognize women's contributions and leadership but also offer an expanded awareness of the wide varieties of gifts, ministries, and service offered by the whole people of God, not only the clergy. He has also argued that demands to see women ordained and in magisterial leadership are themselves marked by clericalism. He notes the erasure of women's leadership that happens in the Church when Church leadership is perceived to be exclusively male. As he observes, women do the majority of the Church's work around the world: in parishes, schools, hospitals, and other organizations.[47] As he notes, specifically pointing to women in the Amazon, "To say that they aren't truly leaders because they aren't priests is clericalist and disrespectful."[48] Many in the Church, particularly women, remain critical of Francis's unwillingness to expand women's role to ordination. And it seems disingenuous to suggest that women's leadership is truly recognized while the institutional structures of the Church remain male dominated. However, Francis's emphasis on the Church as a whole is not merely a deflection but is also a move toward greater recognition of the baptismal equality shared among all members of the Church, which is more capable of recognizing the wide variety of ways in which people serve the Church's mission.

In light of his commitment to recognizing that the Church is composed of not only the ordained but also all the baptized, Francis argues that arguments demanding women's ordination limit the Church to "her functional structures."[49] Further, he assumes that women's contributions should challenge assumptions about power. Questioning that notion that women's influence is only made possible by putting women in positions of power, he argues that putting women in positions of power may not necessarily change institutional culture. Instead, he asks us to consider how to incorporate women's presence, in light of "asking if there are other ways of allowing women's perspectives to challenge existing assumptions."[50] If read with a hermeneutic of suspicion against the backdrop of the gender essentialism of gender complementarity, this approach of Francis's could sound like a reiteration of *Querida Amazonia*'s warning to avoid clericalizing women. But it is worth noting that many feminist theologians, while wanting to see women in all forms of ecclesial ministry and leadership, also question the approach of adding women to the ecclesial structures as they exist, instead imagining a feminist theological method that promotes a new reality in both Church and society.[51]

Francis has fostered opportunities for women's direct engagement within institutional Church structures and ecclesial spaces. He has changed Canon Law to formally allow lay people to serve as lectors and catechists, which has allowed for women to be formally installed in these roles. Though women, and lay men, have certainly served in these roles before, there is now stability and public visibility to their contribution, as he called for in *Querida Amazonia*.[52]

He has also convened two commissions to investigate the ordination of women to the permanent diaconate at the request of women religious.[53] Allowing the line of questioning to be investigated reflects the general openness that characterizes much of his papacy (and that Bryan Massingale explores in chapter 9 of this volume), even as it does not extend to questioning the existing teaching on the male priesthood, despite his unwillingness thus far to ordain women to the diaconate without a commission consensus. Despite not admitting women in the priesthood and the magisterium, Francis has expanded the leadership of women at the Vatican and has allowed a woman to vote at a synod for the first time.[54] These moves, though small, point the Church in a new direction.

He emphasizes that he sought out particular qualifications, but he also expresses that, in his view, women make better administrators than men because of the way that women often have experience running households. His warning against clericalizing women implicitly suggests an ongoing complementarian worldview; however, in his discussion of women's administrative contribution, his emphasis seems more closely aligned to a recognition of the lived experience of women. Aware that the "housewife" has often been considered demeaning, he explains that the "Spanish, *ama de casa* ('mistress of the house') carries the meaning of the Greek *oikos* and *nomos*, from where we get the word 'economics': household management."[55] Thus, while he is still here linking women with the household in distinctive ways that echo John Paul II's gender essentialism, the emphasis on experience could also be a recognition of the disproportionate share of household labor and management carried by women in practice, rather than an idealized sense of the romanticized feminine sphere. As Francis explains, in his experience as an archbishop working with women in leadership, "the sharpest advice came from women who were able to see from different angles, and who were above all *practical*, with a realistic understanding of how things work and people's limitations and potential" (emphasis in the original).[56]

Here Francis not only reflects on what women can bring to the Church, but an awareness of women's contribution and leadership in the world more broadly. Reflecting on the COVID-19 pandemic, he pays attention to the high number of women working in health care. In his view, "countries with women as presidents or prime ministers have on the whole reacted better and more quickly than others, making decisions swiftly and communicating them with empathy."[57] He also observes a trend in the work of women economists who often bring to their work their real-world experience as parents or in managing households. Francis does specifically say that he views women's contribution to economics as "maternal." But, as elsewhere in *Let Us Dream*, his discussion emphasizes lived experience, rather than Marian ideals.

Although early in his papacy Francis relied heavily on the language of the "feminine genius" in his consideration of the roles women should hold in the Church, this language falls out in exchange for a stronger emphasis on the particularity of women's experience in more recent reflections.[58] In *Let Us Dream*, Francis notes that in his own thinking about how to increase the presence of women in Vatican decision-making, "The challenge . . . has been to create spaces where women can lead, but in ways that allow them to shape the culture, ensuring they are valued, respected, and recognized."[59] Though he maintains the desire to avoid "clericalizing" women, he notes that he has included women according to "their skills and experience, but also to influence the vision and mindset of the Church's bureaucracy."[60] Here, we see another shift from his predecessors. While they both articulated women's "special" contribution to the Church, their emphasis remained on women's contribution through family life and spiritual motherhood, not to finding concrete ways of increasing women's leadership and service to the institutional Church.

POPE FRANCIS ON FEMINISM

Francis demonstrates both an appreciation for and a suspicion of feminism. Although he has not offered a systematic discussion of his views on feminism, his overall perspective emerges from his various comments and writings on the topic sprinkled throughout his papacy. He does express suspicion of feminism and has, at times, offered dismissive remarks, such as when he called feminism "machismo with a skirt."[61] This negative assessment appears to be twofold. First, he is critical of feminist thought and approaches to gender when it is, in his view, too rigid or is an "isolated conscience." This view, as noted above, is consistent with his overall approach to rigid ways of thinking and is not isolated to feminism alone. Second, his critiques of feminism are often leveled against ideological approaches and theory, including as applied to theology. However, his critiques are less pointed than those outlined by both John Paul II and Benedict XVI. Unlike these two, Francis outlines in detail favorable assessment of on-the-ground movements that support the concrete human flourishing of women, including support for women's rights. Thus, his critique seems to be directed at ideology and theory, and his approval is directed at improvements to lived experience. Perhaps the difference in his comments can also be attributed to his commitment to listening, which James Keenan, SJ, explores in chapter 2 of this volume.[62]

Similar to his suspicion of gender ideology, he offers warnings about feminism, which, in his view, can be a problem if it requires rigid uniformity or "negate[s] motherhood."[63] In all this, Francis's suspicion seems to be directed at "rigid ideologies" related to feminist and gender theory. Yet, in *Let Us Dream*, Francis's critique of rigidity extends across the ideological spectrum. He does not target feminism or thinking about gender in an isolated way, but includes critiques of those who critique the Church for being too open to change and to the secular world. Still, to the dismay of some, he does specifically name advocates for women's ordination.[64] He is particularly concerned with "those who claim that until the Church ordains women as proof of its commitment to gender equality, the local parish or bishop cannot count on their involvement. Outwardly, the reasons appear coherent and principled, but they disguise the spirit of the isolated conscience, which refuses to act as a disciple of Christ within His Church."[65] His primary concern does not appear to be the ideas themselves, and he has not attempted to squash out discussion of the issue or other concerns facing women. Instead, he indicts the danger of self-righteousness or the way in which some are limited to a single issue.[66]

One of his most significant departures from his predecessors is his appreciation for the contributions of feminism. Francis's warnings about gender ideology and feminism do not result in a total rejection of the feminist movement. It is true that in statements about feminism he expresses suspicion, at times relying on stereotypes. Yet he also appears to have been, perhaps unknowingly, influenced by the feminist movement. And he expresses appreciation for the social and political changes made possible by feminism. Both trends in his thought show up in *Amoris laetitia* when he writes, "If certain forms of feminism have arisen which we must consider inadequate, we must nonetheless see in the women's movement the working of the Spirit for a clearer recognition of the dignity and rights of women."[67] Francis here celebrates the improvement to the concrete well-being of women, with specific attention to the global increased recognition of women's rights, the recognized equal dignity of women and men, and the decrease in the acceptance of discrimination against women.[68] He also expresses an appreciation of the improvement in the concrete, material lives of women and girls, which he recognizes as a manifestation of God's activity in the world. He here rejects as male chauvinism the view of some that "feminine emancipation" has been a cause of the world's problems.[69]

In *Let Us Dream*, Francis suggests that the #MeToo movement is one of several recent movements that work toward a new future aligned more closely with God's will. He notes that as God went to the margins, "When God wanted to regenerate creation," so too the margins are where possibilities for a new future and social change can be found.[70] It is in the context of specific attention to movements in which "those people who are now on the edges become protagonists for social change" that he identifies the #MeToo movement among other movements for change, such as the George Floyd protests.[71] The #MeToo movement, in his view, was a vehicle for change by drawing greater awareness to patterns of domination and entitlement enacted largely by powerful men against women. In Francis's view, this kind of entitlement and domination is the same "root sin" of "the cancer of clericalism."[72] Here, Francis not only identifies a feminist social movement with God's activity but also highlights that the work that it did to challenge patterns of entitlement benefits not only society but also the Church. His willingness to turn to the need for the Church to be influenced by feminist movements shows up also in his acknowledgment of the Church's own responsibility for "male authoritarianism, domination, various forms of enslavement, abuse and sexist violence."[73] In *Christus vivit*, Francis notes that "a Church that is overly fearful and tied to its structures can be invariably critical of efforts to defend the rights of women. . . . Instead, a living Church can react by being attentive to the legitimate claims of women who seek greater justice and equality."[74] Here, it is the Church itself that ought not be limited by rigidity. Although he does go on to say that the Church does not agree with everything advocated by feminist groups, the Church ought to participate in the world to promote women's well-being and equality with men. However, as noted above, this willingness for the Church to grow in this way does not extend in a direct way to the Church as an institution.

Critically, however, Francis advocates for women's flourishing in a way that reflects the contributions of feminist thought to both Church and society over the last fifty years. This is not to say that Francis is directly engaging feminist scholarship or participating in on-the-ground feminist movements. However, it does reflect the openness that he has toward the world in general, which is a world that has been marked and changed by feminist influence. In contrast, both John Paul II and Benedict XVI address feminism as a challenge facing the Church, requiring clarification on topics related to women and the Church and gender more broadly. Francis here offers a new way forward, not breaking bluntly with the teaching of his predecessors, but instead shifting the emphasis, with a new appreciation for the significance of feminism in promoting women's flourishing worldwide.

CONCLUSION

Many have observed Francis on the topic of gender and the role of women in Church and society both with expectation and hope and with trepidation and disappointment. Before the election of Francis, issues related to gender and sexuality were a "third rail," in which the teaching of gender complementarity was strictly enforced. Formally, Francis endorses the teaching of his predecessors, talking of the importance of heterosexual union and parenting, the given significance of biological sex for the person, and justification for the denial of women from the priesthood. This ongoing teaching continues to have significant, negative consequences for the flourishing of women and LGTBQ persons, bolstering ongoing enforcement of a strict gender complementarity at local levels. Dioceses across the United States are developing policies regarding gender expression, including dress codes and guidance on pronouns, and the US Conference of Catholic Bishops has released a doctrinal note on medical care for transgender persons.[75] These approaches double down on the rigid approach to gender complementarity as taught by John Paul II and Benedict XVI. They are also happening during a time of the politicization and attempted legislation of gender issues. But Francis is informed by his emphasis on the Church as a "field hospital," in which consideration of persons matters more than ideals, setting him apart from the majority of the US episcopate.[76] Francis's approach to gender has the potential to offer a new way forward in a fraught context. If the US episcopacy took Francis's example seriously, compassionately accompanying persons in the particularity and complexity of their lives would offer a different approach to transgender and gender nonbinary persons, at least opening the space for some degree of dialogue and treating their experiences as a relevant contribution to the conversation.[77]

His emphasis on lived experience also shows up in his perspective of feminism and women's leadership. As a young adult, he benefited directly from women's expertise and leadership, even to the point of discerning his vocation and surviving significant illness. He also saw the disproportionate suffering of women during his time as archbishop of Buenos Aires.[78] This emphasis on lived experience and pastoral care as accompaniment has led to new directions that are both subtle and radical compared with what has come before him. Respect for the full humanity of trans persons, the leadership of women, and the importance of feminism is characteristic of this approach. His statements have the potential to offer hope for a new future, even as they do not yet fulfill the hope for which many long.

NOTES

1. Mary Ann Hinsdale, "Beyond Complementarity: Gender Issues in the Catholic Church," in *T&T Clark Handbook of Theological Anthropology*, ed. Mary Ann Hinsdale and Stephen Okey (London: T&T Clark, 2021), 361.

2. John Paul II, *Mulieris dignitatem*, no. 18.
3. Specifically, John Paul II has in mind consecrated virgins and women religious. Married women without children and single women do not show up in his consideration. John Paul II, no. 21.
4. Hinsdale, "Beyond Complementarity," 363.
5. Joseph Ratzinger, "Letter to the Bishops on the Collaboration of Men and Women in the Church and the World," July 31, 2004, www.vatican.va/roman_curia/congregations/cfaith/documents/rc_con_cfaith_doc_20040731_collaboration_en.html.
6. John Paul II, *Familiaris Consortio*, November 22, 1981, no. 23.
7. Benedict XVI, *Caritas in veritate*, June 29, 2009, no. 51, www.vatican.va/content/benedict-xvi/en/encyclicals/documents/hf_ben-xvi_enc_20090629_caritas-in-veritate.html.
8. Hinsdale, "Beyond Complementarity," 361.
9. John Paul II, *Mulieris dignitatem*, no. 10.
10. John Paul II, no. 10.
11. Ratzinger, "Letter to the Bishops," no. 2.
12. Francis, *Amoris laetitia*, March 19, 2016, no. 56, www.vatican.va/content/dam/francesco/pdf/apost_exhortations/documents/papa-francesco_esortazione-ap_20160319_amoris-laetitia_en.pdf.
13. Francis, no. 56.
14. Francis, "In-Flight Press Conference of His Holiness Pope Francis from Azerbaijan to Rome," October 2, 2016, www.vatican.va/content/francesco/en/speeches/2016/october/documents/papa-francesco_20161002_georgia-azerbaijan-conferenza-stampa.html.
15. Francis and Austen Ivereigh, *Let Us Dream: The Path to a Better Future* (New York: Simon & Schuster, 2020), 34.
16. Francis, *Amoris laetitia*, no. 56.
17. Francis, no. 151.
18. Francis, no. 136.
19. Francis, no. 285.
20. Francis, *Laudato si'*, May 24, 2015, nos. 6, 155, www.vatican.va/content/francesco/en/encyclicals/documents/papa-francesco_20150524_enciclica-laudato-si.html. See also Elizabeth Pyne, "The Diversity of Creaturely Life," *America*, June 18, 2015, www.americamagazine.org/issue/diversity-creaturely-life.
21. Francis, *Laudato si'*, no. 155.
22. See also Pope Francis, "Address to Participants in the General Assembly of the Pontifical Academy for Life," October 5, 2017, www.vatican.va/content/francesco/en/speeches/2017/october/documents/papa-francesco_20171005_assemblea-pav.html.
23. Francis, *Amoris laetitia*, no. 55.
24. Francis, no. 55.
25. Francis, no. 174.
26. Francis, no. 175.
27. Francis, no. 173.
28. Francis, no. 176.
29. Francis, no. 177.
30. Francis, no. 175. Ann Schneible, "Pope Francis: Children Have a Right to a Mother and Father," Catholic News Agency, November 17, 2014, www.catholicnewsagency.com/news/30948/pope-francis-children-have-right-to-a-mother-and-father; Will Stroude, "Pope Francis Says Children Need a Mother and a Father," *Attitude*, November 7, 2017, www.attitude.co.uk/news/world/pope-francis-says-children-need-a-mother-and-a-father-285081/.

31. Francis, "The Family Is Not an Ideology," EWTN, November 21, 2014.
32. Francis, *Amoris laetitia*, no. 286.
33. Francis, no. 286.
34. Francis, no. 175.
35. Francis, no. 286.
36. Francis, no. 286.
37. Megan Brenan, "Women Still Handle Main Household Tasks in US," Gallup, January 29, 2020, https://news.gallup.com/poll/283979/women-handle-main-household-tasks.aspx.
38. John Paul II, *Familiaris consortio*, no. 25.
39. Francis, *Fratelli tutti*, October 3, 2020, no. 23; Francis, *Evangelii gaudium*, November 24, 2013, no. 212.
40. Susan Rakoczy, "The Ordination of Catholic Women as Deacons: The State of the Question," *HTS Theological Studies* 76, no. 2 (2020): 1–10; Elsa Marie Wiberg Pedersen, "The Pope, Power Plays, and Women Priests," *Dialog* 56, no. 2 (June 2017): 112–15.
41. Francis, *Querida Amazonia*, February 2, 2020, no. 99.
42. Francis, no. 101.
43. Francis, no. 101.
44. Francis, no. 100.
45. Antonio Spadaro, "A Big Heart Open to God: An Interview with Pope Francis," *America*, September 30, 2013.
46. Francis, *Querida Amazonia*, 103.
47. Francis and Ivereigh, *Let Us Dream*, 68.
48. Francis and Ivereigh.
49. Francis, *Querida Amazonia*, no. 100; Francis and Ivereigh, *Let Us Dream*, 65.
50. Francis and Ivereigh, *Let Us Dream*, 65–66.
51. Elizabeth A. Johnson, *She Who Is: The Mystery of God in Feminist Theological Discourse*, 3rd ed. (New York: Herder & Herder, 1992); Rosemary R. Ruether, *Sexism and God Talk: Toward a Feminist Theology* (Boston: Beacon Press, 1993).
52. Christopher White, "Pope Installs First Women Lectors and Catechists," *National Catholic Reporter*, February 4, 2022.
53. Joshua McElwee, "Francis Creates New Women Deacons Commission, Naming Entirely Different Membership," www.ncronline.org/spirituality/news/francis-creates-new-women-deacons-commission-naming-entirely-different-membership; Joshua McElwee, "Francis: Decision on Women Deacons Cannot Be Made 'Without Historical Foundation,'" www.ncronline.org/vatican/francis-decision-women-deacons-cannot-be-made-without-historical-foundation.
54. "Pope Francis Gets It Right on Curia Reform and Women," www.ncronline.org/opinion/signs-times/pope-francis-gets-it-right-curia-reform-and-women; "Pope Bolsters Women at Vatican but Resistance Remains," *National Catholic Reporter*, www.ncronline.org/vatican/vatican-news/pope-bolsters-women-vatican-resistance-remains; "Sister Nathalie Becquart Will Be the First Woman to Vote with Bishops at a Synod; Her Advice for Young Women? Listen," *America*, March 30, 2023, www.americamagazine.org/faith/2023/03/30/women-church-clergy-becquart-245004.
55. Francis and Ivereigh, *Let Us Dream*, 67.
56. Francis and Ivereigh.
57. Francis and Ivereigh, 62.
58. Kate McElwee has traced the transformation over time in Francis's thinking on women in the Church. She argues that the shift away from a strict reliance on complementarity reflects Francis's listening mode. Kate McElwee, "The Evolution of

Pope Francis on Women: Some Movement, but More Needed," *National Catholic Reporter*, March 7, 2023, www.ncronline.org/opinion/guest-voices/evolution-pope-francis-women-some-movement-more-needed.

59. Francis and Ivereigh, *Let Us Dream*, 66.
60. Francis and Ivereigh.
61. Francis, "Intervention at 'The Protection of Minors in the Church,'" February 22, 2019, www.vatican.va/content/francesco/en/speeches/2019/february/documents/papa-francesco_20190222_incontro-protezioneminori.html.
62. Kate McElwee, "Evolution."
63. Francis, *Amoris laetitia*, no. 173.
64. McElwee, "Evolution."
65. Francis and Ivereigh, *Let Us Dream*, 71–72.
66. Francis and Ivereigh, 69–73.
67. Francis, *Amoris laetitia*, no. 54.
68. Francis, no. 54.
69. Francis, no. 54.
70. Francis and Ivereigh, *Let Us Dream*, 11.
71. Francis and Ivereigh, 18.
72. Francis and Ivereigh.
73. Francis, *Christus vivi*, March 25, 2019, no. 42.
74. Francis.
75. Katie Collins Scott, "As Catholic Dioceses Release New Gender Policies, Grassroots Groups Demand Input," *National Catholic Reporter*, February 1, 2023, www.ncronline.org/news/catholic-dioceses-release-new-gender-policies-grassroots-groups-demand-input; US Conference of Catholic Bishops, "Doctrinal Note on the Moral Limits to Technological Manipulation of the Human Body," March 20, 2023, www.usccb.org/resources/Doctrinal%20Note%202023-03-20.pdf.
76. Spadaro, "Big Heart."
77. The exclusion of "the stories and the experiences of the LGBTQ community" is a common critique of the current diocesan approach. Brian Roewe, "Milwaukee Archdiocese Takes Aim at Trans Persons in Sweeping New Policy," *National Catholic Reporter*, January 26, 2022, www.ncronline.org/news/people/milwaukee-archdiocese-takes-aim-trans-persons-sweeping-new-policy.
78. Austen Ivereigh, *The Great Reformer: Francis and the Making of a Radical Pope*, expanded ed. (New York: Picador, 2015); Francis and Ivereigh, *Let Us Dream*.

11

A DISCERNING BIOETHICS
Pope Francis's Threefold Approach
Andrea Vicini, SJ

In January 2016, Pope Francis met with the members of the Italian National Committee for Bioethics, which gathers a multidisciplinary group of scholars and publishes reports on debated bioethical issues. In his address, the pope stressed how

> the Church does not claim any privileged space in this field; on the contrary, it is satisfied when the civil conscience, at various levels, is able to reflect, to discern and to work on the basis of free and open rationality and of the constitutive values of the person and of society. Indeed, precisely this responsible civil maturity is the sign that the sowing of the Gospel—this yes, is revealed and entrusted to the Church—has borne fruit, managing to promote the search for truth and good and beauty in complex human and ethical questions.[1]

Together with reaffirming the need for "particular attention and care ... for those who are the weakest and most disadvantaged, who find it difficult to make their voices heard, or cannot, or can no longer, make it heard," the pope expects that "the ecclesial and civil communities meet and are called to collaborate, according to their respective distinct competences."[2] Unlike his predecessors, in engaging bioethical challenges, Francis is far from understanding the ecclesial role and the responsibility of believers in terms of an oversimplified dichotomy, like the conflict between a culture of life and a culture of death.[3]

In praising the work of the committee, and its commitment to foster human dignity and respect "the integrity of the human being and the protection of health from conception to natural death,"[4] Francis highlighted four areas of bioethical interest that deserve attention: first, "biotechnological applications in the medical field, which can never be used in a way that is detrimental to human dignity, nor must be guided solely by industrial and commercial purposes"; second, the need to promote "interdisciplinary analysis of the causes of environmental degradation"; third, the "issue of disability and the marginalization of vulnerable subjects," with a particular attention given to embryos, the sick, and those who are dying; and fourth, the urgency of promoting the "harmonization of the standards and rules of biological and medical activities" to protect fundamental values and rights.[5] For Francis, "humility and realism," as well as "confrontation between different positions," will contribute "to the maturation of the civil conscience" and help address the "complex bioethical problems" that humankind faces.[6]

Although, from a short address, one cannot expect a fully developed theological bioethics, some of the themes and concerns that inform Francis's approach to bioethical issues surface: from praising discernment and interdisciplinary collaboration, which characterize the way of proceeding of Catholic social thought; to the centrality of human dignity and its concretization in making a preferential option for the poor and the marginalized;[7] to the list of priorities that include biotechnological developments, with their applications in health and within society, and to the care for the environment.[8] More recently, in March 2022, Pope Francis invited all believers to pray and offer a Christian response to challenges presented by bioethical advances while promoting human dignity and addressing a throwaway culture.[9]

In this chapter, I discuss Pope Francis's threefold approach to ongoing bioethical issues. First, the centrality of a spiritual relationship with *Jesus* characterizes Christian discipleship in society. Hence, Francis always relies on this relationship to inform one's being, reasoning, discerning, and acting, while considering the concrete implications of discipleship in facing bioethical challenges. Second, the Second Vatican Council's engagement with the world animates a critical, collaborative, and active presence in the social fabric that empowers moral agents and nourishes personal and communal *discernment*.[10] In dealing with the complexity of today's pluralistic and globalized world, Francis embraces the Second Vatican Council, with its contributions and unfinished agenda for the renewal of the faith. At the same time, steeped in Ignatian spirituality, his Jesuit training and diversified ministry throughout his life strengthen his commitment to fostering a greater social justice at the planetary level, and not only in confessional circles and ecclesial contexts. Third, the understanding of a comprehensive and shared common good is rooted in the *experience* of people, particularly those who are marginalized and excluded. Hence, striving to identify and define the common good, and what it concretely implies, is integral to what the Church preaches and what people live.

A CHRISTOCENTRIC BIOETHICS

For Francis, the spiritual relationship with Jesus is central in the lives of his disciples and, in all situations, it informs one's being and acting.[11] Jesus makes a preferential option for humankind and for creation, and every creature responds to Jesus's loving and redeeming action. In the case of human beings, the moral life contributes to God's action, manifested in Jesus and enriched by Jesus's disciples. In such a way, the pope fully embraces the richness of the Christian tradition that, informed by the mystery of the Incarnation and by the gifts of the Holy Spirit given to the disciples, does not separate one's spiritual life from its embodiment in individual actions, communal engagements, and social matters. Morality expresses one's being and acting, and, for Christians, it is informed by one's personal and communal relationship with the risen Jesus. As Antonio Autiero reminds us, in Pope Francis, "the relationship between the proclamation of the Gospel and the transmission of the doctrine about the matters of faith, is modulated in a new way. The former has primacy over the latter. Francis draws inspiration for his pontificate from this principle of the radicality of the Gospel, and he opens up new paths for theology too."[12]

Far from any spiritualizing and moralizing misinterpretations, and from manipulating Jesus to one's own advantage and interests or to support agendas of privileged groups, focusing on the relationship with Jesus nourishes each disciple's life, creates communal interactions, leads to care for the planet, and advances more peaceable and just ways of living. However, believers might want to reduce Jesus to their own biases, race,[13] concerns, and interests, by claiming they have an exclusive access to him. These relational distortions should be identified, named, and resisted. To say it positively, continuous attention should be given to the many ways in which disciples are invited to ask for the gift of conversion, without presuming that they are fully embracing the transformative character of their relationship with Jesus in their social contexts.[14]

The assessment of one's relationship with Jesus is not only based on self-critical questioning; it also depends on what is beyond the self and, particularly, on the concrete reality of those in greater need, who experience vulnerability, fragility, and poverty. It is from the point of view of the poor in our midst that believers can verify whether, on one hand, they are creating a Jesus made in their own image—a Jesus who resembles and embodies their privileges and biases, who belongs exclusively to elites defined by the color of one's skin, religion, culture, education, social status, neighborhood, and financial security—or, on the other hand, they are continuously surprised by the Christ who is Emmanuel, God-with-us.

The disciples receive Jesus's love, and they are transformed by this love, made in the image of such a love. Hence, they can decide and act. Their choices and actions will be informed by such a love, by continuing Jesus's loving presence both as individuals and as communities. Far from being exclusionary, this love is meant to characterize the lives of the disciples toward all people, as the Gospel stresses with poignant images in the parable traditionally called "the Final Judgment" (Matt. 25: 31–46). Independently of their religious upbringing and belonging, what counts will be how people cared for those who were thirsty, hungry, naked, homeless, migrants, sick, and prisoners.

A Christologically focused morality is not exclusivist, as if it would concern only Christians; on the contrary, it is anthropologically based and, hence, is inclusive. As *Gaudium et spes* stresses in its opening words, "The joys and the hopes, the griefs and the anxieties of the men of this age, especially those who are poor or in any way afflicted, these are the joys and hopes, the griefs and anxieties of the followers of Christ."[15]

Such a recentering of Christian morality on a continuously renewed relationship with Jesus leads the Church to appreciate moral agents and their ability to discern and act, which is informed by their beliefs, experiences, and commitments. At the same time, to emphasize the relational approach to morality situates the role played by moral norms and leads to their critical assessment. As Alessandro Rovati writes, "Francis's approach to Christian morality represents both a correction of certain legalistic attitudes that reduce faith to the application of rules of conduct and a bold reaffirmation of the Church's moral proposal that stressing the attractiveness of the Christian life makes the rejection of certain evils more understandable."[16] Others prefer to name this approach as pastoral. As Joseph Boyle writes, "Pope Francis's primary concern is pastoral. His pastoral goal for morality is to *situate* Christian moral teaching and practice within the broader context of the redeeming actions of Jesus and their effective proclamation in evangelizing. That situating provides context and practical understanding; it is not the rejection of any moral truth" (emphasis in the original).[17]

The being and acting of people of goodwill neither occurs in a vacuum nor is exclusively centered on isolated individuals. On the contrary, the moral agency of individuals and communities is informed by contexts and experiences, particularly by relating with those in need and by caring for them in concrete ways that address their lived realities. The Christian faith is a lived faith that is challenged, tested, and renewed by the complexity of ordinary life. In doing so, our faith leads to work to change oneself and the world, by helping people to be more caring, just, and loving and by leading humankind to strive for personal and social flourishing. In Francis's words, "Before all else, the Gospel invites us to respond to the God of love who saves us, to see God in others and to go forth from ourselves to seek the good of others."[18]

For the pope, both the centrality of the relationship with Jesus, lived in examined and critical ways, and the concerns for those who are in need and poor in our world inform people's faith and actions. These two polarities also shape his understanding of bioethics and its agenda.

During his pontificate, Francis continues to show how, for believers and any person of goodwill, the quality of life of human beings, of living and nonliving creatures, and of the whole planet should be front and center. Hence, it is not surprising that he focuses his attention, teaching, and engagement on environmental concerns and health issues that affect humankind globally (e.g., the global pandemic caused by COVID-19), with a preferential attention given to those who are less well off, marginalized, excluded, and discriminated against, whether in the Global South or the peripheries of the Global North.

Considering Francis's papal ministry, sustainability and global health are two priorities that humankind faces both now and in the coming years. These two choices manifest how, as Jesus's disciple and bishop of Rome, he listens to the cry of the poor and to the cry of the planet. Moreover, he responds to these deafening cries with his personal engagement, leadership, advocacy, humble lifestyle, prayer, and concrete actions, while also appreciating the ongoing commitments of many individuals and groups, and while calling many others—from those who are poor to leaders, from nations to international organizations—to join in addressing these demanding bioethical priorities.[19]

The pope is urging national and international agents to be accountable and to act. His commitment to promoting concrete global actions further stresses how policies and actions are urgently needed to promote environmental sustainability and health, because these goods are integral to his vision of social justice. In this way, Pope Francis embodies, in renewed ways, the spirit of the Second Vatican Council, which is careful to discern the signs of the times, to join people of goodwill in their shared commitment to promote the common good, and to embody a vision of the Church that is engaged in fostering the flourishing of humankind and of the Earth.[20] Moreover, both sustainability and health benefit from the richness of the Catholic tradition in addressing social matters, confirming how the theological and practical resources that characterize Catholic social teaching are integral to facing bioethical issues.[21]

DISCERNMENT

In social contexts, some address bioethical issues by relying on theoretical and practical approaches that aim at reducing their complexity, messiness, and ambiguity. For others, and among them Pope Francis, what is complex can be discerned, and discernment leads to enlightened, realistic, and even pragmatic analyses, decisions, and strategies for action.

In reflecting on end-of-life issues, for example, while Pope Francis reaffirms the traditional teaching articulated in previous magisterial documents—which promotes pain control and palliative care, resists overzealous treatment, and rejects euthanasia and physician assisted suicide—he has also stressed the urgency to discern.[22] In his words, "Needless to say, in the face of critical situations and in clinical practice, the factors that come into play are often difficult to evaluate. To determine whether a clinically appropriate medical intervention is actually proportionate, the mechanical application of a general rule is not sufficient. There needs to be a careful discernment of the moral object, the attending circumstances, and the intentions of those involved."[23]

Discernment is not opposed to relying on principles, norms, and rules; but it aims at addressing the complexity of situations that moral agents face by considering significant factors that could be left unaddressed by a narrow and exclusive focus on principles, norms, and rules. Hence, for Francis, discernment is both theoretical and practical, strengthens moral agency, relies on one's informed conscience, critically examines one's experience, empowers moral agents, and benefits pastoral action in caring for people and communities.

Others are suspicious of discernment, whether in the case of bioethical issues or political contexts. On the contrary, the pope's bioethical agenda is informed by ongoing discernment, which aims to avoid a focus on exclusively or predominantly one single moral issue, no matter how important it might be. For example, while sharing the magisterial approach on the gravity of abortion, Francis has considered abortion neither the exclusive nor primary moral concern in contemporary society. By contrast, since 1989 the members of the US Conference of Catholic Bishops have stressed that "abortion has become the fundamental human rights issue for all men and women of goodwill."[24] They continue, "For us abortion is of overriding concern because it negates two of our most fundamental moral imperatives: respect for innocent life, and preferential concern for the weak and defenseless."[25] Moreover, though some US bishops want to deny the Eucharist to Catholic politicians if they have somehow defended the legality of abortion, Pope Francis has distanced himself from using the Eucharist as a political weapon, instead stressing his pastoral approach.[26]

Discernment, however, is not only limited to pastoral action, because it informs and makes possible decision-making and action that aim at promoting the common good. The 2016 Post-Synodal Exhortation *Amoris laetitia* exemplifies this approach by focusing on love in family life and on the needed discernment—theological, ecclesial, and pastoral—of what families experience while they strive to foster the common good in society and within the Church.[27]

THE CHALLENGING EXPERIENCE OF PEOPLE

Learning from the experience of people, with its wisdom and constraints, and accompanying humankind in addressing ongoing challenges also inform Pope Francis's approach to bioethical issues.[28] Together with a renewed attention to Catholic health care, Francis responded to the struggle of humankind experiencing the global pandemic caused by COVID-19 and its multiplying variants.[29] He also engaged the rapidly developing field of biotechnological innovations, which involves scores of researchers, companies, and users around the globe.[30] Francis is aware of the bioethical urgency that characterizes each one of these areas of human and societal experience. In striving to foster concrete practical engagements, he joins others who are working to address at least some aspects of these challenging issues.

As described by Daniel DiLeo in chapter 13 of this volume, Francis's 2015 encyclical *Laudato si'* aims to promote greater awareness about the urgency of addressing climate change and its consequences for people's lives, economic production, all living creatures, and the whole planet.[31] In recent years, multiple initiatives—involving economic agents, educational and health care institutions, parishes, and dioceses—characterize the "*Laudato si'* Action Platform" and care for our common home in concrete ways.[32]

Moreover, the 2020 Post-Synodal Apostolic Exhortation *Querida Amazonia*, which followed the Synod of Bishops for the Pan-Amazon Region in 2019, actualized *Laudato si'* by gathering multiple constituencies of the Amazonian Church, learning from them, and joining their efforts to protect one of the "lungs" of the planet.[33] Moreover, the Dicastery for Promoting Integral Human Development supports the pope's social agenda and the concrete commitments inspired and animated by Catholic social thought.[34] This approach also expresses a consistent, integral, and comprehensive ethic of life that does not separate theoretical reflections from concrete actions and effective engagements supporting people, groups, and organizations in both ecclesial contexts and civil society.[35]

TWO GLOBAL EXAMPLES

These threefold dimensions inform a Catholic theological bioethics that is less attentive to pursuing a single-issue ethical agenda (e.g., by focusing in a privileged way on abortion or euthanasia, as it is largely stressed in the US Catholic Church) and, instead strives for social justice as well as personal and social flourishing, reinterprets Catholic health care, and is animated by global health concerns (e.g., worldwide COVID-19 vaccinations). Two practical examples reveal the impact of Francis's reprioritization.

Health Care

Todd Salzman and Michael Lawler contrast Pope Francis's approach with the ethical presuppositions that inform the sixth edition of the *Ethical and Religious Directives for Catholic Health Care Services* (*ERDs*) issued by the US Conference of Catholic Bishops in 2018, which regulate health care practice for US Catholic health care institutions.[36] As they stress, the *ERDs* guide Catholic institutions in the provision of health care in ways that intend to embody Jesus's healing ministry, and the commitment of Christianity to care for those who are sick, while striving to promote their well-being and healing whenever possible and, at the same time, they manifest in concrete ways what human dignity deserves and requires.

For Salzman and Lawler, while Catholic health care should be renewed by Francis's transforming ecclesiological, methodological, and anthropological visions, which they define as based on a personalist ethical approach, the revised *ERDs* continue to prioritize a rule-based approach, with an emphasis on absolute norms that proscribe specific medical acts. Within the Catholic Church and wider society, the institutional crisis manifested by the clerical sexual abuse scandal should have generated a more radical process of conversion and reform of Catholic health care institutions as well as collaborations between Catholic and non-Catholic health care providers.[37] Inspired by Pope Francis, Salzman and Lawler propose an increasing pluralism in the norms and directives that facilitate realizing human dignity in Catholic health care contexts. Moreover, together with discernment, the importance assigned to conscience characterizes Francis's approach,[38] and guides believers and people of goodwill in their reasoning, decision-making, and actions.[39] Finally, the pope's emphasis on mercy and care should help in curtailing the stress on norms and inform patients and health care professionals in their conscientious discernment of health care decisions.

Other authors engage differently the pope's bioethical approach to Catholic health care by emphasizing his commitment to a consistent ethic of life, caring for the needy, and promoting a more equitable and just health care distribution.[40] In particular, Cathleen Kaveny discusses, first, how, for the pope, the Christian goals of forming moral identities and empowering moral discernment are nourished by joy and mercy, where, in the centuries-long theological tradition, joy stands for happiness and flourishing, for individuals and communities, and mercy stands for appropriate care.[41]

In Kaveny's assessment, Francis "made a significant contribution to the integration of all levels of Catholic moral thought, a project that was embarked upon after the Second Vatican Council."[42] At the same time, he shifted "the mode of ethical reflection," by focusing on the Good News, with an inclusive social agenda centered on the marginalized and on their needs, and shaped by the concerns and methodologies of Catholic social teaching.[43]

Moreover, Kaveny comments on Francis's call to "go to the periphery." First, she highlights its epistemological relevance, centering on those excluded. Second, the marginalized are the social priority. Third and finally, "go to the periphery" calls people and believers to walk together with the poor, to accompany one another.[44] The pope's repeated criticism of any throwaway culture, and his advocacy for a culture of encounter and global fraternity, reinforce his message.[45] Listening to the cry of the poor and of the Earth, as he invites us to do, leads humankind to both be changed by these cries and to respond to them with concrete actions.[46]

Joining Kaveny's reflection, one could add that Francis's call is shaped by his coming from the world's periphery. He is not simply exhorting us out of a detached concern for what could appear to many to be an ideological choice or condescending and patronizing attitudes. He is indicating how essential it is to embrace the incarnational dynamic of going to those frontiers, being there, and staying there, on those peripheries where mixing, complexity, and messiness are the dominant and characterizing elements. God is there. Jesus's disciples are called to be there, too. God journeys with those who are on the world's peripheries, or cross borders (as Kristin Heyer explores in chapter 7 of this volume), joining those who are often marginalized, excluded, and considered irrelevant because they are too far away from the palaces of power and prestige. The pope invites people of goodwill to embrace this incarnational option, join those who are on those peripheries and frontiers, keep learning from them, and strive with them to transform those contexts in places where social engagement leads to cultural, political, and religious transformations and, ultimately, to improving the quality of life of citizens and communities, and to strengthening personal and social agency.

One example highlights how Francis's vision can be concretely embodied. Cancer has been defined as a rising pandemic. As Philip Landrigan writes, "Cancer has become one of the top two causes of death in 134 countries, the leading cause of death in most high-income countries, and the leading cause of death by disease among children in high-income countries. Nearly 20 million new cancer cases are diagnosed across the world each year."[47] Cancer is a very isolating disease, which affects people and disempowers them.[48] However, discerning how to address the challenges of a cancer diagnosis and its therapy, as well as being in remission and then becoming a survivor, could lead to experiencing communal support and engagement, which aims at fostering a greater cancer awareness, conscientization, advocacy, and social transformation. By focusing on the experiences of Black women who struggled with breast cancer, and by relying on womanist ethics, Elizabeth Williams describes the discernment process that led to the creation of initiatives (like Sista Strut) and associations (like Sisters Network, Inc.). These initiatives contribute to raise awareness about breast cancer, support thousands of women, and gather a significant number of chapters across the United States to challenge disparities in cancer prevention, diagnosis, and therapy that greatly affect Black women.[49] Constructive and virtuous strategies aimed at reducing and eliminating inequities, fostering accompaniment, and promoting social justice can address health care "peripheries."

In Francis's understanding, going to and being on the peripheries of our world changes one's assessment of which priorities must be addressed to promote personal and social flourishing, the common good, and health. Being situated on these peripheries transforms bioethics, both in terms of its agenda and methods. The lack of healthy living conditions, the insufficient quality and availability of health services or the limited access to them, the food deserts, the exposure to toxic pollutants, the lack of green spaces, and the urban architectural chaos that characterize the world's peripheries affect the quality of life of citizens, and their health suffers. Further, sustainability, which aims to protect, preserve, and promote the conditions of life on Earth, is threatened at the peripheries. Inequities should be addressed and eliminated, fostering social justice. In health care, whether locally or globally, this commitment to promoting social justice depends on and implies *discernment* about how scarce health care resources are allocated, which priorities and strategies are chosen, and which social forces are involved or excluded.

Facing the Global Pandemic

The COVID-19 global pandemic actualized this discernment when the whole world, facing this challenging ordeal, became a periphery. Francis's response to this pandemic both exemplifies and confirms such a resolved engagement. Tirelessly, since the beginning of the pandemic, he has invited all to care for those who are more vulnerable around the planet and, when vaccines became available, he pleaded for distributing them fairly around the globe, particularly in the Global South—a call that went largely unheard.[50]

When the world struggled because of this global pandemic to promote the common good of health, the pope denounced any attempt to embrace vaccine nationalism. Confirming instead his appreciation and support for the leadership role of international institutions, Francis addressed the United Nations General Assembly to make the case for a concerted global response.[51] He acknowledged how the COVID-19 pandemic "has led to the loss of so many lives," and continued, "This crisis is changing our way of life, calling into question our economic, health and social systems, and exposing our human fragility."[52] The pope advocated for "the consolidation of multilateralism as the expression of a renewed sense of global co-responsibility, a solidarity grounded in justice and the attainment of peace and unity within the human family."[53] He also urged leaders to embrace global solidarity by providing COVID-19 vaccines as well as essential health care technologies to "the poorest, the most vulnerable, those who so often experience discrimination because they have neither power nor economic resources."[54]

There are practical consequences for Francis's priorities: fostering solidarity with the marginalized, addressing global disparities in access to quality health care services,[55] and promoting population health on Earth that includes refugees and migrants, who have greatly suffered from the Coronavirus pandemic.[56] All should be vaccinated free of charge. In the case of migrants, a resolute commitment to dispel any attempt to gather data about their migration status or related retaliation remains urgent for moral and public health reasons.[57] Analogously, in both the United States and abroad, because of the high percentage of COVID-19 infections in jails and prisons, due to close quarters and living conditions, considering decarceration for selected offenders and facilitating the vaccination of prisoners should be priorities.[58]

As the US National Academies of Sciences, Engineering, and Medicine have stressed,[59] and the World Health Organization has advocated,[60] the COVID-19 global vaccination campaign should serve the goal of promoting health around the planet in integral, equitable, and inclusive ways. Current and future generations will benefit from and appreciate this urgent, complex, and demanding endeavor.

REACTIONS

In recent years, scholars, people of goodwill, and bishops' conferences have manifested their appreciation for the various ways in which Francis has broadened and diversified the ecclesial bioethical agenda by including, in particular, environmental concerns and global health issues as integral to what Catholic bioethics aims to achieve.[61] In all these cases, scholars have appreciated Francis's renewed and expanded set of concerns and have embraced a positive reception of what science is offering, to show how it is possible to form partnerships with researchers, scientists, administrators, politicians, international organizations, believers, and civil society groups in striving to address these ongoing challenges to health and flourishing. This approach does not dismiss the traditional bioethical agenda centered on the beginning and the end of human life or the ethics of research and practice in health care. As confirmation, it is sufficient to consider examples of Francis's statements, on various occasions—addressing, for example, abortion and euthanasia.[62]

As one might expect, the pope's expanded bioethical agenda and his theological approach have been either criticized or received insufficient attention,[63] and were outright resisted or explicitly rejected,[64] particularly by a large majority of the US Catholic hierarchy, which continues to privilege one bioethical and social challenge (i.e., abortion) instead of embracing a discerning stance and a more comprehensive moral agenda. To these criticisms, which need to be critically assessed, one should add that greater attention given to women's reproductive health and agency could further strengthen Francis's contributions to a renewed Catholic theological bioethics, something Megan McCabe's contributions in chapter 10 of this volume help us imagine.

A WAY FORWARD

Both appreciations and resistances, or even rejections, could help in continuing to address bioethical issues that affect people today by striving to improve the quality of their lives, reducing and possibly eliminating inequities, and promoting social justice in ways that will also protect the planet. Confirming this process, a 2022 volume published by the Pontifical Academy for Life explores possible trajectories for the development of the Catholic bioethical agenda and methodology inspired by the pope's approach.[65] The volume features an original document, called a primary text (*testo base*), prepared by eight authors, which "aimed to recast a 'theological ethics of life' in light of Pope Francis's more recent doctrinal impulse, especially his encyclicals and apostolic exhortations."[66] A group of scholars from various continents engaged this text from different theological perspectives, with a privileged attention given to foundational anthropological and eschatological questions and to bioethical issues regarding both the beginning and the end of human life, as well as biotechnologies. Together with this attempt, other efforts are still needed to go to the peripheries of our world and further articulate the Christological, discerning, and experientially based bioethical reflection and action that Pope Francis inspires and nourishes.

NOTES

1. Francis, "Al Comitato Nazionale per la Bioetica," January 28, 2016, www.vatican.va/content/francesco/it/speeches/2016/january/documents/papa-francesco_20160128_comitato-nazionale-bioetica.html. English translations for this text are the author's own.

2. Francis, "Al Comitato Nazionale."
3. See Vincenzo Paglia, "Los Desafíos de la Cultura de la Vida," *Ecclesia* 33, no. 2 (2019): 157–65.
4. Francis, "Al Comitato Nazionale."
5. Francis.
6. Francis.
7. See chapter 6 in this volume by M. T. Dávila. See also Ronaldo Zacharias and Maria Inês de Castro, ed., *A Moral do Papa Francisco: Um Projeto a Partir dos Descartados* (São Paulo: Santuário, 2020).
8. See Francis, "Address to the Members of the Italian National Committee for Biosecurity, Biotechnologies and Life Sciences," April 10, 2017, www.vatican.va/content/francesco/en/speeches/2017/april/documents/papa-francesco_20170410_biotecnologie.html; John A. Gallagher, "Pope Francis' Potential Impact on American Bioethics," *Christian Bioethics* 21, no. 1 (April 2015): 11–34; and Paul Scherz, "The Challenge of Technology to Moral Theology," *Journal of Moral Theology* 10, no. 2 (2021): 239–68.
9. See Devin Watkins, "Pope's March Prayer Intention: For a Christian Response to Bioethical Challenges," *Vatican News*, March 8, 2022, www.vaticannews.va/en/pope/news/2022-03/pope-francis-march-2022-prayer-intention-bioethical-challenges.html.
10. See Christina G. McRorie, "Moral Reasoning in the 'World,'" *Theological Studies* 82, no. 2 (June 2021): 213–37.
11. See Alessandro Rovati, "Mercy Is a Person: Pope Francis and the Christological Turn in Moral Theology," *Journal of Moral Theology* 6, no. 2 (2021): 48–69, at 49. For a reflection on Francis's Jesuit sources, see the introduction in this volume. See also Thomas Massaro, SJ, "'He Drinks from His Own Wells': The Jesuit Roots of the Ethical Teachings of Pope Francis," *Journal of Catholic Social Thought* 15, no. 2 (Summer 2018): 353–73.
12. Antonio Autiero, "On the Ecclesial Vocation of the Moral Theologian: Some Significant Shifts of Emphasis," in *The Catholic Ethicist in the Local Church*, ed. A. Autiero and L. Magesa, Catholic Theological Ethics in the World Church Series (Maryknoll, NY: Orbis Books, 2018), 101. See also Francis, *Evangelii gaudium* (November 24, 2013), no. 39, www.vatican.va/content/francesco/en/apost_exhortations/documents/papa-francesco_esortazione-ap_20131124_evangelii-gaudium.html.
13. For more on the temptations of racial exclusivism, see chapter 8 in this volume, by Maureen O'Connell.
14. See M. Therese Lysaught, "The Peripheries of the Eucharist: Pope Francis, the *Teología del Pueblo*, and the Conversion of Catholic Bioethics," *Perspectiva Teológica* (Belo Horizonte) 51, no. 3 (2019): 421–42.
15. Second Vatican Council, *Gaudium et spes* (December 7, 1965), no. 1, www.vatican.va/archive/hist_councils/ii_vatican_council/documents/vat-ii_const_19651207_gaudium-et-spes_en.html.
16. Rovati, "Mercy," 51.
17. Joseph Boyle, "Franciscan Compassion and Catholic Bioethical Engagement," *Christian Bioethics* 21, no. 1 (March 2015): 35–55, at 37. See also Victor Chacón Huertas, "La 'Bioética Oral' del Papa Francisco," *Moralia: Revista de Ciencias Morales* 40, no. 153 (2017): 7–28. See also chapter 1 in this volume, by Lisa Sowle Cahill.
18. Francis, *Evangelii gaudium*, no. 39.
19. See Dicastery for Promoting Integral Human Development, www.humandevelopment.va/en/sviluppo-umano-integrale.html.
20. See *Gaudium et spes*, nos. 4, 26, 84.

21. See M. Therese Lysaught and Michael McCarthy, eds., *Catholic Bioethics and Social Justice: The Praxis of US Health Care in a Globalized World* (Collegeville, MN: Liturgical Press, 2018); M. Therese Lysaught and Michael McCarthy, "A Social Praxis for US Health Care: Revisioning Catholic Bioethics Via Catholic Social Thought," *Journal of the Society of Christian Ethics* 38, no. 2 (Fall–Winter 2018): 111–30; M. Therese Lysaught and Michael P. McCarthy, "Catholic Bioethics Meets Catholic Social Thought: The Problem, a Primer, and a Plan," in *Catholic Bioethics and Social Justice*, ed. Lysaught and McCarthy, 1–23. See also Lisa Sowle Cahill, *Theological Bioethics: Participation, Justice, and Change* (Washington, DC: Georgetown University Press, 2005); Lisa Sowle Cahill, "Social Justice and the Common Good: Improving the Catholic Social Teaching Framework," in *Ethics Challenges in Global Public Health: Climate Change, Pollution, and the Health of the Poor*, ed. P. J. Landrigan and A. Vicini, SJ, Global Theological Ethics 1 (Eugene, OR: Pickwick Publications, by Wipf & Stock, 2021), 239–68.
22. See Congregation for the Doctrine of the Faith, "Declaration of Euthanasia," May 5, 1980, www.vatican.va/roman_curia/congregations/cfaith/documents/rc_con_cfaith_doc_19800505_euthanasia_en.html; *Catechism of the Catholic Church*, nos. 2276–79, www.vatican.va/archive/ENG0015/__P7Z.HTM; John Paul II, *Evangelium vitae* (March 25, 1995), nos. 64–66, www.vatican.va/content/john-paul-ii/en/encyclicals/documents/hf_jp-ii_enc_25031995_evangelium-vitae.html.
23. Francis, "Message to the President of the Pontifical Academy for Life on the Occasion of the European Regional Meeting of the 'World Medical Association' on 'End of Life' Issues (Vatican, 16–17 November 2017)," November 16, 2017, https://press.vatican.va/content/salastampa/en/bollettino/pubblico/2017/11/16/171116d.html.
24. National Conference of Catholic Bishops, "Resolution on Abortion," November 7, 1989, www.usccb.org/issues-and-action/human-life-and-dignity/abortion/resolution-on-abortion.
25. National Conference of Catholic Bishops.
26. See Katie Rogers and Jason Horowitz, "Biden: Pope Said He Should Receive Communion, Despite US Bishops' Rift on Abortion Rights," *New York Times*, October 29, 2021, www.nytimes.com/2021/10/29/world/europe/biden-pope-communion-abortion.html; Stefano Pitrelli and Amy B. Wang, "Pelosi Receives Communion at Vatican after Earlier US Bishop Refusal," *Washington Post*, June 29, 2022, www.washingtonpost.com/world/2022/06/29/pelosi-pope-vatican-communion/.
27. See Francis, *Amoris laetitia* (March 19, 2016), nos. 77, 79, 151, 242–43, 249, 293, 296–98, 300–305, 312, www.vatican.va/content/dam/francesco/pdf/apost_exhortations/documents/papa-francesco_esortazione-ap_20160319_amoris-laetitia_en.pdf. In this volume, see also chapters 1, 2, and 3, by, respectively, Lisa Sowle Cahill, James Keenan, and Conor Kelly.
28. See Dennis J. Billy, "Dialoguing with Human Experience: A Challenge to Catholic Moral Theology," in *Moral Theology: New Directions and Fundamental Issues*, Festshcrift for James P. Haninan, ed. James Keating (Mahwah, NJ: Paulist Press, 2004), 69–87; and Douglas F. Ottati, "Experience," in *The Oxford Handbook of Theological Ethics*, ed. G. Meilaender and W. Werpehowski (Oxford: Oxford University Press, 2007), 168–86.
29. Human trafficking, in all its multiple forms, is another global bioethical challenge that affects many vulnerable people across continents and that has been a major concern of the pope since the beginning of his pontificate. As examples, see Francis, "Video Message on the Occasion of the 8th International Day of Prayer and Awareness against Human Trafficking," February 8, 2022, www.vatican.va/content/francesco/en/messages/pont-messages/2022/documents/20220208_videomessaggio-contro-trattapersone.

html; and Brett O'Neill and Andrea Vicini, "Human Trafficking and the Dignity of Work," *La Civiltà Cattolica, English Edition* 4, no. 1 (2020): 40–52.
30. See Andrea Vicini, "Artificial Intelligence and Social Control: Ethical Issues and Theological Resources," *Journal of Moral Theology* 11, no. 1 (2022): 43–47.
31. Francis, *"Laudato si'* (May 24, 2015), www.vatican.va/content/francesco/en/encyclicals/documents/papa-francesco_20150524_enciclica-laudato-si.html.
32. See Dicastery for Promoting Integral Human Development, *"Laudato si'* Action Platform," 2022, https://laudatosiactionplatform.org/our-journey-together/.
33. Francis, *Querida Amazonia*, February 2, 2020, www.vatican.va/content/francesco/en/apost_exhortations/documents/papa-francesco_esortazione-ap_20200202_querida-amazonia.html.
34. See chapter 5 in this volume, by Thomas Massaro SJ; and Emilce Cuda de Dunbar, "La Ética Teológica Social del Papa Francisco para Sanar el Mundo," *The First*, June 27 2021, https://catholicethics.com/forum/la-etica-teologica-social/.
35. See Dicastery for Promoting Integral Human Development. See also Paul Valadier, "L'humanisme Intégral selon le Pape François," *Études* 11, no. 4265 (2009): 79–90.
36. See Todd A. Salzman and Michael G. Lawler, *Pope Francis and the Transformation of Health Care Ethics* (Washington, DC: Georgetown University Press, 2021).
37. See Marie-Jo Thiel, *L'Église Catholique Face aux Abus Sexuels sur Mineurs* (Montrouge, France: Bayard, 2019); James F. Keenan, "Hierarchicalism," *Theological Studies* 83, no. 1 (March 2022): 84–108; and Daniel J. Fleming, James F. Keenan, and Hans Zollner, eds., *Doing Theology and Theological Ethics in the Face of the Abuse Crisis*, Global Theological Ethics 4 (Eugene, OR: Pickwick Publications, by Wipf & Stock, 2023).
38. See also David E. DeCosse and Thomas A. Nairn, OFM, eds., *Conscience and Catholic Health Care: From Clinical Contexts to Government Mandates* (Maryknoll, NY: Orbis Books, 2017).
39. See Francis, "Message to the Participants in the European Regional Meeting of the World Medical Association," November 7, 2017, http://w2.vatican.va/content/francesco/en/messages/pont-messages/2017/documents/papa-francesco_20171107_messaggio-monspaglia.html.
40. See James F. Keenan, "What Is Pope Francis' Effect on Health Care?" *America* 218, no. 12 (2018): 19–23. On a consistent ethic of life, see Thomas A. Nairn, ed., *The Seamless Garment: Writings on the Consistent Ethic of Life: Card. Joseph Bernardin* (Maryknoll, NY: Orbis Books, 2008); and Thomas A. Nairn, *The Consistent Ethic of Life: Assessing Its Reception and Relevance* (Maryknoll, NY: Orbis Books, 2008).
41. See Cathleen Kaveny, "Pope Francis and Catholic Healthcare Ethics," *Theological Studies* 80, no. 1 (March 2019): 186–201.
42. Kaveny, 192.
43. Kaveny.
44. See Kaveny.
45. See Kaveny. See also Francis, "Address to Participants at the International Conference Organized by the Pontifical Council of Culture on Regenerative Medicine," April 28, 2018, http://w2.vatican.va/content/francesco/en/speeches/2018/april/documents/papa-francesco_20180428_conferenza-pcc.html; Francis, *Fratelli tutti*, October 3, 2020, nos. 18–19, 188–89, www.vatican.va/content/francesco/en/encyclicals/documents/papa-francesco_20201003_enciclica-fratelli-tutti.html; and Carlo Casalone, "'Humana Communitas': La Vita Umana nella Trama delle Relazioni," *La Civiltà Cattolica* 170, no. 1 (2019): 209–21.

46. See Alexandre Andrade Martins, "Preferential Option for the Poor and Equity in Health," *Camillianum* 14, no. 40 (2014): 31–48; Alexandre Andrade Martins, "Healthy Justice: A Liberation Approach to Justice in Health Care," *Health Care USA* 22, no. 3 (2014): 1–14; and Alexandre Andrade Martins, *The Cry of the Poor: Liberation Ethics and Justice in Health Care* (Lanham, MD: Lexington Books, 2019).
47. Philip J. Landrigan, "Driving Forces of the Epidemic: A Polluted and Polluting Planet," in *The Rising Global Cancer Pandemic: Health, Ethics, and Social Justice*, ed. Andrea Vicini, Philip J. Landrigan, and Kurt Straif, Global Theological Ethics 2 (Eugene, OR: Pickwick Publications, by Wipf & Stock, 2023), 22.
48. See James F. Keenan, "Another Reason to Bring Cancer into the Realm of Global Public Health: The Insularity of Cancer Patients and How Global Public Health Might Get Them Better Connected," in *Rising Global Cancer Pandemic*, ed. Vicini et al., 187–98.
49. See Elizabeth A. Williams, "Talking God and Talking Cancer: Why Womanist Ethics Matters for Breast Cancer Prevention and Control among Black Women," in *The Rising Global Cancer Pandemic*, ed. Vicini et al., 82–97. See also Elizabeth A. Williams, *Black Women and Breast Cancer: A Cultural Theology* (Lanham, MD: Lexington Books, 2019).
50. See Alexandre A. Martins, *COVID-19, Política e Fé: Bioética em Diálogo na Realidade Enlouquecida* (São Paulo: Gênio Criador Editora, 2020); and Andrea Vicini, "Pope Francis, Vaccines, and Global Health," *La Civiltà Cattolica English Edition* 5, no. 12 (2021): 423–33.
51. See Francis, "*Urbi et Orbi* Message," December 25 2020, www.vatican.va/content/francesco/en/messages/urbi/documents/papa-francesco_20201225_urbi-et-orbi-natale.html; Francis, "A Culture of Care as a Path to Peace: Message for the Celebration of the 54th World Day of Peace," December 8, 2021, no. 1, www.vatican.va/content/francesco/en/messages/peace/documents/papa-francesco_20201208_messaggio-54giornata-mondiale-pace2021.html; Vatican COVID-19 Commission and in Collaboration with the Pontifical Academy for Life, "Vaccine for All: 20 Points for a Fairer and Healthier World," December 29, 2020, https://press.vatican.va/content/salastampa/it/bollettino/pubblico/2020/12/29/0697/01628.html#notaing.
52. Francis, "Address to the 75th Meeting of the General Assembly of the United Nations," September 25, 2020, www.vatican.va/content/francesco/en/messages/pont-messages/2020/documents/papa-francesco_20200925_videomessaggio-onu.html.
53. Francis.
54. Francis.
55. See Anita Ho and Iulia Dascalu, "Global Disparity and Solidarity in a Pandemic," *Hastings Center Report* 50, no. 3 (2020): 65–67; and Jordan Pascoe and Mitch Stripling, "Surging Solidarity: Reorienting Ethics for Pandemics," *Kennedy Institute of Ethics Journal* 30, nos. 3–4 (2020): 419–44.
56. See Silvia Huerta Lopez, "'If the Virus Doesn't Kill Us, the Stress and Anxiety Will:' Immigrants During COVID," June 24, 2020, www.thehastingscenter.org/if-the-virus-doesnt-kill-us-the-stress-and-anxiety-will-immigrants-during-covid/.
57. See Nishant Uppal, Parsa Erfani, and Raquel Sofia Sandoval, "ICE Must Provide COVID-19 Vaccines to All Detained Migrants," January 12 2021, www.statnews.com/2021/01/12/ice-must-provide-covid-19-vaccines-to-all-detained-migrants/. See also chapter 7 in this volume, by Kristin Heyer.
58. See Lauren Lyons, "Incarceration, COVID-19, and Emergency Release: Reimagining How and When to Punish," *Kennedy Institute of Ethics Journal* 30, nos. 3–4 (2020): 291–317; Emily A. Wang, Bruce Western, Emily P. Backes, and Julie Schuck, eds.,

Decarcerating Correctional Facilities During COVID-19: Advancing Health, Equity, and Safety (Washington, DC: National Academies Press, 2020).

59. See Benjamin Kahn, Lisa Brown, William Foege, and Helene Gayle, eds., *Framework for Equitable Allocation of COVID-19 Vaccine* (Washington, DC: National Academies Press, 2020).

60. See World Health Organization, *WHO Concept for Fair Access and Equitable Allocation of COVID-19 Health Products: Final Working Version* (Geneva: World Health Organization, 2020).

61. See Nicanor Pier Giorgio Austriaco, "Bioethics in *Laudato Si'*: The Ecological Law as a Moral Principle," *National Catholic Bioethics Quarterly* 15, no. 4 (Winter 2015): 657–63; Jason T. Eberl, "A Bioethical Vision," *Journal of Catholic Social Thought* 16, no. 2 (2018): 279–93; Cory Andrew Labrecque, "Catholic Bioethics in the Anthropocene: Integrating Ecology, Religion, and Human Health," *National Catholic Bioethics Quarterly* 15, no. 4 (Winter 2015): 665–71; and Carlos Alberto Rosas Jiménez, "Bioética de la Esperanza: Claves desde la *Laudato Si'*," *Perseitas* 4, no. 2 (2016): 185–201.

62. On abortion, e.g., see Vatican News staff reporter, "Pope Francis Respects US Supreme Court Decision and Condemns Abortion," July 4, 2022, www.vaticannews.va/en/pope/news/2022-07/pope-francis-condemns-abortion-like-hiring-a-hit-man.html. On euthanasia, e.g., see Francis, "General Audience: Catechesis on Saint Joseph: 11—Saint Joseph, Patron of Good Death," February 9, 2022, www.vatican.va/content/francesco/en/audiences/2022/documents/20220209-udienza-generale.html.

63. In the United States, the encyclical *Laudato si'* and Francis's concern for environmental sustainability as integral to the promotion of social justice received a lukewarm response from the Catholic hierarchy. On the contrary, many other national conferences of bishops, on the various continents, embraced his concerns.

64. See Mark J. Cherry, "Pope Francis, Weak Theology, and the Subtle Transformation of Roman Catholic Bioethics," *Christian Bioethics* 21, no. 1 (April 2015): 84–88; H. Tristram Engelhardt, "A New Theological Framework for Roman Catholic Bioethics: Pope Francis Makes a Significant Change in the Moral Framework for Bioethics," *Christian Bioethics* 21, no. 1 (April 2015): 130–34; Bruce Foltz and Peter Schweitzer, "Pope Francis and the Perils of Double Truth," *Christian Bioethics* 21, no. 1 (April 2015): 89–108; Mary Margaret Mooney, "Habemus Papam," *Christian Bioethics* 21, no. 1 (April 2015): 69–72; and Maurizio Mori, "An Address to Doctors by Pope Francis (15 November 2014): A Doctrinal Mistake and a Lot of Common Sense Presented with Savoir-Faire," *Christian Bioethics* 21, no. 1 (April 2015): 109–29.

65. See Vincenzo Paglia, ed., *Etica Teologica della Vita: Scrittura, Tradizione, Sfide Pratiche* (Vatican City: Libreria Editrice Vaticana, 2022). For reviews of the volume, see Jorge José Ferrer, SJ, "Rereading the Theological Ethics of Life in the Light of Pope Francis," *La Civiltà Cattolica English Edition* 6, no. 8, art. 2, July 21, 2022, www.laciviltacattolica.com/rereading-the-theological-ethics-of-life-in-the-light-of-pope-francis/; and Roberto Dell'Oro and M. Therese Lysaught, "*Theological Ethics of Life*: A New Volume by the Pontifical Academy for Life," *Journal of Moral Theology* 11, no. 2 (2022): 65–77.

66. Dell'Oro and Lysaught, "*Theological Ethics of Life*," 65.

12

POPE FRANCIS'S PEACE ETHICS

Beginning from the "Wounded Flesh of the Victims"

Laurie Johnston

Since the end of the Papal States in 1870, and ever more dramatically in the last sixty years, popes have consistently condemned the resort to violence and called upon Christians to work for peace. Shortly after the outbreak of World War I, Pope Benedict XV lamented the terrible destruction that it was already causing, writing, "Surely there are other ways and means whereby violated rights can be rectified. Let them be tried honestly and with goodwill, and let arms meanwhile be laid aside."[1] Decades later, Pope John XXIII put it more bluntly: "It no longer makes sense to maintain that war is a fit instrument with which to repair the violation of justice."[2] And as the United States prepared to invade Iraq in 2003, Pope John Paul II responded with a dramatic "NO TO WAR! War is not always inevitable. It is always a defeat for humanity."[3] In his statements about war and peace, Pope Francis has continued the trajectory of his predecessors and, at times, further extended their arguments. The commonalities between his teaching and that of the other recent popes are far more striking than any differences. Nevertheless, there are some key characteristics of Pope Francis's approach to war and peace that illustrate his distinctive theological approach.

BEGINNING FROM THE "WOUNDED FLESH OF THE VICTIMS"

One distinctive element is found not so much in the conclusions that he draws but the place Pope Francis begins. For centuries, theologians and pastors have reflected on the ethics of war with a particular audience in mind: political leaders and their advisers. For example, elements of just war theory can be found in letters that Saint Augustine wrote to advise political and military leaders such as Marcellinus, who was trying to understand how he should exercise his political role in light of his conversion to Christianity. While of course the popes have also spoken about war and peace with an eye to shaping the consciences of ordinary Christians, there is nevertheless a frequent implication that the primary audience is those who possess political and military power. The ethics of war emerged primarily as a way of advising elites.

Pope Francis's starting point is quite different. Though he certainly addresses world leaders—often in very direct terms—the people he has in mind are first and foremost the ones who are the most vulnerable and marginal. He is speaking for them, and acting with them in mind:

> Let us not remain mired in theoretical discussions, but touch the wounded flesh of the victims. Let us look once more at all those civilians whose killing was considered "collateral damage." Let us ask the victims themselves. Let us think of the refugees and displaced, those who suffered the effects of atomic radiation or chemical attacks, the mothers who lost their children, and the boys and girls maimed or deprived of their childhood. Let us hear the true stories of these victims of violence, look at reality through their eyes, and listen with an open heart to the stories they tell.[4]

He sees his role as calling attention to these wounds and lamenting the plight of the many victims of violence—and in lamenting, he has even been moved to tears in public.[5] In his words, and also in his concrete gestures, he consistently seeks to turn the world's attention to the often-ignored victims of what he terms "throwaway culture." A pope who sees himself as having come from the margins,[6] he is continually directing attention toward those who are marginalized. As Jan de Volder puts it, "one can readily see how Pope Francis identifies with the victims of globalization and capitalism, rather than with the beneficiaries."[7] He has gone to particular lengths to bring the focus to the victims of war, perhaps most dramatically in his 2015 visit to an active war zone in the Central African Republic. It was there, in a poor and landlocked country whose long-standing conflict rarely gains a mention in the international media, that he inaugurated the Jubilee Year of Mercy at the cathedral in Bangui—and also paid a visit to a mosque. At the cathedral, he began the liturgy by saying, "Today Bangui becomes the spiritual capital of the world. The Holy Year of Mercy starts early in this land of Africa."[8] Instead of observing from afar or speaking in abstractions, Francis plunged into this difficult situation with a word of hope. This paints quite a contrast with the typical ways that world leaders often proceed. Indeed, Francis has been critical of the attitude of those in power who engage in what he calls *balconeando*—looking at the world as if watching on high from a balcony—when instead they ought to be willing to immerse themselves in a real encounter with the suffering of the victims. After all, "To embrace the margins is to expand our horizons, for we see more clearly and broadly from the edges of society."[9]

Pope Francis not only seeks to turn the world's attention to the marginalized and the victims of war, however. He also sees himself as a *representative* for them, one who speaks on their behalf. In his 2015 address at the United Nations, he immediately spoke up for the poor by criticizing international financial institutions whose policies "subject people to mechanisms which generate greater poverty, exclusion and dependence."[10] He also exhorted the members of the US Congress: "You are called to defend and preserve the dignity of your fellow citizens in the tireless and demanding pursuit of the common good, for this is the chief aim of all politics. A political society endures when it seeks, as a vocation, to satisfy common needs by stimulating the growth of all its members, especially those in situations of greater vulnerability or risk."[11]

He also spoke quite directly to the political leaders of South Sudan when they came to the Vatican for a retreat, and concluded his time by kneeling to kiss their feet. He begged them to make peace in their country, so that they could become "Fathers of the nation." In his address, he said:

> God's gaze is especially directed to you; it is a look that offers you peace. Yet there is another gaze directed to you: it is the gaze of our people, and it expresses their ardent desire for justice, reconciliation and peace. At this moment, I want to assure all your fellow citizens of my spiritual closeness, especially the refugees and the sick, who have remained in the country with great expectations and with bated breath, awaiting the outcome of this historic day.... Your people is awaiting your return to your country, the reconciliation of all its members, and a new era of peace and prosperity for all.[12]

As usual, he is making the ordinary people, and especially the suffering, the "refugees and the sick," present in the room with the powerful.

Why focus so much on the poor, the marginalized, the wounded victims? Francis's Ignatian formation is certainly evident here, in the inductive approach where personal encounter generates conversion. As the Jesuit superior general Peter-Hans Kolvenbach said, "When the heart is touched by direct experience, the mind may be challenged to change. Personal involvement with innocent suffering, with the injustice others suffer, is the catalyst for solidarity which then gives rise to intellectual inquiry and moral reflection."[13] Furthermore, Francis's attention to the reality of suffering reflects the influence of Latin American liberation theology, particularly in the form of *la teología del pueblo*, which has so profoundly shaped his approach to the world. James

Keenan describes how liberation theologians have brought about a dramatic shift in moral theology in recent decades. "Suffering," he writes, "like the poor themselves, became the object of the theologians' investigations and, in time, it emerged as the predominant interest of theological ethicists."[14] This is clear in the thought of Pope Francis, so much so that *"Fratelli tutti* presumes that suffering is at the heart of the moral agenda."[15]

This focus on suffering also introduces a range of complexities. Pope Francis is suggesting that the suffering of the victims is the starting place for any reflection on the ethics of war and peace, and that we must "look at reality through their eyes, and listen with an open heart to the stories they tell."[16] Yet we cannot assume that observing the destruction that accompanies war will always lead to opposition to all war. Victims have a wide range of responses, and some tell their stories in order to call for violent responses. What are we to do when the victims of war call for war themselves, or when witnessing suffering seems to provoke a desire for revenge rather than a desire for peace? Still, Francis reveals a deep conviction that it is always possible that the encounter with suffering can induce real change in human hearts. Furthermore, the most fundamental response to suffering is compassion—as can be seen in Francis's repeated use of the parable of the Good Samaritan to illustrate the urgent need for compassionate response to those who are in need. It is when we respond compassionately to those who are suffering that we find ourselves in harmony with God, because it means that we have heard "the 'song of a lament' resounding in our time. . . . We have a responsibility to be in tune with God, to move toward the one who is suffering, to find the right rhythm with Him."[17] (All the translations provided in this chapter are the author's.) Indeed, lament is an accurate term for the way Francis frequently speaks about war. His voice is a mournful one, more so than a strategic one.

Still, Francis's emphasis on the victims of war is also quite pragmatic. He thinks that an honest appraisal of the suffering that is caused by war will lead any rational observer to conclude that war is fruitless and illogical. If we really pay attention to the impact of war, it becomes clear that in the modern day, war is indeed "no longer . . . a fit instrument with which to repair the violation of justice."[18] As Francis said a few months into the war in Ukraine, "I did not cease praying for the battered and martyred Ukrainian people, asking God to free them from the scourge of war. If one looked at what is happening *objectively*, considering the harm that war brings every day to those people, but also to the entire world, the only reasonable thing to do would be to stop and negotiate" (emphasis added).[19] The rejection of war as a legitimate option has become particularly pressing as the war in Ukraine has revived fears of a nuclear attack. As his predecessors have done for decades, Pope Francis draws attention to the particular evil of nuclear weapons—even going so far as to condemn the mere ownership of them.[20] Nuclear deterrence, he argues, cannot be morally justified and certainly cannot create real peace and stability in the international arena. For Catholics in the United States—the only country to ever carry out a nuclear attack, and a nation that has long relied on nuclear deterrence as a security strategy—this poses a major moral challenge.[21]

Overall, Francis is convinced that if we look seriously at the actual effects of war, we will be unable to claim that the benefits can ever outweigh the costs; the very nature of modern warfare is unavoidably extreme in its damaging effects and thus can never be justifiable. As Michael Cardinal Czerny and Christian Barone point out simply, "If the response to an offense has the effect of injuring or denying the very values and rights it is intended to preserve, the outcome will be the encouragement of a disposition towards violence in society."[22] Summarizing Francis's perspective, they go on to explain:

> Every war must be "felt" as a failure of politics and a defeat for humanity, because it "leaves the world worse than before" (*Fratelli tutti*, 261). That is why it is important to be compelled by the tragedy experienced by the civilians involved and to attend to the pain of the victims, the refugees, the orphans, those whose bodies and hearts are maimed, and who are often regarded as the inevitable "collateral damage" of the overwhelming events that are taking place. If it is true that "reality is more important than ideas" (*Evangelii gaudium*, 231–33), the reality of war as experienced by the victims outweighs the opinion of those who see it as a short-term or long-term benefit.[23]

Here again, we see that Francis is deeply concerned to speak on behalf of the poor and marginalized—and far less interested in paying attention to the geopolitical concerns of political theorists or world leaders. This is not out of naivete, however. Rather, those who are naive are the ones who would justify war, because they have failed to "grasp the abyss of evil at the heart of war."[24]

It is not only the sheer destructiveness of modern warfare that makes war always a defeat for humanity. The very complexity of the modern world also means that a war in one part of the world inevitably has reverberations elsewhere. As the first pope from the Global South, Francis is aware that superpower rivalries often create collateral damage all over the world. As Czerny and Barone put it, "Globalization causes conflicts that take place in one region of the world to produce a series of ripple effects that affect the entire planet. We are experiencing a 'world war fought piecemeal' (*Fratelli tutti*, 25, 259), and it is naive to believe that what goes on in another continent does not affect us directly."[25] Indeed, the many complex sources of violence today have led to a situation in which, globally, more civilians than soldiers are dying violent deaths—and that does not even account for the many deaths from hunger and disease due to the economic, political, and environmental disruptions that accompany violent conflicts. In essence, Pope Francis is arguing that contemporary war is never proportional to the harms it seeks to rectify—and thus can never meet one of the traditional criteria for a just war.

JUST (?) WAR AND PROPHETIC TENSION

The question of whether modern war can ever be just, and whether it is ever legitimate for a country to use violence in defense of itself, brings us to a point of real tension in the thought of Pope Francis, and in the broader field of contemporary moral theology. Just war theory was developed primarily as a response to the problem of how to protect the victims of war—the same types of victims with which Pope Francis is particularly concerned. While Francis's concern for them is clear, there is a real ambiguity in his discussion of how the world should respond to their suffering. On one hand, Francis refuses to ever openly endorse the use of force as a morally justified response and argues that just war theory—long a part of the Church's ethical reasoning about war—is no longer serving its purpose and should become a relic of the past. Yet on several occasions, he also acknowledges that some elements of the just war theory, particularly the concept of legitimate defense, may still be necessary.

Overall, this tension in his thought reflects a broader tension in the Church's moral teaching in recent decades. Ultimately, this tension cannot be avoided, as it reflects the broader eschatological tension of our human lives in this in-between time. Christian Braun notes how that eschatological tension is manifest even in the very role of the papacy. Pope Francis's ambiguous remarks, he writes,

> must be seen before the background of a general historical tension within the Catholic Church between Christian pacifists and advocates of the just war idea, between peace in heaven and peace on earth, between the pope's roles as "Vicar of Christ" and "sovereign authority." Any pontiff, as the leader of the Catholic Church, has had to maneuver between these two competing streams. As the result of this delicate balancing task modern popes have foregrounded the tools of nonviolence while, at the same time, their teaching for the temporal realm continues to depend on the just war framework. Only in their role as leader of the Church with its eschatological vision do the popes reject all violence.... The observer faces the challenging task of disentwining the Church's understanding of its own role from its comprehension of the function of political leadership.[26]

When calling for an end to all violence, then, the popes are playing a pastoral role as the vicar of Christ. This is certainly the role with which

Pope Francis is primarily concerned. As Lisa Cahill has put it, "Even if killing is sometimes morally necessary and justified, it is not the job of the popes as Christian leaders, pastors and teachers, to justify it."[27] Thus, when it comes to actual political choices, Pope Francis is reluctant to be drawn into such discussions, much less to justify specific courses of action that may involve violent force.

This reluctance also reflects Francis's desire to be a pope for the entire world; he wants to avoid being drawn into a geopolitical dynamic that far too often ignores the concerns of the many people who live outside Europe or North America. In his afterword to a volume that collected the statements of Pope Francis on peace, Andrea Tornielli describes the pope's effort to speak about the invasion of Ukraine in a way that is morally clear but avoids blessing those who would like to claim the pope's mantle for their own purposes:

> Francis's no to the war, a radical and convinced no, like that pronounced by his predecessors, has nothing to do with a partisan position nor is it motivated by politico-diplomatic calculations. In the war in Ukraine there are the aggressors and there are the attacked. There are those who attacked and invaded by killing defenseless civilians, hypocritically masking the conflict under the guise of a "special military operation"; and there are those who defend themselves by fighting for their land. Francis has said this several times in very clear words, condemning the invasion and martyrdom of Ukraine. However, this does not mean "blessing" the acceleration of the arms race, because the Pope is not the "chaplain of the West" and because he repeats that today being on the right side of history means being against war by seeking peace and never leaving any stone unturned.[28]

Although the hypocrisy of the aggressor in the Ukraine invasion may be clear, Francis is alert to the danger of hypocrisy on all sides. As the pope of the margins, he cannot permit his words to be used to justify violence as if he were merely the "chaplain of the West," ready to legitimate whatever is the policy currently in vogue among Western elites. However, this means that his prescriptions must necessarily remain somewhat vague. This was evident during the discussion about the rise of the Islamic State, when many world leaders were wrestling with how to respond to the extreme and genocidal violence that was taking place. It was a political situation that seemed to merit a forceful response, and so Pope Francis was asked whether US airstrikes might be justified. He replied,

> In these cases where there is unjust aggression, I can only say that it is licit to stop the unjust aggressor. I underscore the verb "stop"; I don't say bomb, make war—stop him. The means by which he may be stopped should be

evaluated. To stop the unjust aggressor is licit, but we nevertheless need to remember how many times, using this excuse of stopping an unjust aggressor, the powerful nations have dominated other peoples, made a real war of conquest. A single nation cannot judge how to stop this, how to stop an unjust aggressor. After the Second World War, there arose the idea of the United Nations. That is where we should discuss: "Is there an unjust aggressor? It seems there is. How do we stop him?" But only that, nothing more.[29]

Indeed, Pope Francis is correct that the excuse of stopping unjust aggression has often provided a pretext for terrible abuses. Yet he also acknowledges the legitimacy of defensive force, at times—and the need to offer moral guidance to the leaders who must make such decisions. He is reluctant to evaluate the details of political strategy, however, pointing only to the importance of multilateralism and of the United Nations. Rather than providing a detailed moral analysis for heads of state (something he is reluctant to do in other moral matters as well, as Cahill and Keenan explain, respectively, in chapters 1 and 2 of this volume), Francis is merely suggesting *where* the conversation ought to take place.

The dilemma of how to respond to "unjust aggression" is precisely where just war theory might be useful, but Pope Francis has been reluctant to speak in those terms, even if he does make use of some traditional just war criteria. He is all too aware of how frequently just war theory has been abused, pointing out trenchantly in *Fratelli tutti* that "war can easily be chosen by invoking all sorts of allegedly humanitarian, defensive or precautionary excuses, and even resorting to the manipulation of information. In recent decades, every single war has been ostensibly 'justified.'"[30] In light of such cynical manipulations, Francis goes on to say that the theory has outlived its usefulness: "Saint Augustine, who forged a concept of' 'just war' that we no longer uphold in our own day, also said that 'it is a higher glory still to stay war itself with a word, than to slay men with the sword, and to procure or maintain peace by peace, not by war.'"[31] Elsewhere, he makes clear that he regards the use of force as a political tool that belongs in the same category as nuclear deterrence or the death penalty. These were conceded to be necessary responses to difficult situations in the past but are now no longer morally acceptable. And in a video call with Patriarch Kirill of Russia near the beginning of the Ukraine invasion, Francis said simply, "Wars are always unjust, since it is the people of God who pay."[32]

The tension between the rejection of all war and the necessity to address political reality is not one that Pope Francis—or any Christian—will escape soon. Even if Pope Francis sees his primary audience as those on the margins, there will always be political and military leaders who seek moral guidance from the papacy. Thus, it is not entirely surprising to see that some of Francis's reflections on the war in Ukraine still draw upon just war reasoning. When asked about the morality of supplying weapons for Ukraine to use in self-defense, he refers to the importance of *right intention*, a key component of just war theory:

> It is a political decision, which can be moral—morally accepted—if it is done according to the conditions of morality, which are many. But it can be immoral if it is done with the intention of provoking more war or selling weapons or discarding those weapons that are no longer needed. The motivation is what largely qualifies the morality of this act. To defend oneself is not only lawful, but is also an expression of love of country. Those who do not defend themselves, those who do not defend something, do not love it, instead those who defend, love. There you get into something else I have spoken on in my speeches, that the concept of just war must be further reflected upon.[33]

Indeed, the concept of a just war merits critical reflection in every era and will always remain in tension with the Christian vocation to be nonviolent peacemakers. We cannot expect the popes to escape this tension. As Paolo Carlotti has put it, "There is certainly a tension present in the magisterium, but also because—even more so—there is a tension present in the very reality of war and more generally in the very reality of history, a reality that no one can fail to consider and which the Christian must consider as a reality that bears an eschatological imprint."[34]

Because this tension is present in history itself, and yet that same history is imprinted by the power of the resurrection, the possibility of redemption remains ever present. Therefore, there always remains scope for the Christian imagination to envision alternative possibilities to violence.

NONVIOLENCE AND ITS REQUISITES

One imaginative alternative to which Francis has drawn our attention is the possibility of nonviolent resistance. His World Day of Peace message for 2017, titled "Nonviolence: A Style of Politics for Peace," declares that "peacebuilding through active nonviolence is the natural and necessary complement to the Church's continuing efforts to limit the use of force by the application of moral norms."[35] Francis goes on to call attention to the many examples of creative and successful nonviolent campaigns for political change:

> The decisive and consistent practice of nonviolence has produced impressive results. The achievements of Mahatma Gandhi and Khan Abdul Ghaffar Khan in the liberation of India, and of Dr. Martin Luther King Jr. in combating racial

discrimination will never be forgotten. Women in particular are often leaders of nonviolence, as for example, was Leymah Gbowee and the thousands of Liberian women, who organized pray-ins and nonviolent protest that resulted in high-level peace talks to end the second civil war in Liberia. Nor can we forget the eventful decade that ended with the fall of Communist regimes in Europe.[36]

This emphasis on nonviolence is a fitting approach for Pope Francis, given his practical approach and his focus on the ordinary people who are often the victims of war; nonviolence is a tool available even to those who seem powerless, and its practical effectiveness is clear.[37]

Nonviolence as an approach often involves gestures or dramatic encounters that reveal a deeper reality. For example, peaceful protesters who face attack without retaliating provide a powerful demonstration of respect for the human dignity of the other, and simultaneously reveal the impotence of violence—since the violence they are experiencing does not dissuade them from protesting. Pope Francis himself has often turned to dramatic gestures as a mode of nonviolent peacemaking, in a way that shows the creative power of the imagination—as we have seen from his visit to Bangui and his act of kissing the feet of South Sudanese leaders. In addition, he used visits to Hiroshima and Nagasaki in 2019 as occasions to remind the world of the devastation that took place there in 1945. As the Jesuit Thomas Massaro writes, "Calling attention to the immorality of nuclear warfare and the pressing need for further negotiations to limit nuclear armaments on the very spots where many thousands died from atomic blasts was an extremely poignant way to publicize this urgent message."[38] Once again, it is by calling attention to the concrete impact of violence that Pope Francis prompts us to imagine alternatives to war.

One aspect of nonviolent strategy that is often overlooked is a willingness to embrace and even escalate conflict while still refusing to employ violent tactics. It is important, therefore, that Francis's approach to conflict reflects a willingness to directly engage, and an emphasis on taking concrete steps to reach across the divides of the world in order to build trust. This is quite different from mere pacification, which would merely attempt to suppress conflict. Instead, in *Evangelii gaudium*, Francis writes,

> When conflict arises, some people simply look at it and go their way as if nothing happened; they wash their hands of it and get on with their lives. Others embrace it in such a way that they become its prisoners; they lose their bearings, project onto institutions their own confusion and dissatisfaction and thus make unity impossible. But there is also a third way, and it is the best way to deal with conflict. It is the willingness to face conflict head on, to resolve it and to make it a link in the chain of a new process. "Blessed are the peacemakers!" (Mt. 5:9).[39]

While much attention has been paid to Francis's emphasis on creating a "culture of encounter," it is important to acknowledge that such a culture requires a certain level of comfort with differences and even conflict. Genuine encounter does not overlook conflict, and genuine peace requires a real reckoning with grievances. As Massaro points out,

> Respectful encounter with the other is part of what Jesuits refer to as "our way of proceeding. . . ." A most constructive basis for any conversation is the assumption that one may readily learn from the other. . . . Regarding the specific ministry of peacemaking, it is clear that any peace settlement that aspires to be sustainable must be based on the kind of trust that is generated when each side is able to acknowledge that it has been listened to thoroughly, so that no perceived grievance is merely swept under the rug, but rather that all legitimate perspectives have been aired and attended to in a respectful way.[40]

Francis's emphasis on the transformative power of encounter to promote peace is rooted in his conviction that "unity is greater than conflict."[41] This hopeful perspective enables him to imagine real alternatives to the violence and geopolitical rivalries that shape our world. Francis speaks instead of a "geopolitics of mercy," in which "the power of mercy changes the meaning of historical processes: no thing and no one is ever to be considered as definitely 'lost' even when speaking of relations between peoples and nations."[42] Indeed, the message of the Gospel is that "Peace is possible because the Lord has overcome the world and its constant conflict,"[43] and therefore Christians must never resign themselves to the inevitability of violence and war. Even amidst the challenges we see all around us, "The aim of Francis's peace praxeology is . . . the fearless realization of the *magis*, the greater good in the perspective of God. . . . He is convinced that it is precisely in the real world with all its ambiguities, that something new and better can always emerge."[44]

A NEW VISION OF POSITIVE PEACE: THE POLYHEDRON OF RECONCILED DIVERSITY

Francis's faith that "unity is greater than conflict" undergirds his most important contribution to the theology of peace: a way of envisioning *positive peace* that is genuinely new, and ought to have particular resonance for Catholics in the United States. This vision is rooted in the theology of *Gaudium et spes*, which emphasizes two important things: first, that peace is not merely the absence of war; and second, that peace is something we are all called to build up. Francis frequently echoes the insights of *Gaudium et spes* that a balance of power does not constitute real peace, and that genuine peace is an enterprise of justice that is the fruit of fraternity and love.[45] Yet he goes on to speak of peace as also the fruit of what he calls *reconciled diversity*. He is particularly concerned to point out that peace is a far cry from *uniformity*. His vision of peace is as a dynamic reality, not a static *tranquilitas ordinis*. It is precisely by bringing together a diversity of perspectives—especially voices from the margins, as Keenan emphasizes in chapter 2 of this volume, that peace emerges. This takes place via dialogue and encounter, a process that Francis describes as "a continuing adventure that makes every periphery converge in a greater sense of mutual belonging."[46] Indeed, one can sense exhilaration in the way that Francis describes this "adventure." He has a strong sense that uniformity is stultifying and diversity is a genuine good, something to be enjoyed and embraced, rather than feared. This sense of the richness of differences emerges in many places in his thought. For instance, we read in *Evangelii gaudium*,

> The message of peace is not about a negotiated settlement but rather the conviction that the unity brought by the Spirit can harmonize every diversity. It overcomes every conflict by creating a new and promising synthesis. Diversity is a beautiful thing when it can constantly enter into a process of reconciliation and seal a sort of cultural covenant resulting in a "reconciled diversity" As the bishops of the Congo have put it: "Our ethnic diversity is our wealth.... It is only in unity, through conversion of hearts and reconciliation, that we will be able to help our country to develop on all levels."[47]

Similarly, in their summary of *Fratelli tutti*, Czerny and Barone point to diversity as an important resource:

> Any exchange in which the identity of the other is not erased or devalued becomes a resource for the civic community and fresh lifeblood circulating in the veins of society (*Fratelli tutti*, 148). The examples of the United States and Argentina... show the goodness of these realities (*Fratelli tutti*, 133–36). ... The protection of diversity, of the plurality of cultures and identities, is the key criterion of a fraternity that aspires to a universality that is not merely abstract (*Fratelli tutti*, 143) and certainly does not impose itself as a power that eliminates diversity. True fraternity does not homogenize, but allows us to remain ourselves together with others; otherwise it is a "false openness to the universal."[48]

This belief in the life-giving potential of diversity, of course, undergirds much of Francis's papacy. As James Keenan points out in chapter 2 of this volume, inclusive and responsive listening is a recurring theme for Francis and is especially clear in his emphasis on synodality. But beyond the importance of inclusive listening and synodality for the life of the Church itself, Pope Francis is also developing a political and social vision that invites us to consider a new way of imagining peace in the world at large: as a *polyhedron*. A trained chemist, Francis may have been inspired by the complex geometric shapes of organic molecules—from hexagonal benzene rings to the three-dimensional buckminsterfullerene. Here is how he explains the idea of the polyhedron in *Evangelii gaudium*:

> Our model is not the sphere, which is no greater than its parts, where every point is equidistant from the centre, and there are no differences between them. Instead, it is the polyhedron, which reflects the convergence of all its parts, each of which preserves its distinctiveness. Pastoral and political activity alike seek to gather in this polyhedron the best of each. There is a place for the poor and their culture, their aspirations and their potential. Even people who can be considered dubious on account of their errors have something to offer which must not be overlooked. It is the convergence of peoples who, within the universal order, maintain their own individuality; it is the sum total of persons within a society which pursues the common good, which truly has a place for everyone.[49]

In the peaceful society that is a polyhedron, there remain genuine differences—edges, one might say. There are distinct facets that represent varying points of view. But without these facets, the polyhedron would be incomplete. The various facets of a snowflake, for instance, are what catch the light and make it beautiful. "May we not be content with being enclosed in one fragment of reality," therefore, Francis writes in *Fratelli tutti*.[50]

CONCLUSION: RECEIVING FRANCIS'S TEACHING ON PEACE AS CATHOLICS IN THE UNITED STATES

For Catholics in the United States, Francis's teaching on peace is challenging indeed. How can we truly attend to the suffering of the victims when war can now be fought by remote-controlled drones, operated far from the theater of war? If the mere possession of nuclear weapons is not morally licit, what does this mean for Catholics who are citizens of a major nuclear power—and particularly those Catholics who serve in the military or work for defense contractors? How do we advocate for the superiority of nonviolent responses to evil in a country originally founded through a violent revolution and a genocide of indigenous peoples, and where today guns outnumber people and arms exports sustain violent conflicts all over the world? Still, the teaching of Pope Francis serves to remind us of the ways in which the United States has, in partial but real ways, demonstrated the power of reconciled diversity in our civic and political life. It is striking to see a papal encyclical mention specific countries by name; yet *Fratelli tutti* specifically points to the United States and Argentina as examples of how the diversity that immigrants bring can be a gift.[51] Thus, Pope Francis is inviting the United States to embrace its potential to live out the positive vision of peace that he envisions. To respond to his invitation, however, US Catholics must find ways to truly demonstrate the attention to the margins, the attention to the suffering victims, the embrace of diversity, and the inclusive listening that make the polyhedron possible. Instead of mirroring the divides in US society, we then might become the leaven that gives rise to richer ways of imagining and living peace in the United States and beyond.

NOTES

1. Benedict XV, *Ad Beatissimi Apostolorum*, April 11, 1914, no. 4, www.vatican.va/content/benedict-xv/en/encyclicals/documents/hf_ben-xv_enc_01111914_ad-beatissimi-apostolorum.html.
2. John XXIII, *Pacem in Terris*, November 4, 1963, no. 127, www.vatican.va/content/john-xxiii/en/encyclicals/documents/hf_j-xxiii_enc_11041963_pacem.html.
3. John Paul II, "Address to the Diplomatic Corps," January 13, 2003, www.vatican.va/content/john-paul-ii/en/speeches/2003/january/documents/hf_jp-ii_spe_20030113_diplomatic-corps.html.
4. Francis, *Fratelli tutti*, October 3, 2020, no. 261, www.vatican.va/content/francesco/en/encyclicals/documents/papa-francesco_20201003_enciclica-fratelli-tutti.html.
5. "Pope Weeps in Rome as He Prays for Peace in Ukraine," AP News, December 8, 2022, https://apnews.com/article/pope-francis-religion-rome-f98677c8b38bd2898a295dbf355d32c1.
6. In his very first words as pope, Francis commented that "it was the duty of the Conclave to give Rome a Bishop. It seems that my brother Cardinals have gone to the ends of the earth to get one; ... but here we are." Francis, "First Greeting of the Holy Father Pope Francis," March 13, 2013, www.vatican.va/content/francesco/en/speeches/2013/march/documents/papa-francesco_20130313_benedizione-urbi-et-orbi.html.
7. Jan de Volder, "Pope Francis's Idiosyncratic Approach to Global Politics," in *The Geopolitics of Pope Francis*, ed. Jan de Volder (Leuven: Peeters, 2019), 6.
8. Francis, "Opening of the Holy Door at the Cathedral of Bangui," November 29, 2015, www.vatican.va/content/francesco/en/homilies/2015/documents/papa-francesco_20151129_repcentrafricana-omelia-cattedrale-bangui.html.
9. Francis and Austen Ivereigh, *Let Us Dream: The Path to a Better Future* (New York: Simon & Schuster, 2020), 126.
10. Francis, "Address to the UN General Assembly," September 25, 2015, www.vatican.va/content/francesco/en/speeches/2015/september/documents/papa-francesco_20150925_onu-visita.html.
11. Francis, "Address to the Joint Session of the US Congress," September 24, 2015, www.vatican.va/content/francesco/en/speeches/2015/september/documents/papa-francesco_20150924_usa-us-congress.html.

12. Francis, "Spiritual Retreat for the Civil and Ecclesiastical Authorities of South Sudan," April 11, 2019, https://press.vatican.va/content/salastampa/en/bollettino/pubblico/2019/04/11/190411c.html.
13. Peter-Hans Kolvenbach, "The Service of Faith and the Promotion of Justice in American Jesuit Higher Education," October 6, 2000, www.scu.edu/ic/programs/ignatian-worldview/kolvenbach/.
14. James Keenan, *A History of Catholic Theological Ethics* (Mahwah, NJ: Paulist Press, 2022), 311.
15. Keenan, 306.
16. Francis, *Fratelli tutti*, no. 261.
17. Michael Czerny and Christian Barone, *Fraternità: Segno dei tempi—Il magistero sociale di Papa Francesco* (Vatican City: Libreria Editrice Vaticana, 2021), 253. Translations of this and other works not in English are the author's own.
18. See, again, John XXIII, *Pacem in Terris*, 127.
19. Francis, "Angelus, Saint Peter's Square, Sunday, 31 July 2022," www.vatican.va/content/francesco/en/angelus/2022/documents/20220731-angelus.html.
20. Francis, "Address of His Holiness Pope Francis to Participants in the International Symposium 'Prospects for a World Free of Nuclear Weapons and for Integral Disarmament,'" November 10, 2017, www.vatican.va/content/francesco/en/speeches/2017/november/documents/papa-francesco_20171110_convegno-disarmointegrale.html.
21. Francis's fellow Jesuit, Drew Christiansen, has collected essays by a range of American theologians who wrestle with the implications of Francis's teaching on nuclear weapons. See Drew Christiansen and Carole Sargent, eds., *Forbidden: Receiving Pope Francis's Condemnation of Nuclear Weapons* (Washington, DC: Georgetown University Press, 2023).
22. Czerny and Barone, *Fraternità*, 190.
23. Czerny and Barone.
24. Francis, *Fratelli tutti*, no. 261.
25. Czerny and Barone, *Fraternità*, 190. Pope Francis has stated that with the invasion of Ukraine, the world is moving closer to an overt "third world war."
26. Christian Braun, "Pope Francis on War and Peace," *Journal of Catholic Social Thought* 15, no. 1 (Winter 2018): 64, 67.
27. Lisa Sowle Cahill, "The Changing Vision of 'Just Peace' in Catholic Social Tradition," *Journal of Moral Theology* 7, no. 2 (2018): 107.
28. Andrea Tornielli, "Afterword," in *Papa Francesco, Contro La Guerra: Il Coraggio Di Construire La Pace* (Vatican City: Libreria Editrice Vaticano, 2022).
29. Quoted by Francis X. Rocca, "Pope Talks Airstrikes in Iraq, His Health, Possible US Visit," *National Catholic Reporter*, August 18, 2014, www.ncronline.org/print/news/world/pope-talks-airstrikes-iraq-his-health-possible-us-visit.
30. Francis, *Fratelli tutti*, no. 258.
31. Francis, no. 242, citing Augustine, Epistola 229, 2: PL 33, 1020.
32. Quoted in "Pope to Russian Patriarch: 'Church Uses Language of Jesus, Not of Politics,'" March 16, 2022, www.vaticannews.va/en/pope/news/2022-03/pope-francis-calls-patriarch-kirill-orthodox-patriarch-ukraine.html.
33. "Pope Francis's Responses to Questions on Giving Weapons to Ukraine, Dialogue with Russia," *Rome Reports*, September 16, 2022, www.romereports.com/en/2022/09/16/pope-francis-responses-to-questions-on-giving-weapons-to-ukraine-dialogue-with-russia/.

34. Paolo Carlotti, "L'invalidazione della guerra: Il recente magistero ecclesiale," in *Ha ancora senso parlare di guerra giusta? Le recenti elaborazioni della teologia morale*, ed. Carlo Bresciani and Luciano Eusebi (Bologna: Edizioni Dehoniane, 2010), 74.
35. Francis, "Nonviolence: A Style of Politics for Peace," December 8, 2016, no. 6, www.vatican.va/content/francesco/en/messages/peace/documents/papa-francesco_20161208_messaggio-l-giornata-mondiale-pace-2017.html.
36. Francis, no. 4.
37. See Erica Chenoweth and Maria Stephan, *Why Civil Resistance Work: The Strategic Logic of Nonviolent Conflict* (New York: Columbia University Press, 2011).
38. Thomas Massaro, "The Peace Advocacy of Pope Francis: Jesuit Perspectives," *Journal of Jesuit Studies* 8, no. 4 (2021): 538.
39. Francis, *Evangelii gaudium*, no. 227. It should be acknowledged that the English translation, "face conflict head on," is significantly stronger than the French, Italian, and Spanish versions of this phrase—"supporter," in French; "accettare di sopportare il conflitto," in Italian; and "aceptar sufrir el conflict," in Spanish—which, instead, imply merely tolerating or putting up with conflict.
40. Massaro, "Peace Advocacy," 532–33.
41. Francis, *Evangelii guadium*, no. 228.
42. De Volder, "Pope Francis's Idiosyncratic Approach," 6, citing Antonio Spadaro, "Francesco e la sfida all'apocalisse," *Limes: Rivista italiana di Geopolitica* 6 (2018): 61–71.
43. Francis, *Evangelii gaudium*, no. 229.
44. Johan Verstraeten, "It Is Better to Build Bridges Than to Build Walls: Pope Francis on Peace and War," in *Geopolitics of Pope Francis*, ed. de Volder, 200.
45. *Gaudium et spes*, no. 78. Francis echoes these themes in *Evangelii gaudium*, nos. 217–19, and in "Fraternity, the Foundation and Pathway to Peace," Message for the World Day of Peace, January 1, 2014, www.vatican.va/content/francesco/en/messages/peace/documents/papa-francesco_20131208_messaggio-xlvii-giornata-mondiale-pace-2014.html.
46. Francis, *Fratelli tutti*, no. 95.
47. Francis, *Evangelii gaudium*, no. 230.
48. Czerny and Barone, *Fraternità*, 156–57.
49. Francis, *Evangelii gaudium*, no. 236.
50. Francis, *Fratelli tutti*, no. 191.
51. Francis, no. 135.

13

POPE FRANCIS'S ECOLOGICAL ETHICS

A Constructive Application for a Climate "Revolution" in the US Catholic Church

Daniel R. DiLeo

"Start a revolution, shake things up. The world is deaf; you have to open its ears."[1] This is the instruction Pope Francis gave in 2021 to a climate activist and others working for social change. Although inspiring, his directive did not provide a clear blueprint for action. In this chapter, I engage Francis's moral theology to suggest how US Catholics can—and should—apply the pope's admonition to the Church itself.

First, I outline Francis's teaching on climate change, which is emblematic of his broader ecological ethics and of particular concern to the pope. Next, I describe how the US Catholic Church—specifically bishops—have refused to share and enact this teaching. Finally, I engage Francis's popular movement writings and ecclesiology to argue that US Catholics should pursue diocesan net zero carbon commitments through community organizing, relational advocacy, and, if necessary, nonviolent direct action.

POPE FRANCIS AND "THE CLIMATE EMERGENCY"

Since at least 1990, Pope John Paul II, Pope Benedict XVI, and many episcopal conferences have explicitly described climate change as a moral crisis that demands action.[2] Francis has built on this precedent as part of his broader ecological ethics, especially in his encyclical *Laudato si'*, the Church's first on ecology, and his subsequent apostolic exhortation *Laudate deum*.[3] However,

Francis's climate change teachings are unique in several ways: analytical method; urgency, frequency, and specificity; Ignatian themes; and calls for action in the institutional Church. Since all are interconnected, this section engages his method—a modified Pastoral Circle—to consider the other dimensions.

Twentieth-century Catholic social action largely followed the see–judge–act model: see concrete realities, judge them in light of social principles from Catholic teaching, and act to better realize the principles. After the Second Vatican Council, Latin American liberation theology developed this inductive method by sharpening the critical analysis of unjust social structures—what the liberationist Paulo Freire called *conscientization*.[4]

Late in the century, Joe Holland and Peter Henriot proposed a method that, in a sense, explicitly incorporated *conscientization* into see–judge–act. Their method, the Pastoral Circle, progresses though four steps: insertion into social reality; social analysis of what causes the experienced situation; theological reflection on the morality of the conditions; and pastoral planning for appropriate action.[5] Since action produces new circumstances into which one must enter, Holland and Henriot stress that their model "is, in fact, more of a 'spiral' than a 'circle.'"[6]

The Pastoral Circle connects to the climate change teaching of the first Latin American and Jesuit pope in several ways. First, Francis gained intellectual and pastoral experience with this approach at the Latin American bishops' 2007 conference in Aparecida: as archbishop of Buenos Aires, he chaired the committee that drafted the *Concluding Document*, which employs a socially critical inductive theological ethics.[7] Similarly, Francis's ecological "awakening" began at the Aparecida conference with the insertion of concerns about Amazonia and continued over years of subsequent "encounters, dialogues, and anecdotes" about ecological degradation.[8]

The dynamics of the Pastoral Circle are also related to Francis's formation as a Jesuit. Freire's emphasis on experience and social analysis shaped Ignatian approaches to educating for the "faith that does justice."[9] Relatedly, socially critical inductive methodology grounds the Jesuits' ecological documents "We Live in a Broken World" (1999) and "Healing a Broken World" (2011).[10] The former underpins the commitment to seek "reconciliation with creation" in the Society of Jesus's General Congregation 35 Decree 3 (2008).[11] The latter was edited by Michael Czerny, SJ, who subsequently helped draft *Laudato si'*.[12]

Given this background, it is unsurprising that Francis describes four similar steps as structuring *Laudato si'*, which outlines his ecological vision, even as he does not name the Pastoral Circle.[13] Interestingly, he begins with experience and concludes with action but inexplicably reverses the second and third steps: before diagnosing the causes of modern environmental degradation, he outlines a theological framework. This "revised" Pastoral Circle provides a framework to consider Francis's climate change teaching.

Insertion: "What Is Happening to Our Common Home"

Francis's climate change ethics is grounded in experiential, dialogical, affective awareness of reality that is notably Ignatian in at least three ways.[14] First, it expresses the Ignatian pedagogical insight that work for justice must be grounded in solidarity, which can only be cultivated through experience in which "the heart is touched."[15] Second, its emphasis on dialogue—the term occurs twenty-five times in *Laudato si'*—echoes the Jesuits' commitment to a collaborative "way of proceeding." Third, it enacts the Ignatian charism of "contemplative in action," which is characterized by a symbiotic relationship between discerning interior reflection and corresponding external action.

Using this approach, Francis describes how the effects of climate change—a phenomenon he affirms is largely caused by humans—makes an impact on both nonhuman creation and human communities, especially the poor.[16] For example, he outlines how droughts and other severe weather events threaten agriculture and subsistence lifestyles, carbon pollution causes ocean acidification that threatens marine ecosystems, and polar ice melting causes rising sea levels that displace coastal communities as climate refugees.[17]

Fueled by such affective awareness, Francis addresses climate change with an urgency, gravity, and frequency unprecedented in papal writings. For example, he declares that climate change "represents one of the principal challenges facing humanity in our day."[18] He also warns the "climate emergency" risks "perpetrating a brutal act of injustice towards the poor and future generations."[19] With an eye to the horizon of climate futures, he addresses warming with scientific specificity that exceeds previous popes. First, he affirms what science calls "climate feedbacks" and "tipping points." The former are processes whereby warming catalyzes additional warming. For example, he describes how polar ice melting emits methane and allows organic material breakdown to emit carbon dioxide—two emissions processes that intensify the greenhouse effect and produce additional warming.[20] The latter are points beyond which climate change will rapidly accelerate and become essentially irreversible. Affirming the Nobel Prize–winning Intergovernmental Panel on Climate Change (IPCC), Francis has repeatedly stressed 1.5°C of postindustrial warming as the critical tipping point that should not be crossed.[21]

Here, additional context is warranted. Since the Industrial Revolution, the planet has warmed 1.1°C. Given the decades-to-centuries lifespan of various greenhouse gases, the planet will almost certainly exceed 1.5°C in this century—likely by 2040.[22] Depending on energy choices in the next few years, the temperature could stabilize at about 1.5°C. Without dramatic emissions cuts and deployment of currently nascent technology to remove carbon from the atmosphere, warming could reach 5.7°C by 2100.[23] The catastrophic nature of such a scenario cannot be understated.

This amount of warming could produce 2 meters (6 feet) of sea level rise by 2100 and 5 meters (16 feet) by 2150.[24] Under high future emissions scenarios, researchers from Cornell University estimate that sea level rise could displace 2 billion people by 2100.[25] The researchers assume that global population will be 9 billion to 11 billion by the end of the century; however, the additional humanitarian effects of climate change (food and water stress, etc.) could prevent this population growth. Summarizing the opinions of two leading climate scientists, one of whom was a member of the Pontifical Academy of Sciences, the theologian Richard Miller describes that "at 4–6°C the carrying capacity of planet could be reduced to between a half a billion and a billion people"—a scenario amounting to the death of at least 87 percent of the current global population.[26]

Theological Reflection: "The Gospel of Creation"

Throughout his papacy, Francis has stressed the immorality of climate change.[27] He emphasizes "the climate is a common good" that underpins human life and describes the climate crisis as driven by the "sin of indifference" that ignores suffering.[28] This sin, he describes more generally, expresses the "rupture" of relationship between, persons, God, and nonhuman creation, catalyzed by human idolatry and manifest in distorted readings of Genesis (especially 1:28) that give divine license for unlimited ecological exploitation.[29] Such exploitation ignores the intrinsic value of nonhuman creation as expressions of God, an insight that echoes the Ignatian charism of "finding God in all things."[30] Quoting African bishops, Francis identifies climate change as "'a tragic and striking example of structural sin.'"[31]

Francis stresses that climate change unduly harms the poor—now and in the future—by straining livelihoods, especially agriculture, and forcibly displacing persons who often lack legal protection as climate refugees.[32] Speaking about ecology more broadly, Francis underscores the need "to hear *both the cry of the earth and the cry of the poor*" (emphasis in the original).[33] This line is particularly emblematic of Francis's vision, since it implicitly invokes his Latin American and socially conscious roots: the italicized text is the title of a book by the Brazilian liberation theologian and former Franciscan priest Leonardo Boff.[34]

Anticipating his recommended actions, Francis underscores the need for *"differentiated responsibilities,"* whereby the rich and those most responsible for causing climate change enact solidarity by leading efforts to address the climate emergency.[35] He notes that, currently, "emissions per individual in the United States are about two times greater than those of individuals living in China, and about seven times greater than the average of the poorest countries."[36] More broadly, it is worth noting that the United States is the world's wealthiest nation and has been most responsible for causing climate change: between 1850 and 2021, the country was responsible for 20.3 percent of historic carbon pollution—more than the next two nations (China and Russia) combined.[37] This fact is especially daunting since the United States has only about 4.2 percent of the world's total population.[38]

Social Analysis: "The Human Roots of the Ecological Crisis" and "Integral Ecology"

Pope Francis diagnoses several interconnected causes of climate change.[39] Scientifically, he affirms that most global warming is due to human activities, particularly fossil fuel combustion and deforestation, a reality the IPCC calls "unequivocal."[40] Sociologically, Francis describes a "tyrannical anthropocentrism" that seeks unbridled control over nonhuman creation.[41] Theologically, and as described in the previous section, Francis perceives the idolatrous, selfish, sinful rupture of humanity's relationship with God and nonhuman creation.

Borrowing the term "technocracy" from Pope Paul VI, Francis describes anthropocentrism as guided by a "technocratic paradigm."[42] This worldview makes human utility the standard of valuing the nonhuman creation, produces a "culture of consumerism, which prioritizes short-term gain and private interest," and absolutizes technological progress, production efficiency, and financial profit.[43] Epistemologically, technocracy yields and is sustained by "the fragmentation of knowledge and the isolation of bits of information" that belie an integrated vision of creation—what Francis calls "integral ecology."[44]

For Francis, technocracy is enacted through and drives a climatically disastrous political economy that excludes environmental costs from financial calculations, glorifies free markets, and is driven by "the intensive use of fossil fuels."[45] Although this analysis exemplifies the Ignatian and Latin American concerns for structural injustice, it is supported by leading economists like Nicholas Stern, former chief economist and senior vice president at the World Bank. Stern declares climate change the "greatest example of market failure we have ever seen" because markets largely encourage fossil fuel dependence by artificially depressing their price through externalization of social and environmental costs.[46]

Critiquing such "a magical conception of the market," Francis further observes that "politics are subject to technology and finance" and subverted by "too many special interests."[47] Relatedly, he laments that climate change denial and diminishment, including in the Church, persist.[48] As a result, political leaders have produced only "weak responses" to the most pressing ecological challenges.[49]

Pastoral Planning: "Lines of Approach and Action" and "Ecological Education and Spirituality"

Informed by insertion, theological reflection, and social analysis, Francis calls for interrelated action to address climate change.[50] As one would expect of the first Jesuit pope, he explicitly emphasizes the need for discernment and embodies the Ignatian charism of living as a "contemplative in action."[51] Animated by this reflection, Francis stresses action in the areas of charitable works, social justice, education, and spirituality.

Charitable works are micro-level actions that directly address a problem, and Francis's climate ethics calls for such ecological activities.[52] For example, he urges "using public transport or car-pooling, planting trees, [and] turning off unnecessary lights."[53] Together with charitable works, the Catholic tradition stresses the concurrent need for social justice that reforms harmful systems, structures, and policies.[54] Francis's ethics highlights that individual actions are necessary but insufficient and stresses the need for much climate-focused social justice.[55]

Francis reifies this position through advocacy for policies to reduce greenhouse gas emissions, facilitate transitions to renewable energy, and limit global warming to 1.5°C.[56] Here, it is important to note that the IPCC estimates that to have *at least a 50 percent chance* of limiting global warming to 1.5°C, global greenhouse gas pollution *must peak by 2025, be cut in nearly half from 2019 levels by 2030*, and the world must reach *net zero carbon by ~2050*.[57] Net zero means eliminating at least 90 percent of emissions and offsetting up to the remaining 10 percent through sinks like forests. Leading by example, the Vatican under Francis has committed to net zero carbon emissions by 2050, does not invest in fossil fuels, and encourages others to consider divestment/reinvestment in renewable energies.[58]

As described in the "Insertion" section above, Francis has a characteristically Ignatian perspective that action is inspired by a pedagogy of an encounter with God's love and the realities of suffering. He thus emphasizes that environmental action must be, respectively, animated by "ecological spirituality" and "ecological education." The former must be rooted in a relationship with God and God's creation and facilitate the unambiguous understanding that care for God's creation is essential to Christianity.[59] Francis's emphasis on a transformative relationship echoes the "culture of encounter" he has sought to build across his papacy.[60] Alongside ecological spirituality, ecological education must be experiential, interdisciplinary, and action-oriented; must exhaustively critique the causes and consequences of problems; and must "take place in a variety of settings: at school, in families, in the media, in catechesis and elsewhere"—including "our seminaries and houses of formation."[61]

Pastoral Planning *Ad Intra*: Fidelity to the Church's Mission

Francis's insistence in *Laudato si'* that ecological education must occur within the Church anticipates a subsequent and unique aspect of his climate change ethics. Although he urges civil society to educate for and take climate action, Francis calls the worldwide Catholic Church to systematically enact its own climate change teaching. This call illustrates the "ecclesial ethics" that Elyse Raby describes in chapter 4 of this volume "as the application of ethical norms or values to the Church's organizational or institutional life."

To help the Church embody its climate change teaching, the Vatican under Francis's leadership launched the *Laudato si'* Action Platform.[62] The Platform identifies seven Catholic "sectors" called to operationalize *Laudato si'*: families, parishes and dioceses, educational institutions, health care and healing, organizations and groups, the economic sector, and religious. Each sector is invited to pursue seven goals: response to the cry of the Earth, response to the cry of the poor, ecological economics, adoption of sustainable lifestyles, ecological education, ecological spirituality, and community resilience and empowerment. Each goal outlines potential activities: response to the cry of the Earth, for example, encourages decarbonization.

The initiative implicitly expresses the socially conscious postconciliar ecclesiology and missiology that Francis outlines in *Evangelii gaudium* and that I have elsewhere considered in the context of the climate emergency.[63] In brief, the Church's mission is to advance God's Kingdom of justice, peace, and the integrity of creation through love and evangelization that require action and engage the "signs of the times."[64] Since love requires social justice that reforms policies—what Francis calls "social love"[65]—and because the Church is structured by policies, the Church's mission requires social justice *ad intra* through internal policies that prudently promote the flourishing of creation.

As the 1971 World Synod of Bishops stressed, the Church must live its mission internally to have credibility in the world.[66]

The responsibility to live the Church's mission in this way especially applies to bishops ordained to the offices of "teaching, sanctifying, and governing" particular churches (dioceses) and whose leadership by example can inspire other Catholics.[67] This insight explains the Vatican's particular call for bishops to "make [*Laudato si'* their] own and share it effectively."[68] It also makes the Platform's parishes and dioceses sector a particularly important locus of missional fidelity.

While bishops should pursue all seven goals in this sector, diocesan net zero commitments under the goal of response to the cry of the Earth could especially help society mitigate the climate crisis. The US Church owns nearly 100,000 buildings that could be committed to net zero carbon emissions.[69] While the bishop does not always govern all Catholic buildings in a diocese, he does administer diocesan-owned buildings, like the chancery, where he could make net zero commitments directly. The bishop can thus also signal governance priorities to those who oversee facilities within but not owned by the diocese.

Following Francis's leadership, bishops could commit all facilities under their control to net zero. This would reduce direct carbon pollution and could also inspire additional action. For example, a diocesan net zero pledge could motivate priests to make parish commitments. This episcopal leadership could also inspire religious communities, universities, and other Catholic institutions in the diocese to make net zero commitments. Such unified Catholic action could in turn catalyze civic action: Catholic net zero commitments across a diocese could move the local utility to pursue renewable energy projects, a step that could spur public policy reforms.

The benefits of net zero would be amplified if each bishop committed their diocese to cut emissions in half from 2019 levels by 2030 and reach net zero carbon by 2040 at the latest. Recall that net zero by 2050 gives only a 50 percent chance of limiting global warming to 1.5°C. As of November 2023, more than 450 companies had signed the Climate Pledge to reach net zero ten years early and thereby give the world a higher chance of avoiding climate catastrophe.[70] Writing to university leaders, Creighton students insist, "If profit-motivated corporations are prudently committed to net zero by 2040, our mission-motivated Jesuit, Catholic university should also commit to this goal."[71] Notably, Christiana Figueres, the UN executive secretary who facilitated the Paris Agreement on climate change and helped launch the Climate Pledge, has called the US Church to reach zero emissions by 2040.[72]

Bishops' net zero commitments could also be an innovative tool for the New Evangelization, especially among young people who are increasingly leaving the Church.[73] Francis reiterates conciliar ecclesiology and missiology that evangelization requires action. The US bishops insist that the New Evangelization of the twenty-first century must be "new in its methods, that must correspond to the times."[74] More than half of young people age 16 to 25 years are "very or extremely worried about climate change," and Generation Z (born in the middle to late 1990s to 2010s) identifies climate change as the most important social issue.[75]

At the confluence of these dynamics, diocesan net zero commitments can be a "new method" that "correspond[s] to the times" of youth and offer the Church as a "living testimony" of hope, which, as a virtue, requires prudent action, in this case action commensurate with climate science.[76] This faithful action would address the ecclesial hypocrisy that Francis laments and that young people addressed in a synodal encounter with Francis: "Young people value authenticity and deplore hypocrisy. We told Pope Francis that US Catholic leaders' failure to share and enact the Church's own climate teachings is causing many in our generation to become disillusioned with the Church."[77]

THE (NON)RECEPTION OF POPE FRANCIS'S CLIMATE CHANGE TEACHING

Despite US bishops' responsibility and opportunity to engage Francis's climate change teaching, they have overwhelmingly failed to do so. Two researchers and I found that between June 2014 (one year before *Laudato si'*) and June 2019 (four years after the encyclical), only 93 of 12,077 columns written by bishops in official diocesan publications—less than 1 percent—even mentioned "climate change," "global warming," or variations.[78] Of those 93 columns, only 56 speak about climate change as real.

Additionally, only 49 columns speak about climate change as a religious issue; only 29 speak about climate change as urgent; only 2 speak about climate change as the result of economic systems; and only 14 mention climate change politics (conversely, 284 mention abortion politics). Several of the 93 columns that mention climate change actually undermine Francis's teaching. Although teaching is not acting, bishops' climate silence corresponds to near total failure to take prudent action. Only 17 of 178 US dioceses signed up for the *Laudato si'* Action Platform ahead of its public launch.[79] As of November 2023, only one diocese (Davenport) had committed to net zero carbon.[80] Our research suggests that bishops' political conservatism fuels their unwillingness to share and, by extension, enact, Pope Francis's climate change teaching. Relatedly, our findings submit that documented widespread nonengagement with *Laudato si'* among US priests is also at least partially a function of their political conservatism. Our assessments are consistent with the "existing literature that political identity/ideology is the strongest predictor of climate change beliefs and conservatism positively correlates with climate change skepticism."[81] It also affirms additional research we cite that US Catholics generally received *Laudato si'* along party lines: politically liberal Catholics were largely receptive, and politically conservative Catholics were widely nonreceptive.

Implications of the US Catholic Bishops' Nonreceipt

Pope Francis wrote *Laudate deum* because since *Laudato si'*, "responses have not been adequate."[82] One implication of US bishops' inadequate responses is thus an ironic contribution to the publication of *Laudate deum*. Elsewhere, I have suggested that Francis's subsequent reference in *Laudate deum* to the US bishops' affirmation of climate change as a moral issue is "a strategic move to hold them to their own standard."[83]

Faced with US bishops' silence and relative inaction regarding Pope Francis's climate change teaching, what can US Catholics do? Grounded in Francis's writings on popular movements and ecclesiology, Catholics should pursue diocesan net zero carbon commitments through community organizing, relational advocacy, and, if necessary, nonviolent direct action.

In 2014, Francis hosted the First World Meeting of Popular Movements. The event convened, affirmed, and encouraged those engaged in "grassroots" organizing and activism to secure "land, housing, and work" with and for the marginalized.[84] Since then, the Vatican has supported World Meetings of Popular Movements nearly annually, at which Francis has given addresses. He has also written the preface to a Vatican book on popular movements.[85]

Across these writings, Francis stresses the need for urgent action to address ecological degradation and celebrates "structural change"—explicitly, "social justice."[86] He recognizes power as "fundamentally in the hands of peoples and in their ability to organize" and affirms lived experience as "authoritative."[87] The pope affirms accompaniment led by "protagonists" who "get organized, study, work, issue demands"[88] and engage in advocacy.[89] Citing Martin Luther King Jr., Francis emphasizes the need for love that eschews hate.[90] In writings beyond those to popular movements, Francis similarly calls King's "nonviolent protest" a form of peacebuilding and celebrates King's "dream" for racial equality.[91] Notably, in his popular movement writings, Francis invites participants to "dream together."[92]

Francis's popular movement writings markedly celebrate the US bishops' Catholic Campaign for Human Development and the PICO National Network founded by the Jesuit John Baumann.[93] This is significant since both are rooted in the tradition of Saul Alinsky who, with support from Chicago auxiliary bishop James Sheil, pioneered US community organizing, by which groups catalyze change by strategically leveraging power.[94] Relatedly, in 2022 Francis met with a delegation from the Industrial Areas Foundation that Alinsky founded and called its work "Good News for the United States."[95]

As with Pope Francis's ecological ethics, his writings on popular movements relate to his Argentine and Jesuit background. Francis describes his support for "people's movements" as fruits of encounters (outlined above as characteristically Latin American and Ignatian) with their persons and activities.[96] Theologically, his writings express the Argentine postconciliar "theology of the people" noted in chapter 1 of this volume by Lisa Sowle Cahill, which emphasizes lay empowerment and transformation of the world.[97] Pastorally, his affirmations echo the celebration of base ecclesial communities—decentralized, often lay-led faith communities generally committed to social action—in the concluding Aparecida document.[98] Moreover, Francis's support reifies the Jesuit charisms of accompaniment, attention to structural reform, and imagination explored throughout this volume, especially in chapter 5, by Thomas Massaro.

Although Francis's writings on popular movements inform social action *ad extra*—that is, outside the Church—they can also guide action *ad intra*. Key to this understanding is recognizing that he has directed many of his insights regarding popular movements to the Church. For example, just as Francis has called popular movements to work for structural (social) justice, Elyse Raby notes his "ecclesial ethics" calls for justice in Church structures. Similarly, Francis's recognition of "people power" and the authority of grassroots voices among popular movements is echoed in what Raby calls his ecclesiology of decentralization that empowers the laity and affirms the *sensus fidei* in a spirit of synodality. Moreover, just as Francis calls activists to be "protagonists," Francis calls young Catholics to be "protagonists of change" in the context of "buil[ding] up and repair[ing] the Church."[99] Richard Gaillardetz observes that as with Francis's writings on popular movements, the pope's ecclesiology is shaped by his Latin American background and experience at Aparecida.[100]

Considering his climate change teachings, popular movement writings, and ecclesiology, Francis's admonition to "start a revolution, shake things up" supports US Catholics' work for diocesan net zero carbon commitments through community organizing, relational advocacy, and, if necessary, nonviolent direct action. This work can take particular inspiration from the prophetic work of Reverend John Markoe, SJ, a Creighton University professor who in the mid–twentieth century organized social action for desegregation in the Church and society.[101]

First, Catholics should engage Francis's support for Alinsky-inspired community organizing to build a diocesan network of persons and groups committed to working for net zero. Here, Catholics should identify their bishop as the "target" with power to set a net zero commitment, perform a "power analysis" to identify potential allies and "secondary targets" that can influence the bishop, and conduct "one-to-one" meetings to build relationships with and recruit collaborators.[102] Next, Catholics should engage Francis's emphasis on encounter and affirmations of advocacy to meet with their bishop and ask for a diocesan net zero commitment. This relational advocacy, what King calls "negotiation," builds on the calls of Jean-Claude Cardinal Hollerich and Blase Cardinal Cupich for young people to meet with their bishop about climate change.[103] To prepare for and structure this encounter, Catholics should apply the "public narrative" theory pioneered by Marshall Ganz. This framework works to catalyze action through systematic storytelling that engages shared values.[104]

If the bishop refuses this request, Catholics should employ King's teaching that out of love, nonviolent direct action—what community organizing calls "tactics"—can follow failed negotiations.[105] Here, Catholics can creatively enact methods from the leading nonviolent theorist Gene Sharp.[106] For example, they could "protest" through marches outside the cathedral, engage in "noncooperation" through boycotting of businesses owned by "secondary targets" like major diocesan donors,[107] and undertake "intervention" through prayer vigil sit-ins at the chancery. These activities would build on Francis's positive response to the suggestion from two students that addressing climate change may require nonviolent direct action.[108] To be effective, Catholics must embrace the insight of the civil rights leader the Reverend James Lawson that successful nonviolent direct action requires systematic training and discerning application.[109]

CONCLUSION

Saint Francis of Assisi was moved to action by God's instruction to "go and build up My house [the Church], which as thou seest, is falling into ruin."[110] Today, the world where God dwells is falling into the ruin of climate change. The US Catholic Church concurrently risks falling into ecclesial and ethical ruin through failure to enact Pope Francis's ecological and ecclesial ethics. In response, I have argued that the ecological ethics, popular movement writings, and ecclesiology of the first pope to take the name Francis calls Catholics to pursue diocesan net zero commitments through community organizing, relational advocacy, and, if necessary, nonviolent direct action. Extending Francis's directive, US Catholics should "start a revolution, shake things up. The [Church] is deaf; you have to open its ears."[111]

NOTES

1. Loup Besmond de Senneville, "Pope Tells Young French Activists to 'Start a Revolution,'" *La Croix*, March 17, 2021, https://international.la-croix.com/news/environment/pope-tells-young-french-activists-to-start-a-revolution/13985.
2. See, e.g., John Paul II, *Peace with God the Creator, Peace with All Creation* (Vatican City: Libreria Editrice Vaticana, 1990), no. 6; Benedict XVI, *If You Want to Cultivate Peace, Protect Creation* (Vatican City: Libreria Editrice Vaticana, 2010), nos. 4, 7, 10; and US Conference of Catholic Bishops, *Global Climate Change: A Plea for Dialogue, Prudence, and the Common Good* (Washington, DC: US Conference of Catholic Bishops, 2001).
3. Francis, *Laudato si'* (Vatican City: Libreria Editrice Vaticana), 2015; Francis, *Laudate deum* (Vatican City: Libreria Editrice Vaticana), 2023.
4. Paulo Freire, *Pedagogy of the Oppressed*, 50th Anniversary / 4th ed., trans. Myra Bergman Ramos (New York: Bloomsbury Academic, 2017); Thomas M. Kelly, *When the Gospel Grows Feet: Rutilio Grande, SJ, and the Church of El Salvador—An Ecclesiology in Context* (Collegeville, MN: Liturgical Press, 2013), 139–40.
5. Joe Holland and Peter Henriot, *Social Analysis: Linking Faith and Justice* (Maryknoll, NY: Orbis Books, 2005), 8–9.
6. Holland and Henriot, 9.
7. Consejo Episcopal Latinoamericano, *Concluding Document: Fifth General Conference of Bishops of Latin America and the Caribbean*, 2007, no. 19, www.celam.org/aparecida/Ingles.pdf.
8. Francis and Austin Ivereigh, *Let Us Dream: The Path to a Better Future* (New York: Simon & Schuster, 2020), 30–31.
9. Thomas Pace and Gina M. Merys, "Paulo Freire and the Jesuit Tradition: Jesuit Rhetoric and Preirean Pedagogy," in *Traditions of Eloquence: The Jesuits and Modern Rhetorical Studies*, ed. Cinthia Gannett and John C. Brereton (New York: Fordham University Press, 2016), 234–47; Thomas M. Kelly, *When the Gospel Grows Feet: Rutilio Grande, SJ, and the Church of El Salvador—An Ecclesiology in Context* (Collegeville, MN: Liturgical Press, 2013), 139–40.
10. Social Apostolate Secretariat at the General Curia of the Society of Jesus, "We Live in a Broken World," *Promotio Iustitiae* 70 (1999); Social Justice and Ecology Secretariat at the General Curia of the Society of Jesus, "Healing a Broken World," *Promotio Justitae* 106, no. 2 (2011): 9; cf. 10–12.
11. General Curia of the Society of Jesus, Official Decrees of General Congregation 35: Decree 3, "Challenges to our Mission Today" (Rome: Society of Jesus, 2008), nos. 31–36.
12. CBC Radio, "The Canadian Who Helped Craft Pope Francis's Statement on Climate Change Will Be Our Fourth Cardinal," September 6, 2019, www.cbc.ca/radio/sunday/the-sunday-edition-for-september-8-2019-1.5270500/the-canadian-who-helped-craft-pope-francis-s-statement-on-climate-change-will-be-our-fourth-cardinal-1.5273000.

13. Francis, *Laudato si'*, no. 15.
14. Francis, *Laudato si'*, chap. 1; Francis, *Laudate deum*, chap. 1.
15. Peter-Hans Kolvenbach, "The Service of Faith and the Promotion of Justice in American Jesuit Higher Education," in *A Jesuit Education Reader: Contemporary Writings on the Jesuit Mission in Education, Principles, the Issue of Catholic Identity, Practical Applications of the Ignatian Way, and More*, ed. George W. Traub (Chicago: Loyola University Press, 2008), 155.
16. For more on the causes and consequences of climate change, see Intergovernmental Panel on Climate Change (IPCC), *Sixth Assessment Report: Climate Change 2022—Impacts, Adaptation, and Vulnerability, Summary for Policymakers* (Cambridge: Cambridge University Press, 2022), SPM.B.1–SPM.B.2.5.
17. Francis, *Laudato si'*, no. 25; Francis, *Laudate deum*, nos. 6-19.
18. Francis, *Laudato si'*, no. 25; cf. Francis, *Laudate deum*, no. 3.
19. Francis, "Address to Participants at the Meeting Promoted by the Dicastery for Promoting Integral Human Development on the Theme: The Energy Transition & Care of Our Common Home," Libreria Editrice Vaticana, June 14, 2019, www.vatican.va/content/francesco/en/speeches/2019/june/documents/papa-francesco_20190614_compagnie-petrolifere.html.
20. Francis, *Laudato si'*, no. 24.
21. Francis, *Laudate deum*, nos. 5, 12, 48, 56.; IPPC, *Global Warming of 1.5°C* (Cambridge: Cambridge University Press, 2018), www.ipcc.ch/sr15/.
22. IPCC, *Climate Change 2021: The Physical Science Basis—Contribution of Working Group I to the Sixth Assessment Report of the Intergovernmental Panel on Climate Change* (Cambridge: Cambridge University Press, 2021), table SPM.1, www.ipcc.ch/report/ar6/wg1/downloads/report/IPCC_AR6_WGI_SPM.pdf.
23. IPCC, *Climate Change 2021*, B.1.1, table SPM.1.
24. IPCC, B.1.1, B.5.3.
25. Charles Geisler and Ben Currens, "Impediments to Inland Resettlement under Conditions of Accelerated Sea Level Rise," *Land Use Policy* 66 (2017): 322–30.
26. Richard W. Miller, "Deep Responsibility for the Deep Future," *Theological Studies* 77, no. 2 (2016): 440.
27. Francis, *Laudato si'*, chap. 1.
28. Francis, nos. 23, 25, 246.
29. Francis, no. 66.
30. Francis, nos. 33, 69.
31. Francis, *Laudate deum*, no. 3.
32. Francis, *Laudato si'*, no. 25.
33. Francis, "Address to Participants at the Meeting Promoted by the Dicastery for Promoting Integral Human Development on the Theme: The Energy Transition and Care of Our Common Home"; Francis, *Laudato si'*, no. 49.
34. Leonardo Boff, *Cry of the Earth, Cry of the Poor* (Maryknoll, NY: Orbis Books, 1997).
35. Francis, *Laudato si'*, nos. 52, 170.
36. Francis, *Laudate deum*, no. 72.
37. Simon Evans, "Analysis: Which Countries Are Historically Responsible for Climate Change?" *Carbon Brief*, May 10, 2021, www.carbonbrief.org/analysis-which-countries-are-historically-responsible-for-climate-change.
38. US Census Bureau, "US and World Population Clock," December 6, 2022, www.census.gov/popclock/.

39. For "The Human Roots of the Ecological Crisis," see Francis, *Laudato si'*, chap. 3. For "Integral Ecology," see Francis, chap. 4.
40. Francis, *Laudato si'*, no. 23; Francis, *Laudate deum*, nos. 11–14; IPCC, *Climate Change 2021*, A.1.
41. Francis, *Laudato si'*, nos. 68–69, 115–22; Francis, *Laudate deum*, no. 67.
42. Francis, *Laudato si'*, no. 184; Francis, *Laudate deum*, chap. 2.
43. Francis, *Laudato si'*, nos. 101, 106–12, 118, 122, 184, 189, 194; cf. *Laudate deum*, no. 13; cf. Pope Paul VI, *Populorum progressio*, March 26, 1967, no. 34, www.vatican.va/content/paul-vi/en/encyclicals/documents/hf_p-vi_enc_26031967_populorum.html.
44. Francis, *Laudato si'*, no. 138.
45. Francis, nos. 23, 56, 190.
46. Nicholas Stern, *Stern Review Report on the Economics of Climate Change* (Cambridge: Cambridge University Press, 2007), 1.
47. Francis, *Laudato si'*, nos. 54, 109.
48. Francis, *Laudate deum*, nos. 5, 14.
49. Francis, *Laudato si'*, no. 54; cf. Francis, *Laudate deum*, chaps. 3–4.
50. For "Lines of Approach and Action," see Francis, *Laudate deum*, chap. 5. For "Ecological Education and Spirituality," see Francis, chap. 6.
51. Francis, *Laudato si'*, no. 185.
52. Kenneth R. Himes and Daniel R. DiLeo, "*Laudato Si'* in the United States: Reflections on Love, Charitable Works, and Social Justice," *Journal of Moral Theology* 9, Special Issue 1 (2020): 90–103.
53. Francis, *Laudato si'*, no. 211.
54. US Conference of Catholic Bishops, "Two Feet of Love in Action," 2022, www.usccb.org/beliefs-and-teachings/what-we-believe/catholic-social-teaching/two-feet-of-love-in-action.
55. Francis, *Laudate deum*, no. 69.
56. Francis, nos. 44–60; Francis, *Laudato si'*, no. 26; Francis, "Message for the Celebration of the World Day of Prayer for the Care of Creation"; Francis, "Message for the Fourth World Day of Prayer for Creation."
57. IPCC, *Sixth Assessment Report: Climate Change 2022*, C.1, C.1.1, C.2.
58. Philip Pullella, "Vatican Urges Catholics to Drop Investments in Fossil Fuels, Arms," Reuters, June 18, 2020, www.reuters.com/article/us-vatican-environment/vatican-urges-catholics-to-drop-investments-in-fossil-fuels-arms-idUSKBN23P1HI/#:~:text=The%20Vatican%20bank%20has%20said,world%20have%20taken%20similar%20positions; Interdicasterial Working Group of the Holy See on Integral Ecology, *Journeying Towards Care for Our Common Home: Five Years After* Laudato Si' (Vatican City: Libreria Editrice Vaticana, 2020), 91, 178–79; Philip Pullella, "Pope Commits Vatican to Net Zero Carbon Emissions by 2050," Reuters, December 12, 2020, www.reuters.com/article/climate-change-un-summit-pope/pope-commits-vatican-to-net-zero-carbon-emissions-by-2050-idUSKBN28M0RP.
59. Francis, *Laudato si'*, no. 217; Francis, *Laudate deum*, nos. 61–65.
60. E.g., Francis, "For a Culture of Encounter," Libreria Editrice Vaticana, September 13, 2016, www.vatican.va/content/francesco/en/cotidie/2016/documents/papa-francesco-cotidie_20160913_for-a-culture-of-encounter.html.
61. Francis, *Laudato si'*, nos. 209–14.
62. Dicastery for Promoting Integral Human Development, "*Laudato Si'* Action Platform," 2021, https://laudatosiactionplatform.org/.

63. Francis, *Evangelii gaudium* (Vatican City: Libreria Editrice Vaticana, 2013), nos. 176–258; Daniel R. DiLeo, "Climate Justice: Essential to the Church's Mission," *Journal of Religion & Society* Supplement 21 (2020): 178–202.
64. Second Vatican Council, *Ad gentes*, nos. 2, 5, 6; Second Vatican Council, *Lumen gentium*, nos. 9, 11, 35–36; Second Vatican Council, *Gaudium et spes*, nos. 4, 11, 24, 43.
65. Francis, *Laudato si'*, no. 231.
66. 1971 World Synod of Bishops, *Justicia in mundo*, no. 47.
67. Second Vatican Council, *Christus Dominus* (Vatican: Libreria Editrice Vaticana, 1965), no. 11.
68. Peter Turkson, "Cardinal Turkson: Bishops Should Promote *Laudato Si'*," Vatican Radio, January 22, 2016, www.archivioradiovaticana.va/storico/2016/01/22/cardinal_turkson_bishops_should_promote_laudato_si/en-1202931.
69. William Driscoll, "Catholic Organizations Go Solar to Save Money, and to Put Faith into Practice," *PV Magazine*, August 31, 2020, https://pv-magazine-usa.com/2020/08/31/catholic-organizations-go-solar-to-save-money-and-to-put-faith-into-practice/.
70. Climate Pledge, "Signatories," 2023, www.theclimatepledge.com/us/en/Signatories.
71. Alex Schultz, José Angel, Henry Glynn, Dana Snider, and Bryce Ferguson, "Letter to Father Hendrickson and Sustainable Governance Committee Members," November 16, 2022.
72. Brian Roewe, "At Catholic Climate Conference, Paris Agreement Architect Challenges US Church to Commit to Net-Zero Emissions," *National Catholic Reporter*, June 16, 2023, www.ncronline.org/earthbeat/justice/catholic-climate-conference-paris-agreement-architect-challenges-us-church-commit.
73. Robert J. McCarty and John M. Vitek, *Going, Going, Gone: The Dynamics of Disaffiliation in Young Catholics* (Winona, MN: Saint Mary's Press, 2017).
74. Second Vatican Council, *Lumen gentium*, no. 35; US Conference of Catholic Bishops, "Disciples Called to Witness, Part II," 2022, www.usccb.org/beliefs-and-teachings/how-we-teach/new-evangelization/disciples-called-to-witness/disciples-called-to-witness-part-ii.
75. Caroline Hickman et al., "Climate Anxiety in Children and Young People and Their Beliefs about Government Responses to Climate Change: A Global Survey," *The Lancet–Planetary Health* 5, no. 12 (2021): E863–73; Amnesty International, "Future of Humanity," 2019, www.amnestyusa.org/press-releases/generation-z-ranks-climate-change-highest-as-vital-issue-of-our-time-in-amnesty-international-survey/.
76. Colleen Griffith, "Christian Hope: A Grace and a Choice," in *Hope: Promise, Possibility, and Fulfillment*, ed. Richard Lennan and Nancy Pineda-Madrid (Mahwah, NJ: Paulist Press, 2013), 9-10.
77. Emily E. Burke and Henry Glynn, "We Told Pope Francis Nonviolent Action May Be Needed to Stop Climate Change," Religion News Service, March 3, 2022, https://religionnews.com/2022/03/03/we-told-pope-francis-nonviolent-action-may-be-needed-to-stop-climate-change/.
78. Sabrina Danielsen, Daniel R. DiLeo, and Emily E. Burke, "US Catholic Bishops' Silence and Denialism on Climate Change," *Environmental Research Letters* 16, no. 11 (2021): 114006. For a popular essay about our research, see Daniel R. DiLeo, Sabrina Danielsen, and Emily E. Burke, "Study: Most US Catholic Bishops Kept Silent on Francis' Climate Change Push," Religion News Service, October 21, 2021, https://religionnews.com/2021/10/19/study-most-u-s-catholic-bishops-kept-silent-on-francis-climate-change-push/.

79. Brian Roewe, "Official Launch of *Laudato Si'* Action Platform Offers Catholics Concrete Steps toward Sustainable Lifestyles," *National Catholic Reporter*, December 29, 2021, www.ncronline.org/earthbeat/justice/official-launch-laudato-si-action-platform-offers-catholics-concrete-steps-toward.
80. Roman Catholic Diocese of San Diego, "Creation Care Action Plan—Version 4.1," www.sdcatholic.org/wp-content/uploads/life-peace-and-justice/care-for-creation-and-environment/documents/Creation-Care-Action-Plan.pdf.
81. Danielsen, DiLeo, and Burke, "Study."
82. Francis, *Laudate deum*, no. 2.
83. Aleja Hertzler-McCain, "Theologians and Scientists Praise, Critique Pope Francis' Climate Exhortation," *National Catholic Reporter*, October 12, 2023, www.ncronline.org/earthbeat/faith/theologians-and-scientists-praise-critique-pope-francis-climate-exhortation.
84. Francis, "Address to the Participants in the World Meeting of Popular Movements," October 28, 2014, www.vatican.va/content/francesco/en/speeches/2014/october/documents/papa-francesco_20141028_incontro-mondiale-movimenti-popolari.html.
85. Uruguayan Guzmán Carriquiry and Gianna La Bella, *La irrupción de los movimientos populares: "Rerum Novarum" de nuestro tiempo* (Vatican: Libreria Editrice Vaticana, 2019).
86. Francis, "Address at the Second World Meeting of Popular Movements," July 9, 2015, www.vatican.va/content/francesco/en/speeches/2015/july/documents/papa-francesco_20150709_bolivia-movimenti-popolari.html; Francis, "Message on the Occasion for the World Meetings of Popular Movements in Modesto (California)," February 10, 2017, www.vatican.va/content/francesco/en/messages/pont-messages/2017/documents/papa-francesco_20170210_movimenti-popolari-modesto.html.
87. Francis, "Address at the Second World Meeting of Popular Movements"; Pope Francis, "Letter to the Popular Movements," April 12, 2020, www.vatican.va/content/francesco/en/letters/2020/documents/papa-francesco_20200412_lettera-movimentipopolari.html.
88. Francis, "Address to the Participants in the World Meeting of Popular Movements," October 28, 2014, www.vatican.va/content/francesco/en/speeches/2014/october/documents/papa-francesco_20141028_incontro-mondiale-movimenti-popolari.html.
89. Francis, "Address to Participants in the 3rd World Meeting of Popular Movements," November 5, 2016, www.vatican.va/content/francesco/en/speeches/2016/november/documents/papa-francesco_20161105_movimenti-popolari.html.
90. Francis, "Address to Participants in the 3rd World Meeting."
91. Francis, "Nonviolence: A Style of Politics," Libreria Editrice Vaticana, 2017, www.vatican.va/content/francesco/en/messages/peace/documents/papa-francesco_20161208_messaggio-l-giornata-mondiale-pace-2017.html, no. 4; Francis, "Address to the Joint Session of the United States Congress," September 24, 2015, www.vatican.va/content/francesco/en/speeches/2015/september/documents/papa-francesco_20150924_usa-us-congress.html.
92. Francis, "Video Message on the Occasion of the Fourth World Meeting of Popular Movements," October 10, 2021, www.vatican.va/content/francesco/en/messages/pont-messages/2021/documents/20211016-videomessaggio-movimentipopolari.html.
93. Francis, "Message on the Occasion for the World Meetings of Popular Movements in Modesto (California)."
94. Lawrence J. Engel, "The Influence of Saul Alinsky on the Campaign for Human Development," *Theological Studies* 59, no. 4 (1998): 636–61; Richard L. Wood and Brad R. Fulton, *A Shared Future: Faith-Based Organizing for Racial Equity and Ethical Democracy*

(Chicago: University of Chicago Press, 2015), 23–24; Nicholas von Hoffman, *Radical: A Portrait of Saul Alinsky* (New York: Nation Books, 2010), 106–12; Loretta Pyles, *Progressive Community Organizing: Transformative Practice in a Globalizing World*, Third Edition (New York: Routledge, 2021), 24.

95. West/Southwest IAF, "Delegation Visits Pope Francis," Industrial Areas Foundation, October 24, 2022, www.industrialareasfoundation.org/2210_pope.
96. Francis and Ivereigh, *Let Us Dream*, 121–22.
97. Juan Carlos Scannone, *Theology of the People: The Pastoral and Theological Roots of Pope Francis* (Mahwah, NJ: Paulist Press, 2021); Rafael Luciani, *Pope Francis and the Theology of the People* (Maryknoll, NY: Orbis Books, 2017).
98. Consejo Episcopal Latinoamericano, *Concluding Document*, nos. 178–80. For background on base ecclesial communities, see Guillermo Cook, *The Expectation of the Poor: Latin American Base Ecclesial Communities in Protestant Perspective* (Eugene, OR: Wipf & Stock, 2021).
99. Francis, "Prayer Vigil with the Young People—Apostolic Journey to Rio de Janeiro on the Occasion of the XXVIII World Youth Day," July 27, 2013, www.vatican.va/content/francesco/en/speeches/2013/july/documents/papa-francesco_20130727_gmg-veglia-giovani.html.
100. Richard R. Gaillardetz, "The 'Francis Moment': A New Kairos for Catholic Ecclesiology," *CTSA Proceedings* 69 (2014): 65–66, 71.
101. Matt Holland, *The Rarest Kind of Courage: The Extraordinary Life of Fr. John Markoe* (Monee, IL: Independently Published, 2023).
102. Aaron Schutz and Marie G. Sandy, *Collective Action for Social Change: An Introduction to Community Organizing* (New York: Palgrave Macmillan, 2011), 221–27, 237–30, 193–206.
103. Martin Luther King Jr., "Letter from Birmingham City Jail," in *A Testament of Hope: The Essential Writings and Speeches*, Reprint Edition, ed. James M. Washington (New York: HarperOne, 2003), 290; Brian Roewe, "Vatican Official: Church Divestment from Fossil Fuels Is 'Moral Imperative,'" *National Catholic Reporter*, May 20, 2021, www.ncronline.org/news/earthbeat/vatican-official-church-divestment-fossil-fuels-moral-imperative; Brian Roewe, "Cardinal Cupich: To Save Planet, US Must Reject 'False Idol' of Money," *National Catholic Reporter*, July 14, 2021, www.ncronline.org/news/earthbeat/cardinal-cupich-save-planet-us-must-reject-false-idol-money.
104. Marshall Ganz, Julia Lee Cunningham, Inbal Ben Ezer, and Alaina Segura, "Crafting Public Narrative to Enable Collective Action: A Pedagogy for Leadership Development," Academy of Management Learning & Education, 2022, https://doi.org/10.5465/amle.2020.0224.
105. Aaron and Schutz, *Collective Action*, 261–83.
106. I am grateful to Richard W. Miller for highlighting the nonviolent direct action theory of Gene Sharp as a resource for climate action.
107. Aaron and Schutz, *Collective Action*, 27–28.
108. Pope Francis, "Construyendo Puentes Norte-Sur: Un Encuentro Sinodal entre el Papa Francisco y Estudiantes," *YouTube*, uploaded by Loyola University Chicago, February 24, 2022, www.youtube.com/watch?v=eM68WVzQzIY&t=0s, at 52:56-58:55.
109. James Lawson, "A Force More Powerful," *YouTube*, uploaded by International Center on Nonviolent Conflict, November 7, 2018, www.youtube.com/watch?v=hpBoHb59iVY, at 32:37.
110. Saint Bonaventure, *The Life of Francis of Assisi* (Charlotte: TAN Books, 2010), 7.
111. Besmond de Senneville, "Pope Tells Young French Activists."

CONCLUSION

Conor M. Kelly and Kristin E. Heyer

As the chapters in this volume have shown, the fact that Pope Francis is not a moral theologian does not mean that he has nothing to offer the field of moral theology. The same distinctive features that have made Francis's pontificate so invigorating for the broader Church are just as applicable to the traditional questions of moral theology and just as relevant for the most pressing issues in applied theological ethics today, provided one does the work to tease out these connections from the implicit moral vision underlying Francis's ministry. Throughout the volume, the contributors have done precisely this work, illuminating the practical implications of Francis's leadership for contemporary ethical concerns related to migration and racism, gender and sexuality, bioethics, war and peace, the environment, and more. The individual contributions are each valuable in their own right, as they show how US Catholics can more fully embrace the Francis revolution in concrete matters of faith and practice. Taken together, however, they also reveal something even more broadly applicable by illuminating the common themes that constitute the heart of Francis's moral vision. Specifically, they show how a stronger emphasis on the poor in the Church, a greater acceptance of ambiguity, and a deeper appreciation of structural forces are not simply indicative of Francis's Jesuit roots and Ignatian perspective but are also illustrative of a new way of proceeding for the Church that is especially pertinent to the field of moral theology. In this conclusion, then, we explore each of these themes to show how they provide a road map for incorporating the two crucial emphases of Francis's papacy identified in the introduction—the centrality of the Gospel's joy, and the priority of mercy—into the heart of moral theology in the United States, expanding the reception of this pope and renewing the work of moral theologians and ethicists in this country.

"A CHURCH WHICH IS POOR AND FOR THE POOR"

Arguably no theme is more prominent in Francis's pontificate, nor more pertinent for the transformation of moral theology in the United States, than his insistence on the priority the Catholic Church owes to those living in poverty. From the moment of his election, Francis explicitly articulated the importance of this priority as an intended hallmark of his pontificate. As he famously explained during his first media appearance after the conclave, he chose the name Francis as an homage to Saint Francis of Assisi and thus a reminder of the importance of poverty, after his dear friend Claudio Cardinal Hummes begged him, "Don't forget the poor."[1] Through his subsequent words and actions, Francis has shown that he took this admonition seriously.

On a practical level, Francis has elevated the work of the papal almoner, the person responsible for performing works of mercy on behalf of the pope. As one observer reflected, "the post had become largely ceremonial, separated from actual contact with the poor," but under Francis the role has become profoundly important, with Archbishop Konrad Krajewski leading a series of initiatives designed not simply to provide care for the poor but also to reaffirm their dignity.[2] From the installation of showers and a dormitory at the Vatican for those experiencing homelessness in Rome to hosting personal meals with the poor to much-publicized trips to the circus, under Francis the papal almoner has displayed a different kind of compassion for the poor that stresses the inherent humanity of all those caught in poverty and challenges the arm's-length response that easily becomes the default mechanism for charity around the globe.[3]

Notably, these actions are consistent with the way Francis has prioritized care for the poor in his magisterial teaching as well. As Krajewski insisted, "I myself could not live the Gospel the way I try to do if Pope Francis didn't show me. He does what he preaches, that's the key to understanding his actions."[4] And, from the very beginning of his pontificate, Francis has been preaching about the need for a renewed attention to the plight of the poor. Describing the theological significance of the option for the poor in Catholicism, Francis proclaimed in his first apostolic exhortation, "This is why I want a Church which is poor and for the poor."[5] In chapter 6 of this volume, M. T. Dávila shows how this mantra has truly served as a guidepost for Francis's papal ministry, reinvigorating the more consequential interpretation of the option for the poor found in liberation theology and making it the standard of fidelity by which to evaluate Catholic action in the world. Dávila nicely illustrates how genuinely embracing this vision of a poor Church has profound implications for Catholic reflection on ethical questions, especially in the United States, where an authentic option for the poor directly contradicts regnant cultural values like individualism and a powerful form of consumerism. Dávila's work thus provides a foundation for understanding how Francis's commitments to the poor can, and should, inspire a change in practical action, so the task of this conclusion is to build on these insights in order to explore more fully the impact of this central vision on the field of moral theology itself.

To embrace Francis's vision of a Church that is poor and for the poor, moral theology must incorporate three crucial elements from Francis's distinctive concern for the poor. First, moral theologians must attend to the fact that Francis's unwavering focus on the plight of the poor is not born of an abstract conception of "the poor" as a generic group but rather emerges from the contextual approach to ethical questions outlined by Lisa Sowle Cahill in chapter 1 of this volume. Francis has the concrete experiences of specific groups and particular people in view when he speaks about the Church's responsibility to care for the poor, whether that be subsistence farmers whose very livelihood is threatened by climate change in *Laudato si'*, the indigenous tribes in the Amazon who are often excluded from regional trends in *Querida Amazonia*, or the individual migrants who are each fleeing distinct personal and social crises in the pope's various appeals to Catholics and world leaders to pay more attention to this issue.[6] As a methodological model, this contextualization and concretization of the preferential option for the poor reveal that moral theology must similarly resist abstractions that paper over the human suffering at the heart of the issues ethicists explore. Francis's characteristic way of proceeding thus criticizes a tendency toward epistemological privilege that assumes the surest path to truth comes through the books and technical reflections of academics and that regard other, less formal analyses from the "uncredentialed" with an inherent—albeit sometimes implicit—degree of suspicion. Embodying something much closer to the "standpoint epistemology" of feminist philosophers like Sandra Harding, who have argued that people's particular social locations often give them unique insights into intellectual challenges that those with formal academic training cannot always see, Francis has prioritized the standpoint of the poor in his efforts to inspire a contextual approach to ethics, as Cahill explores in more detail in chapter 1.[7]

Fortunately, the growth of contextual theologies in the latter half of the twentieth century has already inspired a similar shift toward contextual evaluations of ethical issues, with feminist, womanist, and other liberationist (and decolonial) theologians leading the way.[8] The fact that their work remains labeled with these various modifiers and is not recognized simply as "ethics," however, demonstrates the persistence of an abstraction bias that treats contextual attentiveness as a niche concern rather than the heart of the field. To grapple more honestly with Francis's vision of a Church that is poor and for the poor, moral theology must reject this bifurcation and ensure instead that all moral analyses are rooted in lived reality, especially the lived reality of those who are excluded from systems of power. By letting the concrete experiences of the poor not only establish the slate of issues that moral theology addresses but also shape how the field understands and assess those issues, moral theologians can make the discipline more representative of Francis's vision of a Church that is poor and for the poor.

Second, Francis's own ministry with the poor provides a paradigm for how moral theology can accomplish this task of centering the lived reality of the poor in reflection on ethical issues. Francis has consistently championed the value of a "culture of encounter," and this principle directly informs his support for a Church that is more attentive to the realities of poverty.[9] As Daniel DiLeo notes in chapter 13 of this volume, encounter is a deeply Ignatian priority that seeks authentic interactions with other human beings *as* human beings, with the explicit hope of arriving at new insights from their particular perspectives and experiences. Encounter is thus, as Maureen O'Connell outlines in chapter 8, a tool for elevating the poor and marginalized, a means of generating the recognition and empowerment that James Keenan, SJ, explores with respect to Francis's thought in chapter 2. Practically, pursuing this "'culture of encounter' means that we, as a people, should be passionate about meeting others, seeking points of contact, building bridges, planning a project that includes everyone."[10] Embracing this model, moral theology can search for ways to look at and behold the reality of the poor as they experience it, through a process of accompaniment and engagement that makes their struggles part of the moral theologian's own experience and lived reality as well. There can be no more "*balconeadno*," to borrow the term Laurie Johnston highlights in her description of Francis's contrasting attention to the experiences of the victims of war. Moral theologians must not simply emphasize the lives of the poor in theory; instead, we must enrich our work with actual encounters with poor *people*, if we are going to broaden the impact of the Francis revolution throughout our field.

Third, an essential corollary of the primacy of encounter is the role of the affections as a theological resource in Francis's vision of a Church that is poor and for the poor. By presenting the culture of encounter as a rejection of a "culture of indifference," Francis has stressed the importance of allowing encounters to move the people involved through an affective response that makes the holistic experience of the other part of one's own emotional reality.[11] In chapter 7 of this volume, Kristin Heyer has already shown some of encounter's affective dimensions, and how, much like the reality of encounter itself, the openness to insights through the affections is a decidedly Ignatian trait. To follow the leadership of Francis, then, moral theologians must not merely turn toward the lived reality of those in poverty but must, more importantly, also be open to being moved by encounters with the poor so that they can appreciate the challenges that define life in poverty at the level of felt understanding more than intellectual affirmation.

Ultimately, all three of these ways to prioritize concern for the poor represent meaningful departures from business as usual for the field of Catholic moral theology. Challenging the epistemological privilege of abstraction, relying on insights gleaned through encounters, and leading with the heart as much as the head are not completely novel ideas for moral theologians, but they are approaches that have frequently required justification from the few who have chosen to employ them in the eras before Francis. With Francis calling for a Church that is poor and for the poor, however, these strategies must become the default mode of operation for the field, and that will take some work. The good news is that by embracing this new way of proceeding, moral theologians will find it easier to incorporate the second major theme of Francis's moral vision into their work, because the lives of the poor showcase the depth of life's complexity, and thus the need to account for some degree of ambiguity in the moral life.

"TAKE INTO ACCOUNT THE COMPLEXITY OF VARIOUS SITUATIONS"

There is a direct line between Francis's tolerance for ambiguity and some degree of disagreement on moral matters and his emphasis on the primacy of encounters, because it is precisely his pastoral awareness of the multifaceted challenges besetting people's actual efforts to live as disciples of Christ that prompts him to make room for some degree of variation in the moral life. In chapter 9 of this volume, Bryan Massingale speaks most fully to the positive value of ambiguity in Francis's moral vision, arguing that one of the unique features of Francis's treatment of LGBTQ issues has been his willingness to entertain debates, to the point that contradictory positions are now sometimes promoted by different authorities at the same time. As Massingale explains, the presence of these competing moral judgments is a feature, not a bug, of moral theology in the Francis era, and part of the reason is that Francis sees this type of debate as a critical sign that the faithful are treating the messiness of life with the honesty it deserves. Consider the way Francis defended the synodal process in *Amoris laetitia*, after critics had suggested the bishops' debates about family issues were too heated and free flowing.

It was, according to Francis, "the *complexity* of the issues that arose [that] revealed the need for continued open discussion of a number of doctrinal, moral, spiritual, and pastoral questions" (emphasis added).[12] Thus, in Francis's estimation, the Catholic Church should not attempt to interpret every moral question through the hermetically sealed categories of black and white, because doing so fails to appreciate the ways that human existence is colored in a richly textured palate of grays.

Catholic theologians are not unaware of the ways that ambiguity can benefit the search for truth. Far from conflating ambiguity with the absence of clarity, many have portrayed ambiguity as a sign of a mature moral analysis in much the same way that Francis has championed in his moral vision. Susan Ross, for instance, has argued that the Catholic Church's "prophetic stance when it comes to social justice does have greater credibility, precisely because it is informed by those most affected by these decisions, and it is cognizant of the many complexities involved."[13] On the basis of this experience, she has described how incorporating an increased comfort with ambiguity and a greater acknowledgment of complexity into Catholic teachings on marriage, sexual ethics, and even abortion could strengthen the impact of the Church's moral witness.[14] Her assessment is well aligned with Francis's approach to moral matters, which similarly suggests that the greatest threat in moral reflection is not that disagreement and debate will sacrifice the clarity of the Church's teachings, but that the hunger for certitude will obscure the truth in the name of simplicity.

The danger of this threat is particularly poignant in the United States, where polarization amplifies the type of binary thinking that makes the longing for certitude so acute. An allergy to ambiguity primes Catholics to fall into this trap, which is one major reason why so many US Catholics have retreated to the entrenched positions of the culture wars. Francis's moral vision offers a corrective to these impulses, setting the expectation that Catholics will approach ethical debates with the assumption that matters are inherently more complicated than we can possibly intuit at first glance. Consequently, Catholics should embrace a hermeneutic of suspicion about any explanation that seems too neat, presuming that reductionistic analyses of moral questions are not laudable for their purported "clarity" but are potentially damaging as a result of their artificiality. Indeed, Francis's tolerance—and occasional preference—for ambiguity demonstrates that the most appropriate Catholic disposition entails searching for ways to complicate the assessment of a contested moral question rather than to simplify it. To be consistent with Francis's vision, then, moral theologians should use their work to help the faithful cultivate a new openness to complexity, ideally by pointing out the ways that prevailing discourses fail to account for relevant factors affecting the ethical values at stake.

To offer but one extended example, civic discourse in the United States continues to struggle with how best to respond to the ongoing opioid crisis, which the US Department of Health and Human Services declared a public health emergency in 2017.[15] Part of the problem is the tendency of observers to gravitate toward one of two poles in their analysis of the root causes of addiction, variously describing it as a "choice" or a "disease." Critics of these models—including some theologians—note that "neither of these categories is adequate to the phenomenon of addiction. For instance, the disease concept obscures the extent to which persons may be expected to take responsibility for their addictions, and the choice concept obscures the distinctiveness of the addictive experience."[16] Nevertheless, the models persist, because their simplicity fits with a desire for clear, categorical thinking. By embracing ambiguity as a valuable tool for moral analysis, Catholics can resist the gravitational pull of these two poles, allowing them to see the ways that the categories of choice and disease are often wielded inequitably to exculpate certain individuals or groups and to condemn others, to the point of perpetuating social injustices.[17] Resisting these temptations, Catholics attentive to ambiguity can see that there are ways in which each pole has something, but notably not everything, to contribute to the analysis of addiction, prompting a search for new levels of analysis in the diagnosis of the problem as well as new avenues in the pursuit of a more holistic solution.[18]

Ideally, this perspective will empower a more genuine conversation about the complicated work of recovery, so that communities can acknowledge competing realities like the fact that crackdowns on the overprescription of opioids can indeed lead to less abuse in some cases, but often at the cost of undermining legitimate palliative care options, or that "harm reduction" programs like safe-injection sites can save lives while also enabling some addictions.[19] These interventions, like any human-designed solution, are neither unambiguously good nor unambiguously evil. They have both costs and benefits, and the responsible agent is not the one who pretends that their preferred approach has no flaws, but rather the one who acknowledges the known insufficiencies and then makes the case that their strategy is still the best way to proceed among an array of similarly imperfect options. In this way, embracing ambiguity is not a capitulation to relativism but a theologically honest recognition of our limited humanity in this "time between the times," when the transformative work of God begun in Christ is already changing the world but will not reach its completion until Christ comes again.

A more intentional openness to ambiguity could strengthen Catholics' contemporary moral analyses in a host of other areas as well, but Francis's own tolerance for ambiguity shows that there must be limits to this approach. To begin, the value of ambiguity itself is not unambiguous. Although an openness to debate will indeed allow the Church to explore new complexities in its readings of the ever-changing "signs of the times," not every position should be given equal weight. There is a real risk that harmful claims will be left unchallenged in the name of pluralism if the pendulum swings too far. In chapter 9, Massingale alludes to this problem in the lives of LGBTQ Catholics, but one can imagine the same pitfall in a host of other areas.

The best way to mitigate this risk is to remember that ambiguity is not an intrinsic good but must instead be ordered to a good end. Thus, a Francis-inspired penchant for ambiguity calls attention to all the factors influencing agency and culpability and asks the faithful to grapple with them in good faith, not necessarily to change the judgment but rather to ensure that the moral evaluation does justice to the complexity of the situation. This caveat is crucial, because Francis's openness to ambiguity does not mean that there is no room for norms in his moral vision. On the contrary, Francis has appealed to norms regularly and insistently in order to challenge problematic practices. *Evangelii guadium*, for instance, is replete with negative norms—"no to an economy of exclusion; . . . no to the new idolatry of money; . . . no to warring among ourselves"—that are designed to condemn specific actions and also to inspire more compassionate alternatives.[20] Even in the case of abortion, a perennially charged topic among US Catholics, Francis has emphasized his moral opposition while simultaneously asking the Church to dial down its rhetoric.[21] Francis's promotion of ambiguity is thus not an artifact of some kind of doctrinal uncertainty but rather a pastoral conviction that there is an unavoidable gap between the norm and its application to finite human beings. As Francis insisted in *Amoris laetitia*, after citing Thomas Aquinas's treatise on law, "It is true that general rules set forth a good which can never be disregarded or neglected, but in their formulation they cannot provide absolutely for all particular situations."[22] The point is not to dismiss any existing norms but to "ensure full fidelity to God in the concrete life of a human being."[23]

Attending to ambiguity in this way will take some work, for, as Ross noted in her defense of ambiguity, "a tolerance and an appreciation for ambiguity takes time, and a willingness to think in something more than sound bytes," which few Catholics—and fewer US Catholics—are encouraged, let alone trained, to do.[24] To help develop these traits, moral theologians can benefit from two of Francis's underlying Ignatian commitments. First, moral theologians and theological ethicists can rely on the spiritual value of "indifference" promoted in *The Spiritual Exercises* to hold their individual positions more lightly.[25] If moral theology intends to criticize the idolization of certitude, then moral theologians must be willing to model a different way of entertaining ideas with more humility, beginning with their own claims. Cultivating this indifference does not mean abandoning all convictions, however. Instead, it means presenting those convictions as one's best judgments based on the available evidence, so that one can admit the possibility of being wrong and thus entertain the need for change. By operating in this way, moral theology will invite genuine dialogue, because the gift of indifference is that one no longer needs to feel threatened by disagreement, because reevaluation and, if necessary, revision can be steps on the way to a fuller understanding of the truth. This disposition of indifference would go a long way toward shifting the discussion of divisive issues like abortion, especially if multiple Catholic moral theologians were willing to engage one another across their divisions in a shared spirit of indifference, as at least one recent symposium in the *Journal of Moral Theology* illustrated.[26]

Second, moral theologians must accentuate discernment in the moral life. As this volume's three opening chapters—by, respectively, Cahill, Keenan, and Kelly—show, discernment is a key priority for Francis that reflects his Ignatian roots, and so it is certainly an appropriate resource for incorporating his moral vision into the work of moral theology. Just as important, discernment is particularly valuable for the task of grappling with ambiguity because it provides both the space for ambiguity to emerge and the rationale for allowing it to persist. Hence, discernment can inspire ambiguity because, as both Cahill and Keenan—along with Andrea Vicini, SJ, in chapter 11—explain in this volume, discernment is supposed to be a communal project, and the multitude of voices is unlikely to hit the same note all the time. By viewing competing claims as resources for the shared task of discerning the most fitting solution to practical ethical questions, moral theologians can welcome ambiguity just as Francis does. At the same time, discernment can allow moral theologians to face this ambiguity with more confidence because it expects that different circumstances will lead to different conclusions, and therefore does not assume that contrasts equate with contradiction. To ensure that this process of welcoming ambiguity through indifference and discernment truly leads to an expanded reception of Francis's moral vision in the US Catholic Church, moral theologians must also work to incorporate the final theme of structural concern.

"SUFFERING FROM GRAVE STRUCTURAL DEFICIENCIES"

Francis focuses our attention on another key element of this complexity marking many moral situations: the invisible impact of structures on agents and on those at various peripheries, in particular. His comfort with ambiguity acknowledges these structural constraints and responds to those on the underside of structural violence. The "structural eye" that the pope continually brings to his analysis of social and pastoral issues has been informed by his Ignatian heritage—as Thomas Massaro, SJ, shows in chapter 5—and it summons further developments in the field of moral theology.

The priority Francis gives to structural analysis allows him to probe root causes of economic, environmental, and social injustices and related threats to solidarity. His concern for those who are poor and excluded emerges not from a preoccupation with individual vices or choices, but rather reflects persistent attention to the destructive effects of exploitive economic structures and their desensitizing effects. As Francis stressed in *Fratelli tutti*, "Global society is suffering from grave structural deficiencies that cannot be resolved by piecemeal solutions or quick fixes," creating a duty of charity for Catholics' "work to change the social situations that cause . . . [others'] suffering."[27] In chapter 1, Cahill indicates Francis's concern for how structural sin undermines individual and social discernment, as well. For example, in chapter 13, DiLeo traces how harmful market structures and a technocratic paradigm fuel the climate emergency in *Laudato si'*; and in chapter 7, Heyer connects the pope's attention to the structural drivers of forced migration to abetting cultural legacies and mind-sets.

We see his structural eye at work in some of Francis's internal ecclesial reform efforts as well, whether targeting curial centralization, the "cancer of clericalism," or how certain approaches to knowledge and power can be transmitted through ritual rubrics, bureaucratic policies, and spiritual disciplines that have been handed down, rather than via deliberate individual acts.[28] In chapters 9 and 10, respectively, Massingale and Megan McCabe suggest some ways in which this characteristic attention to structural justice must be further implemented *ad intra*, however. Francis-appointed Robert Cardinal McElroy in San Diego has recently "challenge[d] what he describes as the Church's 'structures and cultures of exclusion,'" in fact, advocating for "a 'radical inclusion' that will bring more women into leadership roles, open paths to divorced and remarried Catholics who want to receive Communion, and listen more attentively to LGBTQ Catholics wounded by the Church."[29] The Synod on Synodality's "Vademecum" also indicates the importance of including the voices and concerns of those who are most marginalized, with some continental reports evidencing synodal efforts and preliminary outcomes in this vein.[30]

Neverthless, Francis's attention to structures ensues amid a Church that has exercised advantage systemically both *ad intra* and *ad extra* and yet that has often avoided power analysis. Even amid the synod processes, theologians have lamented how operative ecclesiologies and hierarchical theologies of synodality, together with inherited ecclesiastical structures, significantly hamper the path.[31] As Vincent Miller's analysis, referenced in chapter 4, underscores, ecclesial structures themselves are "seldom neutral instruments transparent to the interests of the Church," and synodality and structural change face significant challenges not only from within in the Church but also from the "relationship-constructing power" of colonial and neoliberal structures.[32] The Church has not only been formed by but has also colluded with *ad extra* structures and practices that have facilitated domination rather than encounters or communion, and moral theologians cannot claim to genuinely embrace Francis's attentiveness to structural constraints without accounting for this history and working to undo its legacy.

Even as the consistent employment of structural analysis may remain an ongoing task ecclesially, this approach prompts the field of moral theology to better recognize and navigate among the ways that human beings are conditioned and constrained by social forces. For whereas post–Vatican II theological anthropology has deepened trajectories that take seriously "the corporeality, contextuality and communality of the human person," idealized notions of the subject have continued to influence operative conceptions of agency and justice.[33] An atomistic view of autonomy continues to pervade notions of responsibility and sin in Catholic theology, as well.[34] Act-oriented moral theology rooted in a notion of persons rationally choosing rightly ordered ends to secure self-justification has too often led to an emphasis on avoiding transgressions as opposed to pursuing the good.[35] Whereas there is value in a traditional focus on objects of acts and their significance, as well as narrative and virtue ethics' efforts to shift from a focus on acts to a focus on persons, neither is sufficiently informed by the complexities of social structures and cultures, nor are related ecclesial emphases. A primary focus on avoiding sin or vice can occlude the attention to structural context that Francis helpfully highlights.

Recent research on the inadequate confines of certain categories of moral theology indicates the impact of dominant individualistic emphases, from analyses of double effect and cooperation with evil, to avoiding scandal, to "commonplace" understandings of racism.[36] Cristina Traina has shown the shortcomings of Catholic moral theology's assumptions that we can avoid sin, that blameworthiness and sin are identical, and that we have "more ought's than can's."[37] In a related vein, contemporary appeals to a truncated notion of conscience function more as litmus tests than as invitations to the communal discernment and growth discussed by Conor Kelly in chapter 3 of this book. They mask constraints to the pursuit of the good beyond culpable ignorance, vice, or moral confusion, and they reorient "our vision of the moral life toward self-justification and away from accountability to others' needs, which are justifiable claims on us."[38] The focus of the dominant culture wars, discussed in this volume's introduction on the morality of particular acts, has often served to shrink the scope of ethical concern (and the range of relevant moral agents) as well as to coopt the focus of Catholic formation. More work remains to be done on cultivating a personalist understanding of conscience that fully accounts for barriers to genuine freedom in the subject's pursuit of the good, rather than agents' avoidance of cooperation in a discrete range of evil acts.

Despite liberationist insights and relatively recent efforts to "socialize" virtue ethics, then, dominant Catholic conceptions of autonomy, conscience, and virtue have assumed unencumbered agents, underestimating the impact of structural constraints on human agency.[39] Pope Francis's own attention to structures suggests the need to deepen appreciation of the ways in which disordered values and constrained agency shape the moral life. It calls the discipline to more centrally employ insights from those whose experiences have not typically been considered normative in traditional ethical reflection (emphasizing "contextual theologies," as mentioned above), and to enlarge ethical frameworks that often privilege narrow notions of autonomy and efficacy. In the US context in particular, individualistic myths—such as the myths of meritocracy, of the individual agent, and of unfettered freedom—have often further undermined sensitivity to structural injustice. Given the impact of economic, racial, and citizenship constraints sketched in the volume's chapters, there remains a need for greater attention to the contextual and contingent character of agency to improve moral formation and public witness efforts alike.

Cardinal McElroy has noted how a focus on intrinsic evil does not necessarily serve the pope's priorities on poverty, given that the latter is "the result of countless specific human actions with varying degrees of responsibility that give rise to social structures and practices imbued with selfishness and evil."[40] In Francis's own view, casuistry likewise risks detracting from the proper scope of moral theology, characterizing it, in the words of Cathleen Kaveny, as a "cramped" and "self-serving effort to comply with the letter of the law while subverting its spirit and purpose."[41] Hence a focus on a "perfectionist teleology," together with individualistic penitential rites, have obscured the importance of structural analysis and social responsibility in Catholic moral theology.[42]

In a 2022 address to Catholic moral theologians, Francis urged them to "interdisciplinary exchange, including reflection on the work of social scientists."[43] This offers encouragement to those drawing on work in critical social theory to elaborate the relationship between structures, culture, and agency.[44] The work of ethicists showing how critical realist sociologists understand social structures as emerging from the interaction of individual persons as well as influencing them helps resist methodological individualisms, illuminating how "the power of culture and structure is actuated only through the free-but-constrained decisions made by acting persons."[45] Other recent interdisciplinary work on the fragility of virtue,[46] the vulnerability of rationality,[47] and moral intuitionism[48] similarly highlights how social contexts can distort capacities of perception and sympathies.[49] Francis pushes the field further in these directions as he seems to understand, as Cahill has reflected, that "worldviews, individual identities, moral character, practices, culture and structures are all interdependent, take shape together, and together change or resist change," and so "moral responsibility, as both conditioned and free, must address all these factors simultaneously."[50]

Although some observers, including ethicists, may find it frustrating that this renewed attention to structural analysis does not lead to an institutional Church that wields its structural power to implement observers' preferred agendas, Francis seems more prone to characterize effecting structural change as a bottom-up rather than top-down responsibility. In a sense a similar complaint may be lodged against his penchant for ambiguity. As Elyse Raby highlights in chapter 4 of this book, Francis's synodal approach has far-reaching consequences; its processes of consultation and discernment are not about implementing a predetermined agenda or even fixing future diretions via likeminded appointments (e.g., as Keenan's discussion in chapter 2 of Francis's "recognition" of the peripheries illustrates). Rather, these processes are oriented to the realization of a new way of being Church that is defined primarily by the *act* of accompaniment and only secondarily by the "solutions" that accompaniment may produce. Thus, an approach that attends to structural sin both *ad intra* and *ad extra*, by way of the slow work of engaging the peripheries, seems more faithful to Francis's priorities and may augur more thoroughgoing, lasting changes—even if shifts confound the standard categories or ideological divisions typically used as a shorthand way to map the field of moral theology. Joseph Cardinal Tobin has characterized Francis's synodal vision, which he calls Francis's "long game," as a path marked primarily by conversion: "the Church's own conversion, a new way in understanding and approaching how we carry out our mission."[51] As a result of this dynamic focus on the complexities of structural injustice, it is apt that Francis moves in the direction of empowering social movements, signaling perhaps that the field of moral theology is likewise invited to further overcome the silos of theory and praxis (and even activism). As Cahill and DiLeo underscore in chapters 1 and 13, respectively, Francis finds the creative alternatives and proactive mobilization at the grassroots level critical to countering structural injustice and globalized indifference. In the face of pervasive structural violence, Francis finds that the future is in the hands of those on the peripheries, whom he has called to the ecclesial center.

"A RENEWED PERSONAL ENCOUNTER WITH JESUS CHRIST"

While Francis's vision for the Church does entail meaningful changes for the field of moral theology, as both this book and this concluding chapter have shown, one must take care to avoid a reductionistic interpretation that would misconstrue these changes as evidence of an ideological agenda and therefore attempt to read them through the rigid categories of the culture wars.[52] The goal for Francis, as he has insisted from the earliest days of his pontificate, is not a reconfiguration of the Catholic Church in his own image (another point Keenan's discussion of Francis's cardinal appointments demonstrates), but "a renewed personal encounter with Jesus Christ."[53] As Vicini notes in chapter 11, this Christological turn is both crucial to Francis's understanding of discipleship and reflective of his Jesuit roots, for a personal encounter with Christ is at the center of the *Spiritual Exercises*.[54] Unsurprisingly, when Kaveny proposed that Catholic moral theologians could faithfully embody the spirit of Francis by rehabilitating a certain kind of casuistry, she argued that they should "emphasize that the moral law has to be interpreted according to the intention of the lawgiver—Jesus Christ," and asserted that this recentering of Christ "is the most groundbreaking aspect of Pope Francis's approach to moral theology."[55] Kaveny thus connects Francis's Christological focus with another central feature of his pontificate—namely, the priority of mercy—and helps to reveal how the three key themes drawn out of this volume amount to a summons for Catholic moral theologians to put the Gospel encounter with Jesus back at the heart of their work.

Consider first the primacy of the poor. Embracing the preferential option for the poor through an authentic culture of encounter is more than just an attempt to apply an abstract ideal. It is fundamentally an imitation of Jesus's entire way of being in the world. His ministry was marked by a care for the poor and marginalized that brought him into a scandalous degree of contact with these socially and economically excluded human beings (e.g., Matt. 9:10–13).[56] Meanwhile, theologians regularly describe the Incarnation itself as an act of preferential love for the poor, insofar as God not only came to encounter and accompany the creatures whose very humanity had become impoverished as a result of sin but also chose to become enfleshed in a poor family and thus knew the challenges of economic poverty from the inside.[57] By advancing a moral vision that prioritizes the poor, Pope Francis is challenging moral theologians to imitate Christ in an even more holistic fashion that takes the Gospel witness both seriously and literally.

One can similarly see Christ as a model for Francis's promotion of a greater openness to ambiguity in the moral life. Reflecting on his own characteristic emphasis on mercy, Francis once noted that "the scholars of the law . . . represent the principal opposition to Jesus" in the Gospels, and described them as those "who live attached to the letter of the law but who neglect love; men who only know how to close doors and draw boundaries."[58] In contrast to this rigidity, Francis has championed a spirit of flexibility that has led to the embrace of ambiguity described above, insisting that "the true defenders of doctrine are not those who uphold its letter, but its spirit; not ideas but people; not formulae but the gratuitiousness of God's love and forgiveness."[59] This understanding of God comes first and foremost from the encounter with Christ, who reveals God's mercy and shows the priority of people—in all their ambiguity—over abstraction.[60] Jesus's reaction to the woman "caught in adultery" in John's Gospel is emblematic of this response, for he rejects the Pharisees' presumption of legal clarity and instead sees both the woman and her accusers in their full complexity, ultimately freeing her by turning the table on them when he instructs them to "let anyone among you who is without sin be the first to throw a stone at her" (Jn. 8:1–11). Francis's tolerance for ambiguity is rooted in an appeal to this very interaction, for he vividly maintained that "a pastor cannot feel that it is enough to simply apply moral laws to those living in 'irregular' situations, as if they were stones to throw at people's lives."[61] If there is space for variation and room for further growth in Francis's vision for the moral life, it is only because Jesus introduced them in the first place.

Finally, Francis's attentiveness to structural constraints is also an extension of a more radical embrace of the Gospel's ideals. Though scholars have made clear that Jesus was not a revolutionary in the basest political sense of the word, there was nonetheless a direct challenge to the structures of his day in his ministry of the reign of God.[62] More to the point, Jesus was always attentive to the ways that larger social forces influenced the agency of the human beings he encountered, a disposition that both animated his special concern for the poor and marginalized and also supported his preference for compassion over rigidity. Hence, in Matthew's Gospel, Jesus challenged the gender inequities created by divorce, arguing that "anyone who divorces his wife . . . causes her to commit adultery" (Matt. 5:32), thereby calling attention to the fact that divorce greatly constrained the options available to the women left behind in a patriarchal society.[63] Jesus's healing miracles, meanwhile, where as much a challenge to the social mechanisms of exclusion prevalent during his day as they were a transformation for the individuals who were physically healed.[64] Finally, the entire presentation of the "reign of God" was a direct threat to the political structures organizing society at the time, providing the basis for Jesus's ultimate execution at the hands of an imperial power.[65] As a result, the structural concern permeating Francis's comments on ethical

CONCLUSION 249

questions is not merely consistent with the claim that the moral life is best understood as a response to the call to follow Christ; it is also a logical application of that claim and an essential step on the path toward realizing that vision.

The best way to appreciate the moral vision of Pope Francis, then, is to think of it not as Francis's vision for moral theology but rather Francis's account of what he believes Jesus would want for the whole Church. The prioritization of the poor, the acceptance of ambiguity, and the attention to structural influences are all key themes in Francis's moral vision because they target particular shortcomings in the contemporary Catholic approach to moral problems that undermine the Church's efforts to hear and respond faithfully to the call of Jesus. Together, they represent a prescription for a transformation of more than just the field of moral theology, for these emphases are equally challenging for the Church as a whole. Nevertheless, moral theologians and theological ethicists have an opportunity to lead the process of conversion, provided they take this pope more seriously and attend to the ways he is pointing everyone in the Church back to Christ.

NOTES

1. Francis, "Audience to Representatives of the Communications Media: Address of the Holy Father Pope Francis," March 16, 2013, www.vatican.va/content/francesco/en/speeches/2013/march/documents/papa-francesco_20130316_rappresentanti-media.html.
2. Raymond J. de Souza, "Pope's Almoner Reflects Distinctive Difference Francis Has Made," *Crux*, March 11, 2017, https://cruxnow.com/commentary/2017/03/popes-almoner-reflects-distinctive-difference-francis-made.
3. Paulina Guzik, "Papal Almoner Takes 2,000 Poor People to the Circus," *The Compass*, February 28, 2023, www.thecompassnews.org/2023/02/papal-almoner-takes-2000-poor-people-to-the-circus/.
4. Quoted by Paulina Guzik, "He Has 'Changed Our Lives,' Say Those in Need about Francis, the 'Pope of the Poor,'" *Our Sunday Visitor*, March 13, 2023, www.oursundayvisitor.com/he-has-changed-our-lives-say-those-in-need-about-francis-the-pope-of-the-poor/.
5. Francis, *Evangelii gaudium*, November 24, 2013, no. 198, www.vatican.va/content/francesco/en/apost_exhortations/documents/papa-francesco_esortazione-ap_20131124_evangelii-gaudium.html.
6. See Francis, *Laudato si'*, May 24, 2015, no. 25, www.vatican.va/content/francesco/en/encyclicals/documents/papa-francesco_20150524_enciclica-laudato-si.html; Francis, *Querida Amazonia*, February 2, 2020, nos. 17, 84, www.vatican.va/content/francesco/en/apost_exhortations/documents/papa-francesco_esortazione-ap_20200202_querida-amazonia.html; and, e.g., Francis, "Message of His Holiness Pope Francis for the 105th World Day of Migrants and Refugees," September 29, 2019, www.vatican.va/content/francesco/en/messages/migration/documents/papa-francesco_20190527_world-migrants-day-2019.html.

7. Sandra Harding, "Rethinking Standpoint Epistemology: What Is 'Strong Objectivity?'" in *Feminist Epistemologies*, ed. Linda Alcoff and Elizabeth Potter (New York: Routledge, 1993), 49–82.
8. See, e.g., Lisa Sowle Cahill, "Catholic Feminists and Traditions," *Journal of the Society of Christian Ethics* 34, no. 2 (Fall–Winter 2014): 27–51; Katie Geneva Cannon, Emilie M. Townes, and Angela D. Sims, eds., *Womanist Theological Ethics: A Reader* (Louisville: Westminster John Knox Press, 2011); and Anges M. Brazal, *A Theology of Southeast Asia: Liberation-Postcolonial Ethics in the Philippines* (Maryknoll, NY: Orbis Books, 2019).
9. Francis, "Morning Meditation in the Chapel of the *Domus Sanctae Marthae*: For a Culture of Encounter," September 13, 2016, www.vatican.va/content/francesco/en/cotidie/2016/documents/papa-francesco-cotidie_20160913_for-a-culture-of-encounter.html.
10. Francis, *Fratelli tutti*, October 3, 2020, no. 216, www.vatican.va/content/francesco/en/encyclicals/documents/papa-francesco_20201003_enciclica-fratelli-tutti.html.
11. Francis, "For a Culture of Encounter." See also Marcus Mescher, *The Ethics of Encounter: Christian Neighbor Love as a Practice of Solidarity* (Maryknoll, NY: Orbis Books, 2020), xiii–xvi.
12. Francis, *Amoris laetitia*, March 19, 2016, no. 2, www.vatican.va/content/dam/francesco/pdf/apost_exhortations/documents/papa-francesco_esortazione-ap_20160319_amoris-laetitia_en.pdf.
13. Susan A. Ross, "The Complexities and Ambiguities of the 'Prophetic Dimension': A Response," in *American Catholics, American Culture: Tradition and Resistance*, ed. Margaret O'Brien Steinfels, vol. 2, *American Catholics in the Public Square* (Lanham, MD: Sheed & Ward, 2004), 45.
14. Ross, 42–45, 47–48.
15. "Opioid Facts and Statistics," US Department of Health and Human Services, December 16, 2022, www.hhs.gov/opioids/statistics/index.html.
16. Kent Dunnington, *Addiction and Virtue: Beyond the Models of Disease and Choice* (Downers Grove, IL: InterVarsity Press, 2011), 10.
17. Todd Whitmore, "Holy Deviance: Christianity, Race, and Class in the Opioid Crisis," *Journal of the Society of Christian Ethics* 40, no. 1 (Spring–Summer 2020): 145–62.
18. For one example of an added spiritual dimension in the analysis of addiction that takes seriously the insights and limitations of both the choice and disease models, see Andrew Kim, "Newness of Life and Grace-Enabled Recovery from Addiction: Walking the Road to Recovery with Romans 7," *Journal of Moral Theology* 10, special issue 1 (2021): 124–42.
19. See, e.g., Mark A. Rothstein, "The Opioid Crisis and the Need for Comapssion in Pain Management," *American Journal of Public Health* 107, no. 8 (August 2017): 1253–54; and Cara L. Connaughton and Jillian J. Boersteler, "Harm Reduction for Intravenous Substance Use: A Moral Analysis of Common Strategies," *National Catholic Bioethics Quarterly* 21, no. 1 (Spring 2021): 69–84.
20. Francis, *Evangelii guadium*, nos. 53, 55–56, 98–101.
21. See Francis, "Full Text: Pope Francis' In-Flight Press Conference from Slovakia," Catholic News Agency, September 15, 2021, www.catholicnewsagency.com/news/248994/full-text-pope-francis-in-flight-press-conference-from-slovakia; Antonio Spadaro, "A Big Heart Open to God: The Exclusive Interview with Pope Francis," *America*, September 30, 2013, 15–38.

22. Francis, *Amoris laetitia*, no. 304.
23. Francis.
24. Ross, "Complexities and Ambiguities," 45.
25. For more on Ignatius's understanding of "indifference," see Roger Haight, *Christian Spirituality for Seekers: Reflections on the Spiritual Exercises of Ignatius of Loyola* (Maryknoll, NY: Orbis Books, 2012), 104.
26. M. Therese Lysaught, Mari Rapela Heidt, Mary Doyle Roche, and Kate Ward, eds., "Symposium: Dialogue after Dobbs," *Journal of Moral Theology* 12, no. 1 (2023): 89–144.
27. Francis, *Fratelli tutti*, nos. 179, 186.
28. Bradford E. Hinze, "The Ecclesiology of Pope Francis and the Future of the Church in Africa," *Journal of Global Catholicism* 2, no. 1 (2017): 20, 22; Francis, *Let Us Dream: The Path to a Better Future* (New York: Simon & Schuster, 2020), 25.
29. John Gehring, "Pope Francis and the American Church: A Decade Later, He Still Challenges US Catholic Leadership," *New York Daily News*, March 13, 2023, https://www.nydailynews.com/2023/03/13/pope-francis-and-the-american-church-a-decade-later-he-still-challenges-us-catholic-leadership/.
30. Secretary General of the Synod of Bishops, *For a Synodal Church: Communion, Participation and Mission, Vademecum for the Synod on Synodality* (Vatican City: Synod of Bishops, 2021), www.synod.va/content/dam/synod/document/common/vademecum/Vademecum-EN-A4.pdf.
31. See, e.g., Bradford Hinze, "Dreams of Synodality, Specters of Constraint," *Louvain Studies* 43, no. 3 (2020): 297–312, at 297, https://doi.org/10.2143/LS.43.3.3288709; Peter De Mey, "Synodality as a Key Component of the Pontificate of Pope Francis: The Difficult Way from Theory to Practice," in *Changing the Church: Transformations of Christian Belief, Practice, and Life*, ed. Mark D. Chapman and Vladimir Latinovic (Cham, Switzerland: Palgrave-Macmillan, 2021), 323–31; Amanda C. Osheim, "Stepping toward a Synodal Church," *Theological Studies* 80, no. 2 (2019): 370–92, at 373, https://doi.org/10.1177/0040563919836225; and Massimo Faggioli, "From Collegiality to Synodality: Promise and Limits of Francis's 'Listening Primacy,'" *Irish Theological Quarterly* 85, no. 4 (2020): 352–69, at 367, https://doi.org/10.1177/0021140020916034, as highlighted by Vincent J. Miller, "Synodality and the Sacramental Mission of the Church: The Struggle for Communion in a World Divided by Colonialism and Neoliberal Globalization," *Theological Studies* 83, no. 1 (2022): 8–24, https://doi.org/10.1177/00405639221076556.
32. Miller, "Synodality," 8, 10.
33. "Assumptions about the ability of the experience of elite white males to represent the universal human condition have been rightly challenged as distortions that deny the full humanity of all others." See Mary Doak, "Sex, Race, and Culture: Constructing Theological Anthropology for the Twenty-First Century," *Theological Studies* 80, no. 3 (September 2019): 529.
34. Roger Haight, "Sin and Grace," in *Systematic Theology: Roman Catholic Perspectives, Volume II*, ed. F. Schüssler Fiorenza and J. Galvin (Minneapolis: Fortress Press, 1992), 77–141, at 100n32.
35. See, e.g., James F. Keenan, *A History of Moral Theology in the Twentieth Century: From Confessing Sins to Liberating Consciences* (New York: Continuum, 2010); and James F. Keenan, "Redeeming Conscience," *Theological Studies* 76, no. 1 (2015): 129–47; Darlene Fozard Weaver, *The Acting Person and the Christian Moral Life* (Washington, DC: Georgetown University Press, 2011).

36. See, e.g., Cristina L. H. Traina, "Between a Rock and a Hard Place: Unwanted Pregnancy, Mercy and Solidarity," *Journal of Religious Ethics* 46, no. 4 (2018): 658–81; Julie Hanlon Rubio, "Cooperation with Evil Reconsidered: The Moral Duty of Resistance," *Theological Studies* 78, no. 1 (March 2017): 96–120; Christopher Vogt, "The Inevitability of Scandal: A Moral and Biblical Analysis of Firing Gay Teachers and Ministers to Avoid Scandal," in *The Bible and Catholic Theological Ethics*, ed. Yiu Sing Lúcás Chan, James Keenan, and Ronaldo Zacharias (Maryknoll, NY: Orbis Books, 2017), 262–72; and Bryan N. Massingale, *Racial Justice and the Catholic Church* (Maryknoll, NY: Orbis Books, 2010).
37. Traina, "Between a Rock and a Hard Place," 668.
38. Traina, 671.
39. See, e.g., Brian Stiltner, *Toward Thriving Communities: Virtue Ethics as Social Ethics* (Winona, WI: Anselm Academic, 2016); Christopher Vogt, "Virtue: Personal Formation and Social Transformation," *Theological Studies* 77, no. 1 (March 2016): 181–96; Daniel J. Daly, "Structures of Virtue and Vice," *New Blackfriars* 92, no. 1039 (2010): 341–57; and Kevin Ahern, *Structures of Grace: Catholic Organizations Serving the Global Common Good* (Maryknoll, NY: Orbis Books, 2015).
40. Robert W. McElroy, "A Church for the Poor: Pope Francis Makes Addressing Poverty Essential," *America* 209, no. 11 (October 21, 2013): 15.
41. M. Cathleen Kaveny, "A Companion, Not a Judge," *Commonweal* 150, no. 1 (January 2023): 26–30. Kaveny concludes that what the pope is calling for resembles "good" or reformed casuistry, and that it is worth saving.
42. William O'Neill, SJ, "Intrinsic Evil: A Guide for the Perplexed," in *Pope Francis and the Future of Catholicism in the United States*, ed. Erin Brigham, David E. DeCosse, and Michael Duffy (San Francisco: USF Press, 2016), 41–47, at 42.
43. Francis, "Discorso del Santo Padre Francesco ai partecipanti al Convegno Internazionale di Teologia Morale, promosso dalla Pontificia Università Gregoriana e dal Pontificio Istituto Teologico Giovanni Paolo II per le Scienze del Matrimonio e della Famiglia," May 13, 2022, www.vatican.va/content/francesco/it/speeches/2022/may/documents/20220513-convegno-teologia-morale.html.
44. See, e.g., Daniel K. Finn, ed., *Moral Agency within Social Structures and Culture: A Primer on Critical Realism for Christian Ethics* (Washington, DC: Georgetown University Press, 2020); Daniel J. Daly, *The Structures of Virtue and Vice* (Washington, DC: Georgetown University Press, 2020).
45. As David Cloutier puts it, critical realism, "while it takes the causal power of structures seriously, . . . avoids totalizing reductionism, or (even worse) a reification that renders agential responsibility moot." David Cloutier, "How Critical Realism Can Help Christian Social Ethics," in *Moral Agency*, ed. Finn, 4.
46. Kate Ward, "Virtue and Human Fragility," *Theological Studies* 81, no. 1 (March 2020): 150–68.
47. Christina G. McRorie, "Moral Reasoning in 'the World,'" *Theological Studies* 82, no. 2 (June 2021): 213–37.
48. Elizabeth Sweeny Block, "Moral Intuition, Social Sin, and Moral Vision: Attending to the Unconcious Dimensions of Morality and Igniting the Moral Imagination," *Religions* 12, no. 292 (2021): 1–15.
49. McRorie, "Moral Reasoning," 217.
50. Lisa Sowle Cahill, "Afterword," in *Moral Agency*, ed. Finn, 104.
51. Joseph W. Cardinal Tobin, "The Long Game: Pope Francis's Vision of Synodality," *Commonweal*, June 1, 2021, www.commonwealmagazine.org/long-game.

52. Cf., e.g., George Neumayr, *The Political Pope: How Pope Francis Is Delighting the Liberal Left and Abandoning Conservatives* (New York: Center Street, 2017).
53. Francis, *Evangelii gaudium*, no. 3.
54. Kevin F. O'Brien, *The Ignatian Adventure: Experiencing the Spiritual Exercises of Saint Ignatius in Daily Life* (Chicago: Loyola University Press, 2011), 14.
55. Kaveny, "Companion," 30.
56. See Jon Sobrino, *Jesus the Liberator: A Historical-Theological Reading of Jesus of Nazareth*, trans. Paul Burns and Francis McDonagh (Maryknoll, NY: Orbis Books, 1993), 79–104.
57. M. Shawn Copeland, "Poor Is the Color of God," in *The Option for the Poor in Christian Theology*, ed. Daniel G. Groody (Notre Dame, IN: University of Notre Dame Press, 2007), 216–27.
58. Francis, *The Name of God Is Mercy: A Conversation with Andrea Tornielli*, trans. Oonagh Stransky (New York: Random House, 2016), 63, 68–69.
59. Francis, "Conclusion of the Synod of Bishops, Address of His Holiness Pope Francis," October 24, 2015, www.vatican.va/content/francesco/en/speeches/2015/october/documents/papa-francesco_20151024_sinodo-conclusione-lavori.html.
60. Alessandro Rovati, "Mercy Is a Person: Pope Francis and the Christological Turn in Moral Theology," *Journal of Moral Theology* 6, no. 2 (2017): 49, 57–58.
61. Francis, *Amoris laetitia*, no. 305.
62. Gustavo Gutiérrez, *A Theology of Liberation: History, Politics and Salvation*, trans. Caridad Inda and John Eagleson, 15th ann. ed. (Maryknoll, NY: Orbis Books, 1988), 97–105, 171–73.
63. R. Alan Culpepper, *Matthew: A Commentary* (Louisville: Westminster John Knox Press, 2021), 151.
64. John Dominic Crossan, *The Birth of Christianity: Discovering What Happened in the Years Immediately After the Execution of Jesus* (San Francisco: HarperSanFrancisco, 1998), 293–304.
65. James Cone makes these connections repeatedly. See, e.g., James H. Cone, *The Cross and the Lynching Tree* (Maryknoll, NY: Orbis Books, 2011), 156–59.

LIST OF CONTRIBUTORS

Lisa Sowle Cahill is the J. Donald Monan, SJ, Professor at Boston College. She is a past president of the Catholic Theological Society of America (1992–93) and the Society of Christian Ethics (1997–98). She received her MA and PhD from the University of Chicago Divinity School and is a fellow of the American Academy of Arts and Sciences. Her works include *Blessed Are the Peacemakers: Pacifism, Just War and Peacebuilding* (Fortress, 2019); *A Theology and Praxis of Gender Equality* (Dharmaram, 2018); and *Global Justice, Christology, and Christian Ethics* (Cambridge University Press, 2013).

María Teresa (M. T.) Dávila is a visiting associate professor of practice at Merrimack College. As a scholar, she focuses on racial and migrant justice, public theology, and the ethics of the use of force. With Agnes Brazal, she is coeditor of *Living With(out) Border: Theological Ethics and Peoples on the Move* (Orbis Books, 2016). She is a regular contributor to "Theology en la Plaza" in the *National Catholic Reporter*, the first Latin@ column in a national Catholic newspaper. Her work also appears in *Syndicate* and *Political Theology Today*. Since 2016, she has been a consultant for the Science for Seminaries Program, and now the Dialogue on Science, Ethics, and Religion, initiatives that enable seminaries to include sciences in the training of pastors and faith leaders.

Daniel R. DiLeo is associate professor and director of the Justice and Peace Studies Program at Creighton University. His research focuses on Catholic social teaching, climate change, and *Laudato si'*. He recently cowrote "US Catholic Bishops' Silence and Denialism on Climate Change" (*Environmental Research Letters*), and he is the editor of *All Creation Is Connected: Voices in Response to Pope Francis's Encyclical on Ecology* (Anselm Academic, 2018). Since 2009, he has been a consultant with the Catholic Climate Covenant. He received his PhD in theological ethics from Boston College.

LIST OF CONTRIBUTORS

Kristin E. Heyer is professor of theological ethics at Boston College. Her book publications related to this volume include *Christianity and the Law of Migration* (Routledge, 2021); *Building Bridges in Sarajevo: The Plenary Papers from CTEWC 2018* (Orbis Books, 2019); and *Kinship Across Borders: A Christian Ethic of Immigration* (Georgetown University Press, 2012). She received degrees from Brown University and Boston College and serves as cochair of the planning committee for Catholic Theological Ethics in the World Church and president of the Catholic Theological Society of America. She is currently at work on *Moral Agency and the Promise of Freedom*.

Laurie Johnston, is associate professor of theology and religious studies at Emmanuel College in Boston. A social ethicist, she has written and edited works on just war theory, peacebuilding, Catholic–Muslim relations, and political theology, including *The Surprise of Reconciliation in the Catholic Tradition*, with J. J. Carney; and *Can War Be Just in the 21st Century?* with Tobias Winright. She has been a member of the Community of Sant'Egidio for more than twenty years and serves as academic associate of the Sant'Egidio Foundation for Peace and Dialogue. She has received degrees from the University of Virginia, Harvard Divinity School, and Boston College.

James F. Keenan, SJ, is the Canisius Chair and director of the Jesuit Institute and vice provost of global engagement at Boston College. A Jesuit priest since 1982, he received a licentiate and a doctorate from the Pontifical Gregorian University in Rome. He has edited or written twenty-five books and published more than three hundred essays, articles, and reviews in over twenty-five international journals. His most recent books are *A History of Catholic Theological Ethics* (Paulist Press, 2022), and *Preparing for the Moral Life: The D'Arcy Lectures* (Georgetown University Press, 2023). He is the founder of Catholic Theological Ethics in the World Church.

Conor M. Kelly, is associate professor in the Department of Theology at Marquette University. His teaching and research focus on moral discernment in ordinary life. His publications include *The Fullness of Free Time: A Theological Account of Leisure and Recreation in the Moral Life* (Georgetown University Press, 2020); the coedited volume *Poverty: Responding Like Jesus* (Paraclete, 2018, with Kenneth R. Himes); and—especially relevant for this volume; "The Role of the Moral Theologian in the Church: A Proposal in Light of *Amoris Laetitia*"; "From John Paul II to Francis: The Widening Trajectory of the Catholic Theology of Family"; and "Everyday Solidarity: A Framework for Incorporating Theological Ethics and Ordinary Life."

LIST OF CONTRIBUTORS

Megan K. McCabe is an assistant professor of religious studies at Gonzaga University. She works in the fields of moral theology, feminist theologies, social ethics, and liberation theologies. Her current research engages questions of sexual violence, gender, and moral responsibility for social change. She was the cochair of Gonzaga University's Commission on University Response to Catholic Sexual Abuse Crisis and continues to oversee the implementation of the commission's recommendations. She is currently cochairing "Contextualizing the Catholic Sexual Abuse Crisis," a five-year seminar at the American Academy of Religion; and she cofounded an interest group at the Catholic Theological Society of America, "Theology, Sexuality, and Justice: New Frontiers," and cochaired it for three years.

Thomas Massaro, SJ, is professor of moral theology at Fordham University. A Jesuit priest of the US East Province, he has taught as professor of moral theology at the Weston Jesuit School of Theology in Cambridge, Massachusetts; at Boston College; and at the Jesuit School of Theology of Santa Clara University, where he also served as dean. He received a doctorate in Christian social ethics from Emory University. His nine books and over one hundred published articles treat Catholic social teaching and its recommendations for public policies oriented toward social justice, peace, workers' rights, and poverty alleviation. A former columnist for *America* magazine, he writes and lectures frequently on such topics as the ethics of globalization, peacemaking, the environment, the role of conscience in religious participation in public life, and developing a spirituality of justice. His most recent book is *Mercy in Action: The Social Teachings of Pope Francis* (Rowman & Littlefield, 2018).

Bryan N. Massingale is professor of theological and social ethics and holds the James and Nancy Buckman Chair in Applied Christian Ethics at Fordham University. A priest of the Archdiocese of Milwaukee, he is a past president of the Society of Christian Ethics, a past convener of the Black Catholic Theological Symposium, and a former president of the Catholic Theological Society of America. He has written two books and more than 170 articles, book chapters, and book reviews. His monograph, *Racial Justice and the Catholic Church*, received a First Place Book Award from the Catholic Press Association of the United States and Canada. He frequently addresses issues of racial and sexual justice in venues such as NPR, ABC News, the PBS *NewsHour*, the *Huffington Post*, Canadian Public Radio, the *South African Times*, and the Associated Press. He is an active participant in a network of Catholic thought leaders advocating for the full inclusion of LGBTQ persons in both society and the faith community.

Maureen H. O'Connell is associate professor of Christian ethics in the Department of Religion and Theology at La Salle University. She is the author of *Compassion: Loving Our Neighbor in an Age of Globalization* (Orbis Books, 2009); and *If These Walls Could Talk: Community Muralism and the Beauty of Justice* (Liturgical Press, 2012). Her newest book, *Undoing the Knots: Five Generations of American Catholic Anti-Blackness* (Beacon Press, 2021), explores the interplay of her Catholic and racial identities across her family's history in Philadelphia. She is a member of POWER (Philadelphians Organizing to Witness, Empower, and Rebuild), an interfaith coalition of more than fifty congregations committed to making Philadelphia the city of *"just love"* through faith-based community organizing; and she serves on the Board of Cranaleith Spiritual Center, a ministry of the Religious Sisters of Mercy. At Rosemont College, she is a member of the President's Commission on the Legacy of Slavery.

Elyse J. Raby is an assistant professor in the Department of Religious Studies at Santa Clara University. A Catholic systematic theologian, she works at the intersections of ecclesiology, embodiment, and gender. She has written articles on ecclesiology (*Horizons*, 2022), on theologies of the diaconate (*Ecumenical Trends*, 2022), and on intersex theologies of creation (*Theology & Sexuality*, 2018). Her first book will analyze the metaphor of the Church as a body in nineteenth- and twentieth-century Catholic theology and, in particular, how different understandings of embodiment shape our understandings of the Church, its ministry, and its relationship with the world. Long educated in the Jesuit tradition, she received a PhD from Boston College, a master's in theological studies from the Boston College School of Theology and Ministry, and a bachelor's in religious studies from Fairfield University.

Andrea Vicini, SJ, is Michael P. Walsh Professor of Bioethics and professor of theological ethics at Boston College. His recent publications include two coedited volumes—*Reimagining the Moral Life: On Lisa Sowle Cahill's Contributions to Christian Ethics* (2020); and *Ethics of Global Public Health: Climate Change, Pollution, and the Health of the Poor* (2021)—and, among other articles, "COVID-19: A Crisis and a Tragedy—What's Next?" in *Theological Studies* (2021); "Healthcare Practice at the End of Life: Addressing Opposite Attitudes and Diverse Contexts," in *Concilium* (2021); "Posthumanism in Popular Culture: Ongoing Challenges," in *Concilium* (2021); "Artificial Intelligence in Healthcare: Bioethical Challenges and Approaches," in *Asian Horizons* (2020); and "Preserving the Earth and Promoting Health: Challenges for the Common Good," in *Studia Moralia* (2020).

INDEX

abortion, 77, 188, 239, 241
accompaniment: act of, 246; calling of, 127; homosexual persons and, 155; importance of, 20; Jesuit commitment to, 88–89; lived experience and pastoral care as, 179; mercy and, 66; moral theology and, 237; option for the poor and, 105; of outsiders, 117; overview of, 39; paradigm shift and, 40; poor church for the poor and, 108; solidarity with the poor and, 109; vision for, 34
affective motivation, 125, 237–38
agere sequitur esse (action follows being), 51
Allen, John, 2, 42
Alzaga, Fernando Vérgez, 42
ambiguity, 239, 240–41, 242, 247–48
"America First" concept, 125
American Catholicism, 2, 27
Amoris laetitia (Francis): concerns regarding, 6; on conscience, 39, 54, 56; on culture, 19; on discernment, 20, 54, 57, 67, 188; on family life, 19; on feminism, 177; on gender complementarity, 169–70; on general rules, 241; on grace, 25; on growth, 56; mercy in, 5, 67; on moral theology, 5; objective knowledge collaboration in, 16; relations challenges in, 34; synodality and, 38–41, 238–39; Thomistic intellectual-theological framework and, 18–19; tone of, 23; on virtue ethics, 52; virtue ethics and, 52; on ways of being, 171

anamchara (soul-friend), 39–40
Anderson, Elijah, 137
Angels Unawares sculpture, 128
anthropocentrism, 220
antiracism, 143–44
Aparecida, 44; concluding document of, 217
Apostolicam actuositatem (Decree on the Apostolate of the Laity), 84
Apostolic See, 70
Aquinas, Saint Thomas, 18–19, 20, 51, 59, 60
Arabome, Anne, 23–24
Argentina, 85–86, 143
Aristotle, 19–20, 51, 52, 55
Arrupe, Pedro, 88
Augustine of Hippo, Saint, 201, 207
Authenticam charismatis (Francis), 72
Autiero, Antonio, 185

balconeando, 201–2, 237
Baldwin, James, 136
Bangui, 201, 209
baptism, 43
Barnabas, Saint, 38, 41
Barone, Christian, 204
Baumann, John, 225–26
belonging, 93, 140–43
Benedict XV (Pope), 200
Benedict XVI (Pope): advocacy for the poor by, 102–3, 104; apologies of, 68; *Caritas in veritate*, 95, 106;

Benedict XVI (Pope) (*continued*)
  characteristics of, 33; on climate change, 216; on complementarity, 167–68; debate participation by, 49; on feminism, 176, 178; gender teachings of, 166, 173, 179; on migration, 119; moral theology reforms and, 15
Bergoglio, Jorge. *See* Francis (Pope)
Bernard of Clairvaux, 41
bias, 37
bioethics: challenging experience of people and, 189; Christocentric, 185–87; discernment and, 187–88; discipleship in, 10; global examples of, 189–93; overview of, 183–84; reactions regarding, 193–94; way forward regarding, 194
birth control, 17
bishops/US bishops: accountability for, 74; *Authenticam charistmatis* and, 72; ecclesial ethics and, 70–71; "Economic Justice for All" (pastoral letter of US bishops), 95; Eucharist viewpoint of, 188; failures of, 127, 224; justice work of, 76–77, 108, 134; New Evangelization by, 224; nonreceipt by, 225–27; power of, 227; racism addressing by, 139, 140–41, 142, 144; relational role of, 139–40; resistance of, 76, 107; skepticism of, 76
Black Lives Matter, 108
boarding schools, 108
Boff, Leonardo, 219
Book VI (Code of Canon Law), 74
boycotting, 227
Boyle, Gregory, 117
Boyle, Joseph, 186
Brady, Bernard, 125
breast cancer, 191–92
bricoleur, 49
Buenos Aires, Argentina, 86
business, as noble vocation, 92

Cahill, Lisa, 206
cancer, 191–92
Cantoni, Oscar, 42
capitalism, 106
cardinals, choosing of, 73. *See also specific persons*

Caritas Argentina, 100
Caritas in veritate (Benedict XVI), 95, 106
Carlotti, Paolo, 208
Catholic Campaign for Human Development, 225–26
Catholic Church. *See* Church
Catholic moral teaching, 27
Catholic networking, 26
Centesimus annus (John Paul II), 106
Central African Republic, war in, 201
centralization, 71–72
Chan, Lúcás, 55
Chaput, Charles, 155
character, 51–53, 57, 58–59, 60–61, 67
charitable works, 221
charity, 92, 111
China, 220
Christianity, racial and colonial dynamics of, 108
Christus vivit (Francis), 101, 178
Church: advocacy by, 73; care for vulnerable by, 77; centralizing reforms and, 71–72; clericalism in, 74, 76–77; code of ethics for, 65–66; culture wars and, 107, 109; defined, 43; dissent in, 158–61; ecclesial structures and, 244; ecological ethics and, 222–24; empowerment and, 108; as field hospital, 179; Francis's call and vision for, 51, 69–70; importance of local churches to, 70; justice and, 76–77; lay empowerment in, 43; lay listening and, 108; mercy and, 66, 67, 68, 77; migration role of, 128; as missionary, 43, 65; mission of, 222–24; new way of being, 246; option for the poor and, 100–101, 111; as people of God, 84; poor church for the poor and, 24–26, 107–9, 235–38; poor identification by, 85, 92, 104; popular movements and, 226; probabilism and, 160; property of, 223; public witness of, 109; purpose of, 65; as social actor, 119; social justice and, 73, 94–96; subsidiarity and, 76; tension with Francis and, 107; unity of, 28, 71–72; women's role in, 167–68, 172–76
clergy, sexual abuse reporting process of, 71, 74

INDEX

clericalism, 76–77, 174, 178
climate change: differentiated responsibilities regarding, 220; "Ecological Education and Spirituality," 221–22; effects of, 218; efforts regarding, 25; as emergency, 216–24; "The Gospel of Creation," 219–20; "The Human Roots of the Ecological Crisis," 220–21; "Integral Ecology," 220–21; in *Laudato si'* (Francis), 3, 102, 189, 216, 224–25, 236, 243; "Lines of Approach and Action," 221–22; Pastoral Circle and, 217; pastoral planning and, 221–24; poor and, 102, 218; (non)reception of Francis's teaching regarding, 224–27; social analysis regarding, 220–21; statistics regarding, 218–19, 220, 221; theological reflection regarding, 219–20; tipping points and, 218; urgency of addressing, 189; "What Is Happening to Our Common Home," 218–19
"climate feedbacks," 218
Climate Pledge, 223
Code of Canon Law, 74
collaborative discernment, 23, 28. *See also* discernment
College of Cardinals, 41–43
colonialism, 144
common good, 184, 219
compassion, 21–24
Compendium of the Social Doctrine of the Church (Pontifical Council for Justice and Peace), 82
complementarity, 167–68
complexities, impact of, 238–42
Conference of US Catholic Bishops, 133
confession, 39–40
Congregation for the Doctrine of the Faith, 103, 156, 171
connectedness, 16
conscience, 39–40, 54, 56, 136, 244
conscientization, 217
El Consejo Episcopal Latinoamericano y Caribeño (the Latin American and Caribbean Episcopal Council), 124
conspiracy theorizing, 127–28
consumerism, 52–53

Council of Jerusalem, 38–39
COVID-19 pandemic, 36, 37, 175, 189, 192–93
creation, technocratic domination over, 170
Cremer, Douglas, 144
Cuda, Emilce, 98
cultural sin, 126
culture, 2, 19, 99, 101, 139, 141, 160–61
culture of encounter, 128, 210, 237
culture of walls, 136
culture wars, 99, 107, 109, 244–45
Cupich, Blase Cardinal, 227
cura personalis, 119
Curia, 71, 73, 89
Curran, Charles, 22, 158
Czerny, Michael Cardinal, 35, 36, 128, 204, 217

decentralization, 26–27, 68–72
deceptive semblance, 55
Decree on Priestly Formation, 22
dialogue, 139
Dicastery for Promoting Integral Human Development, 119–20, 189
Dicastery for the Doctrine of Faith, 171
difference, integration of, 139
disagreement, 3
discernment: ambiguity and, 242; bioethics and, 187–88; coherence of, 21–24; collaborative, 23, 28; collective, 139; fundamentalism and, 139; goal of, 54; health care and, 192; incumbency of, 54; mercy and, 66; overview of, 20, 21–24; pastoral, 67; as pillar of spirituality, 60; racial justice and, 139; role of, 40; space for, 57; of spirits, 124; virtue ethics and, 53–55, 57
disciples, role of, 41
discipleship, 10, 52, 56, 58–59, 100–102
discrimination, 150
discursive reasoning, 21
dispositions, in virtue ethics, 52
dissent, 158–61
diversity, as resource, 211
divisions, overcoming, 93–94
Doing Theology from the Existential Peripheries, 110–11

double effect principle, 17, 18
Drexler-Dreis, Joseph, 111
dubia, 6

Earth, fate of, 102. *See also* climate change
ecclesial communion, 15
ecclesial ethics: for Church in the United States, 75–77; defined, 65; development of, 65; justice and, 72–75; mercy and, 66–68; overview of, 65–66; structural eye in, 243; subsidiarity and, 68–72
ecclesial structures, 244
ecological ethics: charitable works for, 221; Church's mission regarding, 222–24; climate emergency and, 216–24; "Ecological Education and Spirituality," 221–22; "The Gospel of Creation," 219–20; "The Human Roots of the Ecological Crisis," 220–21; "Integral Ecology," 220–21; "Lines of Approach and Action," 221–22; overview of, 216; pastoral planning and, 221–24; (non)reception of Francis's teaching regarding, 224–27; social analysis regarding, 220–21; spiritual motivation for, 221–22; theological reflection regarding, 219–20; "What Is Happening to Our Common Home," 218–19
economic ethics, 82, 90, 91, 122–23, 126
economic justice, 82–83, 84, 90–94
"Economic Justice for All" (pastoral letter), 95
"Economy of Franceso," 89
Ellacuría, Ignacio, 101
empowerment, 104, 108
encounter, culture of, 128, 210, 237
end-of-life issues, 188
"Enlarge the Space in Your Tent" (Synod on Synodality), 142
Episcopal Commission for Pastoral Practice (Comisión Episcopal de Pastoral Prioridades), 24
episcopal conferences, 70–71
Episcopalis communio (Francis), 69
Erga migratnes caritas Christi (Pontifical Council for the Pastoral Care of Migrants and Itinerant People), 118
Ethical and Religious Directives for Catholic Health Care Services (ERDs), 190

Ethics (Aristotle), 19–20
Eucharist, 173, 188
Evangelii gaudium (Francis): cornerstone of, 41; criticism regarding, 95; on discernment, 53–54; on economic ethics, 82, 83, 90–91; on evangelization, 4, 100–101; on exclusion and inequality, 35, 83; on growth, 55; influence of, 44; on moral standing, 55; negative norms in, 241; on nonviolence, 209; on offense, 95; on papal magisterium, 71; on peace, 211; on politics, 104; on polyhedrons, 212; on the poor, 36, 100; on structures, 125; values of the Gospel in, 5
evangelization, 36, 72, 94–96, 100–102
exclusion, 35, 90
Exsul familia (Pius XII), 118

Faggioli, Massimo, 84, 85, 94
Familiaris consortio (John Paul II), 172
family/family life, 34, 170, 171
fatherhood, 172
fear, 118, 124–25
feedback loop, 55
feminine genius, 167, 173, 176
femininity, 169–72
feminism, 166, 168, 176–79. *See also* gender; women
Figueres, Christina, 223
Final Judgment, 186
Fleming, Julia, 160
Floyd, George, 133, 178
Foglizzo, Paolo, 35, 36
Francis (Pope): as Argentinian, 85–86; call of, 191; characteristics of, 33–34; at Colegio Máximo, 72–73; concerns regarding, 5–6; criticism of, 94, 95, 105, 106; humility of, 95–96; Ignatian spirituality of, 7–8, 87–90, 101, 202; influence of, 4; influences on, 7–8, 24, 60, 87–90, 101; introduction of, 1; Jesuit formation of, 20, 60, 67, 87–90, 184, 202, 217; lamenting by, 201, 203; leadership of, 100; lived experience of, 179; long game of, 246; mercy of, 67–68; ministry of, 98, 100, 237; personal convictions of, 187; priesthood of, 84; reluctance of, 49; as representative for victims, 202; social

location of, 85; strategy of silence of, 94, 95, 168, 169; structural eye of, 90, 123, 243; travels of, 73, 120, 125; work with the poor by, 86
Francis of Assisi, Saint, 227
Fraser, Nancy, 36
Fratelli tutti (Francis): appeals in, 93–94; on cooperation, 108; criticism of, 106; on diversity, 211, 213; on economic justice, 93; on the Good Samaritan, 53; historical consciousness in, 108; on history, 108–9; on love, 56; on migration, 121–23, 213; mutual care in, 16; on nationalism, 125; option for the poor in, 102; on political life, 104; on political transformation, 111; on polyhedrons, 212; on racism, 137; on self-absorption, 125–26; on social sin, 124; on society, 143; speeches in, 35; on structural deficiencies, 243; on suffering, 203; on war, 204, 207
fraternity, 53, 142
Freire, Paulo, 217
La Fuerza del Nostotros (The Power of We) (documentary), 36
Fullam, Lisa, 53
fundamentalism, 139

Gaillardetz, Richard, 226
Galeazzi, Giacomo, 105
Gandhi, Mahatma, 208
Ganz, Marshall, 227
Gaudium et spes (Pastoral Constitution on the Church in the Modern World (Vatican Council II), 15, 16–17, 61, 84, 186, 210–11
Gbowee, Leymah, 209
Gehring, John, 99
gender: communication and, 169–70; complementarity, 169–72; ideology, 169; lens of, 26; overview of, 166, 178–79; rigid categories regarding, 171; roles of, 10; teachings on, 166
General Congregation 35 Decree 3 (2008) (Society of Jesus), 217
general principles, moral truth and, 19
general rules, insufficiency of, 54
Generation Z, 224
generosity, 91

geopolitics of mercy, 210
Gera, Lucio, 24, 101
Giangravé, Claire, 42–43
Global Compact for Safe, Orderly, and Regular Migration, 127
Global Compact on Refugees, 127
globalization, 124, 204
globalization of hope, 26
global warming, 218–19, 220, 221. *See also* climate change
God, communication by, 171
Golden Rule, 120–21
González, Pablo Blanco, 98
Good Samaritan, 28, 53, 203
Gospel, 4, 5, 65, 72, 94–96, 186
grace, 58
Gregory the Great, 41
growth, 55–56, 57, 143–44
Guardado, Leo, 117
Gutiérrez, Gustavo, 99, 103, 105, 111

Harding, Sandra, 236
Häring, Berhard, 22
Hawksley, Theodora, 27
"Healing a Broken World" (2011) (Social Justice Secretariat at the General Curia of the Society of Jesus), 217
health care, 190–93
Henriot, Peter, 217
hermeneutic of suspicion, 239
Hinsdale, Mary Ann, 167
Hiroshima, 209
holiness, 56
Holland, Joe, 217
Hollerich, Jean-Claude Cardinal, 227
Holy Spirit, 38
homosexuality, 150, 153–56, 159. *See also* LGBTQ persons
Honneth, Axel, 36
horizon of possibility, 142
Humanae vitae (Paul VI), 17
humility, 66, 77, 95–96, 140
Hummes, Carlos Cardinal, 98, 235

ideological colonization, 169
idleness, 41
idolatry, 125
Ignatian Family Teach-In for Justice, 128

Ignatius of Loyola, Saint: discernment viewpoint of, 20; influence of, 7–8, 20, 87–90, 123, 202; *Spiritual Exercises*, 8, 20, 23–24, 60, 61, 87, 96, 124, 241, 247; virtue ethics and, 59–61
immigrants, statistics regarding, 27. *See also* migration
incarnational theology, 98–99, 100–105, 247
inclusive listening, 44
indifference, 126, 241–42
individualism, 142
indoctrination, 169
inequality, 35
informality, 35
injustice, 119, 126, 141
"Instruction on Certain Aspects of a Theology of Liberation," 103
integral humanism, 144
integration, as migration theme, 121–22
interdependence, 122
Intergovernmental Panel on Climate Change (IPCC), 218
International Labour Organization, 35
International Theological Commission, 60
isolationism, 125
Israel, 118
Italian National Committee for Bioethics, 183
Ivereigh, Austen, 43–45, 86

Janssen, Louis, 17
Jesuit Curia, 89
Jesuit Refugee Service, 88–89
Jesus Christ, 22, 99, 100–101, 118, 184, 185–87, 247–49
John Paul II (Pope): advocacy for the poor by, 102–3, 104; apologies of, 68; characteristics of, 33; on climate change, 216; complementarity and, 167–168; *Familiaris consortio*, 172; on family life, 170; on feminism, 168, 176, 178; gender teachings of, 166, 172, 173, 175, 179; influence of, 172; on migration, 119; moral theology reforms and, 15, 49; *Mulieris dignitatem*, 167–68; on natural law, 59–60; on socialist materialism, 106; *Sollicitudo rei socialis*, 88; on structural transformation, 104; *Veritatis splendor* of, 18; on war, 200
John XXIII (Pope), 16, 25, 84, 200
Joseph, Saint, 118
joy, 4
Jubilee of Mercy, 5, 201
judgment parable, 28
justice: by the Church, 73; Church's role in, 76–77; ecclesial right relationships and, 72–75; economic, 82–83, 84; labor, 89; for laity, 74–75; in migration, 127; for the poor, 72–73; racial, 108; for sexual abuse survivors, 73–74; for women, 75
Justitia in Mundo, 88

Kalbian, Aline, 18
Kaveny, Cathleen, 190–91, 247
Keenan, James, 22, 202–3
Kelly, Conor, 40
Khan, Khan Abdul Ghaffar, 208
King, Martin Luther, Jr., 208–9, 225, 227
Kino Border Initiative, 128
Kirchner, Nestor, 100
Kolvenbach, Peter-Hans, 202
Krajewski, Konrad, 235

labor justice, 89
laity, 74–75, 76
lament, 34, 203
Lampedusa, 120
Landrigan, Philip, 191
Lantigua, David, 107
Laudate deum (Francis), 216, 225
Laudato si' (Francis): Action Platform, 222, 224; on climate change, 3, 102, 143, 189, 216, 224–25, 236, 243; connectedness and, 16; criticism of, 106; on cry of the poor, 10; on ecological ethics, 217–18, 222; on economic justice, 93; on gender complementarity, 170; on laws, 52; message of, 89; option for the poor in, 102; on popular momentum, 25; resistance to, 106; on sin, 103; use of conflict in, 9; on way of proceeding, 218; on wonder, 137
Lawler, Michael, 190
The Law of Christ (Häring), 22
Lawson, James, 227
lay empowerment, 43

leadership, religious authority, 83
Let's Save Humanity and the Planet, 36
Let Us Dream (Francis), 37–38, 135, 136, 139, 169, 177
LGBTQ persons, 10, 76, 150–58, 159, 238
liberation theology, 24, 99, 102, 105, 202–3, 217
Limbaugh, Rush, 95
listening, 16, 70, 142
local churches, 70–71
love, 16, 21–24, 27–28, 186, 25
Lumen gentium (Dogmatic Constitution on the Church), 84

magisterial authority, 6
magisterial teaching, centering the poor in, 102–4
Marcellinus, 201
marginalized, recognition of, 37–38. *See also* poor
Markoe, John, 226–27
marriage, 171–72, 239
Mary (mother of Jesus), 118
masculinity, 172
Mass, 72
Massaro, Thomas, 123, 209, 210
Massingale, Bryan, 126, 135, 136
McCarrick, Theodore Cardinal, 77
McCormick, Richard, 17–18, 158
McElroy, Robert Cardinal, 243, 245
McQueen, Paddy, 36
mercy: Christian morality and, 16; in the Church, 67, 68, 77; concern for, 5; embodiment of, 27–28; examples of, 67–68; geopolitics of, 210; humility and, 77; meanings of, 66; parable regarding, 5; primacy of the pastoral and, 66–68; priority of, 247; recognition of, 61; social character of, 67
#MeToo movement, 177–78
migration: barriers to, 122; biblical stories of, 118, 119; Church's role regarding, 128; cooperation regarding, 126–27; Doing Theology from the Existential Peripheries and, 110–11; fears regarding, 118, 124–25; forced, 119, 126–27; Francis's solidarity gestures regarding, 120; idolatry and, 125; injustice and, 119; intensification of, 119; justice and, 127; pastoral response to, 127; perils in, 121; scale of, 126–27; social framing of, 9, 117–18; social media regarding, 119; statistics regarding, 27; in the United States, 120–21, 125, 127
migration ethics: affective conversion and, 124–26; community of 'we' in, 117; cultivating an ever wider we in, 126–29; *cura migrantium* among idols of indifference in, 118–21; economic ethics and, 122–23; in *Fratelli tutti* (Francis), 121–23, 213; Golden Rule and, 120–21; ideological threats and, 124–26; overview of, 117–18; right to remain and, 118–19
Miller, Richard, 218–19
Miller, Vincent, 70
modernity, 44
Montgomery, David, 106
moral actions, in virtue ethics, 51
morality/moral life: Christologically focused, 186; complexities regarding, 238–42; Francis's pastoral goal for, 186; Francis's vision for, 55; grace in, 58; holiness in, 56; objective standards of, 16–17; relationship with Jesus and, 185; transformation in, 61; variation and, 57
moral maturity, 56
moral reasoning, 16–20, 21–24
moral theology, 4–6, 15, 22, 49–50, 244
moral truth, 19, 22–23
mortal sins, 18
Mulieris dignitatem (John Paul II), 167–68

Nagasaki, 209
nationalism, 122, 125
nativist populism, 124
natural law, 18–19, 59–60
networking, Catholic, 26
net zero emissions, 221, 223
Neuhaus, Richard John, 106
New Evangelization, 223–24
"Night Will Be No More" (pastoral letter), 140
noncooperation, 227
nonviolence, 208–210
Noonan, John, 160

Novak, Michael, 95, 106
nuclear attacks, 203–4

objective knowledge, 16
opioid crisis, 240
opposition, vice of, 55
Optatam totius (Paul VI), 16
option for the poor: centering the poor in magisterial teaching in, 102–4; Church's role in, 100–101, 111; Francis and, 100–105; imitation of Christ in, 100–101; in liberation theology, 99, 102, 105; overview of, 98–99, 109–10; poor church for the poor and, 107–9; as theocentric option, 99; uphill battle regarding, 105–9
Oropeza, Mauricio López, 41

Pacem in Terris (John XXIII), 25
Palin, Sarah, 95
papal trope of continuity, 82
parable of the Good Samaritan, 28, 53, 203
parenthood, 167, 172
parrhesia, 10, 149, 152, 157, 158, 160–61
Pastoral Circle, 217
pastorality of doctrine, 3, 75
pastoral sensitivity, 66
pastors, 67, 71, 74
Paul, Saint, 38, 41
Paul VI (Pope), 15, 16, 25, 70, 88, 101, 220
peace ethics: culture of encounter and, 210; embodiment of, 27–28; nonviolence and, 208–10; overview of, 200; prophetic tension and, 205–8; receiving, 212–13; reconciled diversity in, 210–12; suffering as focus of, 203; vision of positive peace in, 210–12; war justification and, 205–8; "wounded flesh of the victims" and, 200–205
peacemaking, 10
Penitential Pilgrimage, 68, 134–35, 143
People of God in the Church of El Paso, 140
perfectionist teleology, 245
Perón, Juan, 86
personhood, defined, 17
Peter, Saint, 38
Philadelphia, Pennsylvania, 137–38
PICO National Network, 225–26

Plato, 52
pluralism, 190
pocket veto, 6
polarization, 140, 239
political ideology, 2, 94–95
political love, 104
polyhedron, 212
Pontifical Academy for Life, 194
Pontifical Birth Control Commission, 160
pontifical secret, 74
Pool, Anthony, 135
poor: advocacy for, 102–3, 104; in Argentina, 100; authority of, 24–26; centering of, in evangelization and discipleship, 100–102; centering of, in magisterial teaching, 102–4; Church's role regarding, 92, 104, 235–38; climate change and, 102, 218; ecclesial inclusion and, 16; empowerment of, 25–26, 104; fate of, 102; Francis's work with, 86, 237; health care and, 191, 192; identification with, 85; initiatives of justice and, 16; irruption of, 103; justice for, 72–73; local community's role regarding, 103; political action and, 104; primacy of, 247; priority of, 24–26; recognition of, 37–38; teachings from, 36; as victims of war, 202; voice of, 24–26. *See also* option for the poor
popular movements, 26, 34–38
Populorum progressio (Paul VI), 88
poverty, Church's role regarding, 92. *See also* poor
power, claiming, 141
Praedicate Evangelium (Francis), 43–45
prayer vigil sit-ins, 227
prison system, racism in, 138
probabilism, 10, 27, 158–61
processes of encounter, 139
promotion, as migration theme, 121–22
proportionalists, 18, 160
protection, as migration theme, 121–22
protesting, 141, 178, 209, 225, 227
prudence, 55

Quadragesimo anno (Pius XI), 25
Querida Amazonia (Francis), 25, 101, 108, 173, 174–75, 189, 236

racial justice, 108, 133–34, 135, 139, 140–44
racism: colonialism and, 144; Francis's acknowledgment of, 134–37; Francis's encountering of, 137–40; fuel for, 142; isolated consciences and, 136; national reconciliation regarding, 134; othering impulse regarding, 136; peripheries of, 137; as power, 137; power and, 135–36; in the prison system, 138; self-love and, 136; as sin, 134, 144; as social asphyxiation, 136
Rahner, Karl, 85
Ratzinger, Joseph, 167, 168. *See also* Benedict XVI (Pope)
reciprocal listening, 70
recognition, 36, 37–38
reconciled diversity, 210–12
reconciliation, 27–28
refugees, 89
Relatio (2015 Synod), 21
religious authority, 83
Reno, R. R., 106
responsive listening, 16, 21, 33–34, 37
Ricouer, Paul, 36
right intention, in war theory, 208
right to remain, 118–19
Roman Missal, 72
Ross, Susan, 239
Rovati, Alessandro, 186
Rowlands, Anna, 119
rules, justifiable departures from, 20
Russia, 220
Russo, Charles, 106
Ryan, Paul, 77

Sales, Saint Francis de, 5
Salzman, Todd, 190
same-sex behaviors, 150, 153–56, 159. *See also* LGBTQ persons
same-sex civil unions, 27, 156–57
Scannone, Juan Carlos, 101
scapegoating, 127–28
Schmalz, Timothy, 128
Schönborn, Christoph Cardinal, 54
Second Meeting of Latin American Bishops, 98
Second Vatican Council. *See* Vatican II

see-judge-act model, 217
Segura, Olga, 139, 140, 143
Seitz, Mark, 127, 140
self-absorption, 125–26
self-accusation, 138
selfishness, 53
self-love, 136
sexual abuse, 68, 71, 73–74, 190
sexual morality, 149, 150–52, 159, 239
sexual orientation, 153–56, 157–58. *See also* LGBTQ persons
Sharp, Gene, 227
Shell, James, 226
Simon, William, 95
Simoni, Ernest, 42–43
sins: avoidance of, 244; discernment and, 23; historical conflict and, 103; mortal, 18; power of, 27; problem of, 100; racism as, 134, 144; recognition of, 61; social, 88; structural, 243, 244; structural transformation and, 104
Snyder, Susanna, 118
social action, see-judge-act model for, 217
social anthropology, 122
social conditions, 21
social ethics, 81, 88, 94–95
social justice, 92, 94–96, 239
Social Justice and Ecology Secretariat (SJES), 89
social movements, empowering, 246
social research centers, 89
social sin, 88, 124
social teaching, 82–86, 95, 98, 118
society, women's role in, 172–76
Society of Jesus, 66, 81, 87–90, 123, 153, 217
Sohn, Michael, 36
solidarity, economics and, 93
Sollicitudo rei socialis (John Paul II), 88
Sosa, Arturo, 89
soul-friend *(anamchara)*, 39–40
Spadaro, Antonio, 41, 60
"Special Report on Justice in the Global Economy" (Social Justice and Ecology Secretariat at the General Curia of the Society of Jesus) 89
Spiritual Exercises (Ignatius of Loyola), 8, 20, 23–24, 60, 61, 87, 96, 124, 241, 247

state sovereignty, right to, 119
Stern, Nicholas, 220–21
Stout, Jeffrey, 49
structural analyses, 93, 243, 245–46
structural deficiencies, suffering from, 242–46
structural evil, 123
structural lens, 90
subsidiarity, 68–72, 76
Sudan, 202, 209
suffering, 203
synodality, 23, 38–41, 69–70, 108
Synod of Bishops, 69, 152
Synod on Communion, Participation, and Mission, 141–42
Synod on Synodality, 69, 74, 76, 108, 142, 243
Synod on the Amazon, 15, 23, 69, 73, 108
Synod on the Family, 15, 23, 69, 152–55
Synod on Young People, 69, 155–56
synods, 69–70

Taylor, Charles, 36
technocracy, 220
Teel, Karen, 140
Tello, Rafael, 24, 101
la teología del pueblo, 202–3
Third Meeting of Latin American Bishops, 98
Thirty-Second General Congregation, 88
Thomas Aquinas, 18–19, 20, 41, 51, 59, 60
Thomistic intellectual-theological framework, 18–19
3 Ls (land, lodging, and labor), 35
"throwaway culture," 99, 101, 191, 201
tipping points, 218
Tobin, Joseph Cardinal, 246
Tornielli, Andrea, 42, 105, 206
"Toward the Future," 95
traditionalists, 18
Traditionis custodes (Francis), 72
tranquilitas ordinis, 210–12
Trump, Donald, 121, 125
truth-telling, 160

Ukraine, 203–4, 206–8
uniformity, 210–12

United Nations, 25
United States, 2, 220, 239, 240. *See also* American Catholicism
US bishops. *See* bishops/US bishops
US Conference of Catholic Bishops, 188, 190, 225–27
US National Academies of Sciences, Engineering, and Medicine, 193
utilitarianism, 17

vaccinations, 193
Vatican II, 16–17, 22, 67, 70, 85, 184, 187
Veritatis splendor (John Paul II), 18
virtue ethics: acquisition of, 58; character and, 51–53, 57, 58–59; defined, 50–51; discernment and, 53–55, 57; in discipleship, 58–59; dispositions in, 52; divine-human interaction in, 58; Francis's partial alignments with, 50–56; growth and, 55–56, 57; hierarchy in, 59; implicit expansions from, 57–59; moral actions in, 51; novelty of Francis's approach to, 59–61; overview of, 50, 61–62; socializing of, 245
Volder, Jan de, 201
Vos estis lux mundi, 71
vulnerable, 72–73, 77. *See also* poor

war: Francis as representative for victims of, 202; globalization and, 204; justification for, 205–8; nonviolence and, 208–10; nuclear attacks and, 203–4; prophetic tension and, 205–8; right intention and, 208; suffering and, 203; unjust aggression and, 206–7; viewpoints regarding, 200; "wounded flesh of the victims" and, 200–205
way of proceeding, 69–70
Weigel, George, 95, 106
welcome, as migration theme, 121–22
welfare, benefits of, 92
"We Live in a Broken World" (1999) (Social Apostolate Secretariat at the General Curia of the Society of Jesus), 217
Whelan, Mathew, 35

white supremacy, 126, 127, 138, 139
William, Elizabeth, 191–192
women: as administrators, 175; cancer in, 191–92; in Church, 167–68, 172–76; complementarity and, 167–68; ecclesial justice for, 75; in economics, 175–76; gender lens for, 26; in health care, 175; household role of, 175; inclusion of, 76; ordination of, 174–75; parenthood and, 167–68, 170; participation of, 10; in society, 172–76. *See also* feminism
wonder/wondering, 10, 137–40

workers, 35, 37
World Day of Migrants and Refugees, 101, 117, 125, 128
World Gathering of Popular Movements, 101, 141
World Health Organization, 193
World Meetings of Popular Movements, 26, 34–38, 73, 103, 105, 225
World War I, 200
World Youth Day, 101

xenophobia, 127–28